GETTING AHEAD
Fundamentals of College Reading

JoAnn Yaworski, Ph.D.
West Chester University

PEARSON
Longman

New York   San Francisco   Boston
London   Toronto   Sydney   Tokyo   Singapore   Madrid
Mexico City   Munich   Paris   Cape Town   Hong Kong   Montreal

Senior Acquisitions Editor: Susan Kunchandy
Development Editor: Lai T. Moy
Senior Marketing Manager: Melanie Craig
Senior Supplements Editor: Donna Campion
Managing Editor: Bob Ginsberg
Production Manager: Joseph Vella
Project Coordination, Text Design, and Electronic Page Makeup: Electronic
    Publishing Services Inc., NYC
Cover Design Manager: John Callahan
Cover Designer: Maria Illardi
Cover Photo: Courtesy of JoAnn Yaworski © 2002 of Anderson Hall, West Chester University
    of Pennsylvania.
Manufacturing Manager: Mary Fischer
Senior Manufacturing Buyer: Alfred C. Dorsey
Printer and Binder: R.R. Donnelley and Sons—Harrisonburg
Cover Printer: Phoenix Color Corp.

For permission to use copyrighted material, grateful acknowledgment is made to the copyright holders on pp. 562–566, which are hereby made part of this copyright page.

Library of Congress Cataloging-in-Publication Data

Yaworski, JoAnn.
Getting ahead : fundamentals of college reading / JoAnn Yaworski.
     p. cm.
Includes bibliographical references and index.
ISBN 0-321-99966-4
1. Reading (Higher education) 2. Developmental reading. 3. College reading improvement programs. I. Title.
LB2395.3.Y38 2006
428.4'071'1—dc22   2004025259

Please visit us at http://www.ablongman.com.

ISBN 0-321-09966-4

1 2 3 4 5 6 7 8 9 10—DOH—08 07 06 05

Contents

Preface xi

PART I Reading and Vocabulary Skills 1

INTRODUCTION: FIRST STEPS TO COLLEGE SUCCESS 3

Why Should I Be Motivated to Read My Textbooks? 3

- **Visual Literacy Box I.1** Reading Tables: Workplace Writing 6
- **Getting Ahead in College Box I.1** Pronunciation of Vocabulary 7
- **Getting Ahead in College Box I.2** Sentence Combining: Adjectives 8

What Motivates Us? 9

CHAPTER 1

Getting Ahead in College 12

What Is Motivation and How Do I Build It? 12

What Is Intelligence and How Can I Increase It? 15

What Is Academic Self-Image and How Do I Change Mine If It Is Low? 16

How Can I Improve My Study Habits? 17

How Does Interest Lead to Success? 20

- **Getting Ahead in College Box 1.1** Previewing a Textbook 21

How Can My Career Choice Help Me to Stay Focused? 23

- **Getting Ahead in College Box 1.2** Finding a Major 25
- **Visual Literacy Box 1.1** Hidden Costs of College Education 27

How Does Learning Style Affect Motivation? 27

Teaching Styles and Motivation 30

■ CHAPTER 8

Purpose and Tone   *313*

Preface

The college reading class poses a tremendous challenge to literacy educators. As the following comments indicate, lack of reading skills is the greatest barrier to success in all disciplines.

PHILOSOPHY PROFESSOR: I think they [students] skim through and I don't think they follow trains of thought—they read isolated sentences. They don't see how they connect up. They don't do skimming very well. When you ask, "What did you get out of this?" they have a very hard time articulating anything, even when I say, "Give the major idea; what do you remember?" Most cannot tell me.

ECONOMICS PROFESSOR: They read the wrong thing! If a paragraph starts: "Man has always been in love with the machine," that is what they underline. Throw that away because the next sentence says, "In the global economy of robotics, the following is true. Japan has 20% fewer employees than America." That is what they should have put, but they underline "Man is in love with the machine." They have no idea of what is important in what they read. Consequently, they can't convert what they read into a meaningful test answer.

PSYCHOLOGY PROFESSOR: I'm often surprised that I can give a small selection of only a page and a half and say, "What is the key thing the author wanted to tell us?" The vast majority cannot tell you.

ENGLISH PROFESSOR: I consider them to be nonreaders. Really. I don't think they read fiction. I don't think they read nonfiction. I don't think they read newspapers, magazines. I don't think they read.

SOCIOLOGY PROFESSOR: They look upon reading material as a series of individual items which should be committed to memory…rather than looking for larger structures.

HISTORY PROFESSOR: They all glance over it….I imagine they are skipping over a lot of the words that they don't know and, in essence, don't know what is going on.

BIOLOGY PROFESSOR: I talked with a student yesterday who is now taking a course with me, her second time through it. The first time, she failed…and I somewhat cringed when I saw that she was enrolled in the course again. And she has surprised me because she's a solid B student in the course this time. And I just asked her yesterday, "What is the difference?" And she said that the first time through she did not really read through the material—that she just tried to find the answers to the questions…this time, she's taking the time reading the material.

The main difference between college and high school is reading. High school teachers spend approximately 25 hours per week providing students with academic information via lectures and class activities while students are not required to read much—if at all. In college, students spend only 12–15 hours in classes with the professor covering three times the amount of information. In other words, the college classroom time is reduced by half while the amount of information the student is expected to learn triples.

Getting Ahead seeks to provide the college reading instructor with the tools to help students cope with this academic transition. It aims to assist and motivate students in developing the basic and critical reading skills that will enable them to pass, and excel in, college-level, cross-disciplinary courses.

Getting Ahead provides instruction in basic reading, vocabulary, grammar, critical reading, and study skills. Approximately 200 excerpts from college textbooks reflect the types of reading students are required to comprehend for their college courses and for national or statewide reading exams. Each chapter focuses on a fundamental reading skill and leads students through a progression of readings that become increasingly more difficult. This structure allows students to focus quickly and experience success immediately while learning new skills and strategies for reading college-level materials. The gradual increase in the length and difficulty of the excerpts makes it easier for students to maintain a level of success throughout the chapter without feeling overchallenged. This scaffolding strategy builds a student's confidence and belief that he or she is capable of not only basic comprehension but advanced thinking as well.

OVERVIEW

Chapter 1 focuses on motivation because so much can be accomplished when students are highly motivated to learn.

Chapter 2 addresses time management skills and the PQ4R method for reading textbook chapters. These skills are addressed early on in the text to enable students to immediately begin applying this knowledge to their college studies.

Chapter 3 shows students various ways to learn vocabulary, including context clues, structural analysis (prefixes, suffixes, and roots), and dictionary use.

Chapters 4 and 5 cover main idea and provide scaffolding through the use of practice exercises that segment longer readings.

Chapter 6 presents four simple text structures: (1) term, definition, and example, (2) topic with a list, (3) process, and (4) chronological order. Emphasis is placed on term, definition, and example because it is the most commonly used structure in freshman-level textbooks.

Chapters 7, 8, and 9 respectively cover inference, purpose and tone, and critical thinking. Four different types of inference are highlighted in Chapter 7. In Chapter 8, purpose is looked at from three perspectives: (1) to inform, (2) to entertain, and (3) to persuade. In Chapter 9, reason and consequence are used to show the logical steps in drawing a conclusion.

Note-taking—from both lectures and textbooks—and exam preparation are highlighted in Chapters 10 and 11.

Speed-reading exercises consistent with current research are provided in Chapter 12. Comprehension of thought is emphasized over rapid eye movement with respect to increasing reading speed. Students are shown how to think more quickly instead of sole reliance on moving the eyes faster.

Finally, the Appendix offers a brief English handbook that focuses on grammar with respect to parts of speech (e.g., nouns, pronouns, adjectives, adverbs, and prepositions) and basic sentence structures.

Each chapter includes a demonstration of a reading skill along with practice exercises. The practice exercises include readings that become progressively longer and more difficult. Scaffolding, progressions, and vocabulary terms are provided to ease students from easy to more difficult readings. In this way, it is possible to challenge students without upsetting or discouraging them or making them feel incapable and unprepared. High-interest topics are provided to help students develop confidence in reading expository text information.

FEATURES

Getting Ahead offers a number of innovative features to enhance the learning experience:

- **Over 200 cross-disciplinary readings** provide practice with reading biology, sociology, psychology, chemistry, communications, history, physical science, economics, geography, geology, and English.

- **Emphasis on inference and critical-thinking skills** encourages students to believe that they are capable of not just basic reading comprehension but advanced thinking as well.

- **"Getting Ahead" boxes** provide short exercises for sentence combining and related grammar exercises to support basic reading comprehension and critical thinking.

- **"Visual Literacy" boxes** provide practice with comprehending visual aids (e.g., maps, charts, graphs, diagrams) and illustrate how those aids support students' overall understanding of a reading.

- **A comprehensive vocabulary chapter** teaches students to improve and practice essential vocabulary skills and focuses on the learning of vocabulary *in context*.

- **A grammar appendix** covers the basics of English grammar, including parts of speech and sentence structure.

- **Time management and study skills** are emphasized in the first few chapters.

- **Reading speed** is discussed in Chapter 12 in the context of not merely increasing the movement of eyes across the page but, more importantly, increasing reading comprehension.

THE TEACHING AND LEARNING PACKAGE

Getting Ahead comes with supplements to ensure that the course is a rewarding experience for both the students and instructors.

For Instructors

The Instructor's Manual for *Getting Ahead* (0-321-09968-0) includes sample syllabi, transparencies, and other teaching resources.

Vocabulary and Reader Supplement to accompany *Getting Ahead*. This text-specific supplement cross-references to the complete chapter on vocabulary skills and reduces the need to purchase additional vocabulary supplements. Also included are ten additional readings of five expository and five narrative selections.

Printed Test Bank for Developmental Reading (Instructor / 0-321-08596-5) offers more than 3,000 questions in all areas of reading, including vocabulary, main idea, supporting details, patterns of organization, critical thinking, analytical reasoning, inference, point of view, visual aids, and textbook reading.

Electronic Test Bank for Developmental Reading (Instructor/CD 0-321-08179-X) offers more than 3,000 questions in all areas of reading, including vocabulary, main idea, supporting details, patterns of organization, critical thinking, analytical reasoning, inference, point of view, visual aids, and textbook reading. Instructors simply choose questions, then print out the completed test for distribution or offer the test online.

Instructor's Manual for Reading Road Trip 3.0 (Instructor / 0-321-16195-5) provides detailed instruction on how to use all versions of Reading Road Trip 3.0: CD, Web, and Course Compass. Suggested activities and assessment for in-class use of RRTrip 3.0 and sample student progress report, sample course activity sheet, and answers to suggested activities are included.

For Students

The Longman Textbook Reader, **Revised Edition (with answers Student / 0-321-11895-2 or without answers Student / 0-321-12223-2)** offers five complete chapters from our textbooks: computer science, biology, psychology, communications, and business. Each chapter includes additional comprehension quizzes, critical-thinking questions, and group activities.

The Longman Reader's Portfolio (Student/ 0-321-16366-4). This unique supplement provides students with a space to plan, think about, and present their work. The portfolio includes a diagnostic area (including a learning-style questionnaire), a working area (including calendars, vocabulary logs, reading response sheets, book club tips, and other valuable materials), and a display area (including a progress chart, a final table of contents, and a final assessment). Also includes 10 Practices of Highly Effective Students.

The Longman Reader's Journal, **by Kathleen McWhorter (Student / 0-321-08843-3).** The first journal for readers, The Longman Reader's Journal offers a place for students to record their reactions to and questions about any reading.

Newsweek **Discount Subscription Coupon (12 weeks) (Student / 0-321-08895-6).** *Newsweek* gets students reading, writing, and thinking about what's going on in the world around them. The price of the subscription is added to the cost of the book. Instructors receive weekly lesson plans, quizzes, and curriculum guides as well as a complimentary *Newsweek* subscription. The price of the subscription is 59 cents per issue (a total of $7.08 for the subscription).

Interactive Guide to *Newsweek* (Student / 0-321-05528-4). Available with the 12-week subscription to *Newsweek*, this guide serves as a workbook for students who are using the magazine. FREE with the adoption of a Longman textbook / VALUEPACK ONLY. Sample through Socrates.

Reading Road Trip 4.0 Multimedia Software (www.ablongman.com/ readingroadtrip). Taking students on a tour of 16 cities and landmarks throughout the United States, each of the 16 modules corresponds to a reading or study skill (e.g., finding the main idea, understanding patterns of organization, thinking critically). All modules contain a tour of the location, instruction and tutorial, exercises, interactive feedback, and mastery tests. This new release includes all-new additional exercises and tests, additional exercises at the lowest level, and a brand-new module of longer readings that help students integrate all the skills and prepare for exit exams. An Instructor's Manual for Reading Roadtrip is also available. Please contact your Longman sales representative for further information.

MySkillsLab 2.0 (www.ablongman/myskillslab) (Student Pin Card/0-321-26323-5 or Instructor/ 0-321-26322-7). This Website houses all media tools for developmental English (reading, writing, and study skills) in one place: Avoiding Plagiarism, Exercise Zone, Research Navigator, Longman Writer's Warehouse, Reading Road Trip, Longman Vocabulary Website, and Longman Study Skills Website.

Penguin Discount Novel Program. In cooperation with Penguin Putnam, Inc., Longman is proud to offer a variety of Penguin paperbacks at a significant discount when packaged with any Longman title. Excellent additions to any Developmental Reading or English course, Penguin titles give students the opportunity to explore contemporary and classical fiction and drama. The available titles include works by authors as diverse as Toni Morrison, Julia Alvarez, Mary Shelley, and Shakespeare. To review the complete list of titles available, visit the Longman-Penguin-Putnam Website: http://www.ablongman.com/penguin.

STATE SPECIFIC SUPPLEMENTS

For Florida Adopters

Thinking Through the Test: A Study Guide for the Florida College Basic Skills Exit Test, by D. J. Henry (with answers Student / 0-321-08066-1 or without answers Student / 0-321-09988-5). FOR FLORIDA ADOPTIONS ONLY. This workbook helps students strengthen their reading skills in preparation for the Florida College Basic Skills Exit Test. It features both diagnostic tests to help assess areas that may need improvement and exit tests to help test skill mastery. Detailed explanatory answers have been provided for almost all of the questions.

For Texas Adopters

The Longman THEA Study Guide, by Jeannette Harris (Student/ 0-321-20271-6). Created specifically for students in Texas, this study guide includes straightforward explanations and numerous practice exercises to help students prepare for the reading and writing sections of THEA Test.

For New York/CUNY Adopters

Preparing for the CUNY-ACT Reading and Writing Test, edited by Patricia Licklider (Student/ 0-321-19608-2). This booklet, prepared by reading and writing faculty from across the CUNY system, is designed to help students prepare for the CUNY-ACT exit test. It includes test-taking tips, reading passages, typical exam questions, and sample writing prompts to help students become familiar with each portion of the test.

ACKNOWLEDGMENTS

I would like to thank Michael Yaworski, Cecilia Yaworski, and Glenn A. Usher for their love, friendship, and steadfast support during the writing of this text.

I have been very fortunate to work with development editor Lai T. Moy, who went the extra miles to help me develop organization, clarity, and variation in the writing of the text.

I would also like to thank editor Susan Kunchandy for her interest and input during the publication process.

Finally, thank you to our reviewers across the country for their knowledgeable feedback: Lisa Barnes, Delaware Community College; Paula Ferrell, Mesa Community College; Tammy Frankland, Casper College; Sarah Garman, Miami-Dade College; Reginald Gerlica, Henry Ford Community College; Ralph Gillespie, Pellissippi State Technical Community College; Jean Gorgie, Austin Community College; Pamela L. Gray, Santa Monica College; Ellen Hernandez, Camden County College; Paul H. Parent, Montgomery College; Richard Randolph, Kauai Community College; Karen Taylor, University of Texas Pan American; and Amelia Wilson, Mesa Community College.

ABOUT THE AUTHOR

Dr. JoAnn Yaworski teaches developmental reading, study skills, and teacher education classes in the Department of Literacy at *West Chester University of Pennsylvania*. She has been teaching reading, study skills, and other academic disciplines including History, World Cultures, English, and the Russian Language for public and private high schools, colleges, and universities for over 25 years.

Dr. Yaworski is the content provider for over 12 web-site companions to best-selling reading and study skills textbooks.

Dr. Yaworski received her Ph.D. in Reading and Educational Psychology from the University at Albany, the State University of New York in 1996. Her dissertation concerning student success won the "Distinguished Doctoral Dissertation Award" from this same institution. She has been named in *Who's Who in America* (51st Edition), *Who's Who in the World* (12th, 13th, 14th, & 15th Editions), *Who's Who in the East* (24th, 25th, & 26th Editions*), Who's Who of American Women,* (19th & 20th Editions) and *Who's Who in American Education* (4th & 5th Editions) for her work with college students.

Dr. Yaworski's research interests include student success and teaching reading and study skills with technology. She has been a frequent presenter at conferences sponsored by the College Reading & Learning Association and many of her practical application articles appear in *the Journal of College Reading & Learning* and in the *Journal of Developmental Education*.

JoAnn Yaworski, Ph.D

PART I

Reading and Vocabulary Skills

INTRODUCTION

First Steps to College Success

WHY SHOULD I BE MOTIVATED TO READ MY TEXTBOOKS?

Sometimes we may not understand why we are taking a college reading course or what exactly this type of class can do for us. In the following letters, students explain how college reading courses have helped them:

- Pass required entrance exams;
- Pass college courses;
- Do well in their careers.

> Dear Dr. Yaworski,
>
> I just passed English 101. I was a student in your Reading class first semester Fall 1998. I learned to not only become a better reader, but also how to comprehend reading material in a more efficient manner. I'm also a more avid reader now.
>
> No doubt this class helped me to achieve passing Nelson-Denny and CPE scores.
>
> Thanks,
> *Daniel Bradshaw*

Dear Dr. Yaworski:

This class is what the student makes of it. A student can easily do the assignments and not care about learning. However, not only did I complete the assignments, but I learned valuable skills. After learning the Cornell method of note-taking, I applied it to my criminal law class. After our last reading class, I had my criminal law class. We got our test back and I got the second highest grade in the room. Just an example of how your class can be a beneficial class when applying oneself. Take care, and have a good summer.

Sincerely,

Scott K. Drissel Jr.

Dear Dr. Yaworski,

It is Scott Drissel from your EDR100 Reading and Study Skills Class last semester. I regret to inform you that I have withdrawn from the university and accepted a position as a Philadelphia Police Officer. I leave with a cumulative GPA (grade point average) of a 3.7. I am making 33,000 dollars a year in the police academy; I will be in there for a 10 month period. Upon graduation my salary will increase to $37,000/year. I started on August 5th, and am currently in my 4th week there. Believe it or not, the academic aspect of the police academy is extremely tough. We have intense lectures for about 6 hours a day, 5 days a week. I thought of you on the 1st day of classes, when the instructors basically taught a crash course of EDR100!!! The instructor asked the class if anyone has heard of the Cornell method. While the class looked around puzzled my hand was the only one in the air. As I explained what it was and how it operated, students and teachers looked at me as if I was Albert Einstein. I remember sitting in your class and people acting as if the material taught would only be useful in college. Well, I got news for them; they will continue to use it. We have had 4 tests to date, and my test scores are 87, 100, 100, and 100. I accredit part of that to my note-taking techniques and reading strategies. I thank you even more now for what you taught me in your class.

If there is anything I think we should pass on to your current students it is that no matter how far in their careers they go, they must have a good basis for reading, studying, and note-taking. Also, they should not take things for granted.

I still have the same dedication to getting my degree as I had last spring. I am 4 semesters away from a bachelor's degree, and the city will pay for a good portion of it. I still plan to go to law school; it will take me a little longer. But I feel as if I will learn more in the field of

Law and Law Enforcement this way. I hope this information is of some help to your incoming students.

Best wishes,
Scott K. Drissel Jr.

All of the students who wrote the above letters felt that learning to read their textbooks had a direct effect on their college success. And, as our friend Scott points out, it is extremely important to be successful in your first year.

The first course we take for each different field of study—for example, biology, sociology, or psychology—provides us with a general introduction to the subject. Our textbooks act as *big dictionaries.* They define terms, provide examples, and offer interesting details to help us understand what we are reading. Our textbooks also act as *tour guides* to our college classrooms; they explain the major concepts from our professors' lectures so we can follow along and make sense of them. In addition to being dictionaries and tour guides, our textbooks are our *best friends.* Over a period of two to four years, they help us to become experts in our chosen fields. However, in order for all of this to take place, we need to become expert readers.

Our Reading Textbook

A college *reading* textbook is different from a subject-specific textbook because it is not a body of information to be memorized. Instead, it provides the *directions* or *roadmap* for learning how to read and study the textbooks for our other courses.

Getting Ahead: Fundamentals for College Reading is a reading textbook. It will be one of the most important books that you will own in college. In it, you will find the basic keys that unlock the information to all of your other college texts. Each chapter presents a key strategy to help you increase your reading ability and efficiency so that it will become easier for you to understand your other courses' reading assignments.

Visual Literacy Boxes Sometimes it is easier to understand written text if we can first see a picture of what the text is describing. For this reason, authors often use tables, charts, graphs, and diagrams to provide visual images of ideas and information. Thus, in order to help us learn how to read and interpret the images in our college textbooks, each chapter of *Getting Ahead* includes Visual Literacy Boxes that place these images within context. For example, suppose we are reading an article about skills needed in the workplace. The main topic discusses the different types of writing skills that we need in order to be successful in the field of business. To illustrate which skills are the most important, the author may use a table such as the one that appears in Visual Literacy Box I.1.

As we study the table in the box, we can quickly see that "Writing clearly and succinctly" is the most important writing technique, since it is listed first and has the highest percentage. This means that it is the most useful skill needed in the workplace. Although this conclusion is not stated in the table, we have considered the information, thought about it, and as a result are able to make a reasonable guess.

Visual Literacy Box I.1 ■ ■ ■ ■ ■ ■ ■ ■ ■ ■ ■ ■ ■ ■ ■

Reading Tables: Workplace Writing

Employers very much want the people they hire to have good writing skills. The table below shows how college graduates ranked the usefulness of different types of writing skills at work. In this table, four writing skills are listed. Next to each skill is listed the percentage of graduates who found that particular skill useful at work.

1. Which writing technique did students think was the most useful?

2. Which writing technique did students think was the second most useful?

3. "Incorporating data in reports" is ranked last. Does this mean it is not a useful skill in the workplace? Why or why not?

In our survey, we listed various writing techniques and asked how useful graduates felt these techniques are for performing effectively on the job. Table I.1 shows the rank order by mean of writing techniques from high to low.

Table I.1   Usefulness of Specific Writing Techniques

Technique	% Useful or Better
Writing clearly and succinctly	96.2
Writing grammatically correct English	94.7
Giving oral presentations	85.6
Incorporating data in reports	83.2

(Singh-Gupta and Troutt-Ervin)

Getting Ahead in College Boxes   In all fields, professors and employers expect students and graduates to be able to read fluently and to communicate clearly their ideas in writing. Therefore, in addition to the Visual Literacy Boxes, we will also come across two types of Getting Ahead in College Boxes. One type of box will teach us how to build our reading vocabulary through pronunciation guidelines. Another box will teach us how to improve our writing through sentence-combining techniques.

For most people, the listening vocabulary is much greater than the reading vocabulary. In other words, most people know and use many words that they may not recognize when they read. If, however, we can pronounce an unknown word by sounding it out, we may find that we already know what it means. In this case, it is not necessary to learn and understand the concept because we already "know" the word. We just need to be able to pronounce it. The Getting Ahead in College Boxes will present a series of clues and exercises that will help us with the pronunciation of new words. Once we have completed the series of Getting Ahead Boxes, we will be better equipped to increase our recognition of already-known words when we see them in print.

To figure out how to pronounce a word correctly, first, read the explanation of the spelling pattern. Then, look for the same pattern in the words from the reading. Use the pattern to help pronounce the words. For practice, see Getting Ahead in College Box I.1.

Getting Ahead in College Box I.1

PRONUNCIATION OF VOCABULARY

In our alphabet the letter **c** takes the sound of two other letters, **s** or **k**. When it has the sound of **s,** as in **c**enter, we say that it has a soft sound. When it sounds like **k,** as in **C**anada, we say it has a hard sound. **C** is generally soft when it come in front of e, i, and y. **C** is usually hard in front of a, o, and u.

Using these rules, identify the soft and hard sounds in **c** in the following sentences. On the line following each word that has a **c** in it, write **s** if the **c** has a soft sound and **k** if the **c** has a hard sound.

The Millionaire Next Door

Twenty years ago we began studying how people be<u>c</u>ome (1)__k__ wealthy. At first, we did it just as we might imagine, by surveying people in so-<u>c</u>alled (2)_____ ups<u>c</u>ale (3)_____ neighborhoods a<u>c</u>ross (4)_____ the <u>c</u>ountry

(continued on next page)

(continued from previous page)

(5)_____. In time, we discovered (6)_____ something odd. Many people who live in expensive homes and drive luxury cars (7)_____ do not actually (8)_____ have much wealth. Then, we discovered (9)_____ something even odder: Many people who have a great deal of wealth do not even live in upscale (10)_____ neighborhoods.

How do we become wealthy? (11)_____ Here, too, people have it wrong. It is seldom luck (12)_____ or inheritance (13)_____ or advanced (14)_____ degrees or even intelligence (15)_____ that enables people to amass fortunes. Wealth is more often the result of a lifestyle of hard work, perseverance (16)_____, planning, and, most of all, self-discipline (17)_____.

(Stanley and Danko 1–2)

As we can see from the information presented in Visual Literacy Box I.1, "writing clearly" and "writing grammatically correct English" are as important in the workplace as they are in college. Therefore, the second type of Getting Ahead in College box will present sentence-combining exercises. This series of exercises will help us increase our ability to write clearly *and* to write grammatically correct sentences. When completing these exercises, we are asked to combine two or more sentences to make one sentence. Without repeating any words, our sentence should include all the important information. See Getting Ahead Box I.2 for examples and exercises.

Getting Ahead in College Box I.2

SENTENCE COMBINING: ADJECTIVES

Combine the following sentences into one sentence. Keep the most important information without repeating any words.

1. Twenty years ago we began studying.

We studied how people become wealthy.

Twenty years ago we began studying how people become wealthy.

2. We surveyed people.

The people were in neighborhoods.

The neighborhoods were upscale.

The neighborhoods were across the country.

_____

3. We discovered something.

It was odd.

_____

4. Many people do not have much wealth.

They are the people who live in expensive homes.

They are the people who drive expensive cars.

_____

5. Many people who have a great deal of wealth live in neighborhoods.

Their neighborhoods are middle class.

_____

WHAT MOTIVATES US?

I Made It

1   Hello, my name is Jamal Dawson, and where I'm from, it ain't nothing nice. It's like the sun never shines. I know one thing, I am proud to be here to tell you guys [that] out of my whole neighborhood I'm the only one who went to college. My neighborhood is full of negativity. It is drugs on every corner. We can't even sleep at night, because we hear loud gunshots. In my neighborhood I have witnessed so much. I can remember the day before I started the Academic Development Program, a young man was shot and killed right in front of me. That's just one

Pittsburgh #1, *Oil painting by J. E. Miller, Copyright © 2000.*

of the many murders I have witnessed. That night I said to myself, "I have to get out of here." Through all the negativity I stood strong. Not only is the neighborhood proud of me, but I'm most proud of myself.

2   Although my brother didn't grow up in the neighborhood, he set a goal and achieved it. He went to college and graduated. His college education paid off. He is 40 years old, has a wonderful family, and has a great job as a pharmaceutical sales representative. My brother lives such a stress free life. That's the life I'm trying to live. That man is such a great role model. All my life I have looked up to my brother. He made my mother and father so proud. My brother told me "if you push for what you want, it will come." That's the model he lives by. Everything my brother said he wanted, he got it. All because he worked hard for what he wanted. That's why we should set a goal.

3   There are many children in the neighborhood who don't further their education. There are reasons for that. A lot of children don't have both parents in their corner to push them. I was blessed to have both of my parents in my life. Most children don't have the proper guidance. That's how most of them fall victim. If my brother didn't have the proper guidance, he wouldn't have made it as far as he has. Neither would I. If there were more positive things in the neighborhood for the children to do, maybe we wouldn't have so many young kids on the corners. It would also help to further their education; many don't even make it out of high school. That is really sad. I just thank God for blessing me.

4   By me making it this far, I know I must stay focused. I've come too far to turn back. My mother always told me "get as much as you can

while you are here." That I will do. I'm going to try my best to graduate at the top of the class. Once I graduate I will go on and pursue my career. I just want to live a wonderful and comfortable life.

5   Coming from a bad neighborhood, I have been strong and I have overcome all the negativity around me. Once I make it, I will give back to the neighborhood. Give the children a chance to make something of themselves. Living in my neighborhood is a struggle, but it is only what you make of it. If you want something bad enough, go for it. Remember, "Only the Strong Survive."

Jamal's message is clear. It takes motivation to become successful. As he points out, goals can be very motivating. What are some of Jamal's goals? What are some of your goals?

When we look at ourselves in the future, we can see what we would like to become. For example, Jamal would like to become a person who graduates at the top of his class and lives a comfortable life.

Having a vision of who we hope to become is very important because it helps keep us focused on where we are going. In order to get to that place, we establish goals. Jamal's immediate goal is to do well in college and graduate with honors. However, his main goal is to live comfortably and to give back to others, particularly to those who do not have supportive parents or a brother to serve as a good role model.

But how does Jamal reach his main goal? What steps must he take? Jamal needs to set a series of smaller goals to help carry him through:

Go to college

↓

Do well in college

↓

Graduate and get a good job

↓

Create a comfortable life

↓

Give back to others who need help

As Jamal's experience shows, setting goals is the first step to achieving success in life. However, as Jamal reminds us, we need to "stay focused," and carry through with our plans.

Getting Ahead in College

In this chapter, "Getting Ahead in College," we learn about motivation and how staying motivated keeps us focused on our schoolwork. The more focused we are, the more successful we become. We discuss the following topics:

- What is motivation and how do I build it?

- What is intelligence and how can I increase it?

- What is academic self-image and how do I change mine if it is low?

- How can I improve my study habits?

- How does interest lead to success?

- How can my career choice help me to stay focused?

- How does learning style affect motivation?

WHAT IS MOTIVATION AND HOW DO I BUILD IT?

Motivation is *a feeling or desire* that makes a person want to do something. Motivation is easy enough to define, but not that easy to *build*—especially if we do *not* want to do something. Thus, the first step to building motivation is to figure out what we really want to do by looking at our reasons for doing it.

How Do I Build the Motivation to Read and Study in College?

If we reread Jamal's essay in the Introduction, we notice that Jamal has reasons for being in college. He believes college can lead to a high-paying job, and he understands that the high-paying job will give him the power to live the type of life that he sees his brother living.

More education can certainly open doors and provide us with a greater number of career choices. Before we identify our reasons for being in college, however, let us first ask ourselves the following questions:

- What do I want to become?

- What do I want my life to be like in the future?

- What type of life would make me happy?

EXERCISE
1-1

What Would You Do?

Think about the following questions and write short answers. Discuss the questions and answers with classmates.

1. If you had all the time and money in the world and could do anything you wanted, how would you spend your time?

   _____

   _____

   _____

2. What activities do you enjoy most?

   _____

   _____

   _____

3. With whom do you enjoy spending your time?

_____

_____

_____

4. What places do you enjoy going to the most?

_____

_____

_____

EXERCISE
1-2

Choosing Your Major

List two courses of study you think you might want to choose as your major. How closely related are these majors to the activities and lifestyle that you described above? If they are very different, can you think of any majors that are related to your interests? Discuss these with your classmates.

1. _____

2. _____

EXERCISE
1-3

College Success

List five reasons you want to be successful in college. Put a star next to the ones that are powerful enough to keep you going when things get tough. Discuss these with your classmates.

1. _____

2. _____

3. _____

4. _____

5. _____

WHAT IS INTELLIGENCE AND HOW CAN I INCREASE IT?

INSTRUCTOR: Do you know anyone who is a good student?

TESS: Mary Hall.

INSTRUCTOR: What does she do to become a good student when she reads and studies?

TESS: I think she does it by divine right, by the will of God . . . I swear . . . I never see her study.

POLINA: I know a lot of people who are really smart who just don't study at all. Some people are smarter than other people are.

Like Tess and Polina, some people think that intelligence is a fixed quality that one is born with and has no control over. However, intelligence has two parts: (1) *knowledge* of what we know about the world, and (2) the *ability to learn* new things. When we think of intelligence in this way, we understand that everyone can increase and improve his or her intelligence. We can all increase the amount of information that we know by:

■ experiencing new things

■ asking others questions and listening to their answers

■ reading new information

By the same token, we can increase our knowledge faster and more easily if we can improve our ability to learn. Taking reading and study skills courses helps us do this. Through them, we learn strategies that help us "learn how to learn." As a result, our knowledge increases as well as our ability to gain new knowledge.

WHAT IS ACADEMIC SELF-IMAGE AND HOW DO I CHANGE MINE IF IT IS LOW?

Some of us come to college believing we are not very intelligent—that we are really not "A" students, "B" students, or even "C" students. Where do we get this image of ourselves? Our self-image depends largely on the perception and opinions of others. We develop a sense of who we are from the way others react to us, what they say about us, and how we feel about ourselves. Through other people, we "look in the mirror" at ourselves.

Our **academic self-image** is what we think of ourselves as learners or students. This image is based on the reactions of our teachers, parents, and fellow students as well as on our grades, because grades reflect how well we can do in school. A poor academic self-image can develop if we do not try to live up to our potential. In fact, we can even develop a "fear of failure." Take a look at the comments one student with a poor academic self-image made:

> I didn't study for an exam and did poorly on it. My confidence got shaken a little. Now when I think about the next test, I'm not so sure whether I can really pass it. I might as well not study for the next exam because if I study and fail it, then I will know I am not smart. However, if I do not study for the exam and fail it, at least I can say that I failed the exam because I did not study, not because I am not smart.

This type of thinking is a problem because it eventually destroys our confidence; we no longer have the motivation we need to try in college. Soon we find it harder and harder to study for exams because we have become very fearful of failure—even with a lot of effort.

Fortunately, each semester can provide a new chance to change our academic self-image. From the interviews below, which students decided to change their academic self-image and which students did not?

INNA: For the most part I was kind of a slacker in high school; I did just enough to squeeze by and now . . . a lot more things get me excited as far as learning. I'm very conscious of my grades, which I wasn't in high school at all. I got mostly Cs and Ds; now I get all As and Bs.

TIEN: I was pretty much lazy [in high school]; I didn't do much and I'm pretty much the same way. I'm still the same.

ANIKA: I probably am doing the same [as I did in high school] except that I get caught for it here a lot more easily than when I did it in high school: not going to classes, not turning in homework.

FERN: In high school I was very lazy; I wasn't into school at all. I just was there and didn't pay attention. [Now] I consider myself a good student; I'm always doing homework, studying.

CARLOS: Some teachers would say that you can't do it. . . . Now that I'm in college, I'm considered a smart student here. Top of the class, made the Dean's List.

AARON: I did my best work in high school to get by, but I never pushed myself very hard and I'm about the same kind of student now.

POLINA: I was an average student in high school and I would say I'm still an average student.

MEI: I was a terrible student in high school. I got bad grades. I've improved a lot since I've come to college.

ROSS: In high school I was an average student . . . but here [college] I'm doing much better. My lowest GPA is 2.8.

EXERCISE 1-4

Defining Your Academic Self-Image

What was your academic self-image in high school? What is your academic self-image in college? Has it changed or has it stayed the same? Discuss your responses with your classmates.

_____

_____

HOW CAN I IMPROVE MY STUDY HABITS?

One thing that happens quite frequently with college freshmen is they miscalculate how much time and effort they must invest in order to excel in college. Often, it is hard for them to believe that it takes two hours to prepare for every hour spent in class (also known as the "2-to-1 rule"), especially when this adds up to 25 and 30 hours per week. Many take a full load of classes and try to get by with only 6 hours of reading and studying each week. By the end of the semester their grades confirm that they have not put enough time and effort into their studies. If their grades are low for more than one or two semesters, they are often asked to leave the college. This lack of success, of course, lowers their academic self-concept. To avoid this scenario, we need to develop two habits:

■ trying

■ strategic learning

First, we need to convince ourselves that we should always try. Second, we need to accept the fact that sometimes we will fail and that failing is a part of the learning process. Trial and error learning, for example, is based on failing. If you try one thing and it doesn't work, you try something else. You repeat this process of trying until you find the thing that does work, or the solution. Many major discoveries were made through trial and error learning.

However, we still need to recognize that there *are* easier ways to learn than trial and error. *Learning strategies* involve thinking about how to accomplish the task, calculating what we need to do to succeed at the task, and acting on our plan. If we fail at the task, we write down reasons why we believe we failed. We think about what went wrong and how we can correct the problem. This reading book is a guide to many types of learning strategies that you can use for reading and studying college textbooks. As you go through the exercises in *Getting Ahead in College*, think about how you will use these skills and strategies to read your other college textbooks.

EXERCISE 1-5

Maintaining a High Academic Self-Image

Read the following interviews of students who have high academic self-images. As you read, think about the steps they are taking and the strategies they are using to make sure they keep a high academic self-image.

NINH: I study 20 hours [per week], more or less, depending on my workload.

CARLOS: Sunday mornings I always study. . . . I get all my homework done by Friday night. [I study] at least 38–40 hours [per week].

INGRID: While I'm reading I will . . . highlight the titles and then the subtitles. . . . I'll highlight the most important parts and then I'll read the whole thing. And then I'll go back, and either I'll reread it or . . . I will reiterate in my mind the part that I highlighted.

ROSE: When I'm reading a chapter, I read every word and I highlight the important information . . . what the teacher has gone over in class. So, I know exactly where it is.

ENRIQUE: I read it three times. First, I read it once completely, second, I read it again completely and highlight. The third time I read it and copy the highlights into study notes.

RITA: I participate all the time, every class . . . if I can.

NINH: Anything that's written on the board, I write down, anything the teacher writes at all, I write down, and if I come across anything that's interesting or that I find relevant to what we're doing, I'll write that down. If it's a really important lecture, I'll bring a recorder with me.

ENRIQUE: I study my notes and study the notes from the lecture, and go back to the text to correlate it.

TINA: I read the textbook, read my notes from class, and get my own notes from the textbook.

INGRID: I write down everything, everything he says I write down because I work in the computer lab and when I have nothing to do, I type all my notes. . . . the best part is in the last half of the semester. I got a D-minus and that is when I started typing my notes and I came out with an A-minus.

NINH: In math, if I don't know a problem, I'll go back to the book and rework the problems until I know it. If I do know a problem, I'll pass it and go to the next one.

ENRIQUE: In general, I take notes from the lecture. I read the book before class so I know what's going on and so I can distinguish what's important from what's not. I participate in class discussions, and I ask the professor if I don't know something.

ROSS: I write myself review sheets. . . . I'll take the major points from the notes in the book and write those all down so that . . . I won't even really have to deal with my books or my notes anymore. I will have it all laid out.

CARLOS: I take the important things that I think are going to be in the exam and put a key phrase on the side of the index card. . . . I think flash cards help a lot.

ROSS: It's important to make sure that you can understand it, for your own benefit. I mean, you write down what the teacher says, of course, but if that's not easily understandable, then I'd paraphrase it in my own words so that when I'm reviewing my notes, it's a lot easier.

Now list ten strategies these students are using to maintain high grades so that they themselves, their professors, their parents, and their peers will think of them as "A" students. Discuss these with your classmates.

1. _____

2. _____

3. _____

4. _____

5. _____

6. _____

7. _____

8. _____

9. _____

10. _____

HOW DOES INTEREST LEAD TO SUCCESS?

LOUISA: College is easier [than high school] in a lot of ways, but I think it has to do with the fact that we're learning more things we're interested in . . . we get to decide what we want to take.

ROSS: [In college] you're apt to be more interested in what you're learning.

LOUISA: I want to know most of the things that I'm learning about. I'm interested in them and . . . [I want] to know about the field that I am going into . . . so that I can communicate with people and understand what people are saying.

RITA: You have to be interested in the subject you are studying.

NEAL: With any free time outside of school, I am always involved in some kind of art project . . . my main interest is, of course, art, but I hope to pursue that even further, into a degree in Art Education.

Motivation to succeed in college is greatly affected by personal interests. If we are not interested in a subject, it will be very difficult to focus our attention on it for 20 to 30 hours each week. For this reason, it is extremely important for us to study a subject and choose a major that we find fascinating.

How do we find a subject that interests us?

1. Read through the course catalog every semester and study the descriptions of the "core" courses that are offered at the college. (In most col-

leges, students must take courses totaling about 60 credits from a variety of disciplines called the "core." This requirement helps students become well-rounded thinkers instead of specialists who are exposed to information from only one field.)

2. Choose five courses that sound interesting.

3. Speak with the professors who teach them and the students who have already taken them.

4. In light of this information, discard any courses that sound uninteresting and replace them with new choices.

5. Go to class the first day to get the syllabus and listen very carefully to the professor's introduction to the course. If the course sounds uninteresting, drop it before the drop deadline and add another course (before the add deadline).

Getting Ahead in College Box 1.1

Previewing a Textbook

When we are not sure if we are interested in reading a particular textbook, we use a strategy called previewing to find out. Follow the steps below to preview either a textbook that you will be using for one of your classes or a textbook for a course that you are considering taking in the future.

1. Read the title and information on the jacket for general information about the topic.

2. Read the preface to find out why the author wrote the book and what he expects people to get out of it.

3. Read the table of contents to find out specifically what the book includes.

4. Read any conclusions or summaries at the end of the textbook for the overall picture.

5. Look at the pictures, charts, diagrams, and other visuals to see if the subject matter looks interesting.

(continued on next page)

(continued from previous page)

6. Choose a chapter from the table of contents that looks interesting and read selected parts.

   a. Read the introduction.

   b. Read the summary.

   c. Read the major headings and subheadings.

   d. Look at the visuals.

   e. Stop and read any parts that are interesting.

Another way to find out what subjects are interesting is to go the campus bookstore and browse the textbooks that various courses require. Open one or more of these books and **preview** them (see Getting Ahead in College Box 1.1). Take a few minutes and read a couple of paragraphs from each book. We may find ourselves drawn in by a passage from a "Marriage and Family" textbook on dating rules, or we may find ourselves absorbed in a passage from a biology text about the dangers of smoking cigarettes. We might find that we can't help reading an account from a history book about college students being shot and killed by the National Guard. Or we may find ourselves interested in a passage from a chemistry book that helps us figure out the amount of vitamin C there is in an 8-ounce glass of orange juice. We may also find ourselves picking up a psychology book because it explains why money doesn't buy happiness. We should do our best to make note of the textbooks that have caught and absorbed our attention; these are the subjects that we may want to explore further or select as a major.

EXERCISE 1-6

Practice Previewing

Go to your campus bookstore and preview ten textbooks from the subjects listed. Use the chart below to help you keep track of your interests.

Subject	Not Interesting	Interesting	Very Interesting
Psychology			
Sociology			
Biology			
Chemistry			
History			
Spanish			
Education			
Computer Science			
Finance			
Geology			

HOW CAN MY CAREER CHOICE HELP ME TO STAY FOCUSED?

In general, the students whose career goals are closely related to their academic majors often make it on the Dean's List. Those who have no specific goals for college tend to fall under academic probation (see J. Yaworski, "Why Do Students Succeed or Fail? Theories of Underachieving Affluent College Students," doctoral dissertation, State University of New York, Albany, 1996). Compare the comments below made by students on the Dean's List with those made by students on academic probation. What do you notice?

Dean's List

"The reason I'm here [at college] is I want to be a high school chemistry teacher" (Rose, a secondary education major).

"I realized how much I love working with children; college will give me a chance to pursue my goal to become a teacher" (Rita, an elementary education major).

"Art is my most important interest in life. I hope to pursue it further by getting a degree in art education" (Carlos, an art education major).

Academic Probation

"I would like to get a good paying job; I'm not sure what kind of job" (Sarita, a recreation major).

"I would like to get a degree and make a lot of money in a job" (Mei, an undeclared major).

"I want to graduate, hopefully get a job out of it, and I don't know, have a good time" (Lynn, a business major).

As these students make clear, career interests greatly affect how willing we are to invest our time and energy into doing school work.

Knowing Why We're in College

It is important to know why we are in college. What is our overall goal? What skill or skills did we come to college to learn? What will we do with those skills when we graduate? How much will we really enjoy using those skills? The answers to these questions will greatly affect our willingness to work at becoming an expert in a certain field. For example, if we have always wanted to be an elementary school teacher, and we are enrolled in a teacher education program and know that we want to teach second grade when we graduate, we will probably be motivated to read and study our education textbooks. Our textbooks and classes will become very important to us because they contain the guidelines for our future success. However, if we do not have a specific career in mind, reading and studying will be more difficult because we will not see any real need for learning the information.

Getting in Touch with Our Career Center

From the beginning of our college career, in addition to being in touch with our academic advisor, we should also be in touch with our career counseling center or placement center. There are many informational tests that we can take to learn more about our personality and which careers are best suited for our personality type (see Getting Ahead in College Box 1.2).

Another reason we should be in touch with our career center is to become familiar with the type of jobs that are available to us while we are in school. The first question an employer will ask is "What experience do you have doing this type of work?" People with experience will be considered first.

Therefore, the best thing to do would be to take courses with a specific job in mind, layering our book study with actual work experience. If we do this, by the time we graduate, we will have both the degree and experience in our field.

How do we get experience while we are in school? Go to the career center to find out:

■ Are there any part-time jobs related to our field of interest?

■ What relevant internships are available?

■ What type of volunteer work is needed?

Often people working part-time, interning, or volunteering for a company while they are in college are hired by that organization when they graduate.

Getting Ahead in College Box 1.2

FINDING A MAJOR

For some people, it is difficult to know how to choose a major course of study. During our freshmen year, we should go to the career center and ask to take one or more of the following career assessments. These tools try to match our personality with a career that best suits it.

Career/Personality Assessment Tools
■ The Myers-Briggs Type Indicator
■ The Holland Self-Directed Search
■ The Campbell Inventory and Skills Survey
■ The Harrington O'Shea Career Decision-Making System
■ The Career Occupational Preference System

The organization knows the person already and knows what they can do. Companies are more likely to hire someone whose work they know than someone they have not tried out.

Ask the career center about companies that cooperate with colleges and universities to hire students to work for them. For example, some organizations will hire college students to work every other semester at full pay and let the students take off the other semesters to study full-time. This is so the students can make enough money to support themselves through college while still going to school full-time.

Finally, we should go to our career center at the very beginning of our college career to find out about the job opportunities in various fields. It is important to know the answers to the following questions before deciding on a major course of study:

■ What type of jobs can I do if I major in this particular subject?

■ How much money can I make if I get this type of job?

■ What part of the country or world must I live in to do this job?

■ Are there jobs available if I choose this particular major?

■ How much more training is needed beyond the associate's and bachelor's degree to actually get a job? A master's degree? A Ph.D.?

■ How much internship is required to get a job after obtaining the degree?

■ How much competition will there be? (One job for every 300 applications? Ten jobs for every one application?)

For every year we are in college, we are losing one year's salary and paying additional costs for tuition, room, and board (see Visual Literacy Box 1.1).

With these expenses in mind, *we will want to know that we can get a job* when we graduate. If the field is flooded with qualified professionals and there are 300 applications for every one job, we have a better chance of playing the lottery. If, on the other hand, there are more openings than qualified people, we can feel a lot more confident that we will get a good job when we graduate.

Therefore, we can increase our motivation to study in college if we go in a direction that will lead to success instead of a direction that will lead to a dead end. Our career center can provide career research tools, such as the *Occupational Outlook Handbook*, to help us find the right direction.

Visual Literacy Box 1.1

Hidden Costs of College Education

It costs more to go to college than just the tuition. We also must consider how much money we would make if we were working full-time instead of going to college. In addition to our time away from working, we must count the amount of money that it costs for us to live, such as rent, food, and transportation (car payments, gas, subway expenses, etc.). Look at the following chart. How much will a two- or four-year degree cost if our tuition is $6,000 per year? $18,000 per year?

1. Add tuition, rent, food, transportation, and lost salary for the $6,000/yr. tuition (add across). Then multiply the total by 2 or 4 for a 2- to 4-year degree.

2. Add tuition, rent, food, transportation, and lost salary for the $18,000/yr. tuition (add across). Then multiply the total by 2 or 4 for a 2- to 4-year degree.

Tuition	Rent	Food	Transportation	Salary lost from time away from work
$6,000/year ($3,000/ semester)	$7,200/year ($600/month)	$4,800/year ($400/month)	$2,400/year ($200/month car payment)	$25,000
$18,000/year ($900/ semester)	$7,200/year ($600/month)	$4,800/year ($400/month)	$2,400/year ($200/month car payment)	$25,000

Cost for 2- to 4-year degree at $18,000 tuition? Cost for 2- 4-year degree at $6,000 tuition?

_____ per year   _____ per year

_____ for 4 years   _____ for 4 years

HOW DOES LEARNING STYLE AFFECT MOTIVATION?

Another factor has a tremendous influence on how successfully we can function in college and in life: *learning style*. The three main methods of taking in information, or learning, include:

- learning by seeing

- learning by hearing

- learning by doing

We use all three modes of learning, but most of us rely more heavily on one more than on the others. As a result, our learning styles may consist of various combinations of the three.

Learning by Seeing

Some people learn best when they can see information displayed as written text, pictures, diagrams, charts, graphs, maps, video demonstrations, overhead transparencies, PowerPoint presentations, or handouts. It is difficult for those who learn by seeing to process information unless they can see it in print or on screen. If, for example, you give directions to this type of learner, he or she will probably ask to see a roadmap, want to draw a map, or try to write down the directions. Otherwise, he or she will most likely forget the directions immediately, confuse the details, or remember only parts of the information.

Learning by Hearing

Some people learn best by hearing spoken information. They have a difficult time understanding and remembering information that is written or presented in visual displays. They are most comfortable listening to lectures, participating in class discussions, and studying in groups. Auditory learners may not feel comfortable studying in the library unless they are in the language lab or media center, because they often need to read written text out loud or play a tape recording of the lecture.

Learning by Doing

Some people learn new information best by being physically and actively involved in the process. They will make the extra effort to write notes as they read a book and take notes as they listen to a lecture. They may retype their notes on a computer because they learn through motion, not by seeing or hearing. They may also write out the questions on an exam as well as the answers as a way of using their motor memory to think through the questions. Often they will not understand what they are learning until after they have gone through the process of experiencing what they have studied.

Other Ways of Learning

Not only do we process information by seeing, hearing, and doing, but we use various combinations of other modes.

Type of Learner	Characteristics
Social learners	■ Prefer to learn together with others. ■ Enjoy the social contact of a class discussion or a study group
Independent learners	■ Goal oriented ■ Self-directed; less people oriented ■ Prefer to work alone
Applied learners	■ Prefer to apply what they learn to real-world situations
Conceptual learners	■ Like to think about theories and ideas
Creative learners	■ Imaginative ■ Prefer to learn through discovery and experimentation
Pragmatic learners	■ Organized ■ Systematic
Inductive learners	■ Comfortable with facts from which they can draw conclusions
Deductive learners	■ Prefer to know the overall principle of a situation ■ Seek evidence to prove whether the situation is true or false
Active learners	■ Prefer to process information through physical activity
Passive learners	■ Less active; more thoughtful, quiet, and still *(continued on next page)*

Type of Learner	Characteristics
Global learners	■ Prefer to see the whole picture; want general information first
Sequential learners	■ Prefer a step-by-step process to learning so they can piece all details together

TEACHING STYLES AND MOTIVATION

As we think about the various ways that we process and learn information, we must also consider that our professors have their own teaching style preferences. The more quickly we can recognize the professor's teaching style, the easier it will be for us to understand what the professor is expecting from us.

Teaching Style	Characteristics	How to Succeed as Students
Expert	Transmits detailed information to the students through lectures and class discussions	Understand, remember, and explain the information given
		Read and take notes from textbook and lectures
		Put all information together and learn it *before* class
		Participate in class discussions
Formal authority	Teaches by the book	Read the textbook
	Provides students with very structured and explicit directions to completing assignments	Follow the guidelines of the syllabus
		(continued on next page)

Teaching Style	Characteristics	How to Succeed as Students
	Writes feedback on students' work to let them know whether work has been done correctly	Do *not* make up your own formats for papers or substitute assignments
		Read and think about *all* (positive and negative) feedback the instructor provides
Personal model	Models and demonstrates concepts and information	Imitate by example
Facilitator	Encourages learning through inquiry	Ask a lot of questions
	Acts as a helper, guide, and consultant	
	Emphasizes independent thinking, without losing focus on student as learner	
Delegator	Acts as a resource for students	Ask questions and try to find the answers independently
	Encourages active learning	

EXERCISE
1-7

Learning Styles

Read through all of the learning styles mentioned and list the top three styles that best describe the ways you like to learn.

1. _____

2. _____

3. _____

Think of two professors whose classes you've attended and describe their teaching styles. Then read through the descriptions of the professors' teaching styles again and identify which style best fits your description. With which style are you most comfortable?

1. _____

2. _____

Reading: Habits and Skills

● ●

In this chapter, we will start with the basics:

■ How to manage your time;

■ How to read a textbook.

RESIDENT HALL DIRECTOR 1:   I think the freshmen have a lot of free time because they think of free time in terms of "I blew off my last two classes, it's Thursday afternoon, I have nothing to do. You know, I have so much time to spend, you know, what am I gonna do?"

TESS: In high school there was a time and place to be somewhere every minute of the day, every hour of the day. I don't remember any free time, whereas college is all free time.

RESIDENT HALL DIRECTOR 2:   The freshmen will miss at least two classes in a week; they will definitely, absolutely, positively take a nap at least once during the day. The sleeping is a definite constant for every day.

YOSHIE: I can sleep from the day I get here until the day I have to go home for summer break if I want to. Whereas, in high school, my alarm would go off and I would get myself up—half way—and my father would come in and say, "Get out of bed!" It was easier for me to go to school at home.

TESS: I think it's harder to run on an all-free time schedule than a really rigid schedule.

LYNN: It's easier not to do the work in college; it's easier to get caught behind and slack off.

NOEL: You can slack off pretty much in college. Like this morning, I skipped my class. I didn't mean to skip it; my alarm didn't go off. In high school, I always had my mom there to tell me to do the work: "Do your homework, do your homework! " Now there's nobody to tell me to do it, you know. It's definitely harder to get up and get something done . . . so you have to tell yourself and that's a lot harder.

As the students and resident hall directors in the above interviews indicate, there are many adjustments to college life. One of the most important is time management; another is reading ability.

MANAGING TIME

Time management can be a major roadblock for many college students. Whether you have just graduated from high school or are an adult returning to school from the workforce, the ability to manage time is a "make or break" factor when it comes to success in college.

The College Schedule

The most common mistake that you can make is in thinking that the college schedule is "all free time." For example, let's say that you are taking 5 courses in one semester. Each course is generally worth 3 credit hours, so your course load would be 15 credits (5 courses × 3 credit hours). **Credit hours** are defined as the number of hours that you spend in class each week. Here is where you can make the mistake in thinking that college is "all free time." You remember spending 40 hours each week sitting in high school classes and are overjoyed to find out that you only need to be in class 15 hours each week in college. You just gained 30 hours of free time!

Not so!!! The college schedule is set up as a 45-hour work week if you are taking a normal load of classes. You are only in class for 15 hours each week *because you will need the remaining 30 hours for reading and studying* your college textbooks. For every hour spent in class, you will need two hours outside of class to read, study, and prepare for each class meeting. Whether you are a freshman living in the dorms or a working adult, you must set aside 45 hours each week for school. (See Getting Ahead in College Box 2.1.)

If you are living in the dorms, you have to tell yourself when to go to class and when to study—you have to become your own "mom or dad." If you are a working adult with a family, you need to be realistic about how many credits you can actually take without overwhelming yourself and becoming frustrated. Creating a schedule can help you do this.

Getting Ahead in College Box 2.1

CALCULATING YOUR SCHOOL WEEK

Most people spend about 40 hours each week at work. This is called a **work week**. A **school week** is the number of hours per week that you spend on school-related activities. Before you create a personal schedule, you need to know how many hours you should leave open for school. Go through the following steps to find out what your school week should be. Then answer the following questions.

Step 1: Determine your credit hours. Multiply the number of credits by the number of classes you are taking.

Example: 3 credits × 5 classes = 15 credit hours

Step 2: Use the 2 to 1 rule to determine your study time. Multiply your credit hours by 2.

Example: 2 × 15 credit hours = 30 study hours

Step 3: Add the number of credit hours to the number of study hours to determine your school week.

Example: 15 credit hours + 30 study hours = 45-hour school week

1. Determine your school week if you are taking 12 credit hours.

_____

2. Determine your school week if you are taking a 4-credit biology class and 4 courses that are worth 3 credits each.

_____

Following a Schedule

At the beginning of each semester you should work out three types of schedules:

1. a semester schedule

2. a weekly schedule

3. a daily priority list

Semester Schedule You will need a semester schedule to get the big picture of all your assignments due. You will need to go through each syllabus for every class and figure out which assignments are graded and what day each assignment has to be turned in. Once you have gathered this information, you should put it all on four monthly calendars that span the entire semester and keep it in your notebook (see Visual Literacy Box 2.1). If you follow this calendar throughout the semester, you will always know when your assignments are due.

Visual Literacy Box 2.1   ● ● ● ● ● ● ● ● ● ● ● ● ● ● ●

Following Your Syllabi

If each course has 7 graded assignments and you have 5 courses, you must keep track of 35 assignments on 5 different syllabi. An easy way of doing this is to put everything on one calendar that you keep in your main notebook. Follow the directions below to organize your assignments on a semester calendar.

1. Gather the syllabi from all of the courses you are taking this semester.

2. Photocopy the monthly calendar below four times and write in the months and dates.

3. Map out all assignments from each one of your courses for the entire semester.

4. Start with one course syllabus and mark the date of every graded assignment on the calendar. Then, do the same thing for all other syllabi. Include the following types of graded assignments:

■ mid-terms and final exams

■ tests

■ quizzes

■ papers

■ projects

(continued on next page)

■ presentations

■ graded homework assignments

5. Check your calendar each week to see what is due one and two weeks ahead.

Monthly Schedule

Month _____

Sunday	Monday	Tuesday	Wednesday	Thursday	Friday	Saturday

Weekly Schedule It is very important to map out a weekly schedule so that you can see what your time "looks like." If you have a set schedule, you need to do this only once so that you can get a picture of the routine that you will follow all semester. If your work schedule changes every week, then you should map out your schedule on a weekly basis (see Visual Literacy Box 2.2).

Daily Priority Lists A daily priority list, often called a "to-do" list, is essential to make every day. It is simply a list of things that you have to do in the order in which they should be done. If you are most alert during the morning hours, it is the first business task that you should complete. If you are a night owl and can think most clearly during the evening hours, it is very important for you to make your to-do list the night before.

Although a simple task, the to-do list is a powerful organizational tool. There are many tasks that we must complete every day, some more important than others. When you write out your list of things to do, you should write the most important tasks first and the least important tasks toward the bottom of the list. As you complete each task, you simply check this item off your list. Whatever items are not checked off go on the next day's to-do list. The list makes it easier to get started in the morning because you know exactly what to do. It cuts down on the frustration we feel when we forget something important. And it helps us do the most necessary tasks first. (See Visual Literacy Box 2.3 to create a to-do list.)

Visual Literacy Box 2.2

Creating a Weekly Schedule

Using the Weekly Schedule sheet, follow the steps below to create a schedule that shows what your week looks like.

1. Block out the hours that you spend at work and label it "work time."

2. Block out the time that you spend traveling back and forth to work and label it "work travel time."

3. Write in any family commitments or obligations and label it "family."

4. Block out your school schedule and label it "school."

(continued on next page)

5. Block out your travel time to and from school and label it "school travel time."

6. Block out your times when your classes meet and label it "class time."

7. Block out 30 hours for studying (if you are taking 15 credits) and label it "study time."

8. Block out 7–9 hours for sleeping and label it "sleep time."

9. Calculate the number of waking hours that are left and label this "free time."

10. How much free time do you have?

Weekly Schedule

Hours	Monday	Tuesday	Wednesday	Thursday	Friday	Saturday	Sunday
7:00 a.m.							
8:00 a.m.							
9:00 a.m.							
10:00 a.m.							
11:00 a.m.							
12:00 p.m.							
1:00 p.m.							
2:00 p.m.							
3:00 p.m.							
4:00 p.m.							
5:00 p.m.							
6:00 p.m.							
7:00 p.m.							
8:00 p.m.							
9:00 p.m.							

Visual Literacy Box 2.3 ● ■ ■ ■ ■ ■ ■ ■ ■ ■ ■ ■ ■ ■ ■

Creating a "To-Do" List

A "to-do" list is a list of things that you have to do in the order in which they should be done. You can write your list on a tablet, sticky note pad, piece of paper, palm pilot, computer, etc. It doesn't matter what you use to make your list as long as it is handy for you to use. Follow the directions below to create a to-do list that you can use tomorrow.

1. Make a list of all the things you need to do very soon.

2. Add to the list all the things you have to do but could put off for a day or two.

3. Number the items on your list according to what has to be done first, second, third, and so on.

4. Check off each item after completing the task.

Order of Importance	Things to Do

EXERCISE 2-1

Creating a Weekly Schedule

Create a weekly schedule, paying close attention to time for study. Block in 30 hours per week (for a 15-credit course load) for reading and studying. Follow your schedule for one week and then answer the questions below.

1. Did having a schedule change your study habits?_____

2. Were you able to study the recommended number of hours while following a schedule?

   _____

3. If you were not able to study the recommended number of hours, how could you change your schedule to meet this goal?

   _____

EXERCISE 2-2

Managing Your Time

Read the following scenario. Mei has made some mistakes in managing time and now it has caught up with her. How could you help Mei best manage her time so that she can become more successful in school?

Mei is a freshman in college. It is the fifth week of school, and so far things are going all right. However, she suddenly realizes that she has a big week ahead of her. She has a five-class course load.

Monday, she has an exam in her psychology class at 9:00 a.m. She has been breezing through this course so far, not really reading the textbook. This test covers three chapters' worth of material, and at most, Mei has read one-half of one chapter. In addition to this, Mei has to be prepared, with note cards, to discuss the steps in criminal proceedings for her business law class at 1:00 p.m.

Tuesday is an even bigger day. She has another exam in Introduction to Sociology at 9:30 a.m. Again, the test covers roughly four weeks of class. This time, though, the test is mostly from class notes. One problem—the class meets only on Tuesday and Thursday. Four weeks represents eight classes. Mei has missed three of these eight classes and she didn't get the notes from anyone.

Directly after her sociology exam, Mei has two choices. The campus American Idol club, of which she is a member, is having a big competition starting at 11:00 a.m. Also at 11:00 a.m., though, there is a study session for her Marriage and Family course. While this session is not mandatory, there are an up-coming test and paper due on Thursday. This session will help students study and get ideas for papers. In case you haven't guessed, Mei has also winged her way through this course (e.g., participating in class discussions—when she is there). However, she has missed a couple of classes and has not read the textbook.

At 12:45 p.m. on Tuesday, she has the actual Marriage and Family class. She is supposed to read Chapter 20 for class discussion. At 6:00 p.m., Mei has Beginning Drawing. For Tuesday, she only has to do a few blind contour drawings. However, on Thursday, she has to present her portfolio to her professor for mid-semester grading. Needless to say, she has not really done much of the work expected to be in the portfolio. Finally, on Wednesday, Mei is supposed to have prepared a five-page paper on the steps in criminal proceedings for her business law class, based on the notes she is supposed to have for Monday's class.

1. Use the weekly schedule below to map out Mei's week.

Hours	Monday	Tuesday	Wednesday	Thursday	Friday	Saturday	Sunday
7:00 a.m.							
8:00 a.m.							
9:00 a.m.							
10:00 a.m.							
11:00 a.m.							
12:00 p.m.							
1:00 p.m.							
2:00 p.m.							
3:00 p.m.							
4:00 p.m.							
5:00 p.m.							
6:00 p.m.							
7:00 p.m.							
8:00 p.m.							
9:00 p.m.							
10:00 p.m.							
11:00 p.m.							
12:00 a.m.							

2. Make a "to-do" list for Mei for every day of this week.

Order of Importance	Things to Do

3. What suggestions would you give Mei so that the second half of the semester goes more smoothly?

_____

_____

EXERCISE
2-3

Arranging a Schedule

Read the following scenario. Rosa is a working adult with a family. She has decided to go back to school so that she can get a better job to bring in more money for her family. She is, however, finding it difficult to create a schedule that will allow her enough time to take care of her family, work, and go to school. How could you help Rosa arrange her schedule so that she has time for school, family, and work?

Rosa is a working adult with a husband and two small children. She has been out of high school for ten years and is now entering college for the first time. She works from 9:00 a.m. to 5:00 p.m. Monday through Friday. After work, she comes home and cooks dinner at 5:30 p.m. for her husband, who then leaves at 6:30 p.m. to work the evening shift. She spends quality time with her children every night until they go to bed at 9:00 p.m. Then, she does the dishes, cleans and organizes the house, and plans the meals for the following day. On the weekends, she does the grocery shopping, does the laundry, takes the children to the pool, and goes to worship services.

Rosa plans to major in psychology. She is trying to decide whether to take two or three courses because she needs to take 6 to 8 credit hours to keep her financial aid package. There are two sections of the Introduction to Psychology course that she can choose between. The first section meets every day, Monday through Friday, from 7:00 a.m. to 7:50 a.m. The second section meets from 7:15 a.m. to 8:30 a.m. on Tuesdays and Thursdays.

There are three sections of the Introduction to Sociology course: (1) Mondays, Wednesdays, and Fridays from 7:00 p.m. to 7:50 p.m., (2) Mondays, Wednesdays, and Fridays from 8:00 a.m. to 8:50 a.m., and (3) Tuesdays and Thursdays from 7:15 a.m. to 8:30 a.m.

The third course that Rosa is considering is the College Reading course. It is mandatory for her because she scored low on the college placement exam. It meets only on Mondays, Wednesdays, and Fridays from 8:00 a.m. to 8:50 a.m.

Rosa lives 20 minutes from the college. It takes her 10 minutes to get from the college to work.

1. Use the weekly schedule to map out Rosa's week.

2. Map out the classes that you think Rosa should take onto this weekly schedule.

3. According to the "2 to 1" rule, how many hours must Rosa study each week? Map out the study time that Rosa needs and add it to the weekly schedule.

Hours	Monday	Tuesday	Wednesday	Thursday	Friday	Saturday	Sunday
7:00 a.m.							
8:00 a.m.							
9:00 a.m.							
10:00 a.m.							
11:00 a.m.							
12:00 p.m.							
1:00 p.m.							
2:00 p.m.							
3:00 p.m.							
4:00 p.m.							
5:00 p.m.							

	6:00 p.m.							
7:00 p.m.								
8:00 p.m.								
9:00 p.m.								
10:00 p.m.								
11:00 p.m.								
12:00 a.m.								

READING SKILLS: USING THE PQ4R METHOD

The PQ4R is one of the most effective ways to read a textbook. Since the 1940s, when it was developed, much research has proved that this method helps people learn information from a textbook. There are five parts to this system:

1 Previewing
2 Questioning
3 Reading and Reflecting
4 Reciting
5 Reviewing

Previewing

Think about what you can tell from two puzzles that are exactly alike. One is put together and the other one is scrambled into pieces. Which puzzle helps you to see the whole picture? Although the puzzles have all of the same pieces, you can tell what the completed puzzle looks like. However, this is not true for the scrambled puzzle. We would have to put the pieces together to see the picture.

When we read a textbook chapter, it is very much like putting together a puzzle. Starting at the beginning of the chapter and reading sentence by sentence is like trying to make sense of a scrambled puzzle; it is difficult to imagine how the ideas of each sentence will fit together and relate to the whole chapter.

Sometimes we may need to skim individual sentences or paragraphs in order to get a sense of what the whole chapter is about. This is known as **previewing**. Previewing a textbook chapter is similar to looking at a puzzle that has a border with many of the key pieces in place. You try to identify the main pieces to guess what it should look like.

Finding the main pieces of a textbook chapter allows you to see the main points and how they fit together. Previewing reveals the author's outline. Understanding the author's outline helps you to read much faster because you will know what to expect as you read. And, as you read through the chapter, you begin to understand how the details fit in. So how does one preview? Here are six helpful steps:

1. **Read the title**. First, examine the title of the chapter to get a clue to its general content. A title provides lots of information; unfortunately, in our hurry to get through the chapter itself, it is often too easy for us to skip over it. See Getting Ahead Box 2.2 for an example that shows how much easier it is to understand what we read when we pay attention to the title.

Getting Ahead in College Box 2.2

THE IMPORTANCE OF TITLES

Titles help set the stage for a reading. Read the following paragraph and try to guess what it is about without the title.

> You should get to know a little bit about the person. Ask him very politely what you would like to know. Ask him, for example, where he is from, where has he studied, and what topic he would like to talk about. Everyone else will also want to know this information. It is up to you to get everybody's attention and tell them what you have found out.

Until we find out the title of the passage above, we may not really be certain what it is about. Once we know that the title is "Introducing a Guest Speaker," all of the details begin to make sense and the passage becomes understandable.

2. **Read the introduction**. After reading the title, the next step in previewing is to read the introduction of the chapter. In the introduction, the author announces the general content and tells us the main point of the chapter.

3. **Read the summary**. At this point, it is a good idea to compare the introduction with the summary. It should look pretty similar. Just as the introduction points out the main ideas in the chapter, the conclusion sums up all of the main points that were explained in the chapter. The author wraps up the important content and reviews the major principles and concepts.

   There are two reasons you should be aware of a chapter's main points as you read. First, the knowledge will help you focus on the important information. Second, reading the summary first will help you recognize the information most likely to appear on an exam. If a point is made in both the introduction and in the summary, there is a good chance that you will be tested on this information.

4. **Skim the body of the chapter**. After reading the title, introduction, and summary, you should read the chapter headings. These generally appear in dark **boldface** print and provide the general subject of each section. Herein lies the author's outline. The chapter division headings and subheadings set off the author's main thoughts and announce the subtopics.

There are usually four to five major headings in a chapter and three to six subheadings under each of these. The subheadings may appear in smaller dark print or italics.

5. **Read the first and last sentences of each paragraph**. The first sentence of each paragraph is usually the topic sentence, and the last sentence is usually a transition (link) to the next paragraph. By reading the first and last sentences of each paragraph, you will find out what the main ideas are, how they are related to the topic, and how they are linked to the next main idea. Often it is possible to get a general understanding of an article simply by reading the first and last sentences. You will not know the details, but you will know what the article is about.

6. **Look at graphic aids: pictures, charts, graphs, and diagrams**. Sometimes difficult ideas may be hard to understand if they are explained in words alone. It may take pages for an author to explain, for example, a scientific process. However, it may be easier to understand the process if you can see a picture of it or if you can see the ideas laid out in a chart, diagram, or graph. Once you understand the idea by studying the diagram or chart, it becomes much easier to read the words that explain it. See Visual Literacy Box 2.4 for an example of how diagrams make text easier to understand.

Visual Literacy Box 2.4 ● ● ● ● ● ● ● ● ● ● ● ● ● ●

Graphic Aids Help Understanding

Read the passage below and try to interpret its meaning.

[1]The sun's rays pass through the collectors. [2]The collectors convert the sun's rays into heat. [3]Fluid is heated as it flows through the collectors. [4]Heat fluid is pumped through pipes to the storage tank and back to the collectors. [5]Water in the storage tank is heated by the pipes of hot fluid and pumped to the heating unit and back. [6]A fan blows air that is heated by hot-water pipes from the heating unit into the living space.

It probably did not make much sense. Now look at the diagram below. Before you see the diagram, the passage looks like a real brainteaser. After you see the diagram, however, it is much easier to understand the meaning of the words. Starting with sentence number 1, reread the paragraph. Stop after every sentence to study the diagram and answer the questions.

(continued on next page)

1. Read the first sentence and then look at #1 in the diagram. What do you think a "collector" collects or gathers up?

2. Read the second sentence and look at #2 in the diagram. What type of heating system does this diagram represent?

3. Read the third sentence and look at #3 in the diagram. What is holding the fluid? What is it in?

4. Read the fourth sentence and look at #4 on the diagram. Why is the fluid sent back to the collectors?

5. Read the fifth sentence and look at #5 on the diagram. How is the water in the storage unit heated?

6. Read the sixth sentence and look at #6 on the diagram. What do the hot-water pipes heat?

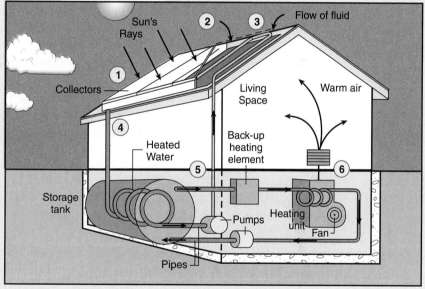

From *Social Study Skills.* Copyright © 1978 by Scholastic Magazines, Inc. Reprinted by permission of Scholastic, Inc.

EXERCISE
2-4

PQ4R: Previewing

Use the following guidelines for previewing the selection below and answer the questions that follow. The first answer has been provided for you.

Preview

1. Read title and introduction of chapter.

2. Read summary to find out what information is important and what to concentrate and spend most time on.

3. Read major headings (main ideas)—this makes an outline of the chapter.

4. Read subheadings (subtopics).

5. Read first and last sentences of each paragraph (topic sentences and transition sentences).

6. Figure out charts, graphs, diagrams.

Handling Conflict

[1]   People who care about each other will get angry, but their closeness should enable them to get through a healthy, productive conflict. They use words, not to hurt, but to find out what is bothering each person. Then, bottled-up stresses can be released.

[2]   There is a big difference between this type of arguing and the destructive kind. Whereas healthy conflict stresses the facts, destructive conflict aims for the ego (the inner self) with statements such as "You're ridiculous," and "Me? You should see yourself." The goal of an argument should be **conflict management**, not insults aimed at the other person's character. Better to say "I don't like your behavior choice" than to say "I don't like you right now."

[3]   There are six principles for managing conflicts that happen between people effectively and efficiently.

1. *Recognize that conflicts can be settled in a calm and reasonable way.* A conflict has a better chance of being settled if you do not pretend it doesn't exist, withdraw from discussing it, surrender to the other person, find fault or lay blame, or attempt to force the other person to take your view.

2. *Define the conflict.* Ask yourself: Why are we in conflict? What is the nature of the conflict? Which of us feels more strongly about the issue? Then try to figure out a way that all can "win."

3. *Check your point of view.* It is possible to misunderstand the other person's behavior, position, or motivations. At this time, try to determine whether you understand one another.

4. *Suggest possible solutions.* The goal at this stage is to put your heads together and come up with a variety of solutions. However, neither you

nor the other person(s) should judge or "put down" the suggested solutions at this time.

5. *Consider all possible solutions and choose the best one.* Determine which solutions will let one party "win" at the other's cost, which solutions would allow both parties to lose, and which solutions will let both parties win. Then choose the one that allows both people to win.

6. *Try out the solution and see how it works.* Decide how well the selected solution is working or not working. Then make the proper changes in the plan.

[4]   As you can see, conflict between persons can be managed successfully. However, doing so means taking the time and spending the necessary energy to talk through the conflict.

From Larry L. Barker and Deborah Roach Gaut. *Communication,* 8e. Published by Allyn and Bacon, Boston, MA. Copyright © 2002 by Pearson Education. Reprinted by permission of the publishers, pp. 137–38.

_____ b _____ 1. What is this selection about?

    a. argument

    b. managing conflict

    c. possible solutions

_____ C _____ 2. The best title for this selection is:

    a. "All People Become Angry at One Time or Another"

    b. "Destructive Argument Aims for the Ego"

    c. "Productive Conflict Involves the Use of Words to Find Out What Is Bothering Each Person"

_____ A _____ 3. In which section will the authors tell you how to settle an argument rationally?

    a. Paragraph 3, section 1

    b. Paragraph 3, section 2

    c. Paragraph 3, section 3

_____ C _____ 4. In which section will the authors tell you how to suggest solutions to an argument?

    a. Paragraph 3, section 2

    b. Paragraph 3, section 3

    c. Paragraph 3, section 4

_____*b*_____ 5. In which section will the authors tell you how to choose the best solution to your argument?

    a. Paragraph 3, section 4

    b. Paragraph 3, section 5

    c. Paragraph 3, section 6

Questioning

The next step in the PQ4R method will keep you from falling asleep when you read. It is much like playing the television game show *Jeopardy*. You must review a section heading and the information from that section and figure out what test question that section answers. You will not fall asleep if your mind is active in creating questions and searching for answers.

The questioning step is a simple process. Start by changing a section heading into a question. Next, read further to see if the information that follows answers your question. As you continue to read, you may find that your question is too broad or too narrow. In either case, you need to change your question to reflect the information in the passage.

For example, imagine you are reading for your chemistry course and come across a section heading in your textbook that reads "Mixing Genes: Improving on Nature." You may ask yourself, "How does mixing genes improve on nature?" As you read, however, you realize that instead of improving on nature, mixing genes creates a lot of problems. You would then revise your question accordingly so that it asks, "What problems arise from mixing genes?"

If the reading has no section headings or subheadings, you can generally turn the first sentence of a paragraph into a question. If you cannot locate the topic sentence, search the content. Glance through the paragraph and ask yourself, "What question was the author trying to answer when he wrote this?"

If you create a section in your notebook for this phase of reading, you will save quite a bit of time when it comes to studying for exams. (See Visual Literacy Box 2.5.) If you choose to take notes like this for every chapter of your textbooks, you will probably have many, if not all, of the test questions and their answers. Foremost, all the material you need to know will already be organized. When it comes time to study for your exams, you will be prepared to sit down and learn everything.

Visual Literacy Box 2.5

Question/Answer Charts

As you read your textbook, make note of all headings. Draw a line down the center of your notebook page and write all of the questions from your section headings in the left-hand space. Write the answers opposite from the questions in the right-hand space.

Chemistry

Section Heading: You Are What You Eat **Question:** Why do we need to eat food?	**Answer:** Food contains the 4 types of materials that keep our bodies functioning: **1.** water **2.** energy sources **3.** raw materials **4.** metabolic regulators
Section Heading: Malnutrition **Question:** What causes malnutrition?	**Answer:** Malnutrition is caused by a diet lacking in the proper mix of nutrients, even if you have enough calories.
Question: What is the difference between malnutrition and undernourishment?	**Answer:** Undernourished people do not have enough calories to meet their metabolic needs.

1. Choose a chapter from one of your textbooks that you will be tested on in the future.

2. Change all of the section headings into questions.

3. Read each section to find the answer to your question.

4. Record all questions and answers in a notebook in the same way as the "Chemistry" example above.

5. Do this for all of the chapters that your next exam will cover.

6. After the exam, compare the questions that you created with those that were actually on the exam. How many of your questions did you find on the exam?

| EXERCISE 2-5 | PQ4R: Questioning |

Read the selection below. Then follow guidelines for the questioning step in the PQ4R to create question/answer notes from the reading below.

Question

1. Convert each section heading (subheading) into a question.

2. If headings are missing, make the topic sentence into a question.

3. Read to find the answer to your question.

4. turn boldface words into Qs

Where Does Drinking Water Come From?

[1]   What journey does water take to get from its natural source to your tap or bottle? Water is widely distributed on planet Earth. On the surface, it is found in oceans, lakes, rivers, snow, and glaciers. In the atmosphere it exists as water vapor and as tiny droplets in clouds that serve to replenish surface water by means of rain and snow.

[2]   Water is also found underground in **aquifers**, *great pools of water trapped in sand and gravel 50 to 500 feet below the surface.* Some aquifers are enormous, such as the Ogallala Aquifer in the center of the United States that underlies parts of eight states from South Dakota to Texas.

[3]   Water that can be made suitable for drinking normally comes from either surface water or ground water. **Surface water**—*lakes, rivers, and reservoirs*—frequently contains substances that must be removed before it can be used as drinking water. By contrast, **ground water** is *pumped from wells that have been drilled into underground aquifers* and is usually free of harmful contaminants.

[4]   Large-scale water supply systems for cities tend to rely on surface water resources; smaller cities, towns, and private wells tend to rely on ground water, the source of drinking water for a little over half of the U.S. population. If an aquifer becomes contaminated, it may take decades to become clean again. Prudence suggests that steps be taken to protect aquifers from contamination. (Stanitski et al. 186–87)

8|9

Chemistry	
Section Heading/Question: Where Does Drinking Water Come From?	Answer: oceans, lakes 1
First sentence/Question (Para. 1): What journey does water take to get from its natural source to your tap or bottle?	Answer: water vaper 2
First sentence/Questions (Para. 2): Where is water also found? What is an aquifer?	Answer: aquifer 3 Answer: 50ft below surface 4
First sentence/Questions (Para. 3): Where does water that can be made suitable for drinking come from? What is surface water? What is ground water?	Answer: surface water 5 Answer: wells 6 Answer: pumped ground 7
First sentence/Questions (Para. 4): What type of source for drinking water do cities tend to rely on? What type of source do smaller cities and towns rely on?	Answer: surface 1 Answer: aquafers

Reading and Reflecting

During the reading and reflecting step of the PQ4R, you are looking for answers to the questions created in the questioning step. However, you are also thinking over each sentence to be sure the meaning is clear. Often, concepts build upon earlier information, so it is important to stop and deal with any information that you do not understand.

When you come to something you do not understand, there are many strategies you could use. You could go to an encyclopedia or dictionary for more information. You could reread the part that is troubling. You could read ahead to see if your questions are answered at a later point in the passage. Or you may ask another student or even meet with your professor.

During the reflecting step of the PQ4R, we may slow down our reading speed for difficult paragraphs. We may even simply stop and think about what we are reading. There are many questions that we can ask ourselves that will help us understand the information:

- Can I give an example of this?

- What is the basic meaning of this?

- Can I sum this up into a generalization?

- What evidence supports this?

- How does this relate to the main topic?

- How would I explain this to someone else?

- How could I summarize this?

- How does this relate to my life?

- How does this relate to the professor's lecture or the information discussed in class?

It is wise to use your seeing, hearing, and motor memory. As your eyes look at the print, you are using your seeing memory. Saying the information out loud involves your hearing memory. Writing the information down, typing notes, or drawing a sketch or diagram involves the motor memory. You can increase your memory power by using all three modes of learning.

EXERCISE
2-6

PQ4R: Reading and Reflecting

Use the guidelines for the reading and reflecting stage below to think about the passage that follows. Then answer the questions at the end of the passage.

Read and Reflect

1. Think over each sentence to be sure the meaning is clear.

2. Mentally, summarize each paragraph after reading it.

3. Ask yourself:
   a. Can I give an example of this?
   b. What is the basic meaning of this?
   c. Can I sum this up into a generalization?
   d. What evidence supports this?
   e. How does this relate to the main topic?

Simplify Your Rules

Having too may rules can be an invitation for children to rebel. It works better to limit your rules to a half dozen or so that are the most crucial to the harmony of your household. You can decide what these are by reviewing the most recent confrontations and noting which ones made you the angriest. It will also help to examine what is most important to you and your family. For example, if weekday mornings are stressful, you could relax the rule about tidying bedrooms before leaving for school. But the rule that homework must be finished before TV remains on the books. A limited number of clear rules that children can keep track of will help you to prevent frustrating incidents that tempt you to spin out of control. (From "The Parent Trap: Breaking Free fromCycles of Anger and Guilt" by Nancy Marriott in Manis 127–28)

1. Sum up the meaning of this passage in one or two sentences.

   _____

   _____

2. Can you think of a time in your childhood when you had too many rules? If you are a parent, can you think of a time when you gave your children too many rules? What happened? Was your experience similar to or different from the information in the passage?

   _____

   _____

3. What conclusion can you draw about rules?

   _____

   _____

4. What is the author's solution for having too many rules?

   _____

   _____

5. How does the author's example for relaxing the rule for tidy bedrooms on weekdays and keeping the rule for homework relate to the title of the passage?

_____

_____

Reciting

Reciting is the most powerful study technique known to psychologists. During this step of the PQ4R, you should close your book, think about the main points, and ask yourself, "What have I just read?" Then put these ideas into your own words.

Write down what you want to remember. Choose about 10–15 facts. If, for example, a sociology exam will cover three chapters and there will be 30 questions on the exam, that leaves 10 questions for each chapter. In this case, you should choose 10 main points, write them down, and memorize them. Some chapters may have over 500 facts crowded into them. You cannot remember all of them, so you need to select the most important concepts and make an effort to understand and remember them.

EXERCISE 2-7	PQ4R: Reciting

Read the selection below. Then follow guidelines for the reciting step in the PQ4R to memorize the points that you choose as being important.

RECITE

1. Use an index card to cover paragraphs. Look at subject headings and try to remember what each section is about.

2. Choose 10–15 facts that you want to remember.

3. Write them down.

4. Memorize them.

Three Types of Friendships

[1]   Not all friendships are the same. But how do they differ? One way of answering this question is by distinguishing among the three major types of friendship: reciprocity, receptivity, and association.

[2]   The friendship of **reciprocity** is the ideal type, characterized by loyalty, self-sacrifice, mutual affection, and generosity. A friendship of reciprocity is based on equality: each individual shares equally in giving and receiving the benefits and rewards of the relationship. In the friendship of **receptivity**, in contrast, there is an imbalance in giving and receiving; one person is the primary giver and one the primary receiver. This imbalance, however, is a positive one because each person gains something from the relationship. The different needs of both the person who receives and the person who gives affection are satisfied. This is the friendship that may develop between a teacher and a student or between a doctor and a patient. In fact, a difference in status is essential for the friendship of receptivity to develop.

[3]   The friendship of **association** is a transitory one. It might be described as a friendly relationship rather than a true friendship. Associative friendships are the kind we often have with classmates, neighbors, or coworkers. There is no great loyalty, no great trust, no great giving or receiving. The association is cordial but not intense. (Barker and Gaut 399–400)

1. List 5 facts that you would want to remember about friendships of reciprocity.

   ■ _____

   ■ _____

   ■ _____

   ■ _____

   ■ _____

2. List 5 facts that you would want to remember about friendships of receptivity.

   ■ _____

- _____
- _____
- _____
- _____

3. List 5 facts that you would want to remember about friendships of association.

- _____
- _____
- _____
- _____
- _____

4. Which type of friendship would you look for in your neighbors?

- _____

5. Which type of friendship would you look for in a husband or wife?

- _____

Reviewing

When we finish reading a chapter in a textbook, our first instinct is to put the book away. We know we have read the assignment and believe we have understood it. However, if we took a test on that information a week later, we would probably fail it.

What happens to the material we just learned over the course of the week? A few things may occur. It is possible to understand something we have read but not remember it. It is also possible not to understand something we have read but still remember it. Finally, it is possible both to understand *and* remember what we have read. As readers, we should all try to reach this goal. If we do not review the material immediately after we read it, within two weeks we will lose 80 percent of it. This means we will only remember 20 percent. Reviewing will help us to retain 80 percent and lose only 20 percent.

Consider what would happen if you type something on the computer and forget to click on the save button. Of course you would certainly understand what you wrote, but because you did not save it, you cannot recall that information from the computer again—it is gone! Our brains function in a similar fashion. Even if we read information and understand it, we will lose what we have learned if we do not schedule immediate and spaced reviews.

The forgetting curve drops after the first hour and then drops sharply after the first 24 hours. Therefore, it is important that we do not close the book after reading a chapter, but immediately go back to the beginning of the chapter and quiz ourselves on what we just read.

Ideally, we should complete a broad review of the chapter. We do this by returning to the beginning of the chapter to recite its broad organization and to recall the big thought patterns or divisions. Our goal is to look at the author's total picture or identify the major idea.

Next, we should check our memory for and understanding of the important subpoints. We can do this by taking an index card and holding it over each paragraph, leaving only the headings and subheadings visible. Then we try to remember what is in each paragraph by looking at the headings and subheadings. If we cannot remember the information, then we should reread the parts we have forgotten. To aid our memories, we find the main points, say them out loud, and write down cue phrases as a memory aid.

Just as an actor memorizes lines well enough to deliver them without error, once we understand the material, we should memorize it so that it becomes automatic. This memory technique is called **over-learning**, and in most cases it will help you overcome test anxiety. For it is possible to understand information and not remember it, remember information that you do not understand, and understand and remember information. If you can both understand and remember the information on a test, the anxiety will diminish.

In addition to over-learning, we should use **spaced reviews**. This means that we will recite and review the information several times on different days to prepare for an exam. For example, if we read a psychology chapter on Sunday night for a Friday exam, we would do an immediate review after reading, and then another review on Tuesday. Again, we might review on Thursday evening and once again before the exam on Friday.

At first, this seems to be a lot of work. However, if you spend 2–3 hours reading a chapter and neglect to do a review, chances are that you will not pass the exam. Even if you remember 50 percent of the material, that is still not enough. Furthermore, as we have said, without a review you will probably only remember 20 percent of the material. If you take the time to complete the reviewing step of the PQ4R and remember 80 percent of the information for an exam, it will make the time you spent reading the textbook worthwhile.

EXERCISE
2-8

PQ4R: Reviewing

Follow the guidelines below to review the information that you read in Exercise 2.7, completing an immediate review and two reviews over the next two days. Then take the quiz that follows. The first one has been provided for you.

Review

Repeat the reciting step several times as spaced reviews before the exam.

Example: If you read the chapter Sunday night and the exam is on Friday morning, you might repeat the recite step on Monday night, Wednesday night, and Friday morning before your exam.

_____b_____ 1. The friendship of reciprocity is characterized by:
    a. no great loyalty.
    b. self-sacrifice.
    c. a difference in status.

_____ 2. The friendship of association is characterized by:
    a. mutual affection.
    b. generosity.
    c. cordial behavior.

_____ **3.** The friendship of receptivity is characterized by:
   a. an imbalance in giving.

   b. equality in giving.

   c. no great giving.

_____ **4.** Which of the following is the ideal type of friendship?
   a. The friendship of receptivity.

   b. The friendship of association.

   c. The friendship of reciprocity.

_____ **5.** The type of friendship that develops between a teacher and student is that of:

   a. receptivity.

   b. association.

   c. reciprocity.

A Reading in Chemistry

Chemistry impacts every aspect of our lives whether we are aware of it or not. Read the following selection to find out how chemistry is related to drinking water.

Vocabulary in Context

Complete the vocabulary exercise before reading the selection to learn the new terms. After reading the selection, complete the comprehension exercises that follow it. The first vocabulary answer has been provided for you.

a. privileged—lucky, fortunate, advantaged

b. access—availability; ease of use

c. discretionary—optional; up to one's own judgment

d. arid—dry, waterless

e. scarce—in short supply

_____c_____ 1. Most peoples of the world do not have the option to choose bottled water; many factors prevent them from having this _____ option.

_____ 2. Although fresh water is _____ in many parts of the world, salt water can be found in abundance.

_____ 3. Fresh water is scarce in _____ regions such as the Middle East.

_____ 4. One in five people do not have _____ to safe drinking water.

_____ 5. Those who are _____ or fortunate enough to have many drinking water choices often take water for granted.

International Needs for Safe Drinking Water

[1]   Those who live in the United States are **privileged** to have drinking water choices available. We can select from tap, bottled, or filtered water, all generally of high quality. Such is not the case for people in most of the rest of the world. The reality there is that more than a billion people (one in five), principally in developing nations, lack **access** to safe drinking water. Whereas bottled water is a **discretionary** option for many in the United States, the majority of the world's population does not have that option.

_____ 1. The majority of the world's population must drink:

   a. tap water.

   b. bottled water.

   c. unsafe water.

_____ 2. How many of the world's people do not have safe drinking water?

   a. one thousand

   b. one million

   c. one billion

[2]   For those living in **arid** regions, such as the Middle East, fresh water is **scarce**. Seawater is readily available in many such areas, but its high salt concentration makes it unfit for human consumption. Ocean water contains 3.5% salt compared to only about 0.9% salt in

body cells. Consequently, seawater can be drunk only after most of the salt is removed. Fortunately, there are ways to do this, but they require large amounts of energy. Collectively the methods are known as **desalination**, a broad general term describing any process that removes ions from salty water.

From *Chemistry in Context: Applying Chemistry to Society*, 3e by Conrad L. Stanitski, Lucy Pryde Eubanks, Catherine H. Middlecamp, and Wilmer J. Stratton. A project of the American Chemical Society. Boston: Mcgraw-Hill. Copyright © 2000, p. 223.

_____ **3.** Any process that removes ions from salty water is called:

   a. desalination.

   b. consumption.

   c. scarcity.

_____ **4.** What percentage of salt can be found in our bodies?

   a. 0.09%

   b. 0.9%

   c. 3.5% salt

_____ **5.** People in arid regions do not drink ocean water because it:

   a. has salt in it.

   b. is not abundant enough.

   c. is not available.

A Reading in Interpersonal Communications

Friends are special people in our lives. Read the following selection to find out what characteristics are necessary for friendships to develop.

Vocabulary in Context

Complete the vocabulary exercise before reading the selection to learn the new terms. After reading the selection, complete the comprehension exercises that follow it. The first vocabulary answer has been provided for you.

a. **array**—group; collection

b. **mutually**—jointly; showing shared feelings or actions

c. **regard**—respect, high opinion, admiration

d. **irreplaceable**—unique, exceptional, matchless; cannot be replaced

e. **essential**—necessary, important, key

_____a_____ **1.** In your lifetime, you will meet a wide _____ (collection) of people, but you will develop relatively few friendships.

_____ **2.** People often become friends when they engage in _____ (equally) enjoyable activities.

_____ **3.** It is _____ (very important) to like people that you call "friends."

_____ **4.** Because friends treat each other in a genuine manner, they are _____ (cannot be replaced) individuals.

_____ **5.** Both people in a friendship must have mutual positive _____ (respect; high opinion) for each other.

Friends

[1]   Friendship has engaged the attention and imagination of poets, novelists, and artists of all kinds. In television, our most influential mass medium, friendships have become almost as important as romantic pairings.

[2]   Throughout your life, you will meet many people, but out of this wide **array** you'll develop relatively few relationships you would call friendships. Yet despite the low number of friendships you may form, their importance is great.

_____c_____ **1.** According to the author, throughout your life you will:

a. make large numbers of friends.

b. meet very few people.

c. have a relatively low number of friends.

[3]   Friendship is an interpersonal relationship between two persons that is **mutually** productive and characterized by mutual positive **regard**.

[4]   Friendship is an interpersonal relationship; communication interactions must have taken place between the people. The interpersonal relationship involves a "personalisitic focus" (Wright 1978, 1984). Friends react to each other as complete persons, as unique, genuine, and **irreplaceable** individuals.

_____   **2.** Friends treat each other as if:

      a. they can be easily replaced.

      b. they are similar to other friends.

      c. they are valuable and unique.

[5]   Friendships must be mutually productive; this qualifier emphasizes that, by definition, they cannot be destructive either to oneself or to the other person. Once destructiveness enters into a relationship, it can no longer be characterized as friendship. Lover relationships, marriage relationships, parent-child relationships, and just about any other possible relationship can be either destructive or productive. But friendship must enhance the potential of each person and can only be productive.

_____   **3.** In order for friendships to last, they must be:

      a. positive and helpful.

      b. destructive.

      c. unproductive.

[6]   Friendships are characterized by mutual positive regard. Liking people is **essential** if we are to call them friends. Three major characteristics of friends—trust, emotional support, and sharing of interests—testify to this positive regard.

[7]   The closer friends are, the more interdependent they become; that is, when friends are especially close, the actions of one will impact more significantly on the other than they would if the friends were just casual acquaintances. At the same time, however, the closer friends are, the more independent they are of, for example, the attitudes and behaviors of others. Also, they are less influenced by the societal rules that govern more casual relationships. Close friends are likely to make up their own rules for interacting with each other; they

decide what they will talk about and when, what they can say to each other without offending and what they can't, when and for what reasons you can call the other person, and so on.

_____ 4. Three major characteristics of friendships include:

    a. trust, emotional support, and sharing of interests.

    b. trust, independence, and sharing.

    c. independence, acquaintance, and emotional support.

[8] In North America, friendships clearly are a matter of choice; you choose—within limits—who your friends will be. The density of the cities and the ease of communication and relocation make friendships voluntary, a matter of choice. But, in many parts of the world—small villages miles away from urban centers, where people are born, live, and die without venturing much beyond their birthplace, for example—relationships are not voluntary. In these cases, you simply form relationships with those in your village. Here you do not have the luxury of selecting certain people to interact with and others to ignore. You must interact with and form relationships with members of the community simply because these people are the only ones you come into contact with regularly. (Barker and Gaut 398–99)

_____ 5. In small villages miles away from urban centers, where people are born, live, and die without venturing much beyond their birthplace, friendships are:

    a. a matter of choice.

    b. a matter of location.

    c. a matter of communication.

Getting Ahead in College Box 2.3

THE PRONUNCIATION OF VOCABULARY

In our alphabet the letter **g** has two sounds. It can sound like itself as in the word **girl** or it can take the sound of **j** as in **giraffe**. The **g** in girl is called the hard **g** while the g in giraffe is called the soft **g**.

The hard **g** usually comes in front of **a**, **o**, and **u**. The soft **g** usually comes in front of **e**, **i**, and **y**.

(continued on next page)

Using these rules, identify the soft and hard sounds in **g** in the following sentences. On the line, write **j** if the **g** has a soft sound and **g** if it has a hard sound.

_____j_____ **1.** There are more children than parents with every **g**eneration.

_____ **2.** One hypothesis for the increase in singlehood is the **g**rowth of cohabitation.

_____ **3.** Very few families live below the poverty line as officially defined by the U.S. **g**overnment.

_____ **4.** Most families move into poverty as wa**g**e earners lose a job, get, sick, or get divorced.

_____ **5.** Families move out of poverty as wage earners **g**et well or remarry.

_____ **6.** In the thirty years since 1965, divorces have **g**enerally increased each year.

_____ **7.** Beginning in the 1960s, these patterns began to chan**g**e.

_____ **8.** Young people be**g**an to demand more freedom.

_____ **9.** The highest divorce rate was in 1945 when soldiers returned to marria**g**es hastily arranged before going to war.

_____ **10.** One-fifth of all women worked outside of the home at the be**g**inning of the century.

A Reading in Sociology

Family has changed in North America. Read the following selection to find out how it has changed and if these changes were for the better or worse.

Vocabulary in Context

Complete the vocabulary exercise before reading the selection to learn the new terms. The first one has been answered for you. After reading the selection, complete the comprehension exercise that follow it.

a. **contemporary**—modern, present day, up-to-date

b. **landscape**—scene, background, backdrop

c. **hypocritical**—not sincere; phony, deceitful

d. **dissolve**—break up; end

e. **commentator**—reviewer, observer, reporter, person giving an opinion

_____d_____ 1. Today, if a couple is unhappy in their marriage, they usually _____ (break up; end) the marriage.

_____ 2. Teenage pregnancies increased because of _____ (insincere) attitudes of adults who were against teenagers having contraceptives.

_____ 3. Some _____ (observers) suggest that the social institution we call "family" may not survive.

_____ 4. The authors question what is happening to the _____ (present day) American family.

_____ 5. The authors suggest that the reader take a good look at the _____ (background) of the American family to decide whether the family is falling apart or not.

Contemporary American Families

[1]   What is happening to the American family? Every place we look we see dysfunctional families, divorced single parents, teen-age mothers . . . Where is it all leading? Every day we are bombarded—by politicians, experts, talk-show hosts—with images that the family is changing, threatened or even dying. Perhaps the best way to find out is by surveying the **landscape** of the modern American family, finding out what is "out there," and finding out what is not.

[2]   There has been a dramatic change in family life in many parts of American society in the last forty years. And there has been a dramatic change in the way we think about the family as well. In the 1950s, as now, most people hoped to marry and have children and stay together until "death do us part." But those who didn't were seen as strange and different and perhaps even a little dangerous.

[3]   Beginning in the 1960s, these patterns began to change. Driven by the development of the birth control pill, women's liberation, and the sexual freedom of the "hippies," young people in particular began to demand more freedom in their sexual behavior and lifestyle. Age of first intercourse dropped for both males and females. And perhaps partially due to the **hypocritical** attitudes of adults who discouraged distribution of contraceptives to teenagers, teenage pregnancies boomed.

[4]   The economic changes in the U.S. which began in the 1970s added fuel to these trends. No longer were the majority of American families able to survive on a single income. Women poured into the workplace. The new economic freedoms and changes in the legal code making divorce easier allowed many unhappy marriages to **dissolve**. But now many fear that the changes have gone too far, and that even couples who want to stay together may not survive the hard times. It seems to many people that the search for new freedoms and the attempts to solve age-old problems went too far, or created problems that were worse than the ones before. Some **commentators** even go so far as to say that the very survival of the family as an institution is threatened. What do you think? Take this quiz based on an article, *Prophets of Doom* by Edward Kain, and see whether these fears are true:

[5]   **Family Trend Quiz**

1. The divorce rate in the U.S. was highest in which of the following years?
   a. 1935   b. 1945   c. 1955   d. 1965

2. What percentage of women worked outside the home at the beginning of the century?
   a. 2%   b. 5%   c. 10%   d. 20%

3. **True or false**: Due to the great increase in divorce, children are much more likely to live in single-parent households than 100 years ago.

4. **True or false**: One hundred years ago, most families lived in three-generational households, as opposed to now when grandparents are likely to be placed in nursing homes.

5. **True or false**: Over the past century, fewer and fewer believe in marriage so the number of singles in increasing.

6. **True or false**: Few poor families live below the poverty line for five years or more.

[6]   Before giving the answers, you should know that if you didn't do well, you are not alone. Edward Kain gave this test to hundreds of students and professionals and found that the majority did not score well. What this suggests is that most people are fairly uninformed about history of the family and its problems but are "well-informed" about the stereotypes of families past and present, as promoted by politicians, talk-show hosts and purveyors of gloom and doom. Following the answers will be some explanations.

ANSWERS:
1. b   2. d   3. f   4. f   5. f   6. t

[7]   #1. Most people think "c" is the answer, believing that the farther from the good old days, the worse things became. Actually 1965 had the lowest divorce rate. The highest was in 1945, when soldiers returned to marriages hastily arranged before going to war or disrupted by WWII, and found them unworkable. In the thirty years since 1965, divorces have generally, though not consistently, increased each year. Most experts believe social disruptions affect the divorce rate, as societal stresses increase the pressures felt in marriages by increasing economic difficulties or creating changes in values of other disruptions.

[8]   #2. We have an image that women started to work outside the home during WWII, but fully one-fifth of all women worked outside of the home at the beginning of the century. Many women worked in agriculture and as domestic servants, and many more worked in the newly emerging textile industry, and as teachers and clerks. Many other women who did not work outside the home supplemented family incomes by working within the home, doing sewing, laundry and other part-time work.

[9]   #3. This question throws nearly everyone. Kain points out that few people are aware of the profound effects on family life that have resulted from the decline in mortality rates due to modern medicine and health practices. While divorce has increased tremendously, it has been more than offset by the incredible decline in the numbers of parents who died at an early age, leaving behind vast numbers of widows, widowers and orphans.

[10]   #4. For a number of years, most experts have believed that extended families were the norm until they were supplanted by the smaller, more mobile nuclear family during the industrial revolution. This view has

recently been challenged by a number of recent studies which demonstrate that the nuclear family, at least in Northern Europe and America, was the dominant form even before industrialization. Given the predominance of the nuclear family, three-generational families being the majority is a mathematical impossibility since there are more children than parents with every generation. More likely was the temporary addition of a relative, whether sibling, parent, or even child, which lasted until they married, remarried, or [at a much earlier age than now] died.

[11]   #5. Despite the increase in divorce, and the increase in singlehood, most Americans believe in marriage. Nearly all singles would like to get married eventually, and 75% of divorcees remarry. One hypothesis for the increase in singlehood is the growth of cohabitation. Most couples believe that "living together" will lead to marriage, but in two-thirds of all cases it does not. Probably the majority of singles who never marry will cohabit one or more times, but that cohabitation will end before marriage occurs.

[12]   #6. Despite concerns about a "culture of poverty" or "cycle of poverty," very few families live below the poverty line [as officially defined by the U.S. government] for five consecutive years. Major studies by the University of Michigan showed that only 4% of families remain consistently below the poverty line. Most families move in and out of poverty as wage earners lose a job, get sick, divorced, give birth to an additional child or are rehired, get well or remarry. (Manis 15–17)

Comprehension Questions

_____b_____ 1. The author suggests that:
  a. the very survival of the family as an institution is threatened.
  b. the survival of the family is not threatened because most Americans believe in marriage.
  c. the changes that have taken place in American society are for the worse.

_____ 2. The economic changes in the United States which began in the 1970s:
  a. made it easier for the majority of American families to live on one income.

    b. made it hard for the majority of American families to live on one income.

    c. made it more difficult for people to get divorced.

_____ 3. In the 30 years since 1965, the number of divorces:

    a. stayed the same.

    b. decreased.

    c. increased.

_____ 4. How many women worked outside the home at the beginning of the century?

    a. 1%

    b. 5%

    c. 20%

_____ 5. Children today are not any more likely to live in a single-parent home than they were 100 years ago because:

    a. just as many people were getting divorced 100 years ago.

    b. the death rate of parents was higher 100 years ago than it is today.

    c. the death rate of parents was lower 100 years ago than it is today.

_____ 6. Today nearly all single people:

    a. would like to get married.

    b. do not want to get married.

    c. believe marriage is good for some people, but not for them.

_____ 7. How many divorced people remarry today?

    a. Half of the population.

    b. Two-thirds of the population.

    c. Three-quarters of the population.

_____ 8. Today, the majority of people who are "living together" will:

    a. eventually get married.

b. never marry.

c. eventually get married, but then divorce.

_____ 9. One reason that a family will live below the poverty line is:

    a. job loss.

    b. recovery from an illness.

    c. remarriage.

_____ 10. One reason that a family will not live below the poverty line for more than five years is:

    a. job loss.

    b. remarriage.

    c. illness.

Getting Ahead in College Box 2.4

SENTENCE COMBINING: MULTIPLE ADJECTIVES

Combine the sentences in each group into one sentence. Keep the most important information (especially the words that are underlined) without repeating any words.

1. Most experts believe disruptions affect the divorce rate.
    The disruptions are <u>social</u>.
    The disruptions are <u>tremendous</u>.
    <u>Most experts believe tremendous social disruptions affect the divorce rate</u>.

2. Stresses increase the pressures felt in marriages.
    The stresses are <u>societal</u>.
    The stresses are <u>many</u>.

(continued on next page)

(continued from previous page)

3. Some think the family is threatened.
   The family is <u>modern.</u>
   The family is <u>American</u>.

_____

4. The changes began in the 1970s.
   The changes were <u>economic</u>.
   The changes were <u>lasting</u>.

_____

5. No longer were the majority of American families able to survive on an income.
   The income was <u>single</u>.
   The income was <u>average</u>.

_____

CHAPTER

3

Vocabulary: Development and Practice

• •

Vocabulary knowledge is very important to reading comprehension. Without a good sense of vocabulary, we would not be able to understand what we read. In this chapter we:

■ Learn how textbook authors define words;

■ Understand how to use context clues;

■ Learn how to use the glossary to cross-check;

■ Learn how to use the dictionary and thesaurus effectively;

■ Learn how to analyze word parts for meaning;

■ Learn how to tell the differences between commonly confused words.

LEARNING WORDS FROM TEXTBOOKS

When interviewed, a number of professors pointed out how important vocabulary is to reading comprehension. For example, one professor explained why some of his students did not understanding the assigned readings.

Professor Cohen: Simply because their vocabulary is limited, they are not getting it and they are not looking in the dictionary or using some other way to try and figure it out.

Professor Cohen's comment above suggests that knowing what words mean is key to understanding what we read. Also, the professor's comment suggests that there is more than one way to figure out what a word means.

Using the dictionary is the most commonly known strategy for finding out what an unknown word means. However, it should not be the first step you take. There are other strategies that may save you some time if you try them first.

Context Clues

How do textbook authors define words? In many cases, an author may give the definition of a word right in the same sentence. In other cases, the author may give clues to the definition instead. Thus, we can learn many new words simply by paying attention to the other words in the sentence. These other words are called **context clues** because they surround the unfamiliar words with hints toward their meaning within the sentence or paragraph.

Definitions   Textbook authors may help us out by directly defining a word in the same sentence or in the surrounding paragraph in which it is used. Authors often define new terms within the context of a sentence by setting the definition apart with the verbs "is," "is called," "are," and "are called." In the example below, notice how the term is joined to the definition by the word "is."

term   definition

A **professional portfolio is** <u>a collection of work that documents an individual's accomplishments in an area of professional practice</u>.

Usually the author will **boldface**, *italicize*, or highlight a word that is being defined. From the clues in this sentence, we know that "professional portfolio" is the word being defined because it appears in boldface print. We also know the definition of a professional portfolio is "a collection of work that documents an individual's accomplishments in an area of professional practice" because the word "is" tells us this.

Authors may also use commas (,), dashes (—), or parentheses ( ) to insert a definition into the sentence after introducing the new term. Notice how the definition of "professional portfolio" is included in the sentences below:

A **professional portfolio,** <u>a collection of work that documents an individual's accomplishments in an area of professional practice,</u> is often required as part of the job application process.

A **professional portfolio**—a collection of work that documents an individual's accomplishments in an area of professional practice—is often required as part of the job application process.

A **professional portfolio** (a collection of work that documents an individual's accomplishments in an area of professional practice) is often required as part of the job application process.

We know that the phrase "a collection of work that documents an individual's accomplishments in an area of professional practice" is the definition of "professional portfolio" because the commas, dashes, and parentheses set it apart from the sentence. This sentence would still make sense without the definition. It is up to us to look for the definition of a word when we come across sentences constructed in these ways.

Copyright © 2006 by Pearson Education, Inc.

| EXERCISE 3-1 | Definitions |

Read the following sentences selected from an education textbook. Identify the word that is being defined along with its definition. The first word has been identified and defined for you.

1. A **practicum** is a short-term field-based experience that allows teacher education students to spend time observing and assisting in classrooms.

   Term: practicum

   Definition: a short-term field-based experience that allows teacher education students to spend time observing and assisting in classrooms.

2. A new model of teacher preparation that provides students with extensive practical field experiences is known as **school-based education**.

   Term: _____

   Definition: _____

3. **Teaching simulations** (a practice in which students analyze teaching situations that are presented on videotape) provide opportunities for practicing a wide range of teaching skills.

   Term: Teaching simulation

   Definition: a practice which students analyze teaching sits. that

4. **Distance learning**—the use of technology that enables students to receive instruction at several remote sites—now enables teacher education programs to use models for learning how to teach.

Term: Distance learning

Definition: _____

5. **Substitute teachers** are teachers who replace regular teachers when they are absent due to illness, family responsibilities, personal reasons, or professional workshops and conferences.

Term: Substitute teachers

Definition: _____

(Parkay and Stanford 54–61)

What Are Some Other Types of Context Clues?

Details   Sometimes it takes more than a simple definition to understand a concept. In this case, an author will define a word by including *details* that explain the meaning of the word. Details may include:

■ physical descriptions

■ places of origin

■ names

■ functions

It is up to the reader to choose the most important details and to create a definition from those details. Read the following paragraph about music. Which details would you use to define the term "rhythm"?

As we have seen, the term **rhythm** in its broadest sense refers to the time aspect of music. In a more specific sense, a rhythm refers to the actual arrangement of durations—long and short notes—in a particular melody or some other musical passage. Of course, the term is also used in other contexts, about golfers, quarterbacks, poems, and even paintings. But no sport and no other art handles rhythm with such precision and refinement as does music. (Kerman and Tomlinson 6)

Before going into the details of the term "rhythm," we should first recognize its basic definition: the time aspect of music. But what does this mean, exactly? The definition alone does not tell us much about the purpose of rhythm or how you create a rhythm. This is where details are necessary. For example, to understand how to create a rhythm, we can explain that the rhythm is made up of long and short notes that are arranged into a melody or musical passage. Thus, a more complete definition might look like this:

Rhythm—the arrangement of long and short notes into a melody or musical passage for the purpose of keeping time.

EXERCISE 3-2	**Using Details**

Read the following sentences selected from a music textbook. Identify the word being defined and create a definition from the details provided.

1. The term *rhythmic* is often used to describe music that features simple patterns, such as ONE *two* ONE *two*, repeating over and over again, but that is not really correct (think about what a golfer or tennis player means by rhythm). Such patterns should be described as *metrical*, or strongly metrical, not rhythmic.

   Term: <u>metrical</u>

   Definition: <u>music that features simple patterns, such as ONE *two* ONE *two*,</u> <u>repeating over and over again.</u>

2. The basic unit for measuring time in music is the **beat.** When listening to a marching band, to take a clear example, we surely sense a regular recurrence of short durational units. These units serve as a steady, vigorous background for more complicated durational patterns that we discern at the same time. We can't help beating time to the music, waving a hand or tapping a foot, following the motion of the drum major's baton and of the

big-drum players' drumsticks. The simple durational pattern that is being signaled by waving, tapping, or thumping is the music's beat.

Term: _____

Definition: _____

3. Beats provide the basic unit of measurement for time; if ordinary clock time is measured in seconds, musical time is measured in beats. There is, however, an all-important difference between a clock ticking and a drum beating time. Mechanically produced ticks all sound exactly the same, but it is virtually impossible to beat time without making some beats more emphatic than others. This is called giving certain beats an **accent.**

Term: _____

Definition: _____

4. And accents are really what enable us to beat time, since the simplest way to do this is to alternate accented ("strong") and unaccented ("weak") beats in patterns such as ONE *two*, ONE *two*, ONE *two* . . . or ONE *two three*, ONE *two three*, ONE *two three* . . . To beat time, then, is not only to measure time but also to organize it, at least into these two- and three-beat patterns. That is why a drum is a musical instrument and a clock is not.

Term: _____

Definition: _____

5. Any recurring pattern of strong and weak beats, such as we have already referred to and illustrated above, is called a **meter**. Meter is a strong/weak pattern repeated again and again. Each occurrence of this repeated pattern, consisting of a principal strong beat and one or more weaker beats, is called a **measure**, or **bar**. In musical notation, measures are indicated by vertical lines called **bar lines**. (Kerman and Tomlinson 6–7)

Term: _____

Definition: _____

Term: _____

Definition: _____

Term: _____

Definition: _____

Visual Literacy Box 3.1 ● ● ● ● ● ● ● ● ● ● ● ● ●

Reading in Music

Reading in the field of music requires that you translate symbols into sounds just as you would translate letters into sounds. The paragraph below explains how to measure and organize time by creating "beat" patterns. When composers want a particularly strong accent, they put the sign > above or below a note. This is called an accent mark. Thus a pattern of alternating very strong and weak beats looks like this:

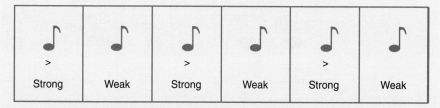

This pattern above shows a rhythm such as ONE *two*, ONE *two*, ONE *two*, with the strong beats coming first and the weak beats following. Draw accent marks in the boxes below and label them "strong" or "weak" to show the following pattern:

ONE *two three*, ONE *two three*, ONE *two three*

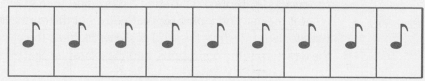

Visual Literacy Box 3.2 ● ■ ■ ■ ■ ■ ■ ■ ■ ■ ■ ■ ■ ■ ■ ■ ■

More Reading in Music

Reread the paragraph below on meters and label the following terms on the numbered lines in the diagram:

■ measure

■ bar lines

■ accent marks

Meter is a strong/weak pattern repeated again and again. Each occurrence of this repeated pattern, consisting of a principal strong beat and one or more weaker beats, is called a (1) **measure**, or **bar**. In musical notation, measures are indicated by vertical lines called **bar lines**.

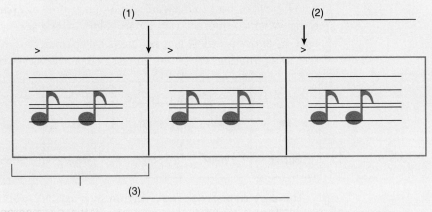

(Kerman and Tomlinson 6–7)

Examples Authors often define a word and then give an example to show what it means. Some phrases that point out the examples include: *for example, such as, to illustrate this,* and *as shown by.* Read the passage below and find the new terms, the definitions, and the examples that explain the definitions.

A **market** is a mechanism through which buyers and sellers interact to set prices and exchange goods and services.

In a market system, everything has a **price**, which is the value of the good in terms of money. Prices represent the terms on which people and firms voluntarily exchange different commodities. For example, when I agree to buy a used Ford from a dealer for $4,050, this agreement indicates that the Ford is worth at least $4,050 to me and that the $4,050 is worth at least as much as the Ford to the dealer. The used-car market has determined the price of a used Ford and, through voluntary trading, has allocated this good to the person for whom it has the highest value. (Samuelson and Nordhaus 27)

In the first paragraph, "market" is defined as "a mechanism through which buyers and sellers interact to set prices and exchange goods and services." No example is given for the term market.

However, in the second paragraph, the term "price" is defined as "the value of the good in terms of money" and an example of this term is introduced with the words "For example." By using the example of the person buying a Ford from a dealer for $4,050 in the used-car market, the author further defines the term "price."

Signals to Examples

for example	to illustrate
such as	as shown by
for instance	include/including

EXERCISE
3-3

Using Examples

Read the following excerpts taken from the same macroeconomics textbook as the above passage. Identify the term being defined, and find examples that support the meaning of the term. The first term has been identified for you.

term   *def*

1. In addition, prices serve as **signals** to producers and consumers. If consumers want more of any good, the price will rise, sending a signal to producers that more supply is needed. For instance, when a terrible disease reduces beef production, the supply of beef decreases (making people want more beef than is available) and raises the price of hamburgers. The higher price encourages farmers to increase their production of beef and, at the same time, encourages consumers to substitute other foods for hamburgers and beef products.

Term: <u>signals</u>

Example: <u>For instance, when a terrible disease reduces beef production, the</u>
<u>supply of beef decreases and raises the price of hamburgers. The higher price is</u>
<u>a signal for farmers to increase their production of beef</u>

Visual Literacy Box 3.3

Picture Charts in Economics

Pictures help us visualize new concepts. Read the following paragraph and then study the picture chart to determine if the production of beef increased or decreased between the years 2003 and 2005. Based on the information provided in the paragraph, do you think hamburger would be more or less expensive in 2005 than it was in 2003 and 2004?

In addition, prices serve as signals to producers and consumers. If consumers want more of any goods, the price will rise, sending a signal to producers that more supply is needed. For instance, when a terrible disease reduces beef production, the supply of beef decreases (making people want more beef than is available) and raises the price of hamburgers.

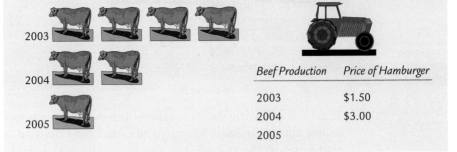

	Beef Production	Price of Hamburger
	2003	$1.50
	2004	$3.00
	2005	

2. What is true of the markets for consumer goods is also true of **markets for factors of production**, such as land or labor. For example, if more computer programmers are needed to run Internet businesses, the price of computer programmers (their hourly wage) will tend to rise. The rise in relative wages will attract workers into the growing occupation.

Term: _____

Example: _____

3. A **market equilibrium** represents a balance among all the different buyers and sellers. Depending upon the price, households and firms all want to buy or sell different quantities. The market finds the equilibrium price that meets the desires of buyers and sellers at the same time. For example, too high a price would mean a glut of goods (too many goods), with too much output; too low a price would produce long lines in stores and a deficiency of goods. Those prices for which buyers desire to buy exactly the quantity that sellers desire to sell yield an equilibrium of supply and demand.

Term: _____

Example: _____

4. We have just described how prices help balance demand and supply in an **individual market**. *What happens when we put all the different market's together*—beef, cars, land, labor, capital, and everything else? These markets work all at the same time to determine a general equilibrium of prices and production.

Term: _____

Example: _____

5. Firms, in turn, are motivated by the desire to get the most profits. **Profits** are the difference between total sales and total costs. Firms let go of areas where they are losing profits; by the same token, firms are lured by high profits into production of goods in high demand. Some of the most profitable activities today are producing and marketing legal drugs—drugs for depression, anxiety, etc. Lured by the high profits, companies are investing billions in research to come up with yet more new and improved chemicals. (Samuelson and Nordhaus 27)

Term:_____

Example: _____

Compare/Contrast

Authors compare two or more persons, places, or things to show how they are alike, and they contrast them to show how they are different. Sometimes authors will define a new word by telling how it is like or different from something that they think their readers know about. They can show similarity by using words such as *like, just as, similar to, the same as*. Can you tell from the information provided in the following sentence what the word "irregular" means?

> The smallest asteroids are **irregular** in shape, like boulders.

We can tell the word "irregular" means *unevenly shaped* because the sentence tells us that asteroids are shaped like boulders and we know that boulders are not perfectly round.

When a contrast clue is present, the meaning of the new word is shown to be different from an idea that is familiar to us. Some word clues that show differences include: *in contrast, different from this, on the other hand, however, whereas,* and *although.* Look at the following sentence.

> Whereas asteroids travel between the planets in roughly circular orbits, the orbits of comets are highly **elliptical**, extending far beyond Pluto's orbit. (Hewitt, Suchocki and Hewitt 702)

The first part of the sentence describes the asteroids as traveling in circle-shaped orbits. In the second sentence, the word "however" tells us to switch our thinking away from this idea, that "elliptical" and "circular" have different or opposite meanings. We can guess that the comets' orbits are oval shaped because they go around the planet, but the sentence tells us that they "extend far beyond Pluto's orbit."

Signals to Compare	Signals to Contrast	
like	the same as	on the other hand
just as	in contrast	however
similar to	different from this	although

the same as

EXERCISE 3-4

Compare and Contrast

Read the following sentences. Identify the word clue and the definition of the boldface term. The first one has been done for you.

1. The **freshman** year of college is the first year of college study; it is like grade thirteen in that it is the 13th year that students will be in school.

Word Clue: like

Definition: First year of college study

2. The associate's degree requires two years of successful college study. The **bachelor's degree** is different from the associate's degree in that it requires four years of college study.

Word Clue: _____

Definition: _____

3. In contrast to the bachelor's degree, the **master's degree** requires six years of college study—fours years to obtain the bachelor's degree and an additional two years for the master's degree.

Word Clue: _____

Definition: _____

4. A master's degree takes six years of full-time study. However, a **doctoral degree** takes nine years of full-time study. After obtaining a master's degree, it takes three more years of full-time study to gain a Ph.D.

Word Clue: _____

Definition: _____

5. Just as high school **seniors** are in their last year of high school, college seniors are in their last year of college if they are going for a bachelor's degree.

Word Clue: _____

Definition: _____

Multiple Meanings All fields have their own specialized terminology or vocabulary. As we read the textbooks for each new field, we recognize many familiar terms. However, we quickly realize that many of the terms that we know and use in our everyday conversations have taken on a new meaning—one particular to the subject. For example, we know what *concrete* is—cement used for sidewalks and buildings. We know that a *stage* is a place where actors and dancers perform. And we know that we go to the hospital for an *operation* if we are very ill. But as we open an education textbook, we see our familiar words used in a new way:

> During the school years, students move through the **preoperational stage**, the **concrete operations stage**, and the formal **operations stage**.

As this sentence illustrates, in educational terms, our familiar words *stage*, *concrete*, and *operations* have very different meanings. In this sentence:

■ *stage* means a period of development.

■ *concrete* means that things are physical instead of ideas.

■ *operations* means interactions with surroundings.

Hard money is another good example of a term with multiple meanings, depending on the context in which it appears. Of course, everyone knows what the word *money* means! And we know that *hard* is the opposite of *soft*. However, when we see these two words put together in a new way in a government textbook, we are not so sure of their combined meaning. It is not until we read the explanation in our textbook that we understand that *hard money* refers to money specifically set aside for federal election campaigns. And so, it is very important to pay attention to the way familiar words are used in various subject areas.

EXERCISE 3-5	Words with Multiple Meanings

Each sentence contains an italicized word or phrase that has multiple meanings. Read through the list of possible meanings and choose the meaning that makes the most sense. The first one has been done for you.

___b___ 1. His peers called him a *free rider* when he received a raise even though he didn't join the union or go out on strike.
    a. The second name listed on a voter's ballot.
    b. Someone who doesn't join a group but receives the benefits.
    c. Free airline ticket during economic downturns.

_✓_ 2. Unlike socialist countries, the United States has a *free market* economy because the government does not control the price of goods.
   a. Giving out free items in the market to encourage shoppers.
   b. A stock market condition when the economy is not in either a bull market or a bear market.
   c. A market economy in which supply and demand set prices.

_✓_ 3. As *First Lady*, Hillary Clinton worked very hard to help children in need.
   a. A woman president.
   b. The first woman to become president.
   c. The president's wife.

_✗_ 4. I voted a *split ticket* because I thought the Republican candidate would do a good job as lieutenant governor and the Democratic candidate would do a good job as governor.
   a. Voting for candidates of different parties in the same election.
   b. Sharing a ballot when voting.
   c. Tearing a ticket in half.

_✓_ 5. The *turnout* for the presidential election was over ten million.
   a. Turning something inside out.
   b. Manufacturing or producing.
   c. The proportion of the voting-age public that votes.

USING A GLOSSARY TO CROSS-CHECK MEANING

Most textbooks have a glossary at the end of the book, but some also have one running along the outside margin to help readers understand new vocabulary as they read the text. A **glossary** is like a dictionary, but only the new terms from that particular book are used. The terms are listed in alphabetical order (or, if it's a running glossary, in the order that they appear) with their definitions. Below is an excerpt of one section of a glossary from a physical science textbook.

Glossary

Extrusive rocks Igneous rocks that form at the Earth's surface.

Intrusive rocks Rocks that crystallize below the Earth's surface.

Lava Magma once it reaches the Earth's surface.

Valence electron Any electron in the outermost shell of an atom.

Velocity The speed of an object and specification of its direction of motion.

Velocity vector An arrow drawn to scale that represents the magnitude and direction of a given velocity.

Virtual image An image formed by light rays that do not converge at the location of the image.

Volcano A central vent through which lava, gases, and ash erupt and flow.

Volt The unit of electric potential; a potential of 1 volt equals 1 joule of energy per 1 coulomb of charge; $1 V = 1 J/C$

Water table The upper boundary of the zone of saturation; the area where every pore space is filled with water.

Wave A disturbance or vibration propagated from point to point in a medium or in space.

Look through the above section of a glossary and find the definition of *velocity*. As you can see, *velocity* is defined as "the speed of an object and specification of its direction of motion."

When you come to an unfamiliar word or new vocabulary word, you should use context clues to figure out its meaning. You can then use the glossary to **cross-check** your understanding of the word. Cross-checking means to check your understanding by using two different strategies. In this case, your first strategy would be the use of context clues to gain an understanding of the word, and the second strategy would be the use of the glossary to cross-check your guess, or to see if your guess was right.

EXERCISE 3-6

Using a Glossary

Read the following excerpt from a physical science textbook and use context clues to answer the questions that follow. Then use your glossary to cross-check your answers. The first answer has been done for you.

[1]   [1]Igneous rocks may form either at or below the Earth's surface. [2]Igneous rocks that form at the Earth's surface are called **extrusive**

rocks. [3]Igneous rocks that form beneath the Earth's surface are called **intrusive** rocks.

[2]   [1]Magma that moves upward from inside the Earth and extrudes onto the surface is called **lava**. [2]The term lava refers to both the molten material itself and to rocks that form from it. [3]Lava may be extruded through cracks and fractures in the Earth's surface, or through a central vent—a **volcano**. [4]Although eruptions from a volcano are more familiar, the outpourings of magma through fissures are much more common. (Hewitt, Suchocki, and Hewitt 543)

1. What is the difference between extrusive and intrusive rocks? Use the glossary to cross-check your understanding of these terms.

   Extrusive rocks form at the Earth's surface while intrusive rocks form below the Earth's surface.

2. From what the passage tells you and from what you found in the glossary, explain the two ways in which lava comes to the surface of the Earth.

   _____

   _____

3. What is the most common way for magma to come to the surface?

   _____

   _____

4. Using both context clues and the glossary, explain what the word *extruded* means?

   _____

   _____

5. Which sentences show that igneous rocks can form both at the Earth's surface and under the Earth's surface?

   _____

   _____

USING THE DICTIONARY

The dictionary is one of the most useful tools available for learning new words. It provides:

- spelling *(guide words)*
- pronunciation *(stressed syllable)*
- word meanings *(synonyms / antonyms)*
- word endings *(variants / inflections)*
- parts of speech *(n., adj., adv., v.)*
- ~~word origins~~ *word origin [etymology]*

The entry below shows the various types of information you will find when you look up a word. In this case, the word is *imaginary*.

> **imaginary** (i-'ma-jə-,ner-ē) adj. **a.** existing only in the imagination; lacking factual reality **b.** containing or relating to the imaginary unit—imag.i.nari.ly (i-,ma-jə-'ner-e-lē) *adverb*—imag.i.nari.ness (i-'ma-jə-,ner-ē-nəs) *noun*
>
> ***syn*** IMAGINARY, FANCIFUL, VISIONARY, FANTASTIC mean unreal or unbelievable. *Imaginary* applies to something which is fictitious and unreal; the product of one's imagination; *fanciful* suggests the free play of the imagination; *visionary* stresses impracticality or incapability of realization; *fantastic* implies incredibility or strangeness beyond belief.
>
> *By permission, From* Merriam-Webster's Collegiate® Dictionary, Eleventh Edition© *2004 by Merriam-Webster, Incorporated (www.Merriam-Webster)*

Spelling

At the top of each page of the dictionary, you will find two **guide words**— these are the first and last words on the page. The guide word on the top left refers to the first word on the page and the guide word on the top right refers to the last word on the page. Since words in the dictionary are listed alphabetically, we can tell by the guide words on which page we will find our target word. For example, we know the word *imaginary* can be found on the page with the guide words *imagery* and *immerse* because the *imagi* in imaginary comes after the *image* in imagery (first word on the page). Also, the *ima* in imaginary comes before the *imm* in *immerse* (the last word on the page.

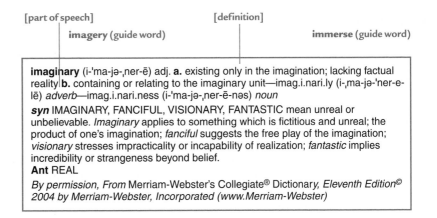

[part of speech]

imagery (guide word)

[definition]

immerse (guide word)

imaginary (i-'ma-jə-ˌner-ē) adj. **a.** existing only in the imagination; lacking factual reality **b.** containing or relating to the imaginary unit—imag.i.nari.ly (i-ˌma-jə-'ner-e-lē) *adverb*—imag.i.nari.ness (i-'ma-jə-ˌner-ē-nəs) *noun*

syn IMAGINARY, FANCIFUL, VISIONARY, FANTASTIC mean unreal or unbelievable. *Imaginary* applies to something which is fictitious and unreal; the product of one's imagination; *fanciful* suggests the free play of the imagination; *visionary* stresses impracticality or incapability of realization; *fantastic* implies incredibility or strangeness beyond belief.

Ant REAL

By permission, From Merriam-Webster's Collegiate® Dictionary, *Eleventh Edition*© *2004 by Merriam-Webster, Incorporated (www.Merriam-Webster)*

Pronunciation

If you do not know how to pronounce a word, look for a pronunciation guide such as the one below at the bottom of each dictionary page.

a	cat	ō	go	û	fur	ə	= a in ago
ā	ape	ô	fall, for	ch	chin		= e in agent
ä	cot, car	oo	look	sh	she		= i in pencil
e	ten	ōō	tool	th	thin		= o in atom
ē	me	oi	oil	*th*	*then*		= u in circus
i	fit	ou	out	zh	measure		
ī	ice	u	up	ŋ	ring		

After the main entry, you will see the word again, but it will look different because it is spelled *phonetically*, or as it sounds. For example, the word **imaginary** is spelled with symbols and letters (i maj' i ner' ē) and broken into five parts. The stress mark (') tells us to emphasize the second and fourth parts of the word when we say it. Looking at the pronunciation chart, we can see that the first part of the word is pronounced like the "i" in fit. In the second part of the word, the "a" is pronounced as the "a" in cat. The third part of the word is pronounced the same as the first syllable. In the fourth part of the word, the "e" is pronounced as the "e" in ten. Finally, in the fifth part of the word, the symbol "ē" stands for the long ē sound as in mē. Put the five parts together and you have the pronunciation for *imaginary*.

Word Meaning

Most words have more than one meaning and several different shades of the same meaning. When we look up a word in the dictionary, we need to read through all of the entries and choose one. Then we should reread our sentence or passage with the meaning in mind to see if it makes sense. For example, after reading the sentences below, we quickly recognize that the meaning of *imaginary* lies in the first entry and not the second.

> As teenagers imagine what others must be thinking, two distorted images of the relation between self and other appear. The first is called the **imaginary audience**. Young teenagers regard themselves as always on stage.

> **imaginary** (i-'ma-jə-,ner-ē) adj. **a.** existing only in the imagination; lacking factual reality **b.** containing or relating to the imaginary unit—imag.i.nari.ly (i-,ma-jə-'ner-e-lē) *adverb*—imag.i.nari.ness (i-'ma-jə-,ner-ē-nəs) *noun*
> *ant* **real**

In this case "imaginary" is best defined by the first entry because the word *imaginary* in this sentence refers to the idea that an "imagined audience" exists only in the minds of teenagers.

For many words in the dictionary, a **synonym** (a word that has the same meaning as another) will follow the definition. For the word *imaginary*, three synonyms are provided at the end of the definition entries. The **syn** stands for synonym. It tells us that *imaginary* can carry the same meaning as the words *fanciful, visionary*, and *fantastic*, depending upon the context of a sentence. Sometimes, an **antonym** or opposite of the word is provided; its symbol is **ant**. In this case, the opposite of *imaginary* is *real*.

Word Endings

Some dictionaries also provide a word's **variants** and **inflections**. *Variants* are word endings that ~~slightly~~ change the meaning of the word. For example, look at the word *psychological* in the following sentence.

> Adolescents' ability to reflect on their own thoughts, combined with the physical and **psychological** changes they are undergoing, means that they are starting to think more about themselves.

We could replace *psychological* with its variant *psychologic* without changing the meaning of the word. The adolescent changes could be *psychological* or *psychologic*. In this case, the different endings have no effect on the meaning or use of the word.

```
Main entry: psy•cho•log•i•cal
Pronunciation: sī-kə-'lä-ji-kəl
Variant(s): also psy•cho•log•ic /-jik/
Function: adjective
```

Inflections are word changes that slightly alter the meaning of the word. They include (1) making a word plural (boy, boy<u>s</u>); (2) making a word show ownership (Jerome'<u>s</u> car); (3) making a word show that the action took place in the present or the past (play<u>s</u>, play<u>ing</u>, play<u>ed</u>); and (4) making the word show a comparison (slow, slow<u>er</u>, slow<u>est</u>).

For example, let's look at the inflection of the word *inflate* in the following sentence.

Because teenagers are so sure that others are observing and thinking about them, they develop an <u>inflated</u> opinion of their own importance.

The inflections given in the dictionary are *inflat**ed*** and *inflat**ing***.

```
Main entry: in•flate
Pronunciation: in-'flāt
Function: verb
Inflected form(s): in•flat•ed; in•flat•ing
```

Parts of Speech

The dictionary also tells us what function a word has in a sentence—a noun, a verb, an adjective, an adverb, and so forth. For example, if we look up the word *invulnerable* (*unable to be harmed*), we will find out that it is an adjective.

We will also find that it has other forms; it can also be an adverb (*invulnerably*) or a noun (*invulnerability*).

Teenagers who . . . weave in and out of traffic at 80 miles an hour seem, at least for the moment, convinced of their uniqueness and <u>invulnerability</u>.

Some dictionaries will spell out the part of speech, and others will abbreviate it: *n.* for noun; *adj.* for adjective; *adv.* for adverb; *v.* for verb.

```
Main entry: in•vul•ner•a•ble
Pronunciation: (")in-'vəl-n(ə-)rə-bəl, -nər-bəl
Function: adjective
in•vul•ner•a•bil•i•ty /-"vəl-n(ə-)rə-'bi-lə-tē/ noun
-in•vul•ner•a•ble•ness /-'v l-n(ə-)rə-bəl-nəs, -nər-bəl-/ noun
-in•vul•ner•a•bly /-blE/ adverb
```

All dictionaries have an abbreviation guide or key either at the beginning or end of the dictionary.

EXERCISE 3-7	Using a Dictionary

Read the passage below about teenagers and self-focusing from a psychology textbook. Then use what you have learned about the dictionary to answer the questions that follow. The first answer is provided for you.

Self-Consciousness and Self-Focusing

1 Adolescents' ability to reflect on their own thoughts, combined with the physical and <u>psychological</u> changes they are undergoing, means that they start to think more about themselves. As teenagers imagine what others must be thinking, two <u>distorted</u> images of the relation between self and other appear.

Main entry: **dist•tort**
Pronunciation: di-'stort
Function: *verb*
transitive senses
1 : to twist out of the true meaning or proportion <*distorted* the facts>
2 : to twist out of a natural, normal, or original shape or condition <a face *distorted* by pain>; *also* **:** to cause to be perceived unnaturally <the new lights *distorted* colors>
3 : <u>PERVERT</u>
intransitive senses **:** to become <u>distorted</u>; *also* **:** to cause a twisting from the true, natural, or normal
synonym see <u>DEFORM</u>
- **dist•tort•er** *noun*

_____a_____ **1.** As used in the passage, the best meaning for the word
           distorted is:

              a. entry 1.

              b. entry 2.

              c. entry 3.

_____ **2.** When we pronounce the word *distort*, we would put the
           emphasis on:

              a. the first syllable (first part of the word).

b. the second syllable (second part of the word).

c. both the first and second syllables.

Main entry: **psy·cho·log·i·cal**
Pronunciation: sī-kə-' lä-ji-kəl
Variant(s): *also* **psy·cho·log·ic** /-jik/
Function: *adjective*
1 a : of or relating to psychology **b :** MENTAL
2 : directed toward the will or toward the mind specifically in its cognitive function
<*psychological* warfare>
- **psy·cho·log·i·cal·ly** /-ji-k(-)lē/ *adverb*

_____ **3.** One variant of *psychological* is:

a. psychologically.

b. psychologic.

c. psychology.

2   The first is called the **imaginary audience**. Young teenagers regard themselves as always on stage. They are convinced that they are the focus of everyone else's attention and concern. As a result, they become extremely self-conscious, often going to great lengths to avoid embarrassment. Sabrina, for example, woke up one Sunday morning with a large pimple on her chin. "I can't possibly go to church!" she cried. "Everyone will notice how ugly I look." The imaginary audience helps us understand the hours adolescents spend inspecting every detail of their appearance. It also accounts for their sensitivity to public criticism. To teenagers, who believe that everyone is monitoring their performance, a critical remark from a parent or teacher can be mortifying.

Main entry: **mor·ti·fy**
Pronunciation: 'mor-tə-fī
Function: *verb*
Inflected forms(s): **-fied; -fy·ing**
Etymology: Middle English *mortifien*, from Middle French *mortifier*, from Late Latin *mortificare*, from Latin *mort-, mors*
Date: 14th century
transitive senses
1 *obsolete* **:** to destroy the strength, vitality, or functioning of
2 : to subdue or deaden (as the body or bodily appetites) especially by abstinence or self-inflicted pain or discomfort
3 : to subject to severe embarrassment **:** SHAME
intransitive senses

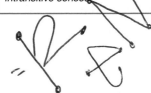

* word origin

_____ **4.** Which of the following is an inflected form of *mortify*?

      a. mortifier.

      b. mortifying.

      c. shame.

_____ **5.** The word *mortifying* is:

      a. a noun.

      b. an adjective.

      c. a verb.

_____ **6.** As used in the passage, the word *mortifying* means:

      a. entry 1.

      b. entry 2.

      c. entry 3.

3   A second cognitive distortion is the personal <u>fable</u>. Because teenagers are so sure that others are observing and thinking about them, they develop an <u>inflated</u> opinion of their own importance. They start to feel that they are special and unique. Many adolescents view themselves as reaching great heights of glory as well as sinking to unusual depths of <u>despair</u>—experiences that others could not possibly understand. On one occasion, for example, Sabrina had a crush on a boy who failed to return her affections. As she lay on the sofa feeling depressed, Franca tried to <u>assure</u> her that there would be other boys. "Mom!" Sabrina snapped, "you don't know what it's like to be in love!" The personal fable may contribute to adolescent risk taking. Teenagers who have sex without contraceptives or weave in and out of traffic at 80 miles an hour seem, at least for the moment, convinced of their <u>uniqueness</u> and invulnerability.

From Laura E. Berk, *Development Through the Lifespan*, 2e. Published by Allyn and Bacon, Boston, MA. Copyright © 1998 by Pearson Education, pp. 374–75.

Main entry: **in•flate**
Pronunciation: in-ˈflāt
Function: *verb*
Inflected form(s): **in•flat•ed**; **in•flat•ing**
transitive senses
1 : to swell or distend with air or gas
2 : to puff up : <u>ELATE</u>
3 : to expand or increase abnormally or imprudently
intransitive senses **:** to become <u>inflated</u>
synonym see <u>EXPAND</u>
- **in•fla•tor** *or* **in•fla•ter** /-ˈflā-tər/ *noun*

_____ **7.** A synonym for the word *inflate* is:

      a. to puff up.

      b. to swell.

      c. to expand.

_____ **8.** As used in the passage, the best meaning for the word *despair* is:

      a. to swell or distend with air or gas.

      b. to expand or increase abnormally.

      c. to puff up.

_____ **9.** Inflated is:

      a. a verb.

      b. a noun.

      c. an adjective.

_____ **10.** The "a" in "inflate" would be pronounced the same as:

      a. the a in c**a**t.

      b. the a in **a**pe.

      c. the a in **a**go.

USING A THESAURUS

A **thesaurus** is like a dictionary. It provides a definition, the part of speech, an example of the word used in a sentence or phrase, a list of synonyms (words with similar meanings), and a list of related words. This tool can help you with both reading and writing. When we come to an unfamiliar word while reading, we can look up the word in a thesaurus and find a substitute for the word we don't know to make sense of the passage. Not all synonyms are exactly interchangeable. Therefore, we need to pay careful attention to the context of the sentence to be sure the word supplies the accurate meaning.

EXERCISE
3-8

Using a Thesaurus

Use a thesaurus and the previous reading on "Self-Consciousness and Self-Focusing" to answer the following questions. The first answer is provided for you.

_____a_____ **1.** A synonym that could correctly be substituted for the word
fable in the above passage is:
  a. story.

  b. falsehood.

  c. lie.

_____ **2.** A synonym for the word *mortify* is:
  a. mortifying.

  b. shame.

  c. mortified.

_____ **3.** A synonym for the word *unique* as used in this passage is:
  a. single.

  b. alone.

  c. exceptional.

_____ **4.** The meaning of the word *assure* as used in the passage is:
  a. convince.

  b. persuade.

  c. alarm.

_____ **5.** In this passage, the word *despair* means:
  a. reach great heights of glory.

  b. lose all hope or confidence.

  c. be misunderstood.

Getting Ahead in College Box 3.1

PARTS OF SPEECH:
PREPOSITIONAL PHRASES

Prepositional phrases always begin with a preposition, or joining word.
The joining words generally show position, direction of motion, or
condition. Below is a list of prepositions:

at	of	above	below	except	through
by	on	across	beside	into	toward

(continued on next page)

for	to	against	between	like	under
from	with	among	down	off	up
in	around	during	over	without	

Combine the following sentences into one sentence. Keep the most important information without repeating any words. Use the word "and" to separate two prepositional phrases within a sentence. Use commas to separate more than two phrases in a sentence.

1. He chased Mikey and me.

He chased us around the yellow house.

He chased us up a backyard path.

He chased Mikey and me around the yellow house and up a backyard path.

2. He continued to chase us.

He chased us under a low tree.

He chased us up a bank.

He chased us through a hedge.

He chased us down some snow steps.

He chased us across the grocery store's delivery driveway.

_____

_____

3. We smashed through a gap.

The gap was in another hedge.

_____

_____

4. We entered a scruffy backyard.

We ran around its back porch.

We ran tight between houses to Edgerton Avenue.

_____

_____

(continued on next page)

(continued from previous page)

5. We ran across Edgerton.

We ran to an alley.

We ran up our own sliding woodpile.

We ran to the Hall's front yard.

_____

_____

6. We ran up Lloyd Street.

We wound through mazy backyards.

We ran toward the steep hilltop.

The hilltop was at Willard and Lang.

_____

_____

7. He chased us silently.

He chased us over picket fences.

He chased us through thorny hedges.

He chased us between houses.

He chased us around garbage cans.

He chased us across streets.

_____

_____

WORD PARTS

An understanding of word parts can greatly increase our ability to learn new words, often without going to a dictionary. A **word part** is a letter combination that carries a specific meaning when it appears at the *beginning, middle,* or *end* of a word. When it appears at the beginning of the word, it is called a *prefix.* When it appears at the end of a word, it is called a *suffix.* A word part that is the main part of the word, occurring either in the middle or at the beginning, is called a *root.* For example:

The **prefix** *auto* means *self*.

The Greek **root** *bio* means *life*.

The Greek **root** *graph* means *to write*.

The **suffix** *fy* means *to make*.

Thus, the word *autobiography* means *to write a life story about oneself* (**auto**[self] + **bio**[life] + **graph**[write] + **fy**[to make] = **autobiography**).

Below are lists of prefixes, suffixes, and roots. Study the lists and examples and complete the exercises that follow.

Prefixes	Meaning	Examples
re-	back, again	reverted; redundant
trans-	across or through	translucent
sol-	alone	solitude
un-	not	unfair; unzipped
in-; im-	not; opposite	incredibly; impelled
com-	with; together	compelled
dis-	not	dismembered; dismantled
ex-	out	exhausted
inter-	between	intervals
Suffixes		
-less	without	fearlessly; breathless
-ic	pertaining to	enthusiastic
-ous	full of	furious; joyous; righteous
-al	pertaining to	spherical
-or	person or thing	captor
Roots		
cap-	to take	captor
cred-	to believe	credibly
cor-	heart	courage
-luc	to be light	translucent

A Reading in Memoir

Read the passage below and identify the prefix, suffix, or root within the underlined words. Then explain the meaning of the word based on the identified word part (prefix, suffix, or root). Cross-check your answer by looking for context clues in the sentence. Sometimes a word part does not provide a good clue to the meaning. In these cases, use both the dictionary and context clues to determine their definitions.

Example

<u>a</u>   <u>un</u>familiar

      a. prefix   b. suffix   c. root

      Meaning of word part: <u>un</u> → <u>not</u>

      Meaning of word: <u>not familiar with</u>

An American Childhood by Annie Dillard

[1]   Some boys taught me to play football. This was fine sport. You thought up a new strategy for every play and whispered it to the others. You went out for a pass, fooling everyone. Best, you got to throw yourself mightily at someone's running legs. Either you brought him down or you hit the ground flat out on your chin, with your arms empty before you. It was all or nothing. If you hesitated in fear, you would miss and get hurt; you would take a hard fall while the kid got away, or you would get kicked in the face while the kid got away. But if you flung yourself wholeheartedly at the back of his knees—if you gathered and joined body and soul and pointed them diving (1) <u>fear<u>lessly</u></u>—then you likely wouldn't get hurt, and you'd stop the ball. Your fate, and your team's score, depended on your concentration and (2) <u>courage</u>. Nothing girls did could compare with it.

[2]   Boys welcomed me at baseball, too, for I had, through (3) <u>enthusiastic</u> practice, what was weirdly known as a boy's arm. In winter, in the snow, there was neither baseball nor football, so the boys and I threw snowballs at passing cars. I got in trouble throwing snowballs, and have seldom been happier since.

_____ **1.** fear<u>lessly</u>

      a. prefix   b. suffix   c. root

      Meaning of word part: _____

Meaning of word: _____

_____ **2.** <u>courage</u>
    a. prefix   b. suffix   c. root

Meaning of word part: _____

Meaning of word: _____

_____ **3.** enthusias<u>tic</u>
    a. prefix   b. suffix   c. root

Meaning of word part: _____

Meaning of word: _____

[3]   On one weekday morning after Christmas, six inches of new snow had just fallen. We were standing up to our boot tops in snow on a front yard on trafficked Reynolds Street, waiting for cars. The cars traveled Reynolds Street slowly and evenly; they were targets all but wrapped in red ribbons, cream puffs. We couldn't miss.

Courtesy of John E. Miller, Copyright © 1997.

[4]   I was seven; the boys were eight, nine, and ten. The oldest two Fahey boys were there—Mikey and Peter—polite blond boys who lived near me on Lloyd Street, and who already had four brothers and sisters. My parents approved of Mikey and Peter Fahey. Chuckie McBride was there, a rough kid, and Billy Paul and Mackie Kean too, from across Reynolds, where the boys grew up dark and (4) <u>furious</u>, skinny, knowing, and skilled. We had all drifted from our houses that morning looking for action, and had found it here on Reynolds Street.

[5]   It was cloudy but cold. The cars' tires laid behind them on the snowy street a complex trail of beige chunks like (5) crenellated castle walls. I had stepped on some earlier; they squeaked. We could have wished for more traffic. When a car came, we all popped it one. In the intervals between cars we reverted to the natural (6) solitude of children.

_____ **4.** furious

    a. prefix   b. suffix   c. root

    Meaning of word part: _____

    Meaning of word: _____

_____ **5.** crenellated

    a. prefix   b. suffix   c. root

    Meaning of word part: _____

    Meaning of word: _____

_____ **6.** solitude

    a. prefix   b. suffix   c. root

    Meaning of word part: _____

    Meaning of word: _____

[6]   I started making an iceball—a perfect iceball, from perfectly white snow, perfectly (7) spherical, and squeezed perfectly (8) translucent so no snow remained all the way through. (The Fahey boys and I considered it (9) unfair actually to throw an iceball at somebody, but it had been known to happen.)

_____ **7.** spherical

    a. prefix   b. suffix   c. root

    Meaning of word part: _____

    Meaning of word: _____

_____ **8.** translucent

    a. prefix   b. suffix   c. root

    Meaning of word part: _____

Meaning of word: _____

_____ **9.** <u>un</u>fair

a. prefix　　　　b. suffix　　　　c. root

Meaning of word part: _____

Meaning of word: _____

[7]　I had just embarked on the iceball project when we heard tire chains come clanking from afar. A black Buick was moving toward us down the street. We all spread out, banged together some regular snowballs, took aim, and, when the Buick drew nigh, fired.

[8]　A soft snowball hit the driver's windshield right before the driver's face. It made a smashed star with a hump in the middle.

[9]　Often, of course, we hit our target, but this time, the only time in all of life, the car pulled over and stopped. Its wide black door opened; a man got out of it, running. He didn't even close the car door.

[10]　He ran after us, and we ran away from him, up the snowy Reynolds sidewalk. At the corner, I looked back; (10) <u>incredibly</u>, he was still after us. He was in city clothes: a suit and tie, street shoes. Any normal adult would have quit, having sprung us into flight and made his point. This man was gaining on us. He was a thin man, all action. All of a sudden, we were running for our lives.

[11]　Wordless, we split up. We were on our turf; we could lose ourselves in the neighborhood backyards, everyone for himself. I paused and considered. Everyone had vanished except Mikey Fahey, who was just rounding the corner of a yellow brick house. Poor Mikey, I trailed him. The driver of the Buick sensibly picked the two of us to follow. The man (11) <u>apparently</u> had all day.

_____ **10.** in<u>cred</u>ibly

a. prefix　　　　b. suffix　　　　c. root

Meaning of word part: _____

Meaning of word: _____

_____ **11.** <u>apparent</u>ly

a. prefix　　　　b. suffix　　　　c. root

Meaning of word part: _____

Meaning of word: _____

[12]   He chased Mikey and me around the yellow house and up a backyard path we knew by heart: under a low tree, up a bank, through a
hedge, down some snowy steps, and across the grocery store's delivery driveway. We smashed through a gap in another hedge, entered
a scruffy backyard and ran around its back porch and tight between
houses to Edgerton Avenue; we ran across Edgerton to an alley and
up our own sliding woodpile to the Hall's front yard; he kept coming.
We ran up Lloyd Street and wound through mazy backyards toward
the steep hilltop at Willard and Lang.

Visual Literacy Box 3.4 ● ─ ● ─ ● ─ ● ─ ● ─ ● ─ ● ─ ● ─ ● ─ ●

Drawing Maps for Comprehension

It is important to see in your "mind's eye" the pictures that authors
paint with words when they write literature. Reread the following
paragraph. Then finish drawing the map showing where Mikey and the
author were chased.

He chased Mikey and me around the yellow house and up a backyard path
we knew by heart: under a low tree, up a bank, through a hedge, down some
snowy steps, and across the grocery store's delivery driveway. We smashed
through a gap in another hedge, entered a scruffy backyard and ran around
its back porch and tight between houses to Edgerton Avenue; we ran across
Edgerton to an alley and up our own sliding woodpile to the Hall's front
yard; he kept coming. We ran up Lloyd Street and wound through mazy
backyards toward the steep hilltop at Willard and Lang.

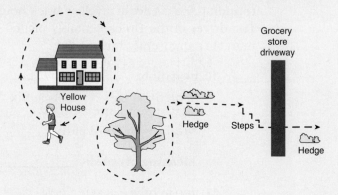

[13]   He chased us silently, block after block. He chased us silently over
picket fences, through thorny hedges, between houses, around garbage
cans, and across streets. Every time I glanced back, choking for breath,
I expected he would have quit. He must have been as (12) <u>breathless</u> as

we were. His jacket strained over his body. It was an immense discovery, pounding into my hot head with every sliding, (13) <u>joyous</u> step, that this ordinary adult evidently knew what I thought only children who trained at football knew; that you have to fling yourself at what you're doing, you have to point yourself, forget yourself, aim, dive.

_____ **12.** breath<u>less</u>

        a. prefix   b. suffix   c. root

        Meaning of word part: _____

        Meaning of word: _____

_____ **13.** joy<u>ous</u>

        a. prefix   b. suffix   c. root

        Meaning of word part: _____

        Meaning of word: _____

[14]   Mikey and I had nowhere to go, in our own neighborhood or out of it, but away from this man who was chasing us. He (14) <u>impelled</u> us forward; we (15) <u>compelled</u> him to follow our route. The air was cold; every breath tore my throat. We kept running, block after block; we kept (16) <u>improvising</u>, backyard after backyard, running a frantic course and choosing it (17) <u>simultaneously</u>, failing always to find small places or hard places to slow him down, and discovering always, (18) <u>exhilarated</u>, (19) <u>dismayed,</u> that only bare speed could save us—for he would never give up, this man—and we were losing speed.

_____ **14.** <u>im</u>pelled

        a. prefix   b. suffix   c. dictionary

        Meaning of word part: _____
        (Hint: *pellare* is the French word for "to drive")

        Meaning of word: _____

_____ **15.** <u>com</u>pelled

        a. prefix   b. suffix   c. dictionary

        Meaning of word part: _____

        Meaning of word: _____

_____ **16.** u̲nderlined improvising

    a. prefix   b. suffix   c. dictionary

Meaning of word part: _____

Meaning of word: _____

_____ **17.** simultane̲ous̲ly

    a. prefix   b. suffix   c. dictionary

Meaning of word part: _____

Meaning of word: _____

_____ **18.** e̲xhilarated

    a. prefix   b. suffix   c. dictionary

Meaning of word part: _____

Meaning of word: _____

_____ **19.** di̲smayed

    a. prefix   b. suffix   c. dictionary

Meaning of word part: _____

Meaning of word: _____

[15]   He chased us through the backyard (20) labyrinths of ten blocks before he caught us by our jackets. He caught us and we all stopped.

[16]   We three stood staggering, half blinded, coughing, in an (21) obscure hilltop backyard: a man in his twenties, a boy, a girl. He had released our jackets, our pursuer, our (22) captor, our hero: he knew we weren't going anywhere. We all played by the rules. Mikey and I unzipped our jackets. I pulled off my sopping mittens. Our tracks multiplied in the backyard's new snow. We had been breaking new snow all morning. We didn't look at each other. I was (23) cherishing my excitement. The man's lower pants legs were wet; his cuffs were full of snow and there was a (24) prow of snow beneath them on his shoes and socks. Some trees bordered the little flat backyard, some messy winter trees. There was no one around: a clearing in a grove, and we the only players.

[17]   It was a long time before he could speak. I had some difficulty at first (25) <u>recalling</u> why we were there. My lips felt swollen; I couldn't see out of the sides of my eyes; I kept coughing.

_____ **20.** labyrinths

     a. prefix   b. suffix   c. dictionary

     Meaning of word: _____

_____ **21.** obscure

     a. prefix   b. suffix   c. dictionary

     Meaning of word: _____

_____ **22.** <u>cap</u>tor

     a. prefix   b. suffix   c. dictionary

     Meaning of word part: _____

     Meaning of word: _____

_____ **23.** cherishing

     a. prefix   b. suffix   c. dictionary

     Meaning of word: _____

_____ **24.** prow

     a. prefix   b. suffix   c. dictionary

     Meaning of word: _____

_____ **25.** <u>re</u>calling

     a. prefix   b. suffix   c. dictionary

     Meaning of word part: _____

     Meaning of word: _____

[18]   "You stupid kids," he began (26) <u>perfunctorily</u>.

[19]   We listened perfunctorily indeed, if we listened at all, for the chewing out was (27) <u>redundant</u>, a mere formality, and beside the point. The point was that he had chased us passionately without giving up, and so he had caught us. Now he came down to earth. I wanted the glory to last forever.

[20]   But how could the glory have lasted forever? We could have run through every backyard in North America until we got to Panama. But when he trapped us at the lip of the Panama Canal, what precisely could he have done to prolong the drama of the chase and cap its glory? I brooded about this for the next few years. He could only have fried Mikey Fahey and me in boiling oil, say, or (28) <u>dismembered</u> us piecemeal, or staked us to anthills. None of which I really wanted, and none of which any adult was likely to do, even in the spirit of fun. He could only chew us out there in the Panamanian jungle, after months or years of exalting pursuit. He could only begin, "You stupid kids," and continue in his ordinary Pittsburgh accent with his normal (29) <u>righteous</u> anger and the usual common sense.

[21]   If in that snowy backyard the driver of the black Buick had cut off our heads, Mikey's and mine, I would have died happy, for nothing has required so much of me since as being chased all over Pittsburgh in the middle of winter—running terrified, (30) <u>exhausted</u>—by this sainted, skinny, furious redheaded man who wished to have a word with us. I don't know how he found his way back to his car. (Dillard)

_____ **26.** perfunctorily

      a. prefix   b. suffix   c. dictionary

      Meaning of word: _____

_____ **27.** <u>re</u>dundant

      a. prefix   b. suffix   c. dictionary

      Meaning of word part: _____

      Meaning of word: _____

_____ **28.** <u>dis</u>membered

      a. prefix   b. suffix   c. dictionary

      Meaning of word part: _____

      Meaning of word: _____

_____ **29.** right<u>eous</u>

      a. prefix   b. suffix   c. dictionary

      Meaning of word part: _____

      Meaning of word: _____

_____ **30.** <u>ex</u>hausted

      a. prefix   b. suffix   c. dictionary

Meaning of word part: _____

Meaning of word: _____

Getting Ahead in College Box 3.2

THE PRONUNCIATION OF VOCABULARY

When two or three consonants (letters that are not vowels) are grouped together, the combination of the letters makes one sound. For example, the **p** and the **l** sounds in please, plan, and play are blended together to make one sound. Thus, they are called consonant blends. Complete the following sentences with words that begin with blends. Use the following examples as a pronunciation guide.

bl	as in	**bl**end
cl	as in	**cl**oth
fl	as in	**fl**at
gl	as in	**gl**ass
pl	as in	**pl**an

1. Some boys taught me to _____ football. (play, coach)

2. Either you brought him down or you hit the ground _____ out. (flat, hard)

3. If you _____ yourself at the back of his knees, you'd stop the ball. (flung, hurled)

4. Mikey and Peter were polite _____ boys who lived near me on Lloyd. (blond, big)

5. We heard tire chains come _____ from afar. (clanking, making noise)

6. A _____ Buick was moving toward us down the street. (tan, black)

7. He didn't even _____ the car door. (close, lock)

8. He was in city _____. (garments, clothes)

9. Having sprung us into _____, he had made his point. (flight, fear)

10. We kept running _____ after _____. (mile, block)

COMMONLY CONFUSED WORDS

Words that are similar in sound or in spelling can often be *confused*. For example, the words *their*, *there*, and *they're* all sound the same but have different spellings and different meanings. *Their* is a possessive for the pronoun *them*, as in the sentence "Tell them to bring <u>their</u> cell phones." *There* is an adverb that shows place, as in the sentence "We can go <u>there</u> to buy a cell phone." *They're* is a contraction for *they are*, as in "<u>They're</u> going to buy another cell phone." Study the list of commonly confused words below and complete the exercise that follows.

1. all ready	fully prepared	"Our family was <u>all ready</u> to go on vacation."
already	before; earlier	"Our family has <u>already</u> returned from vacation; we went to the mountains last week."
2. any one	a certain person or thing from a group	"<u>Any one</u> of the business school graduates can apply for this position."
anyone	any person	"<u>Anyone</u> can apply for this job."
3. beside	next to	"I am going to sit <u>beside</u> the president of the college during the graduation ceremony."
besides	except	"No one <u>besides</u> the president can sit in that seat."
	in addition to	"The president needs to sit in the chair by the podium because she will be the first to speak at the ceremony. <u>Besides</u>, it is traditional for the president to sit in that chair.
4. learn	to gain knowledge	"I can <u>learn</u> a lot from this teacher."
teach	to give knowledge	"I can <u>teach</u> this information to my friends."
5. your	possessive pronoun for *you*	"Bring <u>your</u> books with you to the study session."
you're	contraction for *you are*	"<u>You're</u> the leader of this study session."

6. **loose**	unfastened	"The wheels will fall off if the bolts become <u>loose</u>."
lose	to misplace not win	"Did you <u>lose</u> the keys to your car?" "Did you <u>lose</u> the race because your wheels were <u>loose</u>?"
7. **to**	preposition that shows movement and direction	"Magali and Cliff are going <u>to</u> school; they have to be there by 8:00a.m."
too	adverb that means "in addition to" or "also"	"They invited me to go with them and so, I am going <u>too</u>."
two	adjective that describes a number that is greater than one and less than three	"We will stop at <u>two</u> schools—one is a community college and the other is university."
8. **have**	verb that shows possession	"They <u>have</u> a huge assignment due on Wednesday."
have got	*got* should never be used with *have*	"They have a <u>huge</u> assignment due on Wednesday."
9. **here**	adverb that shows place	"We came <u>here</u> to listen to the concert."
hear	to perceive sound	"I cannot <u>hear</u> you because the music is too loud."
10. **good**	adjective, modifies a noun	"She has an A in accounting; she is a <u>good</u> student."
well	adverb, modifies a verb, adjective, or adverb	"She has an A in accounting; she did <u>well</u> on the last three exams."

EXERCISE
3-9

Commonly Confused Words

Read the following sentences and fill in the blank with the letter for the correct word. The first one has been done for you.

_____b_____ **1.** The semester has _____ started. The first day of classes was last week.

(a) all ready   (b) already

_____ **2.** The entire class did _____ in the organic chemistry class. Not a single person earned less than a B.

(a) good   (b) well

_____ **3.** You need at least five references for the English paper. Eileen has seven, but Gerd still needs_____ more.

(a) to   (b) too   (c) two

_____ **4.** Julio is not going to the party tonight because he has a research paper due tomorrow. _____ that, he has two exams scheduled for the next day.

(a) Beside   (b) Besides

_____ **5.** Because of the holiday, we will not have class on Friday. _____ next assignment will be due on Monday.

(a) Your   (b) You're

_____ **6.** Patrick is taller than _____ I know.

(a) anyone   (b) any one

_____ **7.** _____ meeting at 7:00 p.m.; you can either study with them or wait until our study group meets.

(a) Their   (b) There   (c) They're

_____ **8.** We asked our chemistry instructor to _____ us how to balance the equation since it was different from the examples in the textbook.

(a) teach   (b) learn

_____ **9.** I did not _____ what the professor said because I was late for class.

(a) here   (b) hear

_____ **10.** Sidney spends five hours every night on his school work because he does not want to _____ his scholarship.

(a) lose   (b) loose

EIGHT EXERCISES FOR VOCABULARY

| EXERCISE 3-10 | **Terms and Definitions** |

Read the following passage taken from an astronomy textbook. Then identify the new terms along with their definitions.

[1]   In any particular location, some days may be hotter or cooler than others, some may be clearer or cloudier, some may be calmer or stormier. This ever-varying combination of winds, clouds, temperature, and pressure is what we call **weather**.

[2]   Local weather can vary dramatically from one day to the next, or even from hour to hour. The weather can also vary greatly between places just a short distance apart. For example, temperatures on a warm day may be several degrees hotter just a few kilometers inland form a coastal city. The complexity of weather makes it difficult to predict, although modern-day *meteorologists* (people who study weather) often can predict weather quite accurately a few days in advance.

[3]   **Climate** is the long-term average of weather and is generally stabler than weather. Deserts remain deserts and rain forests remain rain forests over periods of hundreds or thousands of years, while the day-to-day and even year-to-year weather may vary dramatically. (Bennett et al. 270)

_____ **1.** In the first paragraph, the term being defined is:

    a. weather.

    b. temperature.

    c. pressure.

_____ **2.** The term *meteorologist* means:

    a. the complexity of the weather.

    b. people who study weather.

    c. accuracy in predicting weather.

_____ **3.** In the third paragraph, the term being defined is:

    a. deserts.

    b. climate.

    c. rain forests.

4. As used in the passage, the word *stabler* means:
   a. unpredictable.
   b. varying or changing.
   c. unchanging.

 5. Climate is defined as:
   a. the long-term average of weather.
   b. the day-to-day weather.
   c. ever-varying combination of winds, clouds, temperature, and pressure.

EXERCISE 3-11

Using Details

Read the following excerpts from a communications textbook. Identify the word or phrase being defined and create a definition from the details provided.

Personality Traits

1. *Personality traits* are those qualities that distinguish one personality from another. As the following examples indicate, some personality traits aid communication, but many are barriers to communication.

Term: personality traits

Definition: those qualities that distinguish one personality from another aiding or creating barriers to communication.

2. People vary with regard to the characteristic of *manipulation*, or the degree to which they attempt to achieve goals by dominating and controlling others. However, research has shown that people who have an *external locus of control* (that is, who believe that the world is ordered and controlled by others) often desire that control for themselves and tend to exhibit greater manipulative behaviors than do people who have an internal locus of control. People with an *internal locus of control* believe that they control their own fates, and do not generally manifest excessive degrees of manipulation.

+1 Term: manipulation

+1 Definition: the degree which ppl attempt to acchrive goals by manipulating others

+1 Term: external locust of control

+1 Definition: ppl who believe the world is ordered and controlled by others

+1 Term: internal locust of controll

+1 Definition: ppl who believe they control there own fates

3. One of the most difficult personality traits encountered in a communication situation is **dogmatism**. Dogmatic individuals have closed minds and are reluctant to accept new ideas and opinions. Yet they may accept without question the word of certain authorities and expect the same kind of blind acceptance from those they consider their inferiors. Dogmatic individuals often remain steadfast to ideas or opinions in spite of contradictory evidence. (Barker and Gaut 109–10)

+1 Term: dogmatism

+1 Definition: closed minds & are reluntant to accept New Ideas and opinions

+8/8

<table>
<tr><td>EXERCISE
3-12</td><td>**Compare and Contrast**</td></tr>
</table>

Read the sentences below. Identify the word clue and the definition of the italicized or boldfaced word.

1. While some people can live with shades of gray, others insist on things being clearly defined and unambiguous. This varying **tolerance of ambiguity** frequently affects the communication process.

   Word clue: _while_

   Word meaning: _The ability for some people to live with shades of gray, while_

   others insist on things being clearly defined and unambiguous

2. Communication is also affected by the self-esteem of the sender and the receiver. **Self-esteem,** which is your enduring evaluation of yourself, often determines your confidence in what you are saying and your readiness to accept the view of others.

   Word clue: _which is_

   Word meaning: _your how feel about yourself_

3. Therefore, in the communication process, it is important to use your perception of another person's self-esteem as a means of evaluating certain messages. For example, individuals with *high self-esteem* may state an opinion confidently even without sufficient evidence.

   Word clue: _therefore_

   Word meaning: _you think highly of urself_

4. On the other hand, you might be quicker to question their veracity than that of speakers whose *low self-esteem* would prevent them from supporting unproven viewpoints.

   Word clue: _on the other hand_

   Word meaning: _you think low of urself_

5. Of the many personality variables, the one that most strongly affects communication is level of *maturity*. It is difficult to pinpoint the stage at which a person matures psychologically, but we usually judge a person as mature when he or she is able to function independently in a social setting. One measure of such maturity is the individual's ability to satisfy psychological needs for things such as independence, approval, affection, and so forth. With maturity comes the absence of intrapersonal

CY6

conflicts in a communication setting. In contrast, a lack of maturity presents intrapersonal conflicts that might intrude on objective transmission and interpretation of messages. (Barker and Gaut 109–10)

Word clue: *IN CONTRAST*

Word meaning: *to function independently*

EXERCISE
3-13

Using Examples

Read the following excerpt from a communication textbook. Use the example of the roommates' relationships to figure out the meanings of the underlined words and to answer the questions below.

> Even when you have triads, <u>dyads</u> are still <u>primary</u>; dyads are always central to <u>interpersonal</u> relationships. Consider, for example, the following situation: Al and Bob (a dyad) have been roommates for their first two years of college. Expenses have increased, and so they ask Carl to join them and become a third roommate. Now a <u>triad</u> exists. But the <u>original</u> dyad has not gone away; in fact, now there are three dyads: Al and Bob, Al and Carl, and Bob and Carl. Al and Bob are ballplayers and interact a lot about sports. Al and Carl are both studying communication and talk about their classes. Bob and Carl belong to the same religious club and frequently discuss the club's activities. At times, of course, all three interact, but even then the topic of conversation will determine who talks primarily to whom. If the topic is sports, Al and Bob will primarily address each other; Carl will be a kind of outsider. When the topic is classes, Bob is an outsider.

From Joseph A. Devito, The *Interpersonal Communication Book*, 8e. Published by Allyn and Bacon, Boston, MA. Copyright © 1998 by Pearson Education, pp. 7–8.

_____a_____ **1.** The word *dyad* means:
   a. two-person relationship.
   b. three-person relationship
   c. five-person relationship

_____b_____ **2.** The word *triad* means:
   a. group of two people.
   b. group of three people.
   c. group of five people.

3. The word *primary* refers to:
   a. first in time or order.
   b. from which others are taken or made.
   c. first in importance.

 4. As used in the passage, the word *interpersonal* means:
   a. ability to communicate.
   b. individual.
   c. between persons.

 5. The term *original dyad* refers to:
   a. Al and Bob.
   b. Al and Carl.
   c. Bob and Carl.

EXERCISE 3-14	**Words with Multiple Meanings**

Each sentence contains a boldfaced term from the field of interpersonal communications. Read through the list of possible meanings and choose the one that makes the most sense for the field of communications.

_____b_____ **1.** The *channel* acts like a bridge connecting source and receiver.
   a. television station.
   b. medium through which signals are sent.
   c. the deeper part of a river.

 2. Trademarks, nameplates, and initials on a shirt are all examples of *ear markers*.
   a. marks made on a person's ears.
   b. marker that identifies an item as belonging to a specific person.
   c. hearing aids.

3. Gunnysacking refers to the practice of storing up grievances so they may be unloaded at another time.
   a. storing items in large burlap bags.

b. dumping all one's complaints onto another person at one time.

 c. talking about the listener or some third party.

_____ **4.** Should you decide that you want to **repair** your relationship, you might discuss this with your partner, the interpersonal repair phase.

    a. physically fix items that are broken.

    b. seek to improve the relationship.

    c. go or leave.

 _____ **5.** With most interpersonal relationships, especially those of long standing, you know where the belt line is. Hitting below the belt line, or **belt-lining**, causes added problems for all persons involved. (DeVito 16–385)

    a. stopped or slow-moving traffic on a beltway or freeway.

    b. arranging clothing belts in a closet to make them easier to find.

    c. ineffective conflict strategy in which a person's criticism of another is harsh enough to damage the relationship.

EXERCISE 3-15   Using a Glossary

Read the excerpt below and use context clues to answer the questions that follow. Then use your glossary to cross-check your answers.

ferment—to cause a slow chemical change to take place in a substance by means of yeast, bacteria, etc.

transform—to change the form of through chemical reaction.

gaseous—in the form of gas (neither liquid nor solid).

synthesize—to put together elements to make a whole.

reassemble—to put together again.

When a substance undergoes a chemical change, it changes its identity. Grape juice treated with yeast <u>ferments</u> into wine; iron exposed to air and water <u>transforms</u> into rust; dynamite explodes into a variety of <u>gaseous</u> compounds; wood burns to ashes, and aspirin is <u>synthesized</u> from petroleum. During these changes, chemical bonds are broken and new ones are formed—molecules are plucked apart and their atoms <u>reassembled</u> in different arrangements. This shuffling of atoms is what we call a chemical reaction. (Hewitt, Suchocki and Hewitt 449)

_____ **1.** "Grape juice treated with yeast ferments into wine" means:
    a. a slow chemical change caused by yeast makes wine become grape juice.
    b. yeast becomes grape juice by adding wine to the yeast.
    c. a slow chemical change caused by the yeast causes grape juice to become wine.

_____ **2.** "Iron exposed to air and water transforms into rust" means:
    a. you can clean off rusted iron by exposing it to air and water.
    b. when air and water touch iron, a chemical reaction causes it to rust.
    c. iron will rust if it is not exposed to enough air and water.

_____ **3.** "Dynamite explodes into a variety of gaseous compounds" means:
    a. dynamite becomes a solid.
    b. dynamite becomes a liquid.
    c. dynamite becomes a gas.

_____ **4.** Which of the following best explains the phrase "aspirin is synthesized from petroleum"?
    a. Aspirin comes from petroleum.
    b. Petroleum comes from aspirin.
    c. Aspirin and yeast molecules are put together to make petroleum.

_____ **5.** Which of the following best explains the phrase "molecules are plucked apart and their atoms reassembled in different arrangements"?
    a. A chemical reaction occurs when atoms are broken up.
    b. A chemical reaction occurs when molecules are broken up and put back together in the same way.
    c. A chemical reaction occurs when molecules are broken up and their atoms are put together in a new way.

EXERCISE 3-16

Using the Dictionary

Use the sentence below to answer the questions that follow. Use the dictionary as a reference.

Teachers may <u>reinforce</u> <u>stereotypical</u> <u>gender</u> behavior by selecting instructional materials that encourage male students toward aggression and achievement and female students toward <u>passivity</u> and <u>domesticity</u>. (Davidson and Moore 61).

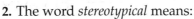

_____ **1.** The word *reinforce* means:
  a. to make stronger by adding something.
  b. to select instructional materials.
  c. to stereotype.

_____ **2.** The word *stereotypical* means:
  a. carefully considering individual differences.
  b. pertaining to a fixed pattern of thinking that consistently favors males.
  c. pertaining to a fixed pattern of thinking without consideration for individual differences.

_____ **3.** The word *gender* means:
  a. a person's sex (male or female).
  b. aggressive behavior.
  c. favoring male students.

_____ **4.** As used in the passage, the word *passivity* means:
  a. active toward achievement.
  b. aggressive.
  c. behavior that is not active.

_____ **5.** Which gender is encouraged to have their lives revolve around the home?
  a. male.
  b. female.
  c. both male and female.

EXERCISE
3-17

Word Parts

Study the word parts below and use them to figure out the meanings of the words that follow.

un = not; opposite   **pre** = before

in = not   **mis** = wrong; bad

dis = not; opposite

1. unreal (un + real) = ~~not real~~
2. preheat (pre + heat) = ~~preheat~~ heat before
3. inactive (in + active) = not active
4. mislead (mis + lead) = bad directions lead
5. dislike (dis + like) = don't like

EXERCISE
3-18

Practice with Commonly Confused Words

Read the following sentences and fill in the blank with the letter for the correct word.

_____b_____ 1. I was late for class because my car would not start. By the time I arrived on campus the professor had _____ given the exam.

(a) all ready   (b) already

_____A_____ 2. This work/study position is open to _____ of the freshman students.

(a) any one   (b) anyone

_____A_____ 3. We must _____ all of the elements in the periodic table for our chemistry exam tomorrow.

(a) learn   (b) teach

_____A_____ 4. I sit _____ Fernando every day in the biology class.

(a) beside   (b) besides

_____A_____ 5. Carlene is a really _____ student; she was on the Dean's List every semester since she started college.

(a) good   (b) well

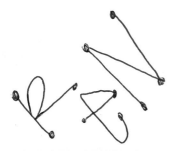

CHAPTER

4

Main Idea and Supporting Details

• •

In this chapter we learn how to:

■ Recognize the topic of a paragraph;

■ Find the main idea of a paragraph.

NADINE: While I'm reading, I will highlight the titles and then the subtitles, and then usually right after the subtitles, there's either a statement or a question that gets answered in the text of the paragraph.

REGINALD: Usually I look at the headings and look for sentences that summarize things and the general topic, take things and just put things together.

What exactly do Nadine and Reginald mean when they say they are looking for sentences that "answer questions" and "sentences that summarize" so that they can "put things together"?

First of all, good readers look for the overall topic of a selection so they know what the author is writing about. They keep this topic in mind while reading so they can see how the information in each paragraph fits into the general idea of the selection. Thus, the **topic** tells us the general idea of a paragraph or selection in one word or phrase.

While reading each paragraph, good readers also search for a sentence that sums up all of the information in that paragraph. If that sentence were made into a question, the information from the remaining sentences would answer that question. In other words, the **main idea statement** is a general statement that is related to all of the sentences in the paragraph. The other sentences include the supporting details, or the specific facts that give readers more information about the main idea.

If you are not used to looking for the topic and the main idea as you read, this may seem complicated at first. However, once you practice and make this a habit, you will find that this strategy will help you understand what you read much better.

There are three questions to ask yourself when you are looking for the main idea:

1. What is the paragraph about?

2. What words or ideas can be found in all of the sentences in the paragraph?

3. Which sentences have facts that are not found in the other sentences?

TOPICS

A reading can be about anything in the world—people, places, events, and ideas. It is important to know what exactly you will be reading about before you start, or you may not be able to focus your attention on the selection. The *topic* tells us who or what a reading is about. The sentence in a paragraph that introduces the topic is called the **topic sentence**.

Knowing the topic helps us make sense of the reading; it focuses our attention. Have you ever tried to join a conversation that had started before you entered a room? At first, you may not know what people are talking about. But as you listen, you begin to pick up on clues, and then you put those clues together. When you gather enough clues, you can guess the topic and eventually join in the conversation. As with reading, it is difficult to jump in until you are sure of the topic.

How Do We Detect Topics?

Have you ever watched the television show *Jeopardy*? On the show, the players look at a list of clues that relate to different items belonging to a particular category. The players then attempt to guess what each item is, based on those clues. Remember, each unnamed item belongs to a category. A *category* is an overall name for a certain group of *items*, or objects For example, if you saw the following list of items on a menu, you would know that you were looking at the category of beverages, or items to drink.

Soda

Milk

Juice

Coffee

Tea

In other words, "beverages" is the name of the category, and "soda," "milk," "juice," "coffee," and "tea" are the items in that category.

To help us picture this idea, let's review the following organization chart:

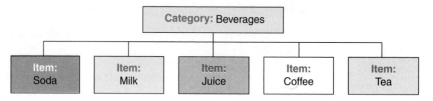

The word "Beverages" is written in the top box to show the overall category. The different types of drinks that are written in the boxes below it show the members of this group. Thus, a category is essentially the topic, and the types of drinks are the "details" that relate to this topic.

Another example of a topic would be the "United States." The words "United States" stand for the overall idea, while New York, California, and Illinois are names that belong to this group. The diagram below helps us to visualize this concept.

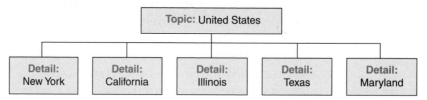

EXERCISE
4-1

Identifying the Topic

Look at the items in each list and ask yourself, "What do all of these items have in common?" Then, identify and circle the topic from the list of items. The first one has been identified for you.

1. (cars)
   Ford
   Chevy
   Honda
   Toyota

2. New York
   Los Angeles
   Chicago
   (cities)
   Houston

$\dagger$ 4/4

3. Georgia
   Florida
   Louisiana
   (Southern states)
   South Carolina

4. mathematics
   (courses)
   English
   sociology
   biology

5. chairs
   table
   couch
   bed
   (furniture)

Copyright © 2006 by Pearson Education, Inc.

EXERCISE
4-2

Identify the Major Category

Look at the items listed below and determine the major category or topic. The first one has been done for you.

1. house, skyscraper, factory, school, post office

   Category: buildings _____

2. United States, Japan, Russia, England, France

Category: _Continents_

3. eggs, bacon, toast, pancakes, waffles

Category: _Breakfast foods_

4. Volkswagen, Toyota, Ford, Chevrolet, Dodge

Category: _Cars_

5. shorts, bathing suit, sandals, t-shirt, short-sleeved dress

Category: _Clothing_

6. dog, cat, horse, cow, sheep

Category: _Animals_

7. computer, monitor, mouse, keyboard, printer

Category: _Electronics_

8. playing sports, going to movies, going to dances, watching television, going to the beach

Category: _Activities_

9. windows, walls, ceilings, doors, floors

Category: _Buildings_

10. lakes, streams, oceans, rivers, ponds

Category: _bodies of water_

10/10

MAIN IDEA

Every paragraph has a **main idea.** It is *always* stated as a sentence and it is *usually* (that is, not always) the first sentence of a paragraph. It tells us the topic—who or what the paragraph is about. You should try to find the author's main idea in each paragraph as you read. Each main idea is connected to the topic. Thus, we can think of the topic as a "group" and the main ideas in each paragraph as "members of the group."

How Do We Detect Main Ideas?

How do we know which idea is the main one? The main idea is found in a sentence that can be related to every sentence in the paragraph. For example, the main idea sentence of a paragraph explaining the topic "beverages" might look like this:

Most restaurants serve a variety of beverages.

The sentences that follow would tell you more about the different kinds of beverages that are available. These sentences contain the supporting details. (Supporting details will be discussed in more detail in Chapter 5.) **Supporting details** give more information about the topic and the topic sentence. For example, one sentence may explain more about the different types of soda that are served. Another sentence might tell you about the different kinds of coffee or cappuccino offered. Yet, another sentence may simply state that white milk and chocolate milk are always available for children. The diagram below shows the connections from the main idea statement to the supporting details in a paragraph. (See Visual Literacy Box 4.1 to learn how to make an organization chart with topics, main ideas, and supporting details.)

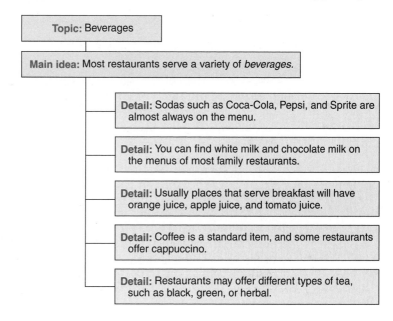

Topic: Beverages

Main idea: Most restaurants serve a variety of *beverages.*

Detail: Sodas such as Coca-Cola, Pepsi, and Sprite are almost always on the menu.

Detail: You can find white milk and chocolate milk on the menus of most family restaurants.

Detail: Usually places that serve breakfast will have orange juice, apple juice, and tomato juice.

Detail: Coffee is a standard item, and some restaurants offer cappuccino.

Detail: Restaurants may offer different types of tea, such as black, green, or herbal.

The first sentence in the chart states the main idea. It tells us the paragraph is about beverages found in restaurants. The remaining sentences are related to the topic; each sentence describes a different kind of beverage that might be on restaurant menus; these sentences contain the supporting details.

Read the paragraph below and decide which sentence is the topic sentence.

[1]Americans are judged by their beauty. [2]First of all, research suggests that physical beauty influences job interviews. [3]Beauty can also affect courtroom decisions. [4]Furthermore, a person's looks can determine their grades in school. [5]Finally, appearance can influence a person's buying behavior. (Barker and Gaut 65)

If you chose the first sentence as the one that states the topic, you are right! The first sentence introduces the topic "beauty and judgment." It makes an overall statement about the power of beauty. The following sentences provide *details*, in this case, *examples* of how people are affected by their looks.

Visual Literacy Box 4.1 ● ● ● ● ● ● ● ● ● ● ● ● ● ● ● ●

Organization Charts

An organization chart shows how information is organized so that we can see how the ideas fit together. Look at the following sentences:

There are five kinds of beverages: soda, coffee, milk, juice, and tea. Soda is a beverage and there are three types of soda: Coca-Cola, Pepsi, and Sprite. Coffee is a beverage and there are three types of coffee: regular, decaf, and cappuccino. Milk is a beverage and there are two kinds of milk: white and chocolate. Juice is a beverage and there are three types of juice: orange, apple, and tomato. Tea is a beverage and there are three kinds of tea: black, green, and herbal.

We would break this information down like this:

■ "Beverages" is the most general word—it could mean anything you drink. So we place it at the top of the organization chart.

(continued on next page)

■ The kinds of beverages are more specific, but these words don't tell us exactly what we are drinking. Therefore, we connect and place them under the topic "beverages."

■ Finally, we look at the most specific words that tell us the brand, flavor, color, etc., of what we are drinking. We connect them to the general type of drink but not to the overall topic. When we follow the lines, we can see how general or specific the word is in relationship to the other names for beverages.

Study the chart below. Then take the missing information from the sentences above and place it in the empty squares below to finish the chart.

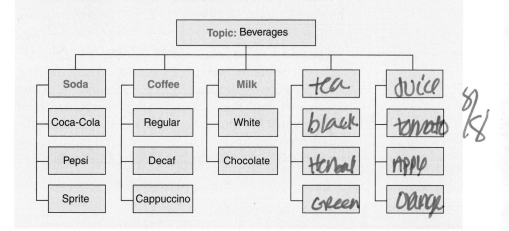

The second sentence would *not* be the main idea because it makes the point that "job interviews are affected by beauty." Although it supports the idea that Americans are judged by their beauty, no other sentences in the paragraph add more information about job interviews.

The third sentence is not the main idea because it narrows the topic to "courtrooms and beauty." No other sentences in the paragraph give more information about courtrooms.

Like sentences 2 and 3, the fourth sentence makes a specific point about "grades and beauty." Again, it supports the idea that "Americans are judged by beauty." But no other sentences go into detail about grades, so it cannot be the main idea.

The last sentence also cannot be the main idea because it specifically mentions "a person's buying behavior." Like the other details, it supports the idea that Americans are judged by their appearance. It is not the topic sentence because the other sentences in the paragraph do not give more details about buying behavior.

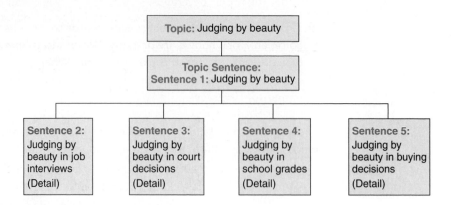

The first sentence makes the point that all of the sentences in the paragraph will be about "judging by beauty." The following sentences are also about "judging by beauty," but each sentence adds something more. The "extra something" that is added to the other sentences are the "details." We would say that the remaining sentences give us more detail about the topic and the topic sentence. In other words, the topic sentence only introduces the topic, while the other sentences add the details.

Main Ideas and Supporting Details

Read the sentences or groups of words below. Label each one as follows: The first one has been started for you.

"T" for topic

"MI" for main idea sentence

"D" for a sentence with details

_____T_____ 1. Self-concept

__D__ Self-concept is the image you have of who you are.

__MI__ Your self-concept is influenced by others' images of you.

2. You can increase your self-awareness by listening to others and actively seeking information about yourself.

Self-awareness

Self-awareness is your knowledge of yourself.

3. Self-esteem is the value you place on yourself.

One way to increase your self-esteem is to work on projects that will result in success.

Self-esteem

4. Self-disclosure

Self-disclosure involves some dangers, such as personal risks and the inability to reverse what was said.

Self-disclosure is the act of revealing normally hidden information about yourself to others.

5. The "open self" includes information known to both yourself and to others.

Self-awareness includes knowledge of your four selves: the open self, the blind self, the hidden self, and the unknown self.

The four selves

(DeVito 89)

EXERCISE
4-4

Choosing the Best Title

Choose the best title for each of the following paragraphs. The first title has been chosen for you.

1. Squids are superbly equipped predators of the open sea. They drift and glide—watching, waiting—then suddenly dart after a fish with knifelike precision. In a chase, a squid can reach almost 25 miles/hour in a matter of seconds, faster than any other invertebrate and most fish. Suction cups on a squid's tentacles and arms grasp prey, and beak-like jaws at the base of the tentacles quickly chop the food into bite-sized pieces. (Campbell, Mitchell, and Reece 562)

   a. Jaws

   b. The Speedy Squid

   c. Predators of the Sea

___B___ **2.** It is the Amazon River system that dominates Brazil. The Amazon Basin is considered the largest single reserve of biological organisms in the world. Scientists estimate that there are anywhere from 800,000 to 5 million species living in the Amazon Basin, 15 to 30 percent of all the species in the world. The Amazon Basin also contains many other assets, including valuable minerals and indigenous Amerindian populations. (Farr and Hammers 30)

   a. Five Million Species

   b. The Assets of the Amazon Basin

   c. Biological Organisms of the Amazon

___A___ **3.** If you were taught to handle disagreements by walking away from them, learn to communicate what is bothering you. On the other hand, if the behavior you grew up with was confrontational (if there was yelling or abuse), strive to change the pattern by, for example, setting a specific time with your partner or your children when troubling matters can be raised, discussed, and resolved. (Berman)

   a. Learn How to Manage Conflict

   b. Quality Time with Your Children

   c. Life's Many Confrontations

_____ **4.** Somewhere around 1950, petroleum surpassed coal as the major energy source in the United States. The reasons are relatively easy to understand. Petroleum, like coal, is partially decomposed organic matter, but it has the distinct advantage of being liquid. It is easily pumped to the surface from its natural, underground reservoirs, transported via pipelines, and fed automatically to its point of use. Moreover, petroleum is a more concentrated energy source than coal, yielding approximately 40–60% more energy per gram. (Stanitski et al. 157–58)

a. Coal Production in the United States
b. Why Petroleum Became the Major Energy Source
c. Petroleum—The Concentrated Energy Source

5. With the development of tools that could be thrown and cooperative hunting techniques, humans began to have profound effects on certain other species. Fossil records indicate that *Homo sapiens* decimated populations of woolly rhinoceroses and giant deer in Europe. About 50,000 years ago, modern humans reached Australia by boat and may have killed off that continent's giant kangaroos. Nomadic hunters migrated from Asia to North America via the Bering land bridge about 30,000 years ago. These early migrants may also have pushed to extinction some large mammals that they hunted. (Campbell, Mitchell and Reese 406).

a. The Development of Tools
b. Nomadic Hunters
c. Hunting and the Extinction of Mammals

Visual Literacy Box 4.2

Circle Graphs

How many species are in the Amazon Basin? Read the sentence below.

Scientists estimate that there are anywhere from 800,000 to 5 million species living in the Amazon Basin, 15 to 30 percent of all the species in the world.

1. Can you give an exact number of species from the details given?

_____

(continued on next page)

2. Can you give an exact percentage from the details provided?

_____

3. Look at the circle chart below. Is there a big difference in the percentages provided?

_____

4. How useful are the statistics?

_____

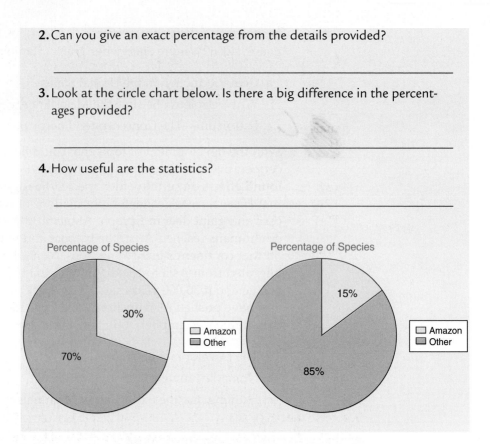

Locating the Main Ideas

The main idea of a paragraph is often found in the first sentence of a paragraph. However, you may also find it in other locations. There are five different places in a paragraph where we can find the main idea, with the fifth being understood but not stated. You can find the main idea:

■ in the first sentence.

■ in the last sentence.

■ in a middle sentence.

4 ▪ split between the first and last sentences.

5 ▪ not stated in the paragraph (implied).

(In Chapter 5, we focus specifically on main idea statements that are implied.)

Study the paragraphs below and make note of the relationship between the main idea statement and the sentences that explain it.

Main Idea in the First Sentence

<u>Self-concept</u>. <u>You no doubt have an image of who you are; this is your self-concept</u>. It consists of your feelings and thoughts about your strengths and weaknesses, your abilities and limitations. Your self-concept develops from at least three sources: (1) the image of you that others have and that they reveal to you, (2) the comparisons you make between yourself and others, and (3) the way you interpret and evaluate your own thoughts and behaviors.(Devito70)

Notice here that the main idea is in the first sentence: "You no doubt have an image of who you are; this is your self-concept." This sentence announces and defines the topic "self-concept." The sentences that follow explain the main idea by further defining it as self-thoughts of strengths and weaknesses and by giving sources for self-concept: (1) others' images, (2) comparisons between self and others, and (3) your own evaluations. The shape of this paragraph looks like an upside-down triangle with the most important idea first and the details following.

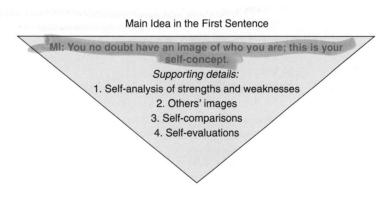

Main Idea in the First Sentence

MI: You no doubt have an image of who you are; this is your self-concept.
Supporting details:
1. Self-analysis of strengths and weaknesses
2. Others' images
3. Self-comparisons
4. Self-evaluations

Main Idea in the Last Sentence

Self-Awareness. The *open self* represents all the information that both you and others know about yourself. The *blind self* represents all the things that you don't know about yourself that others do know. The *hidden self* contains all that you know of yourself and of others that you keep secret. The *unknown self* represents truths about yourself that neither you nor others know. Thus, your self-awareness is how much you know about yourself according to the model of the four selves. (DeVito, 89)

Sometimes authors list all of the details first and then sum them up in the last sentence. Or they may use the last sentence to draw a conclusion based on all of the details. In this case, the author drew the conclusion that *"your self-awareness is how much you know about yourself based on the model of the four selves."* The shape of this paragraph looks like a triangle right side up, where the (supporting) details lead into a final (main idea) sentence that pulls them all together.

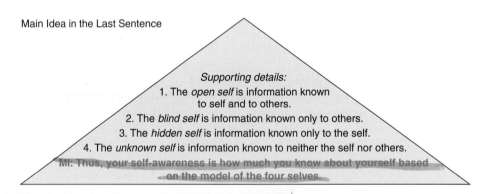

Main Idea in the Last Sentence

Supporting details:
1. The *open self* is information known to self and to others.
2. The *blind self* is information known only to others.
3. The *hidden self* is information known only to the self.
4. The *unknown self* is information known to neither the self nor others.
MI: Thus, your self-awareness is how much you know about yourself based on the model of the four selves.

Main Idea in a Middle Sentence

When you think you're a failure, you're more likely to act like a failure. When you think like a success, you are more likely to act like a success. When you feel good about yourself—about who you are and what you are capable of doing—you will perform better. Self-esteem is very important because success breeds success. Increasing self-esteem will, therefore, help you to function more effectively in school, in interpersonal relationships, and in careers. (DeVito, 75)

As this paragraph shows, sometimes the main idea is found in the middle. First, several details lead up to the main idea. Then, the main idea is stated. Finally, several details follow and explain more about the main idea.

In this case, details are provided about success and failure. They lead up to the main idea that *"self-esteem is very important because success breeds success."* After that, more details emphasize the point that increasing self-esteem will lead to success.

The structure of this paragraph looks like a diamond. Supporting details come before the main idea statement, which ties together the first set of details. Then that statement is followed by yet another supporting detail that further explains it.

Main Idea in a Middle Sentence

1. Thinking like a failure results in acting like a failure.
2. Thinking like a success results in acting like a success.
3. Feeling good about yourself results in better performance.
4. MI: Self-esteem is very important because success breeds success.
5. Increasing self-esteem will help you to function more effectively.

Main Idea Split Between the First and Last Sentences

One of the most important forms of interpersonal communication that you could engage in is talking about yourself, or self-disclosure. It may involve information about (1) your values, beliefs, and desires, (2) your behavior, or (3) your self-qualities or characteristics. You could also self-disclose nonverbally by, for example, wearing gang colors, wedding rings, or shirts with slogans that reveal your political or social concerns. <u>Self-disclosure refers to your communicating infor-mation about yourself to another person.</u> (DeVito 77)

Notice, in this case, how the main idea is split between the first and last sentences. The idea that "self-disclosure" is "talking about yourself" is repeated and explained more in the last sentence. The shape of this paragraph looks like a box, where the main idea serves as bookends to the supporting details.

Main Idea Split Between the First and Last Sentences

1. MI: Talking about yourself is self-disclosure.

2. It may involve information about your values, beliefs, and desires.

3. It may involve information about your behavior.

4. It may involve information about your self-qualities or characteristics.

5. It may involve the communication of nonverbal information such as wearing wedding rings or shirts with slogans.

6. MI: Self-disclosure refers to your communicating information about yourself to another person.

Main Idea Supplied by the Reader (Implied)

People in the United States disclose more than those in Great Britain, Germany, Japan, or Puerto Rico. American students also disclose more than students from nine different Middle East countries. Singaporean-Chinese students consider more topics to be taboo and inappropriate for self-disclosure than their British colleagues. In Japan it is considered undesirable to reveal personal information whereas in much of the United States it is not only considered desirable, it is expected. (DeVito 81)

In this case, there is no main idea statement. <u>Each sentence contains details that lead to a common idea, but it is not stated in writing.</u> In order to arrive at the main idea, we have to compare every sentence and figure out what they all have in common.

■ We discover that all of the sentences are about "self-disclosure."

2. ▪ The subject of each sentence is people from different countries and cultures.

3. ▪ The action part of each sentence is about how much people of different cultures are willing to tell about themselves.

If we put this information all together, we could come up with a main idea statement such as "Culture exerts powerful influence on self-disclosures."

The shape of this type of paragraph looks like a wheel, where each stated supporting detail is a spoke and together all of the spokes are attached to the rim and tire. All of the spokes work together to help the wheel maintain its shape so that it can roll. Likewise, the implied main idea is not actually stated, but it takes shape when we look at all of the details together.

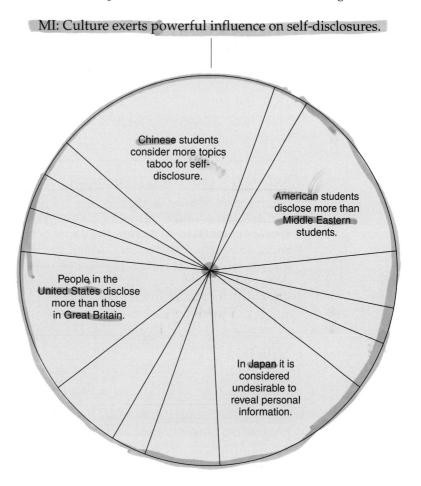

Locating the Topic and Main Idea Sentence

Read each of the paragraphs below. Write the topic of the paragraph in the space provided. Then, determine which sentence contains the main idea and write it out on the space below the topic. The first one has been done for you.

1. When you are in debt, you speak of being "in the red"; when you make a profit you are "in the black." When you are sad, your are "blue"; when you are healthy, you are "in the pink"; when you are jealous, you are "green with envy." To be a coward is to be "yellow" and to be inexperienced is to be "green." When you talk a great deal, you talk "a blue streak"; when you are angry, you "see red." As revealed through these time-worn clichés, language abounds in color symbolism. (DeVito 254)

   Topic: Color Communication

   Main Idea: As revealed through these time-worn clichés, language abounds

   in color symbolism.

2. Although dietary fat is an essential part of a balanced diet, the fact remains that many Americans are consuming too much of it, and too much of the wrong kind. Fats provide about 40% of the calories in the average American diet. Health care specialists recommend that this value should be 30% or less. Much of the concern and controversy regarding cardiac health problems is focused on cholesterol. (Stanitski et al. 157–58)

   Topic: Dieting

   Main Idea: _____

   _____

3. Viewing the Soviet Union as an "evil empire" in his first term, Reagan promoted a bigger atomic arsenal. He argued that a nuclear war could

be fought and won. The administration dropped efforts to obtain Senate ratification of SALT II, the arms reduction plan negotiated under Carter, although it observed the pact's restrictions. Then Reagan proposed the enormously expensive and bitterly criticized Strategic Defense Initiative, popularly known as "Star Wars" after a 1977 movie, to intercept Soviet missiles in outer space. (Nash et al. 830)

Topic: _Nuclear war_

Main Idea: _____

_____

4. From a biological standpoint, fireflies are poorly named. They are bee-tles—not flies. Their light is almost cold, not fiery. In fact, in emitting light, they give off only about one hundred-thousandth of the amount of heat that would be produced by a candle flame of equal brightness. (Campbell, Mitchell and Reese 71)

Topic: _fireflies_

Main Idea: _____

_____

5. South Africa has a life expectancy of approximately 53 for males and 57 for females. It also has an infant mortality rate of approximately 52, meaning that 52 children die in the first year of life for every 1000 born. This relatively high death rate reflects problems with basic sanitation and health care, and is also a result of South Africa's growing crisis with HIV and AIDS. (Farr and Hammers 30)

Topic: _Life in S. Africa_

Main Idea: _____

_____

6. It is estimated that 20 percent of the South African population is infected with the HIV virus. Unlike other diseases which strike mostly small children or the elderly, AIDS kills adults in the prime of their lives, and, at least in Africa, women as well as men. The AIDS crisis is lowering the life expectancy in South Africa, and in the next two decades will lead to tremendous loss of life and human suffering. The American government's Agency for International Development estimates that within 10 years the life expectancy in South Africa will be 35, a drop of 20 years or almost 50 percent. This devastation will leave a population of old people with few able bodied adults to support them. (Farr and Hammers 30)

Topic: _Aids in South Africa_

Main Idea: _____

_____

7. Ask your parents to explain, adult to adult now, why the divorce took place. Don't lecture. Don't judge. Don't personalize. Try to understand the situation they were in and the pressures they grew up with in their own families of origin. Understanding your parents is an important step toward letting go of the pain of the past and moving, with greater confidence, toward the future. (Berman)

Topic: _Divorce (understanding ur parents)_

Main Idea: _____

_____

8. What's in a glass of water? The answer to this question is more than meets the eye because tap water is anything but pure water. Depending on your location, tap water also contains a variety of compounds, such as calcium carbonate; magnesium carbonate; calcium fluoride; chlorine disinfectants; the ions of metals such as iron and potassium; trace amounts of heavy metals such as lead, mercury, and cadmium; and trace amounts of organic compounds in addition to dissolved gaseous mate-

rials such as oxygen, nitrogen, and carbon dioxide. (Hewitt, Suchocki and Hewitt 372)

Topic: _Gases_

Main Idea: _____

_____

9. There is no need to panic and go thirsty, however. While it is surely important to minimize any toxic components of your drinking water, it is unnecessary and undesirable to remove all other substances from it. Some of the dissolved gases and minerals give water a pleasing taste, and many of the other dissolved substances promote human health: The fluoride ion protects teeth; trace amounts of chlorine destroy harmful bacteria; and as much as 10 percent of our daily requirements for iron, potassium, calcium, and magnesium is obtained from ordinary drinking water. (Hewitt, Suchocki and Hewitt 372)

Topic: _toxic components (whats in drinking water)_

Main Idea: _____

_____

10. A nuclear family lasts only as long as the parents and children remain together. Most people belong to at least two nuclear families at different times in their lives. They are born into a family consisting of their parents and siblings. When they reach adulthood, they may marry and establish a nuclear family that includes the spouse and eventually the children. Since most societies permit divorce, some people establish more than one family through marriage. (Kottak 110)

Topic: _Nuclear family_

Main Idea: _____

_____

Visual Literacy Box 4.3

Reading Charts

(Refer to paragraph 6 in Exercise 4.5)

■ First, look at the title of the chart (in this case it is the "Life Expectancy of South Africa's Population").

■ Next, look at the information going across the rows. It gives you the number of years that South Africans are expected to live according to what year it is.

■ Now, look at the information going down the columns. It breaks South Africans into two groups, "male" and "female."

■ We can see from this chart that South African males are expected to live until they are age 53 and South African females are expected to live until they are age 57—*during the year 2003.*

■ We can also see a change for the year 2013. Both South African males and females are expected to live until they reach the age of 35.

Life Expectancy of South Africa's Population		
Year	Males	Females
2003	53	57
2013		

Rows →

Columns

Practice with Charts:

Let's say, for example, that a new medicine came out that would raise the South Africans' life expectancy by 10 years.

1. Fill in the chart below with numbers that would show an increase in life expectancy of 10 years by the year 2013.

2. Fill in the chart below with numbers that would show an increase in life expectancy of 20 years by the year 2013.

3. Fill in the chart below with numbers that would show an increase in life expectancy of 30 years by the year 2013.

	10 years			20 years			30 years	
Life Expectancy of South Africa's Population			Life Expectancy of South Africa's Population			Life Expectancy of South Africa's Population		
Year	Males	Females	Year	Males	Females	Year	Males	Females
2003	53	57	2003	53	57	2003	53	57
2013			2013			2013		

A Reading in History

Would you rather participate in the workforce or take care of children and manage the home? Read the following article to find out how people made these decisions over past decades. Determine the location of the main idea after reading each paragraph. After reading the selection, complete the comprehension exercises that follow it.

Vocabulary in Context

Complete the vocabulary exercise before reading the selection to learn the new terms. The first one has been done for you.

a. gender—sexual category: male or female

b. reaffirmed—firmly said again; repeated

c. conform—do the accepted thing; act in the required way

d. reluctant—unwilling

e. resume—begin again; pick up where you left off

_____c_____ **1.** Although many women wanted to continue working, they had to quit their jobs and _____ to society's rules.

_____ **2.** Women were torn between wanting to _____ their way of life before the war and wanting to continue with their jobs.

_____ **3.** During the war, the _____ roles had changed for women—instead of being homemakers, they supported the family.

_____ **4.** After World War II, many women were _____ to leave their jobs; they liked having jobs outside the home.

_____ **5.** In 1956, examples of women as married homemakers in *Life* magazine _____ traditional standards.

Back to the Kitchen

Read each paragraph and write the number of the sentence that contains the main idea. If the main idea is implied, write a "0." If the main idea is split between the first and last sentence, write the number of both sentences.

_____1_____ **1.** [1]World War II had interrupted traditional patterns of behavior for both men and women. [2]As servicemen went overseas, women went to work. [3]After 1945, there was a period of adjustment as the men returned and many working women were told that they were no longer needed in their jobs. [4]In the 1950s, traditional **gender** roles were **reaffirmed** and women faced tremendous pressure to **conform** to accepted prewar patterns, even though more women entered the workforce than ever before.

_____ **2.** [1]Men and women had different postwar expectations. [2]Most men planned to go to school and then find jobs to support a family. [3]Viewing themselves as the primary breadwinners, they wanted their jobs back after the war. [4]For women, the situation was more complex. [5]While they wanted to **resume** disrupted patterns of family life, many had enjoyed working in the plants and were **reluctant** to retreat to the home, although the government and employers persistently told them to do so.

_____ **2**

3. [1]In 1947, *Life* magazine ran a long photo essay called "The American Woman's Dilemma." [2]Women, it observed, were caught in a conflict between the traditional expectation to stay home and a new desire to have a paid job. [3]Understandably, the sense of dilemma was strongest among white, well-educated, middle-class women; black and lower-class white women usually had to continue working outside the home whether they liked it or not.

_____ **2**

4. [1]By the 1950s, middle-class doubts had largely receded. [2]The baby boom increased average family size and made the decision to remain home easier. [3]The flight to the suburbs gave women more to do, and they settled into the routines of redecorating their homes and gardens and transporting children to and from activities and schools.

_____ **1**

5. [1]In 1956, when *Life* produced a special issue on women, the message had changed strikingly from that of nine years before. [2]Profiling Marjorie Sutton, the magazine spoke of the "Busy Wife's Achievements" as "Home Manager, Mother, Hostess, and Useful Civic Worker." [3]Married at the age of 16, Marjorie was now involved with the PTA, Campfire Girls, and charity causes. [4]She cooked and sewed for her family, which included four children, supported her husband by entertaining 1,500 guests a year, and worked out on the trampoline "to keep her size 12 figure." [5]Marjorie Sutton typified the widespread social emphasis on marriage and home. (Nash 699–700)

Comprehension Questions

_____ a

1. World War II ended in:
   a. 1945.
   b. 1950.
   c. 1956.

2. After 1945, men expected:

    a. to go to school and get their jobs back.

    b. to become homemakers.

    c. to have their wives support them.

 3. Black and lower-class white women continued working because:

    a. they needed the money.

    b. they were not interested in raising a family.

    c. they were not interested in being homemakers.

 4. By the 1950s, white middle-class women more readily chose marriage and home life over work because:

    a. there were no jobs available.

    b. they had to care for many more children.

    c. they moved to the cities where there was more to keep them occupied.

 5. The sentence "Marjorie Sutton typified the widespread social emphasis on marriage and home" means that:

    a. Marjorie Sutton's life was an example of how people believed women should spend their time.

    b. Marjorie Sutton's life was very different from the lives of other women in the 1950s.

    c. Marjorie Sutton's life was an example that showed most people's belief that both the husband and wife should work outside the home.

Visual Literacy Box 4.4 ● ● ● ● ● ● ● ● ● ● ● ● ● ● ●

Vertical Timelines

To make a vertical timeline,

■ List all of the dates of events or trends from the reading in the left-hand column of your timeline.

(continued on next page)

■ Then write each event or trend in the right-hand column next to the date on which it occurred.

When you are finished, you will have a summary of events for that time period and topic. Study the list of events below and answer the following questions. (Refer to the "Back to the Kitchen" excerpt.)

1. How did the workplace change for men between 1945 and 1956?

_____

2. How did the workplace change for women between 1945 and 1956?

_____

3. At first, women did not want to give up their jobs. What persuaded them to go back to homemaking?

_____

Before 1945	"World War II had interrupted traditional patterns of behavior for both men and women. As servicemen went overseas, women went to work."
↓ After 1945	"After 1945, there was a period of adjustment as the men returned and many working women were told that they were no longer needed in their jobs."
↓ 1947	"In 1947, *Life* magazine ran a long photo essay called 'The American Woman's Dilemma.' Women, it observed, were caught in a conflict between the traditional expectation to stay home and a new desire to have a paid job."
↓ 1950	"Women faced tremendous pressure to conform to accepted prewar patterns." "The baby boom increased average family size and made the decision to remain home easier."
↓ 1956	"When *Life* produced a special issue on women, the message had changed strikingly from that of nine years before," placing "widespread social emphasis on marriage and home."

A Reading in Chemistry

What is DNA analysis? Are we really headed toward *Jurassic Park*? Read the following article to find out how DNA analysis and cloning are shaping the future. Determine the location of the main idea after reading each paragraph.

Vocabulary in Context

Complete the vocabulary exercise before reading the selection to learn the new terms. Study the terms below. Then complete the exercise by writing the letter of the term in front of the sentence in which it is best used. The first one has been done for you.

a. DNA (deoxyribonucleic acid)—genetic material that organisms inherit from their parents

b. DNA fingerprinting—the technique of DNA matching that can be used to identify the individual source of a DNA sample

c. unique—only one of its kind

d. encode—create by writing in code; to copy genetic material

e. nonessential—not needed; unnecessary

_____a_____ **1.** Researchers have taken _____ samples from a 2400-year-old Egyptian mummy to gain information about the relationship of ancient peoples, their migration routes, and their diseases.

_____ **2.** The genes that _____ for most proteins are identical in most humans.

_____ **3.** _____ is used in criminal investigation.

_____ **4.** Forensic scientists can see differences in the genetic make-up of people by comparing the _____ DNA.

_____ **5.** Scientists can tell differences between us by looking at our DNA because each of us has his or her own _____ DNA.

DNA Analysis

Read each paragraph and write the number of the sentence that contains the main idea. If the main idea is implied, write a "0." If the main idea is split between the first and last sentence, write the number of both sentences.

___1___ **1.** [1]**DNA fingerprinting** is based on the fact that each of us has his or her own **unique DNA.** [2]It is not surprising that the really important genes, those that **encode** for most proteins, are identical in almost all of us. [3]We differ primarily in the "junk" DNA that makes up about 98% of the three billion base pairs in each human cell nucleus. [4]Therefore, it is to this **nonessential** DNA that forensic scientists look when they seek to determine "who dun it."

_____ **2.** [1]Criminal investigation is not the only use of DNA fingerprinting. [2]It is also a powerful tool in genetic identification. [3]In 1998, DNA fingerprinting was used to determine the identity of a soldier who was killed during the Vietnam War and was buried in the Tomb of the Unknowns at Arlington National Cemetery. [4]The tests resolved the identity of the entombed soldier, which had been narrowed to two possible candidates. [5]The profile of DNA taken from the bones of First Lieutenant Michael Blassie matched sufficiently that of a DNA sample taken from his mother, thus allowing proper identification.

_____ **3.** [1]DNA analysis is not done on just the living and those who recently died. [2]Researchers have cloned and investigated DNA samples obtained from a 2400-year-old Egyptian mummy and some even older human remains. [3]Scientists have interpreted the results to gain information about the relationship of ancient peoples, their migration routes, and their diseases.

Implied Main Idea: _____

_____

_____   **4.** [1]The current DNA age record is held by a bee and a termite that lived about 30 million years ago. [2]Since that time, the insects had been entombed and protected in amber, which is plant resin that has become solid. [3]In 1992, researchers released their perfectly preserved bodies, took out their DNA, and put it through a number of tests. [4]This research gave important information about the ancient bees evolved into the modern species.

Main Idea: _____

_____

_____   **5.** [1]But could 30-million-year-old DNA yield more? [2]Could it be cloned into a living fossil? [3]That was the basic idea for *Jurassic Park*. [4]In the science fiction film and the novel, the chief interest is not in the fossilized insects themselves, but in the dinosaur blood they contain. [5]The blood is the source of the DNA that is cloned and introduced into crocodile egg cells, where it replicates until it creates modern copies of long-extinct creatures. [6]"Could this happen in real life?" [7]That question is posed by I. Edward Alcamo in the book *DNA Technology: The Awesome Skill*. [8]Professor Alcamo's answer may be mildly reassuring for those who would rather not encounter a *Tyrannosaurus rex*: [9]"Possibly. [10]But you would need an entire set of dinosaur chromosomes, and only a minuscule fragment has been obtained up to now. [11]And that's only the first of a thousand problems that must be solved." (Stanitski et al. 478–81)

Comprehension Questions

___a___   **1.** *Jurassic Park* is the name for:
  a. a film.

  b. a crocodile.

  c. dinosaur chromosomes.

_____   **2.** When the authors refer to "junk" DNA, they mean:
  a. the really important genes that encode for most proteins.

  b. the essential DNA.

  c. the nonessential DNA.

_____ **3.** The DNA taken from the bones of First Lieutenant Michael Blassie matched:

    a. the DNA of two possible candidates.

    b. a DNA sample taken from his mother.

    c. the DNA of other Unknowns at Arlington National Cemetery.

_____ **4.** The oldest DNA that researchers studied is from a bee and a termite that lived:

    a. 3 million years ago.

    b. 30 million years ago.

    c. 300 million years ago.

_____ **5.** The reason that a dinosaur is unlikely to be cloned is:

    a. scientists have not found a way to match DNA samples.

    b. scientists have not found any fossilized insects.

    c. scientists have not found an entire set of dinosaur chromosomes.

Getting Ahead in College Box 4.1

THE PRONUNCIATION OF VOCABULARY

When two or three consonants (letters that are not vowels) are grouped together, the combination of the letters makes one sound. For example, the p and the l sounds in please, plan, and play are blended together to make one sound. Thus, they are called consonant blends. Complete the following sentences with words that begin with blends. For each question, choose one of the terms provided, underline the term, and then write it in the blank space. Use the following examples as a pronunciation guide. The first one has been done for you.

    br   as in   **br**ing

    cr   as in   **cr**eam

    dr   as in   **dr**ag

(continued on next page)

(continued from previous page)

gr	as in	**gr**ass
pr	as in	**pr**ice
tr	as in	**tr**y
fr	as in	**fr**om

DNA Analysis

1. It is not surprising that the really important genes, those that encode for most _____ are identical in almost all of us. (<u>proteins</u>, genetic material)

2. _____ investigation is not the only use of DNA fingerprinting. (criminal, forensic)

3. Since that time, the insects had been entombed and _____ in amber, which is plant resin that has become solid. (sealed, protected)

4. But you would need an entire set of dinosaur chromosomes, and only a minuscule _____ has been obtained up to now (amount, fragment).

Birth Order

5. They have an issue with fairness since the oldest has received _____ before them. (privileges, attention)

6. Sometimes middle children are teased and _____ badly by the older sibling. (treated, taunted)

7. When a second child is born, it is said that he or she will "dethrone" the oldest, _____ another child for the parents to pay attention to. (creating, adding)

8. Identical twins can have some special difficulty in families where identity is _____ a competitive effort. (mainly, primarily)

9. Some feel as though they had to _____ up too fast. (give, grow)

10. They often have _____ in developing an identity since older siblings have already taken various family niches. (trouble, difficulty)

A Reading in Psychology

How many brothers and or sisters do you have? The order in which you were born greatly affects your personality. Read the article below to see if any of the situations described are similar to the experiences you had while growing up. Determine the location of the main idea after reading each paragraph. After reading the selection, complete the comprehension exercises that follow it.

Vocabulary in Context

Complete the vocabulary exercise before reading the selection to learn the new terms. The first term has been identified for you.

a. siblings—other children in a family beside oneself; brothers and sisters

b. manipulate—influence, control

c. perceives—sees, understands

d. dominant—leading

e. recessive—taking a secondary place

_____b_____ **1.** The youngest children in the family can learn to _____ (b. manipulate, c. perceive) others into doing what they would like.

_____ **2.** For a twin, finding a place in the family depends on how he or she _____ (c. perceives, a. siblings) himself or herself.

_____ **3.** The youngest in a family can have trouble developing an identity because the older _____ (c. perceives, a. siblings) have taken many of the positions in the family.

_____ **4.** In some families, identity is a competitive effort for identical twins. One twin will become _____ (d. dominant, e. recessive) and assertive.

_____ **5.** When one twin takes the lead, the other becomes more timid and _____ (d. dominant e. recessive).

Birth Order

Read each paragraph and write the number of the sentence that contains the main idea. If the main idea is implied, write a "0." If the main idea is split between the first and last sentence, write the number of both sentences.

<u>   1   </u>   **1.** <u>Oldest Child.</u> [1]First children tend to be very authority conscious, leadership oriented, bossy and are often held up as the family example or hero. [2]They have the unique advantage of having a period of time where they had all the parents' attention and did not have to share it. [3]They are the "family guinea pigs" in the sense that parents are first-time parents when they are born. [4]They tend to be demanding of themselves and others, perfectionists who do not like making mistakes and often rise to leadership positions in organizations. [5]They generally like responsibility and have usually been given a good amount of it early in life. [6]Many respond to their parents expectations, and some in less functional families actually take over the role of the parent. [7]They are independent and like to be in charge. [8]Many oldest children with **siblings** spent time caring for younger children, which further developed their sense of responsibility.

<u>   </u>   **2.** [1]Oldest children sometimes will take responsibility for things that had little to do with them. [2]They can also blame themselves excessively when things do not go well in the family. [3]There are lots of photos in the family albums of first-born children!

<u>   </u>   **3.** <u>Middle Children.</u> [1]A middle child, and particularly a second child, has to make a choice of whether to follow in the footsteps of the oldest and compete or to establish some other sense of identity on his own. [2]Middle children have the advantage of watching the older children grow and then learn from their success or failure. [3]However, they can suffer from being compared to the oldest. [4]They hardly ever get to do anything first. [5]In families with a competitive atmosphere, these children can spend endless hours trying to compete with or keep up with the oldest, leading to feelings of discouragement. [6]Or they can strike out in an opposite direction

to establish their place or identity. [7]When these children are in photographs, they are usually pictured with other siblings.

_____ 4. [1]Middle children are usually cooperative, unseen "peace-makers" in the family, since they are used to dealing with comparisons made by parents and jealous behavior from other siblings. [2]They have an issue with fairness since the oldest has received privileges before them, and sometimes they are compared to them regardless of whether they do good or bad things. [3]Middle children often feel like they receive more chores. [4]When a second child is born, it is said that he or she will "dethrone" the oldest, creating another child for the parents to pay attention to. [5]This can lead in some cases to jealous behavior toward the second child. [6]Sometimes middle children are teased and treated badly by the older sibling.

_____ 5. [1]Middle children are most likely to be dependable workers and easygoing spouses. [2]As they grow, middle children are less likely to aspire to positions of leadership than older children. [3]However, they are experienced by others as solid, dependable workers who are loyal and easy to get along with. [4]As future spouses they "roll with the punches" better than siblings in other positions.

_____ 6. Youngest Children. [1]Folk wisdom would have us believe these children are the spoiled ones. [2]They are referred to as the "babies" of the family and still can have that term applied to them even as adults! [3]They are often given more attention than the middle children and are sometimes held back in the growing-up process. [4]Although the youngest have many advantages, they can experience some challenges. [5]They often have trouble in developing an identity since older siblings have already taken various family niches. [6]Other family members tend to give them too much assistance by readily supplying advice and tying their shoes for them all the time when they are little. [7]They are almost always in the position of being taken care of. [8]Youngest children often have fewer expectations than the older children and are disciplined differently. [9]They have many others to watch to see how they would like to act.

_____ 7. [1]Youngests sometimes feel dependent on the other members of the family and lack confidence in their own decisions. [2]They have little experience in caring for others unless the family sets up experience for them. [3]They can learn to **manipulate** others in the family into doing what they would like. [4]They can be the last one to find out anything that is being planned or any forthcoming change within the family. [5]They are sometimes treated as though they do not have the competence or maturity to handle things. [6]In most families they have more access to financial resources and experience their parents as being more relaxed than the other siblings do. [7]Thus, the youngest's lack of confidence stems from low family expectations and their lack of experience in caring for themselves or for others.

_____ 8. <u>Only Children</u>. [1]With a few exceptions, the experiences of oldest children and only children are similar. [2]The only child has the advantage of remaining the center of the parents' attention permanently. [3]Only children have all the resources of the family focused toward them, but they also have all the expectations of the family to live with.

_____ 9. [1]Only children tend to associate with adults as they grow up, missing significant cooperative experiences with other children. [2]They often feel alone. [3]Some feel as though they had to grow up too fast. [4]They are leadership oriented and responsible, but like the oldest do not care for making mistakes. [5]They are highly independent and individualistic. [6]Only children can find a real difference between the "center of attention" world of their home and the "you're one of the bunch" world outside the home. [7]They sometimes lack the skills of interaction with the group. [8]Only children will often rise to leadership positions as adults, having lived in the adult world all their lives.

_____ 10. <u>Twins</u>. [1]The resulting place in the family for twins depends primarily upon how each **perceives** him or herself and upon the atmosphere (competitive or cooperative) within the family. [2]Identical twins can have some special difficulty in families where identity is primarily a competitive effort. [3]In some cases twins will act more like a first and second child or follow a pattern where one is **dominant** and the other **recessive**. [4]Both of these point to the interpretation each person makes of their role and how to achieve their place. (Pulver 33–36)

Comprehension Questions

_____ 1. Which of the following children are noted as becoming loyal, dependable workers?
   a. oldest child.
   b. middle child.
   c. youngest child.

_____ 2. Which of the following children learn to manipulate family members in order to get what they want?
   a. youngest child.
   b. only child.
   c. twins.

_____ 3. The oldest child tends to:
   a. rise to leadership positions.
   b. become a spouse that is able to "roll with the punches."
   c. be dependent on family members.

_____ 4. "Only children" often rise to leadership positions as adults because:
   a. they grew up with few expectations.
   b. they grew up associating with adults more than other children.
   c. they grew up with too much assistance.

_____ 5. Middle children:
   a. are referred to as the "family guinea pigs."
   b. learn from their older siblings' successes and failures.
   c. often feel alone.

PARTS OF SPEECH: REVIEW OF ADJECTIVES AND PHRASES

Combine the following sentences into one sentence. Use all of the underlined words from the sentences below it. Keep the most important information without repeating any words. Adjectives always come before the noun they describe. Prepositional phrases always begin with a preposition, or joining word. Use the word "and" to separate two prepositional phrases within a sentence. Use commas to separate more than two phrases in a sentence. (The following exercise refers to the "Birth Order" reading.), and the first set of sentences has been combined for you.

1. The oldest child has the advantage.

   The advantage is <u>unique</u>.

   The advantage is <u>of having a period of time</u>.

   The period of time was <u>where they had their parents' attention</u>.

   The parents' attention was <u>all</u>.

   <u>The oldest child has the unique advantage of having a period of time where they had all the parents' attention.</u>

2. A middle child has the advantage.

   The advantage is <u>of watching</u>.

   The watching is to see how <u>the older children grow</u>.

   The advantage is <u>then</u>.

   Then advantage is <u>from learning</u>.

   The learning is from <u>their success or failure</u>.

   _____

   _____

(continued on next page)

3. The youngest child has others.

The others are <u>many</u>.

The others are <u>to watch</u>.

The others are also <u>to see</u>.

The seeing is <u>how they would like to act</u>.

_____

_____

4. The only child has the advantage.

The advantage is <u>of remaining</u>.

The remaining is of <u>the center</u>.

The center is <u>of the parents' attention</u>.

The attention is <u>permanent</u>.

_____

_____

5. In some cases twins will act.

The acting will be <u>more</u>.

The acting will be <u>like a first child</u>.

The acting also be <u>like a second child</u>.

_____

_____

CHAPTER

5

Implied Main Ideas

In this chapter, we:

- review our knowledge of the various main idea patterns;

- apply those patterns to help us distinguish between main idea and supporting details;

- use the details to help us understand the implied main idea.

Finding the author's main point is a very important part of reading. However, that is not enough! As the interviews with professors below show, reading the textbook, *including the details*, is completely necessary if you want to understand the information. The first professor explains the kind of problems students have when they just search for the main ideas without reading the rest of the text.

PROFESSOR YOUNG: The students who do poorly just look at the questions and scan for the answers. I talked with a student yesterday who is now taking a course with me, her second time through it. The first time, she failed . . . and I somewhat cringed when I saw that she was enrolled in the course again. And she has surprised me because she's a solid B student in the course this time. And I just asked her yesterday, "What's the difference?" And she said that the first time she took the course she did not really read through the material, that she just tried to find the answers to the questions. This semester, she's taking the time to read the material.

Another professor describes the opposite problem: students read the details but do not understand how they are related to the main idea.

PROFESSOR DJANG: Some students look upon reading material as a series of individual items which should be committed to memory . . . rather than looking for larger structures.

A third professor explains why some of his students have poor comprehension. His comments show that you need to read both the main ideas and the supporting details. Not only do you need to read both, but you have to think about how they are related.

PROFESSOR PEDRO: I think they skim through and I don't think they follow trains of thought; they read isolated sentences. They don't see how they connect up.

MAIN IDEA PATTERNS

When reading textbooks, we really need to read *all* of the information and then determine how it fits together. We do this by looking for the author's main points and connecting them with the details or examples. We call these main points the **main ideas** and the details or examples the **supporting details**.

The process of *skimming* simply involves looking for the main ideas without reading the other sentences. This is a useful strategy *when you have already learned the information* and you are just refreshing your memory. However, when you are first introduced to new material, it is difficult and sometimes impossible to understand the main ideas without reading all the sentences (that is, the supporting details) that explain those ideas.

When you are learning new information, you need to read all of the sentences in a paragraph to determine which one contains the main idea. If you skip this process and just guess, you will probably not understand what you are reading. Thus, students who only skim their textbooks are not really learning the information and, as a result, will likely not do as well as they could in school.

Where Is the Main Idea Located?

In Chapter 4 we looked at five main idea patterns. Some paragraphs stated the main idea in *the first sentence*. These general statements were followed by sentences that explained or gave more information about them. We called these sentences that followed the "supporting details" because they contained "details" or more information about the first sentence. The order of the paragraph looked like this:

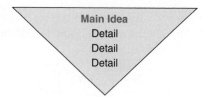

We also looked at paragraphs in which the supporting details came first. Each sentence gave some information about the topic. Then, the last sentence either summed up all of the details or drew a conclusion about them. In this case, the *last sentence* was the main idea.

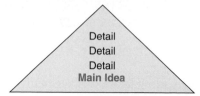

There were also paragraphs in which the main idea was stated *in the middle*. Some details were given at the beginning of the paragraph and other details provided more support for the main idea in the final sentences.

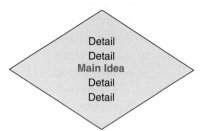

Finally, we looked at paragraphs in which the main idea was *split between the first and last sentences*. We noticed that the first sentence did not include enough information to cover all of the ideas mentioned in the paragraph, nor did the last sentence. But, when combined, the first and last sentences created a general statement that could be related to all of the details in the paragraph.

Partial Main Idea
Detail
Detail
Detail
Complete Main Idea

How Do We Detect Supporting Details?

The supporting details include all of the sentences that are not the main idea; they offer specific facts that give more information about it. Once you have found the main idea, you can usually find the supporting details. For example:

> Bottled water **[TOPIC]** has become more than just a thirst quencher for athletes **[MAIN IDEA]**. Many people, especially students, drink multiple bottles throughout the day [Supporting Detail]. Students carry bottled water with them everywhere, especially to classes [Supporting Detail]. Students can be seen drinking bottled water in the student union, while walking on campus, and at special outdoor events [Supporting Detail]. On college campuses, even the bookstores are well stocked with bottled water **[SUPPORTING DETAILS]**.

Visual Literacy Box 5.1

Visualizing Supporting Details

We can visualize the relationship between the main idea and the supporting details by creating a web. Follow the directions below to finish a web based on the sample paragraph about bottled water.

1. In the center of your paper, draw a circle and place the topic and main idea in it.

2. Count the number of supporting detail sentences in the paragraph and draw that many circles around the "topic" circle.

3. Fill in each circle with a supporting detail sentence.

4. Draw arrows connecting the topic to each supporting detail.

When finished, you can see how the topic and main idea relate to all sentences in the paragraph. Like the topic, all of the sentences are about bottled water. The supporting details extend the main idea by adding more information about the popularity of bottled water.

(continued on next page)

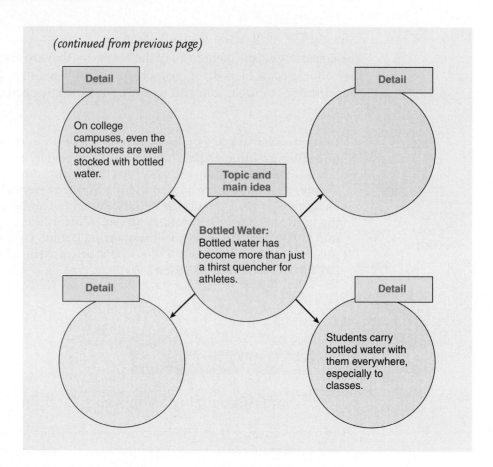

(continued from previous page)

Detail

On college campuses, even the bookstores are well stocked with bottled water.

Detail

Topic and main idea

Bottled Water: Bottled water has become more than just a thirst quencher for athletes.

Detail

Detail

Students carry bottled water with them everywhere, especially to classes.

EXERCISE
5-1

Identifying the Topic, Main Idea, and Supporting Detail

Read the following sentences or groups of words below. Label each one as follows:

"T"   for topic
"MI"   for main idea sentence
"D"   for a supporting detail

One sentence has already been labeled for you.

_____D_____ **1.** The friendship of reciprocity is the ideal type, characterized by loyalty, self-sacrifice, mutual affection, and generosity.

_____MI_____ There are three types of friendship: reciprocity, receptivity, and association.

_____T_____ Friendship

_____D_____ **2.** Friends help us to view ourselves as worthy and competent individuals.

_____D_____ Purposes of Friendships

_____MI_____ There are several purposes of friendships.

_____MI_____ **3.** Men and women make friends in different ways.

_____D_____ Men's friendships are built around shared activities.

_____T_____ Gender Differences

_____T_____ **4.** Types of Love

_____D_____ Agape is the type of love that is self-giving.

_____MI_____ There are six types of love.

_____MI_____ **5.** Men score higher on romanticism.

_____D_____ Men and women have different views of love.

_____T_____ Gender Differences and Love

(DeVito 415)

MAJOR AND MINOR DETAILS

There are two kinds of supporting details: major and minor. The **major supporting details** add more information about the topic by expanding on what was stated in the topic sentence. The **minor supporting details** give more information about the major supporting details. Read the paragraph below and try to find two major details and four minor details.

Pizza

All pizzas are not the same. First of all, the crust can be made in two different ways. Some pizzas, for example, have a thick crust for a chewy texture. Other pizzas have a thin crust for a crispy feel. Secondly, many different types of toppings can be added to pizza. Vegetarians can add mushrooms, onions, and peppers. Meat lovers can add pepperoni, sausage, and sliced steak.

Our topic, of course, is "pizza." Our main point is that pizzas can be different—"All pizzas are not the same." The two major details tell us that (a) the crust can make a pizza different and (b) toppings can make a pizza different. Two minor details explain how a crust can be different: (1) they can be chewy or (2) they can be crispy. Two other minor details explain how toppings can make a pizza different: (1) you can top it with vegetables or (2) you can top it with meat.

We can visualize the relationship between the main idea and the major and minor supporting details as an outline.

Topic: Pizza

I   Main Idea: All pizzas are not the same.

   a. Major Detail: First of all, the crust can be made in two different ways.

      1. Minor Detail: Some pizzas, for example, have a thick crust for a chewy texture.

      2. Minor Detail: Other pizzas have a thin crust for a crispy feel.

   b. Major Detail: Secondly, many different types of toppings can be added to pizza.

      1. Minor Detail: Those who like vegetables can add mushrooms, onions, and peppers.

      2. Minor Detail: Meat lovers can add pepperoni, sausage, and sliced steak.

We can also visualize this relationship in an organization chart.

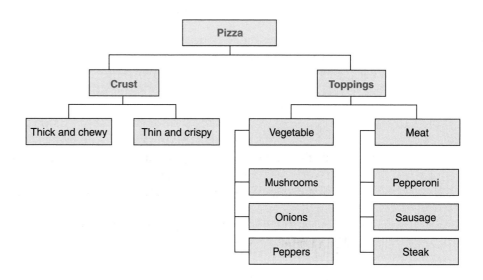

Let's look again at our paragraph on "pizza" and label each part:

- "T" for topic
- "MI" for main idea
- "SD1" for major supporting detail
- "SD2" for minor supporting detail

(T) Pizza

(MI) All pizzas are not the same. (SD1) First of all, the crust can be made in two different ways. (SD2) Some pizzas, for example, have a thick crust for a chewy texture. (SD2) Other pizzas have a thin crust for a crispy feel. (SD1) Secondly, many different types of toppings can be added to pizza. (SD2) Vegetarians can add mushrooms, onions, and peppers. (SD2) Meat lovers can add pepperoni, sausage, and sliced steak.

Distinguishing Between Major and Minor Details

Read the following sentences or groups of words below. Label each one as follows:

- "T" for topic
- "MI" for main idea sentence
- "SD1" for a sentence with major supporting details
- "SD2" for a sentence with minor supporting details

The first group of words has been labeled for you.

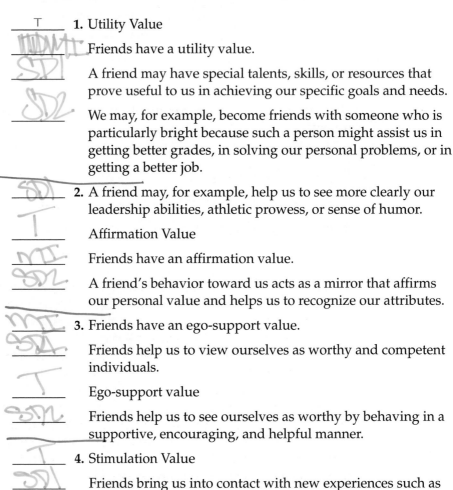

___T___ **1.** Utility Value

_____ Friends have a utility value.

_____ A friend may have special talents, skills, or resources that prove useful to us in achieving our specific goals and needs.

_____ We may, for example, become friends with someone who is particularly bright because such a person might assist us in getting better grades, in solving our personal problems, or in getting a better job.

_____ **2.** A friend may, for example, help us to see more clearly our leadership abilities, athletic prowess, or sense of humor.

_____ Affirmation Value

_____ Friends have an affirmation value.

_____ A friend's behavior toward us acts as a mirror that affirms our personal value and helps us to recognize our attributes.

_____ **3.** Friends have an ego-support value.

_____ Friends help us to view ourselves as worthy and competent individuals.

_____ Ego-support value

_____ Friends help us to see ourselves as worthy by behaving in a supportive, encouraging, and helpful manner.

_____ **4.** Stimulation Value

_____ Friends bring us into contact with new experiences such as modern art, foreign cultures, and new foods.

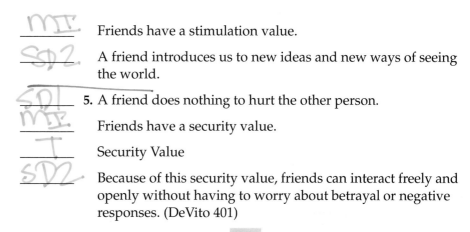

_____ Friends have a stimulation value.

_____ A friend introduces us to new ideas and new ways of seeing the world.

_____ **5.** A friend does nothing to hurt the other person.

_____ Friends have a security value.

_____ Security Value

_____ Because of this security value, friends can interact freely and openly without having to worry about betrayal or negative responses. (DeVito 401)

EXERCISE
5-3

Distinguishing Between Major and Minor Details II

Read the following sentences or groups of words below. Label each one as follows:

- "T" for topic

- "MI" for main idea sentence

- "SD1" for a sentence with major supporting details

- "SD2" for a sentence with minor supporting details

(1) _____ Interviewing
(2) _____ When you are being interviewed, your chief responsibility is to yourself. (3) _____ During an employment interview, you owe it to yourself to obtain as much information as you can. (4) _____ Should you be offered the job, you will need this information so that you can make an intelligent decision. (5) _____ Make sure you understand the requirements of the job (just what it is that you will be expected to do). (6) _____ If you don't understand something, ask questions until you do. (7) _____ State your qualifications in a positive way. (8) _____ Balance potential weaknesses with strengths. (9) _____ The most important thing to do during any kind of interview is to communicate. (10) _____ It is important to listen, speak, question, respond, and understand. (Barker and Gaut 354)

Visual Literacy Box 5.2 ■ ● ● ● ● ● ● ● ● ● ● ● ● ● ● ● ●

Making an Outline:
Major and Minor Supporting Details

Below is a partial outline of the paragraph on "Interviewing." The main idea and the major details are provided. Finish the outline by filling in the minor details.

Interviewing

When you are being interviewed, your chief responsibility is to yourself. During an employment interview, you owe it to yourself to obtain as much information as you can. Should you be offered the job, you will need this information so that you can make an intelligent decision. Make sure you understand the requirements of the job (just what it is that you will be expected to do). If you don't understand something, ask questions until you do. State your qualifications in a positive way. Balance potential weaknesses with strengths. The most important thing to do during any kind of interview is to communicate. It is important to listen, speak, question, respond, and understand.

Topic: Interviewing

I   When you are being interviewed, your chief responsibility is to yourself.
   a. During an employment interview, you owe it to yourself to obtain as much information as you can.

   _____

   _____

   _____

   b. If you don't understand something, ask questions until you do.

   _____

   c. The most important thing to do during any kind of interview is to communicate.

   _____

EXERCISE	**Locating Supporting Details**
5-4	

Look carefully at the topic of each paragraph below. Then read the paragraph for the details that develop the topic. Finally, answer the question that follows each paragraph. The first question has been answered for you.

Paragraph 1

Topic: Document Design and First Impressions
When readers first see your document, they immediately form opinions about you and your information. A well-designed document shows you have respected the assignment and spent enough time to master the required format. In turn, a document that makes a good first impression influences readers positively. (Troyka 239)

 c   Why is it necessary to develop a well-designed document?

    a. Readers form opinions about you when they first see your document.

    b. A well-designed document shows that you have respected the assignment.

    c. Well-designed documents make a positive impression on readers.

Paragraph 2

Topic: The Importance of the Type-Written Paper
Few college instructors accept handwritten essays and research papers. If you do not own a computer, you can use one at your college's computer lab. Find out if you need to sign up in advance or whether it's "first come, first served." Then schedule enough time to get there, wait your turn, and perhaps go again if you need more time. (Troyka 239)

    What should students do if they do not own a computer?

    a. Give the professor a handwritten copy.

    b. Buy a computer.

    c. Go to the college's computer lab.

Getting Ahead in College Box 5.1

IDENTIFYING THE TOPIC

Below is a list of phrases. Identify which one is the topic. Look for a phrase that could sum up all of the other phrases combined.

Topic:

1. Gulping drinks.

2. Drinking to modify uncomfortable feelings.

3. Personality or behavioral changes after drinking.

4. Getting drunk frequently.

5. Experiencing "blackouts"—not being able to remember what happened while drinking.

6. Frequent accidents or illness as a result of drinking.

7. Priming—preparing yourself with alcohol before a social gathering at which alcohol is going to be served.

8. Warning signs of problem drinking—alcoholism

9. Not wanting to talk about the negative consequences of drinking (avoidance).

10. Preoccupation with alcohol.

11. Focusing social situations around alcohol.

12. Sneaking drinks.

Paragraph 3

Topic: Alcohol

Alcohol encompasses a variety of beverages containing ethyl alcohol, such as beers, wines, and distilled spirits. The concentration of ethyl alcohol varies from about 4% in most beers up to 40% in 80-proof liquor, and occasionally more in higher-proof liquors. When people drink heavily, the central effect is a relaxed euphoria that temporarily boosts self-esteem, as problems seem to melt away and inhibitions diminish. Alcohol is the most widely used recreational drug in our society. Because alcohol is legal, many people use it casually without even thinking of it as a drug.

_____ What percentage of alcohol do most beers contain?

    a. 4%

    b. 40%

    c. 400%

Paragraph 4

Heavy drinking is particularly prevalent on college campuses, according to a large-scale survey by researchers at the Harvard School of Public Health. Unfortunately the survey also indicated that drinking contributes to many social problems in college life. With their inhibitions released, some drinkers become argumentative and prone to aggression. In the Harvard survey of over 17,000 undergraduates, 34% of the students from "heavy drinking" schools reported that they had been insulted or humiliated by a drunken student, 20% had experienced serious arguments, and 13% had been pushed or assaulted. (Weiten ch. 5)

_____ What percentage of undergraduates reported being insulted by a drunken student?

    a. 13%

    b. 20%

    c. 34%

Visual Literacy Box 5.3 ● ● ● ● ● ● ● ● ● ● ● ● ● ● ● ● ● ●

Making a Web:
Major and Minor Supporting Details

Reread paragraph 4 of Exercise 5.4. Then, look through the list of phrases below and decide whether they represent (1) a main idea, (2) a major supporting detail, or (3) a minor supporting detail. Place the phrases in the appropriate spaces in the web below.

■ Drinkers become aggressive

■ 34% report insults

■ Heavy drinking is prevalent on college campuses.

(continued on next page)

(continued from previous page)

■ 20% report arguments

■ Harvard School of Public Health's survey

■ 13% report assaults

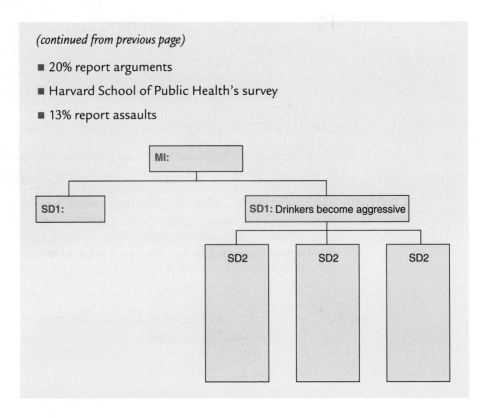

Paragraph 5

Marx believed society essentially consisted of two basic social classes: the "haves" and the "have-nots." According to Marx's viewpoint, the *bourgeoisie* (haves), the powerful ruling class, had assumed power not because they were the "fittest" but because they owned and controlled the means of production. He believed the bourgeoisie used deception, fraud, and violence to take over the production of the *proletariat* (have-nots), or working class, whose labor created most of society's goods—and hence, its profits. (Thompson and Hickey 15)

 In this paragraph the "proletariat" are referred to as:

    a. the ruling class.

    b. the "haves."

    c. the working class.

Step 3: What general statement can we make about the supporting details? One possible observation could be:

- There are four qualities that most people look for in a friend.

Step 4: Do the facts from step 1 give more information about the statement made in step 3?

- Does the statement "A friend is a loyal companion" give us more information about the qualities that people look for in friendships?

- Does the statement "Friends are always supportive" give us more information about the qualities that people look for in friendships?

- Does the statement "Through friends, we find warmth and affection" give us more information about the qualities that people look for in friendships?

- Does the statement "Friends are always willing to make time for us" give us more information about the qualities that people look for in friendships?

Now that we've completed all four steps, we can see that the statement in step 3—"There are four qualities that most people look for in a friend"—expresses the point the author is trying to make. We can safely say, therefore, that this statement contains the implied main idea.

EXERCISE 5-5

Identifying the Category

Each section of the chart below has a list of five items. Think of what they all have in common and name the category in the space provided. The first one has been named for you.

(1) business	(2) Nature	(3) gov't	(4) time	(5) weather
profit	mountains	congress	second	snow
corporation	rivers	governor	hour	rain
merchant	oceans	treaty	week	ice
market	plains	statesman	year	hail
monopoly	deserts	mayor	day	sleet

EXERCISE 5-6	Identifying the Topic

Each group below has a list of three phrases. Think of what each group has in common and name the topic. The first topic has been named for you.

1. Going to College

   Going to lectures

   Writing research papers

   Living in the dorms

2. *PlayING BBall*

   Dribbling the ball

   Making a basket

   Making a foul shot

3. *being social*

   Talking with others

   Listening to others

   Giving and receiving feedback

4. *Driving*

   Going into fifth gear

   Stopping at red lights

   Following the speed limit

5. *Newspapers*

   Looking at the sports section

   Reading the editorial

   Noticing the front-page story

Getting Ahead in College Box 5.2

THE PRONUNCIATION OF VOCABULARY

When two or three consonants (letters that are not vowels) are grouped together, the combination of the letters makes one sound. For example, the p and the l sounds in please, plan, and play are blended together to make one sound. Thus, they are called consonant blends. Complete the following sentences with words that begin with blends. Use the following examples as a pronunciation guide.

sc	as in	**sc**arce
sh	as in	**sh**ip
sl	as in	**sl**im
sn	as in	**sn**ail
sp	as in	**sp**ell
st	as in	**st**reet
sm	as in	**sm**ell

1. Lawn fertilizer runoff pollutes nearby <u>streams</u>. (streams, rivers)

2. This large _____ of greenhouse gases comes from the high North American consumption of fossil fuels. (portion, share)

3. _____ is a combination of industrial air pollution and car exhaust. (Soot, Smog)

4. This combination often results in a thermal inversion—a warm mass of _____ air that is trapped beneath cooler air blowing in off the ocean. (stagnant, settled)

5. Lisa Crawford moved to a rural community because _____ believed it would be a healthy place to raise her son. (she, Lisa)

6. Lisa learned that Fernald was also a major _____ facility for "hot" nuclear waste. (sales, storage)

7. In 1989, the DOE closed the facility, which is now waiting for cleanup under a _____ government program called Superfund. (special, similar)

(continued on next page)

(continued from previous page)

8. Acid rain is _____ along the U.S.-Canadian border. (significant, scattered)

9. Canada generates hazardous waste more _____ than the United States. (subtly, slowly)

10. Acidic water can kill certain forest trees and, when concentrated in lakes and streams and _____ cover, can destroy fish and wildlife. (snow, ice)

EXERCISE
5-7

Creating a Topic Sentence

Each group below has a list of sentences. Think of what each group has in common and create a topic sentence. The first one has been created for you.

Group 1

- Sixty percent of African Americans live in communities with at least one uncontrolled toxic-waste site.

- Fifty percent of Hispanics also live in communities with at least one uncontrolled toxic-waste site.

- Military bases are a major source of hazardous wastes, generating more wastes than the top five U.S. chemical companies combined.

Topic Sentence: An unequal amount of hazardous waste is disposed of in military

bases and in locations where African American and Hispanic people live.

Group 2

- Habitat for wild creatures and plants is lost when new homes are built and on landfills where the solid waste is disposed of.

- Lawn fertilizer runoff pollutes nearby streams.

- The extraction of wood and petroleum products needed for building and maintaining the home causes environmental damage.

use 4 step process from pg 186

Topic Sentence: _There are many different ways of harming the Earths ozone layer._

Group 3

- North America has only 5 percent of the world's population, but produces 26 percent of the greenhouse gasses released globally by human activity.

- This large share of greenhouse gases comes from the high North American consumption of fossil fuels.

- North Americans use fossil fuels for oil-dependent industrial and agricultural processes, the heating of homes and offices, and automobiles.

Topic Sentence: _North America; does it really have more people than the rest of us?_

Group 4

- Smog is a combination of industrial air pollution and car exhaust.

- Los Angeles's smog hovers over the city because the warm land temperatures mix with the moist west coast air.

- This combination often results in a thermal inversion—a warm mass of stagnant air that is trapped beneath cooler air blowing in off the ocean.

- This inversion is held in place, often for days, by the mountains that surround the city.

Topic Sentence: _Los Angeles is a very dirty city._

Group 5

- Acid rain is produced when sulfur dioxide and nitrogen oxide are released into the air.

- Acid rain makes water acidic.

- Acidic water can kill certain forest trees and, when concentrated in lakes and streams and snow cover, can destroy fish and wildlife.

Topic Sentence: _Dioxide and Nitrogen oxide Need to be put away and Never used again_

(Pulsipher and Pulsipher)

Getting Ahead in College Box 5.3

PARTS OF SPEECH: ADVERBS

Adverbs tell "where," "when," "how," or "how often." They describe verbs, adjectives, and other adverbs. Adverbs generally go before or after the word they tell about. But in some cases, the adverb can go anywhere in the sentence.

<u>Often</u> our professor is pleased with our work.

Our professor <u>often</u> is pleased with our work.

Our professor is <u>often</u> pleased with our work.

Our professor is pleased with our work <u>often</u>.

In other cases, there is only one spot in the sentence for the adverb.

Put the desk <u>there</u>.

We wouldn't say "There put the desk" or "Put the there desk." In the sentences below, put the adverb (the underlined word) in the best place in the sentence. Show all of the places it can go while still making sense.

1. Lisa learned that Fernald was a major storage facility for "hot" nuclear waste.

Lisa learned it <u>soon</u>.

(continued on next page)

Soon Lisa learned that Fernald was a major storage facility for "hot" nuclear waste.

_____

_____

_____

2. She was at a loss about how to respond.
She was at a loss <u>completely</u>.

_____

_____

_____

3. She joined with a friend to found a community action group.
She joined <u>eventually</u>.

_____

_____

_____

4. The facility is waiting for cleanup under a special government program called Superfund.
It is waiting for cleanup <u>now.</u>

_____

_____

_____

5. The DOE estimated that it will take 50 years and $50 billion to clean up the Fernald site.
The DOE estimated <u>recently</u>.

(continued on next page)

(continued from previous page)

_____

_____

_____

use 4 gud press on page 1986

EXERCISE
5-8

Identifying the Implied Main Idea

Each paragraph below has an implied main idea. Read the sentences in the paragraph and create an appropriate main idea statement. The first one has been done for you.

Paragraph 1

[1]Lisa Crawford lived in Fernald, a rural community in southern Ohio. [2]In the mid-1980s she and her family occupied a rented farmhouse across the road from a "Feed Materials Production Center." [3]Lisa believed the "Feed Materials Production Center" was an animal feed factory and thought the rural environment would be an excellent place to raise her son—fresh well water, fresh air, clean living.

Implied Main Idea: Lisa Crawford moved to a rural community because she believed it would be a healthy place to raise her son.

Paragraph 2

[1]This thought changed when Lisa learned that she lived across the road from a U.S. Department of Energy (DOE) military nuclear facility producing nuclear materials for weapons. [2]One day her landlord called to say that the well water was contaminated, and soon Lisa learned that Fernald was also a major storage facility for "hot" nuclear waste. [3]For a while she was at a loss about how to respond but eventually joined with a friend to found a community action group called Fernald Residents for Environmental Safety and Health (FRESH), one of the first grassroots groups that brought publicity to environmental conditions at U.S. military facilities.

Implied Main Idea: _One day her land lord_
called & said the well water was
contaminated . . .

Paragraph 3

[1]After years of investigation, the government disclosed that the Fernald facility had released 394,000 pounds of uranium and 14,300 pounds of thorium into the air. [2]Another 167,000 pounds of uranium were discharged into the Ohio River and entered the Great Miami aquifer. [3]In 1989, the DOE closed the facility, which is now waiting for cleanup under a special government program called Superfund. [4]The DOE estimates it will take 50 years and $50 billion to clean up the Fernald site.

Implied Main Idea: _After years of investigation_
the gov't disclosed that Fernald facility
had released 394,000 lbs of ur . . .

Paragraph 4

[1]In the United States, hazardous waste is produced by nuclear power generation and weapons manufacture. [2]It is also produced by mineral mining and drilling and by waste incinerators. [3]Industry in general produces 80 percent of all liquid hazardous waste.

Implied Main Idea: _In the US. hazardous_
waste is produced by nuclear power
generation & weapons mnfr.

Paragraph 5

[1]The United States generates large hazardous wastes each year. [2]With a population of roughly 280 million, each year the United States generates five times the amount of hazardous waste generated by the entire European Union (population more than 300 million). [3]Canada generates much less hazardous waste per capita each year than the United States.

Implied Main Idea: _the US generates large hazardous waste each year._

(Pulsipher 89)

A Reading in Social Psychology

Have you ever thought about starting your own business? What kind of business would you open? What resources would you need and how would you get them? Read the passage below to see how two men started a well-known business without much but an idea. While reading, create an implied main idea for each paragraph. After reading the selection, complete the comprehension exercises that follow it. The first one has been done for you.

Vocabulary in Context

Complete the vocabulary exercise before reading the selection to learn the new terms.

a. **converted**—changed, transformed

b. **profit**—income, earnings, what you have left over after paying business expenses

c. **renovations**—repairs

d. **philanthropic**—charitable

e. **unconventional**—different from usual ways, rules, or standards

_____d_____ 1. The company continues to donate 7.5 percent of its annual profits to _____ causes.

_____A_____ 2. The two young men were thought to be _____ because not many businesses give away "free food for life" or have frog-jumping contests.

_____ B _____ 3. Part of the _____, or the money they had left over after paying their business expenses, was donated to the community to improve the quality of life.

_____ U _____ 4. The two young businessmen promised their building contractor "free food for life" because they didn't have enough money to pay for the building's badly needed _____.

_____ U _____ 5. With the help of a small bank loan, Ben Cohen opened a food shop in an _____ gas station in Burlington, Vermont.

Free Food for Life

[1]   In 1978, boyhood friends Jerry Greenfield and Ben Cohen opened a small homemade food shop in a **converted** gas station in Burlington, Vermont, with the help of a $4,000 bank loan. Their business plan, if you could call it that, was to sell high-quality food in a "fun" way, while using part of their **profit** to improve the quality of life of the community. Greenfield was given the title of president because they had put Cohen's name first when naming the business.

Implied Main Idea: <u>Two friends started a business with a good idea but very little money.</u>

[2]   Having little cash to pay for the building's extensive **renovations**, the two young businessmen promised their building contractor "free food for life" and named him as the third member on their board of directors. Greenfield and Cohen also offered lifetime free food to friends who helped with the renovations. Once operating, they even extended their free food offer to a customer who regularly played ragtime and boogie-woogie tunes on the food shop's decrepit piano.

Implied Main Idea: two buisness men Need renovations done to there building and offer food as payment

[3]   Very quickly, the young business became a popular eating and entertainment spot. The unofficial motto of the business became "If it's not fun, why do it?" Attracted by this philosophy and the commitment to social responsibility, employees worked long hours for little pay to

make the business a success. They did fun things such as showing summer movies on the outside wall of the store and having annual frog-jumping, apple-peeling, and stilt-walking contests.

Implied Main Idea: *The buisness turned into a fun place for many people.*

[4]   Although only a handful of people and two **unconventional** leaders made up this business group in 1978, twenty years later it employed more than several hundred people, had 150 franchises, and sold shares of its company on the stock market. True to their commitment to give back to the community, 7.5 percent annual profits are donated to employee-managed **philanthropic** causes in the country and abroad.

Implied Main Idea: *The buisness grew and made a lot of money.*

[5]   Have you guessed yet what kind of food Cohen and Greenfield serve to their customers? Do their first names, Ben and Jerry, jog your memory? Yes, their product is ice cream. Today, "Ben & Jerry's Homemade" brings annual sales over $170 million and is widely regarded as a model for other socially responsible businesses.

Implied Main Idea: *Cohen & Greenfield are Ben & Jerry's Ice cream company.*

(Franzoi 322)

Recalling Supporting Details

_____c_____ **1.** How much money did Ben and Jerry borrow to get their business started?

a. $40

b. $400

c. $4,000

 2. "Selling high-quality food in a 'fun' way, while using part of their profit to improve the quality of life of the community" was referred to as:

a. Ben & Jerry's business plan.

b. their profit.

c. philosophy.

 3. In what year did Ben & Jerry's Homemade get started?

a. 1979

b. 1997

c. 1999

 4. What percentage of their profits do Ben and Jerry donate to charity?

a. 1.7 %

b. 7.5 %

c. 40 %

 5. How many years did it take Ben and Jerry to make over $170 million?

a. Five

b. Ten

c. Twenty

 ## A Reading in Biology

How much do you know about iguanas? Charles Darwin didn't know anything about them when he first went to the Galapagos Islands. Read the passage below to see what misunderstandings Darwin had about the iguana.

Vocabulary in Context

Complete the vocabulary exercise before reading the selection to learn the new terms. The first one has been done for you.

a. Galapagos—islands off the coast of South America

b. naturalist—biologist

c. iguanas—large lizards of the tropical parts of Central and South America

d. terrestrial—living on land

e. predators—killers and eaters of other animals

___e___ **1.** Darwin thought the iguanas lay on the rocks to keep safe from sea _____.

___A___ **2.** The _____ Islands are off the coast of South America, 600 miles from Ecuador.

___B___ **3.** Charles Darwin was a _____ who studied the plants and animals of the Galapagos Islands because that was the only place in the world where many of them could be found.

___C___ **4.** The _____ do not bite.

___D___ **5.** The two types of iguanas that Darwin studied were marine, those living in the water, and _____, those living on land.

Decide whether the highlighted portion of each paragraph is a (a) topic, (b) main idea, (c) major supporting detail, or (d) minor supporting detail. Write the letter of your choice in the space provided. Then, answer the "supporting detail" questions at the end of the reading.

The Iguana

___a___ **1.** Located some 950 km (570 miles) west of Ecuador, the **Galapagos** are home to many organisms, such as the meter-long marine **iguanas** that are found nowhere else on Earth. Created by volcanoes only about five million years ago, the islands were probably first colonized by a few plants and animals that chanced to reach them from the South American mainland.

   a. topic

   b. main idea

   c. major supporting detail

   d. minor supporting detail

_____ **2.** British **naturalist** Charles Darwin spent part of his 26th year on the Galapagos. Darwin saw that there was much to be learned from the islands' unique forms of life. He was fascinated by the marine iguana's body features and behavior. Watching the iguanas dive into the ocean to feed on algae, Darwin wrote, "This lizard swims with perfect ease and quickness, by serpentine movement of its body and flattened tail." Darwin contrasted the marine iguana's tail with the rounded tail of typical **terrestrial** iguanas. He also noted that the strong claws and partial webbing on the marine iguana's feet probably help steer and pull it along the seafloor. Darwin found he could not frighten the iguanas into the sea. When he chased them to the water's edge, they would stop, and he could easily pick them up by the tail.

   a. topic

   b. main idea

   c. major supporting detail

   d. minor supporting detail

_____ **3.** He wrote, "They do not seem to have any notion of biting; but when much frightened they squirt a drop of fluid from each nostril." Darwin tossed one of the lizards into the water repeatedly; each time, the animal quickly returned to its place on the rocky shore. Darwin supposed that the lizard was safe from **predators** on land and, except when searching for food, remained on the lava rocks to avoid being eaten by sharks.

   a. topic

   b. main idea

   c. major supporting detail

   d. minor supporting detail

4. Many biologists since Darwin have studied the marine iguana, and we now have answers to some of the questions he raised. For instance, the iguana's tendency to remain on dark rocks instead of diving into the sea when approached seems to be related more to keeping warm than to the danger of shark attack. The ocean around the Galapagos is quite cold for marine iguanas. Although they can withstand the water temperature long enough to feed, they must sunbathe to maintain a suitable metabolic rate. When an iguana is out on the warm rocks, blood vessels near its body surface expand, speeding up heat absorption by the blood. Its heart rate also increases, distributing the heat to the rest of its body. When the lizard dives into the ocean, its circulatory system adjusts to cooling. Its surface vessels are constricted and its heart rate slows, keeping much of its blood and heat in deeper tissues.

   a. topic

   b. main idea

   c. major supporting detail

   d. minor supporting detail

5. Biologists have also learned that the fluid Darwin saw squirting from the iguana's nostrils is a highly concentrated salt solution. The marine iguana has salt-excreting glands inside its head just above the eyes. The salt solution drips into its nostrils and passes out in a cloudlike mist as the lizard exhales. This feature enables the marine iguana to dispose of excess salt it obtains from eating marine algae. (Campbell, Mitchell and Reese 562)

   a. topic

   b. main idea

   c. major supporting detail

   d. minor supporting detail

Recalling Supporting Details

1. The Galapagos islands were created by:
   a. volcanoes.

   b. earthquakes.

   c. barrier reefs.

2. To study the iguanas' behavior, Darwin:

    a. tried to chase them into the sea.

    b. tried to feed them.

    c. tried to take pictures of them.

 3. Darwin thought the iguanas stayed on the lava rocks:

    a. to get warmth from the sun.

    b. to find food.

    c. to avoid being eaten by sharks.

 4. The marine iguana must sunbathe to:

    a. constrict surface vessels and slow its heart rate.

    b. distribute heat to the outer part of its body.

    c. keep much of its blood and heat in deeper tissues.

 5. The fluid Darwin saw squirting from the iguana's nostrils is:

    a. a highly concentrated salt solution.

    b. marine algae.

    c. a cloudlike mist of water.

Outlining: Main Ideas and Supporting Details

Below is a list of scrambled sentences from the reading about the iguana. Put these phrases into an outline form. The main points have been provided.

- He wrote, "They do not seem to have any notion of biting; but when much frightened they squirt a drop of fluid from each nostril."

- Darwin found he could not frighten the iguanas into the sea.

- Each time, the animal quickly returned to its place on the rocky shore.

- He watched the iguanas dive into the ocean to feed on algae.

- He also noted that the strong claws and partial webbing on the marine iguana's feet probably help steer and pull it along the seafloor.

- Darwin was fascinated by the marine iguana's behavior.

- Darwin was fascinated by the marine iguana's body features.

- Darwin supposed the iguana came back to shore quickly to avoid being eaten by sharks.

■ He noted that the lizard swims with perfect ease and quickness by serpentine movement of its body and flattened tail.

■ Darwin tossed one of the lizards into the water repeatedly.

■ When he chased them to the water's edge, they would stop, and he could easily pick them up by the tail.

Topic: The Iguana

I. Darwin was fascinated by the marine iguana's body features.

A. _____

_____

_____

1. _____

2. _____

II. Darwin was fascinated by the marine iguana's behavior.

A. _____

_____

_____

1. _____

2. _____

B. Darwin tossed one of the lizards into the water repeatedly.

_____

_____

1. _____

2. _____

 A Reading in Autobiography

Can you imagine going through life without knowing how to read? What types of things would you not be able to do? Read the passage below to see how one very ingenious man taught himself how to read. While reading, create an implied main idea for each paragraph. Finally, answer the "supporting detail" questions at the end.

Vocabulary in Context

Complete the vocabulary exercise before reading the selection to learn the new terms. The first one has been done for you.

a. convey—send from one place to another

b. articulate—express oneself clearly

c. penmanship—handwriting

d. riffling—wildly searching through

e. immensely—very much; enormously

_____d_____ 1. Malcolm X spent two days _____ through the pages of the dictionary, trying to figure out how to use it.

_____a_____ 2. Malcolm X decided to learn how to read and write because he realized that his poorly written letters did not _____ his ideas to other people.

_____b_____ 3. In fact, his letters were so badly written, he realized that he had to become more _____ if he wanted others to be able to understand what he was writing.

_____e_____ 4. He was _____ proud of himself after just being able to copy words that were new to him from the dictionary.

_____c_____ 5. At first Malcolm X just wanted a dictionary, paper, and pencils so that he could improve his _____.

Homemade Education

[1]   It was because of my letters that I happened to stumble upon starting to acquire some kind of a homemade education.

Implied Idea: <u>Malcolm X decided that he needed to learn to write better.</u>

[2]   I became increasingly frustrated at not being able to express what I wanted to **convey** in letters that I wrote, especially those to Mr. Elijah Muhammad. In the street, I had been the most **articulate** hustler out there—I had commanded attention when I said something. But now, trying to write simple English, I not only wasn't articulate, I wasn't even functional. How would I sound writing in slang, the way I would say it, something such as, "Look, daddy, let me pull your coat about a cat, Elijah Muhammad."

Implied Idea: <u>Malcom X needed to write letters to Elijah Muhammad in order to be articulate.</u>

[3]   Many who today hear me somewhere in person, or on television, or those who read something I've said, will think I went to school far beyond the eighth grade. This impression is due entirely to my prison studies.

Implied Idea: <u>Malcom X never went to school passed the 8th grade. He learned to write in prison</u>

[4]   It had really begun back in the Charlestown Prison, when Bimbi first made me feel envy of his stock of knowledge. Bimbi had always taken charge of any conversation he was in, and I had tried to emulate him. But every book I picked up had few sentences which didn't contain anywhere from one to nearly all the words that might as well have been in Chinese. When I just skipped those words, of course, I really ended up with little idea of what the book said. So I had come to the Norfolk Prison Colony still going through only book-reading motions. Pretty soon, I would have quit even these motions, unless I had received the motivation that I did.

Implied Idea: _Bimbi was malcom X's_ _prison body was more_ _educated then him._

[5]   I saw that the best thing I could do was get hold of a dictionary—to study, to learn some words. I was lucky enough to reason also that I should try to improve my **penmanship**. It was sad. I couldn't even write in a straight line. It was both ideas together that moved me to request a dictionary along with some tablets and pencils from the Norfolk Prison Colony school.

Implied Idea: _Malcom learned a lot_ _about his penmenship from_ _the dictonary_

[6]   I spent two days just **riffling** uncertainly through the dictionary's pages. I'd never realized so many words existed! I didn't know which words I needed to learn. Finally, just to start some kind of action, I began copying.

Implied Idea: _He keept looking thru_ _the dictonary looking for_ _new words._

[7]   In my slow, painstaking, ragged handwriting, I copied into my tablet everything printed on the first page, down to the punctuation marks.

Implied Idea: _He copied everything_ _word for word in the dictonary_ _on to a paper._

[8]   I believe it took me a day. Then, aloud, I read back, to myself, everything I'd written on the tablet. Over and over, aloud, to myself, I read my own handwriting.

Implied Idea: _He read what he wrote_ _over again until he could_ _read his own handwriting._

[9]   I woke up the next morning, thinking about those words—**immensely** proud to realize that not only had I written so much at one time, but I'd written words that I never knew were in the world. Moreover, with a little effort, I also could remember what many of these words meant. I reviewed the words whose meanings I didn't remember. Funny thing, from the dictionary's first page right now, that "aardvark" springs to my mind. The dictionary had a picture of it, a long-tailed, long-eared, burrowing African mammal, which lives off termites caught by sticking out its tongue as an anteater does for ants.

Implied Idea: _The next day Malcom_ _realized what he learned._

[10]   I was so fascinated that I went on—I copied the dictionary's next page. And the same experience came when I studied that. With every succeeding page, I also learned of people and places and events from history. Actually the dictionary is like a miniature encyclopedia. Finally the dictionary's A section had filled a whole tablet—and I went on into the B's. That was the way I started copying what eventually became the entire dictionary. It went a lot faster after so much practice helped me pick up handwriting speed. Between what I wrote in my tablet, and writing letters, during the rest of my time in prison I would guess I wrote a million words.

Implied Idea: _He did the same thing_ _with the 2nd page._

[11]   I suppose it was inevitable that as my word-base broadened, I could for the first time pick up a book and read and now begin to understand what the book was saying. Anyone who has read a great deal can imagine the new world that opened. Let me tell you something: from then until I left that prison, in every free moment I had, if I was not reading in the library, I was reading on my bunk. You couldn't have gotten me out of books with a wedge. Between Mr. Muhammad's teachings, my correspondence, my visitors . . . and my reading of books, months passed without my even thinking about being imprisoned. In fact, up to then, I never had been so truly free in my life.

Bonus Question (1 pt. extra credit)

Implied Idea: _____

_____

_____

(Malcolm X)

Recalling Supporting Details

_____b_____ **1.** Before entering jail, Malcolm X had been a:
    a. political leader.
    b. hustler.
    c. teacher.

_____✓_____ **2.** Before copying the dictionary, Malcolm X was:
    a. a good writer.
    b. a good reader.
    c. unable to understand what he read.

_____✓_____ **3.** Malcolm X guesses that between his letter writing and copying the dictionary, he wrote:
    a. nearly one hundred words.
    b. nearly one thousand words.
    c. nearly one million words.

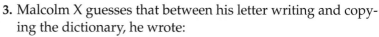

_____ **4.** After copying the dictionary, Malcolm X spent all of his free time in prison:

a. reading.

b. listening to Mr. Muhammad's teachings.

c. meeting visitors.

_____ **5.** In paragraph 3, the author implies that:

a. he only went to school up to the eighth grade.

b. he went to school far beyond the eighth grade.

c. he never went to school.

Visual Literacy Box 5.5 ● ● ● ● ● ● ● ● ● ● ● ● ● ● ● ●

Understanding the Author's Outline

Below is a list of scrambled sentences containing some of the main ideas from the reading about Malcolm X. Complete the outline below by adding the main ideas.

■ When Malcolm X realized that he was learning the meanings of the words that he copied from the dictionary, he was inspired to copy the entire dictionary.

■ Since Malcolm X didn't know where to begin in learning how to read and write, he just began to copy the dictionary word for word.

■ Malcolm X requested a dictionary, paper, and pencils because he realized that he needed to learn both penmanship and vocabulary.

■ Malcolm X decided that he needed to learn to write better.

■ An educated prisoner inspired Malcolm X to want to do more than pretend he could read.

I Malcolm X decided that he needed to learn to write better.

   a. I became increasingly frustrated at not being able to express what I wanted.

   b. But now, trying to write simple English, I not only wasn't articulate, I wasn't even functional.

(continued on next page)

II _____

   a. So I had come to the Norfolk Prison Colony still going through only book-reading motions.
   b. Bimbi first made me feel envy of his stock of knowledge.
   c. Bimbi had always taken charge of any conversation he was in, and I had tried to emulate him.

III _____

   a. I saw that the best thing I could do was get hold of a dictionary—to study, to learn some words.
   b. I was lucky enough to reason also that I should try to improve my penmanship.

IV _____

   a. I spent two days just riffling uncertainly through the dictionary's pages.
   b. I didn't know which words I needed to learn.
   c. Finally, just to start some kind of action, I began copying.

V _____

   a. [After copying the words] I could remember what many of these words meant.
   b. I was so fascinated that I went on—I copied the dictionary's next page.
   c. That was the way I started copying what eventually became the entire dictionary.

VI When Malcolm X increased his reading comprehension, it opened up a whole new world to him, giving him a sense of freedom that he had not felt before.

CHAPTER

6

Text Patterns: Paragraphs

- -

In this chapter we cover the following patterns:

■ term, definition, and example;

■ topic and list;

■ process;

■ chronological order (time order).

TEXT STRUCTURE

INSTRUCTOR: How does the business textbook compare with the English text-book?

KAI: You'd be surprised; the business textbook really isn't that dry. I mean, it has stories . . . it will give you an example of Mr. Smith and how he just went out of business because he isn't doing this and that and it will give you a little story.

Kai makes a very important point in saying that his business text gives examples (in the form of stories) that explain ideas about business. This type of pattern is common in freshman college textbooks.

Textbook authors, when they write, organize their ideas so that others can follow what they are saying. This organization of ideas is called the **text pattern**. If you do *not* look for the pattern of the text while you read, some major clues to understanding the author's point will escape you.

The text is the written or printed information and the pattern refers to how the writing is organized or arranged. There are more than 100 different kinds of text patterns, but here we focus specifically on the most commonly found patterns in college textbooks.

TERM, DEFINITION, AND EXAMPLE

Every subject (business, sociology, psychology, anthropology, political science, biology, philosophy, etc.) has its own vocabulary. We learn this specialized vocabulary in the first (or *prerequisite*) courses taken in a given field. The first course is often, but not always, named as the introductory course or elementary course and have such titles as:

Introduction to Business Management

Introduction to Psychology

Introduction to Sociology

Elementary Algebra

Biology: Concepts and Connections

The textbooks for these courses serve as "big" dictionaries. For instance, when we finish reading these texts, not only do we increase our vocabulary, but we become knowledgeable about the concepts connected to the subject. As a result, we are able to continue taking other courses in the same field without losing our way. How is this possible? The answer is simple; we have learned what the terms mean by reading the course's introductory textbook.

The most common pattern found in freshmen texts is called the **term, definition, and example** pattern. First, a new term is introduced. Then, it is highlighted, underlined, *italicized*, or placed in **boldface** print to make it stand out from the other information. Next, this new term is defined somewhere in the same paragraph in which it was introduced. Finally, one or more examples are given to further define and explain the new term or concept.

Let's look at an example from communications:

Your **social clock** is *a time schedule set by your culture and society that dictates the right time to do a variety of important things.* For example, it tells you the right time to start dating, to finish college, to buy your own home, to have a child. Most people are taught about this clock as they grow up and internalize these lessons. On the basis of this social clock, you then evaluate your own social and professional development. If you are on time with the rest of your peers—for example, you all started dating at around the same age or you're all finishing college at around the same age—then you will feel well adjusted, competent, and a part of the group. If you are late, you will probably experience feelings of dissatisfaction and inadequacy. (DeVito 143)

The term being defined is "social clock." It appears in boldface print. The definition of "social clock" is *"a time schedule set by your culture and society that dictates the right time to do a variety of important things."* The author has placed this definition in italics to help the reader connect the term with the definition. Then, examples are given to help us understand and remember the concept of *social clock*: (1) the right time to start dating, (2) the right time to finish college, (3) the right time to buy your own home, (4) the right time to have a child.

Often students try to cut corners by skipping the examples and reading only the terms and definitions. This doesn't work so well because the examples are provided so that we can relate the new terms to our own experiences. When we relate new information to something we already know, we are more likely to understand and remember it. Therefore, the examples are just as important as the terms and definitions.

Signals

As noted earlier, new words that are being defined are normally highlighted, **boldfaced**, *italicized*, or underlined. In addition, some authors use signals to help us determine the definition of a term without us having to refer to a dictionary. *Signals* are clue words such as "is," "are," "is defined as," and "means." Punctuation symbols such as dashes, parentheses, and commas can also be used to show that a term is about to be defined. For example,

term to be defined	signal	definition
Your social clock	is	*a time schedule set by your culture and society that dictates the right time to do a variety of important things.*

- Your **social clock**—*a time schedule set by your culture and society that dictates the right time to do a variety of important things*—**is** an interesting aspect of cultural time.

- Your **social clock** (*a time schedule set by your culture and society that dictates the right time to do a variety of important things*) **is** an interesting aspect of cultural time.

- Your **social clock,** *a time schedule set by your culture and society that dictates the right time to do a variety of important things*, **is** an interesting aspect of cultural time.

The author may also introduce special terms by using phrases like "for example," "such as," "to illustrate this," and "for instance."

For example, it tells you the right time to start dating, to finish college, to buy your own home, to have a child.

Once you read a paragraph and understand the term, definition, and example, you should mark the textbook so this relationship clearly stands out. Circle the term, underline its definition, and highlight the examples.

Your social clock is *a time schedule set by your culture and society that dictates the right time to do a variety of important things.* For example, it tells you the right time to start dating, to finish college, to buy your own home, to have a child. Most people are taught about this clock as they grow up and internalize these lessons. On the basis of this social clock, you then evaluate your own social and professional development. If you are on time with the rest of your peers—for example, you all started dating at around the same age or you're all finishing college at around the same age—then you will feel well adjusted, competent, and a part of the group. If you are late, you will probably experience feelings of dissatisfaction and inadequacy.

EXERCISE 6-1

Identify the Term, Definition, and Example

Read the following paragraphs and find the term, definition, and examples. Then circle the term, underline the definition, and highlight the examples. The first one has been done for you.

1. Prejudice and discrimination are closely tied yet distinct. Prejudice is a negative attitude directed toward people because they are members of a specific group. Discrimination is a negative action toward members of a specific group. Muttering to yourself or telling others that you dislike someone because of her group membership is an example of prejudice. Throwing a punch at the person because of her group membership is an example of discrimination. (Franzoi 234)

Term: prejudice

Definition: a negative attitude directed toward people because they are members of a specific group

Example: <u>Muttering to yourself or telling others that you dislike someone</u>

<u>because of the person's group membership is an example of prejudice.</u>

Term: <u>discrimination</u>

Definition: <u>a negative action toward members of a specific group</u>

Example: <u>Throwing a punch at someone because of the person's group</u>

<u>membership is an example of discrimination.</u>

2. When atoms of different elements attach to one another, they make a **compound**. Sodium atoms and chlorine atoms, for example, join to make the compound sodium chloride, commonly known as table salt. Iron atoms and oxygen atoms join to make the compound iron oxide, commonly known as rust. (Hewitt, Suchocki and Hewitt 371)

Term: _____

Definition: _____

Example: _____

3. **Personal observation**. Police officers may use their personal training, experience, and expertise to infer probable cause from situations that may not be obviously criminal. If, for example, a police officer observes several people in a car slowly circling a certain building in a high-crime area, that officer may infer that the people are "casing" the building in preparation for a robbery. Probable cause could be established for detaining the suspects. (Gaines, Kaune and Miller 145)

Term: _____

Definition: _____

Example: _____

4. **Kinetic energy** is energy that is actually doing work, such as pedaling a bicycle. A mass of matter that is moving performs work by transferring its motion to other matter, whether it is leg muscles pushing bicycle pedals or firefly wings moving air as they beat. **Heat**, the energy associated with the movement of molecules in a body of matter, is one kind of

+4/4

kinetic energy. Light is another kind of kinetic energy. (Campbell, Mitchell and Reese 72)

Term: _____

Definition: _____

Example: _____

Term: _____

Definition: _____

5. **Cultural time**. Two types of cultural time are especially important: formal and informal time. In the United States and in most of the world, **formal time** is divided into seconds, minutes, hours, days, weeks, months, and years. Some cultures, however, may use phases of the moon or the seasons to delineate time periods. In the United States, if your college is on the semester system, your courses are divided into 50- or 75-minute periods that meet two or three times a week for 14-week periods. Eight semesters of 15 or 15 50-minute periods per week equal a college education. As these examples illustrate, formal time units are arbitrary. The culture establishes them for convenience.

Informal time refers to the use of general time terms—for example, "forever," "immediately," "soon," "right away," "as soon as possible." This type of time creates the most communication problems because the terms have different meanings for different people.

Attitudes toward time vary from one culture to another. In one study, for example, the accuracy of clocks was measured in six cultures—Japan, Indonesia, Italy, England, Taiwan, and the United States. Japan had the most accurate and Indonesia had the least accurate clocks. The speed at which people in these six cultures walked was also measured and results showed that the Japanese walked the fastest; the Indonesians walked the slowest.

From Joseph A. Devito, *Essentials of Human Communication,* 3e © 1999. Published by Allyn and Bacon, Boston, MA. Copyright (c) 2001 by Pearson Education, pp. 142–43.

Term: _formal time, Informal_

Definition: _____

Example: _____

Term: _____

Definition: _____

Example: _____

Visual Literacy Box 6.1 ● ● ● ● ● ● ● ● ● ● ● ● ● ●

Graphic Organizers:
Term, Definition, and Example

Use graphic organizers to display the information from your textbook in a way that will help you visualize and remember it. One way to organize information in the "Term, Definition, Example" pattern is to make an array, with the examples fanned out.

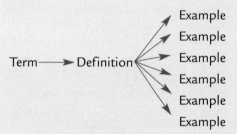

Put the information from the sentence below into a "term, definition, example" array.

Informal time <u>refers to the use of general time terms,</u> such as _forever, immediately, soon, right away, as soon as possible._

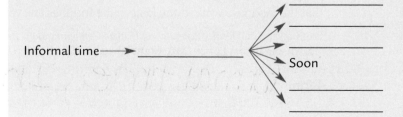

TOPIC AND LIST

Another common textbook pattern is called the "topic and list" or "simple listing" pattern. You will see this pattern quite often in political science, business law, sociology, and psychology texts. It is the easiest to recognize because often the items listed are actually numbered or bulleted. The topic sentence tells you to look for a list by using phrases such as:

- There are many kinds of . . .

- There are many reasons why . . .

- A number of factors contributed to . . .

- Three problems related to the . . .

- There are various types of . . .

- Five types of . . . are

Look at the passage below. What is the topic? How many items are in the list? What do all of the items on the list have in common?

In the United States there are five ways in which silence can be interpreted negatively. At a business meeting or even in informal social groups, the silent member may be seen as:

- not listening

- having nothing interesting to add

- not understanding the issues

- being insensitive

- or being too self-absorbed to focus on the messages of others.

(DeVito 142)

The topic is "negative interpretations of silence." The first sentence tells us that there are five items on the list. It also tells us about the topic—that silence can be seen as a negative behavior. As we look through the passage, we can see the author has organized the five items by making them a bulleted list.

Signals

Since the details in this pattern are equally important, they can be listed in any order. If the list is not obvious through numbering, bulleting, and so forth, then as with the term, definition, and example pattern, the reader must look for signals—clue words or clue phrases—to find the list. These clue words and phrases include the following:

first	second	third	next
finally	also	in addition	moreover

Some paragraphs written in this pattern introduce a clue word at the beginning of each sentence. Others may use just one clue word throughout the entire paragraph. Read the paragraph below and look for clues that signal the list pattern.

[There are four major sections in this book.] First, we review the events leading to the acceptance of the fact that life on Earth has evolved over several billion years. Then, we summarize how evolutionary mechanisms adapt organisms to their environments, and we review the major milestones in the evolution of life on Earth. Finally, we describe briefly how scientists generate new knowledge, how they develop and test hypotheses, and how that knowledge can be used to inform public policy. (Purves et al. 1)

We know we are looking for a list of items because the first sentence explains that there are four parts to the book. Also, in the second sentence, the clue word "first" (first, we review) is used. This signals to us that at least one or more items will follow. As we read the third sentence, we see the clue word "then" (then, we summarize). The word "finally" in the last sentence signals the end of the list. Our list looks like this:

■ First, we review . . .

■ Then, we summarize . . . and review . . .

■ Finally, we describe . . .

Mark your textbook after you have identified the organizational pattern of the reading. First underline the topic or main idea and then number the list. Then, take notes from the paragraph by simply writing down the items that you have marked and by making a topic and a list. Add key words that will help you remember the definitions. Once marked, you will not need to spend time later rereading the passage to recognize the main points. Furthermore, you will be able to see the author's organization at a glance:

> <u>Japan appears to be a country with few problems</u>. [1]First of all, crime rates in Japan are lower than in most industrial countries. [2]Secondly, guns in this society are virtually non-existent. [3]Also, there are few divorces and few births to single teenage mothers. [4]Moreover, the AIDS infection rate is low. [5]In addition to these advantages, the literacy rate is high and unemployment is low. [6]Finally, the Japanese have the longest life expectancy in the world. (Farr and Hammers 6–7)

Topic: Advantages of Japanese Society

1. Crime rates are low.

2. Guns are virtually non-existent.

3. There are few divorces and few births to single teenage mothers.

4. The AIDS infection rate is low.

5. The literacy rate is high and unemployment is low.

6. Japanese have the longest life expectancy in the world.

EXERCISE 6-2	Identifying the Topic and List

Following the previous examples, find the topic and list in each of the paragraphs below. Mark each paragraph and take notes. The first one has been done for you.

1. There are four elements that must be present for an arrest to take place. First of all, the police officer must intend to make the arrest. Also, the police officer must have the authority to arrest. Some states, for example, allow off-duty police officers to make arrests, while others do not.

Furthermore, a seizure or detention must take place. Finally, the person being arrested must understand that she or he has been arrested. (Gaines, Kaune and Miller 150)

Signal: <u>four elements; first of all; also, furthermore, finally</u>

Topic: <u>Elements of an arrest</u>

List:

1. <u>intent to arrest</u>
2. <u>authority to arrest</u>
3. <u>the seizure or detention</u>
4. <u>the understanding of the person that he or she has been arrested</u>

2. Taken in moderation, alcohol can be compatible with good health. The term moderation is important in describing alcohol use. How many drinks constitute moderate use, and how much is "a drink"? First, a drink is any alcoholic beverage that delivers $1/2$ ounce of pure ethanol:

   ■ 5 ounces of wine.
   ■ 10 ounces of wine cooler.
   ■ 12 ounces of beer.
   ■ 1 $1/2$ ounces of distilled liquor (80 proof whiskey, scotch, rum, or vodka).

Second, because people have different tolerances to alcohol, it is impossible to name an exact daily amount of alcohol that is appropriate for everyone. Authorities have attempted to set limits that are acceptable for most healthy people. An accepted definition of moderation is not more than two drinks a day for the average-sized man and not more than one drink a day for the average-sized woman. (Whitney and Rolfes 230)

Signal: _____

Topic: _____

List: _____

_____

_____

_____

3. In many communication situations, and perhaps especially in public speaking, you'll want to use a speaking style that is forceful or powerful. Here are three suggestions for achieving greater power in your speech:

- Eliminate phrases that weaken your sentences or detract from your authority on the subject, such as *It seems to me that . . .* or *I'm not sure about this but . . .*

- Use strong verbs. Instead of saying "He walked through the forest," consider *wandered, prowled, rambled, roamed*. Consult a thesaurus to replace any verb you suspect might be weak.

- Avoid clichés, overused phrases that have lost their novelty and part of their meaning; they call attention to themselves because of their overuse, for example, "in this day and age," "tell it like it is," "no sooner said than done," "it goes without saying," and "few and far between." (DeVito 326)

Signal: _____

Topic: _____

List: _____

_____

_____

_____

4. There are four common fat soluble vitamins:

- Vitamin A can be found in dark green and orange vegetables and fruits, and dairy products.

- Dairy products and egg yolks contain vitamin D. It can also be produced by the skin when exposed to sunlight.

- Vegetable oils, nuts, and seeds contain high amounts of tocopherol, commonly known as vitamin E.

- Vitamin K can be found in green vegetables and tea.

(Stanitski et al. 444)

Signal: _____

Topic: _____

List: _____

_____

_____

_____

5. Most people who become millionaires have confidence in their own abilities. They do not spend time worrying about whether or not their parents were wealthy. They do not believe that one must be born wealthy. Have you ever thought that most millionaires are born with silver spoons in their mouths? If so, consider the following facts that our research uncovered about American millionaires:

- Only 19 percent receive any income or wealth of any kind from a trust fund or an estate.

- Fewer than 20 percent inherited 10 percent or more of their wealth.

- More than half never received as much as $1 in inheritance.

- Fewer than 25 percent ever received "an act of kindness" of $10,000 or more from their parents, grandparents, or other relatives.

- Ninety-one percent never received, as a gift, as much as $1 of the ownership of a family business.

- Nearly half never received any college tuition from their parents or other relatives.

- Fewer than 10 percent believe they will ever receive an inheritance in the future.

(Stanley and Danko 15–16)

Signal: bullits

Topic: American millionares

List: _____

_____

_____

_____

Visual Literacy Box 6.2

Graphic Organizers: Topic and List

Use graphic organizers to display the information from your textbook in a way that will help you visualize and remember it. One way to organize information in the "topic and list" pattern is to make a webbed organizational chart.

(continued on next page)

(continued from previous page)

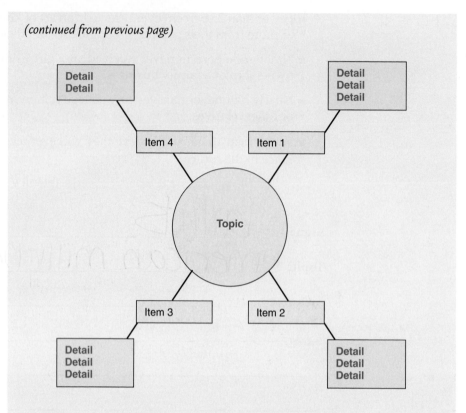

Study the example above. Then put the information from the paragraph below into a "topic and list" webbed organizational chart.

There are four common fat soluble vitamins:

■ Vitamin A can be found in dark green and orange vegetables and fruits, and dairy products.

■ Dairy products and egg yolks contain vitamin D. It can also be produced by the skin when exposed to sunlight.

■ Vegetable oils, nuts, and seeds contain high amounts of tocopherol, commonly known as vitamin E.

■ Vitamin K can be found in green vegetables and tea.

(continued on next page)

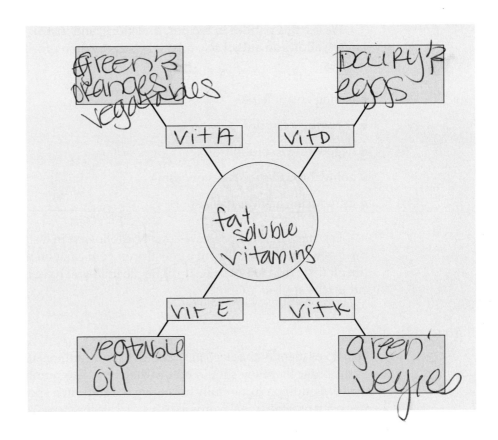

PROCESS

Another text pattern found in introductory course textbooks and found in much of our everyday print, is called the **process pattern**. Authors use this pattern to describe the steps in a process. It is used in almost every type of textbook from biology to computer science.

The process pattern looks a lot like our *topic and list pattern*. Even when we take notes, we write the steps of the process in a list. However, the difference between the two patterns is that the steps in the listing pattern can be written in any order. The steps in the process pattern, however, must follow a specific order.

We see this pattern in recipes, directions, and instructions. This writing pattern allows an author to explain the step-by-step procedure for processes such as:

■ baking an apple pie

■ changing a flat tire

■ negotiating a solution

■ going through the stages of dating

■ introducing a guest speaker

The steps in most processes must be followed in a specific order or the process will not work. To put a new tire on your car, you have to take the old tire off first. You cannot bake an apple pie until you have made the crust and cut up the apples.

Signals

To help us identify the steps in a process pattern, authors usually list the steps in the order that they should occur. They may also number, letter, or bullet them. In addition to carefully arranging the steps in a specific order, authors will often provide signal words to help us locate the steps. You'll note that some of these clues are the same as the ones used to signal a topic with a list.

The first step is	First, Second, Third
Next	During the next step
Then	Now
Once	Once that is finished
At this point	After that
Finally	

Look at the paragraph below. Can you identify the seven signals that the author uses to help us locate the steps in this process?

To make an apple pie, you must *first* mix and roll the dough. *Once* the dough is ready, place it in a glass pie pan. *Then*, peel and cut up 3 large apples. *Next*, place the apples into the pie pan and sprinkle brown sugar on top. *After this*, sprinkle cinnamon on top of the brown sugar. *Next*, place another thin layer of dough on top of the apples and pinch its edges together with the bottom layer of dough. *Then*, place the pie into the oven and bake it until the crust is golden brown. *Finally*, take your apple pie out of the oven, cut a slice, and enjoy!

Would you eat an apple pie if any of the above steps in the process were left out? You would probably say something to the cook if, for example, the apples had been left out. Would you be pleased if the dough was not baked? What if the pie were baked before the apples were peeled and cut up?

EXERCISE 6-3	Identifying the Process and Steps

Read the following paragraphs or passages, find the topic, and write it on the space provided. Then identify the process and record the steps in the correct order below. The first one has been done for you.

1. Changing a Flat Tire

Flat tires are not fun at all, especially on busy streets or freeways in 100° weather. Changing a flat tire, however, is easy to learn. Each tire has a hub cap. First, pull your car over to the side of the road and put up safety flares. Next, remove the hub caps by prying them off with a crowbar. After that, take the lug nuts off each wheel and pull off the old tire. Then, carefully put your new tire in place. Next, secure the new tire by tightening the lug nuts. Finally, place the hub cap over the inner part of the wheel and drive off!

Process: <u>Changing a flat tire</u>

Steps in the Process:

1. <u>Pull over and set up flares.</u>
2. <u>Pry the hub caps off with a crowbar.</u>
3. <u>Take the lug nuts off each wheel and pull off the old tire.</u>

  4. <u>Put the new tire in place.</u>

  5. <u>Secure the new tire by using the lug nuts.</u>

  6. <u>Return the hub cap over to its original place and drive away.</u>

2. Designing a Persuasive Speech

When designing a speech to get listeners to do something, keep the following guidelines in mind. First, be realistic about what you want the audience to do. Remember you have only 10 or 15 minutes. Ask for small, easily performed behaviors—to sign a petition, to vote in the next elections, to donate a small amount of money.

Second, stress the specific advantages of these behaviors to your audience. Don't ask your audience to do something because of abstract reasons. Give them concrete, specific reasons why they will benefit from the actions.

Third, demonstrate your own willingness to do the same. As a general rule, never ask the audience to do what you have not done yourself. (DeVito 391–92)

Process: _____

Steps in the Process: _____

_____

_____

_____

_____

3. Dating Stages

Just as there are stages of development in individual growth that influence the timing and variations in dating, there are sequential stages in the dating process that determine the rules of the dating game. For example, early dating experiences are likely to involve group activities, whereas older teens tend to become more exclusive and intimate. For some time now, the research literature has delineated four stages in the dating continuum: casual dating, steadily dating, seriously dating, and engaged-to-be-engaged (Duval and Miller, 1985). Although the sequence of these stages has remained fairly constant over time, today's young people and their parents do not always speak the same language when communicating about the dating scene.

Casual dating may have been defined by parents in their day as "playing the field," in which the person was dating a number of different people at the same time. Today, this is often called "dating" or "hanging out." *Steadily dating* describes the stage in which persons date each other frequently and decrease their dating of other persons. An increase in interaction, affection, dependence, and control occurs at this stage (Stets, 1993). However, in this stage of the game there is no agreement to date each other exclusively. The term *seriously dating* ("going out with" or "seeing someone") has, to a considerable degree, replaced the term steady dating, particularly among college-age individuals. Seriously dating usually means a commitment to date each other exclusively as well as an emotional commitment in the relationship. The *engaged-to-be-engaged* status involves an understanding that the individuals will eventually marry each other, but there may be no public or formal declaration of this intent. (Davidson and Moore 296)

Process: _____

Steps in the Process: _____

_____

_____

_____

_____

4. Introducing a Guest Speaker

We often have guest speakers in class, at work, and at club functions. Whatever the function, it is extremely important to let the guest know that he or she is welcome. Below are some tips to help you feel more confident when introducing a guest speaker. First, address the audience and tell them the topic and purpose for the talk. Next, tell the audience the speaker's name and discuss his or her background and experience with respect to the topic. Then, ask the audience to help you in welcoming the speaker. Finally, show the speaker a hearty welcome by leading the audience in applause.

Process: _____

Steps in the Process: _____

_____

_____

_____

_____

5. Negotiating a Solution

Now that you and your partner understand each other's needs, the goal becomes finding a way to meet them. This is done by trying to develop as many potential solutions as possible and then evaluating them to decide which one best meets the needs of both. The following steps can help communicators develop a mutually satisfying solution.

1. *Identify and Define the Conflict.* This process consists of discovering each person's problem and needs, setting the stage for meeting all of them.

2. *Generate a Number of Possible Solutions.* In this step, the partners work together to think of as many means as possible to reach their stated ends. The key word here is quantity: It's important to generate as many ideas as you can think of without worrying about which ones are good or bad. Write down every thought that comes up, no matter how unworkable; sometimes a far-fetched idea will lead to a more workable one.

3. *Evaluate the Alternative Solutions.* This is the time to talk about which solutions will work and which ones won't. It's important

for all concerned to be honest about their willingness to accept an idea. If a solution is going to work, everyone involved has to support it.

4. *Decide on the Best Solution.* Now that you've looked at all the alternatives, pick the one that looks best to everyone. It's important to be sure everybody understands the solution and is willing to try it out. Remember: Your decision doesn't have to be final, but it should look potentially successful. (Adler and Rodman 249)

Process: _go in order_

Steps in the Process: _4 steps_

Visual Literacy Box 6.3

Graphic Organizers: Process

Use graphic organizers to display the information from your textbook in a way that will help you visualize and remember it. One way to organize information in the "process" pattern is to make a sequence map.

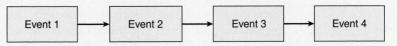

(continued on next page)

(continued from previous page)

Study the example above. Then put the information from the paragraph below into a "sequence map."

Just as there are stages of development in individual growth that influence the timing and variations in dating, there are sequential stages in the dating process that determine the rules of the dating game. For example, early dating experiences are likely to involve group activities, whereas older teens tend to become more exclusive and intimate. For some time now, the research literature has delineated four stages in the dating continuum: casual dating, steadily dating, seriously dating, and engaged-to-be-engaged (Duval & Miller, 1985). Although the sequence of these stages has remained fairly constant over time, today's young people and their parents do not always speak the same language when communicating about the dating scene.

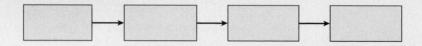

CHRONOLOGICAL PATTERNS

When events need to be introduced in the order in which they occurred, this pattern is known as **chronological order**, or **time order**. This pattern is especially common in history texts where events are documented in the order in which they occurred. It can also be found in most other textbooks when the history or background of a topic is being presented. Authors of sociology and psychology textbooks generally use time order patterns to show trends or the changes that take place over a period of time. Look at the following example. What trend does this information show?

The Polish people were first united into a country in the 10th Century. After a series of foreign invasions the country was pulled together again under the Jagiellonian Dynasty, which lasted from the 1300's to 1562. During this period, Poland experienced great heights of power and cultural achievement—the Golden Age in Polish History. This period was followed by a series of foreign wars, invasions, occupations, and conquests that lasted until the end of WWI. After WWI, Poland went through three dramatic stages including WWII, the domination of Poland by the Soviet Union after WWII, and the fall of the Iron Curtain in 1989. (Farr and Hammers 56)

We can see from the order in which the details were given that this is a brief account of Polish history from sometime before the year 1000 to the year 1989. This information becomes clearer when we lay it out on a timeline.

TimeLine for Polish History

1000	Polish people were first united into a country
1300	Foreign invasions ended and Golden Age began
1562	Golden Age ended
WWI	Series of foreign wars, invasions, occupations, and conquest
Post-WWII	Soviet take-over
1989	Fall of the Iron Curtain

So far we have looked at time order as being **linear**, where the events occur one after another and could be diagrammed in a straight line, as in our timeline above. Time order can also be **cyclical**: the events occur in cycles and can be diagrammed in a circle because the last event leads into the first. Study the following paragraph and the diagram that follows. At what point does the cycle end?

For most young people, the life course takes shape within the family life cycle. In early adulthood, people typically live on their own and marry. They have and raise children. As they become middle-aged and their children leave home, their parenting responsibilities are lessened. Late adulthood brings retirement, growing old, and the death of one's spouse. (As their children enter young adulthood, their children marry, have their own children and the cycle repeats itself.) (Berk 466)

As we can see from reading the above paragraph, the cycle never ends. We can diagram such a cycle by using a circle instead of a straight line, marking points on the circle to show the order of the events and their repetitive nature.

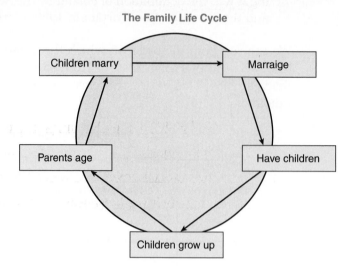

The Family Life Cycle

Signals

Clue words that signal time order patterns include:

since	first	next	then
after	during	later	finally
previously	prior to	follow a cycle	at the beginning of the cycle

EXERCISE
6-4

Creating Timelines

Read each paragraph below and identify the topic. Next, list the events or stages along with the period of time in which they occurred. Then, draw a timeline to show the relationship between the time periods and the events. The first one has been done for you.

1. In 1975, 62.8% of the Mexican population lived in cities. By 1999 almost 75 percent of the population lived in cities. In 1980, only seven cities in Mexico had populations greater than 500,000, but by the year 2000, over 25 cities had populations over 500,000. Mexico City is now estimated to have a population of over 20 million people, making it the largest city in the world. (Farr and Hammers 19)

Topic: <u>Growth of Mexican cities</u>

Events:

1. <u>In 1975, 62.8% of the Mexican population lived in cities.</u>

2. <u>In 1999, almost 75% of the Mexican population lived in cities.</u>

3. <u>By the year 2000, over 25 cities had populations over 500,000.</u>

4. <u>Mexico City is the most heavily populated city in the world.</u>

TIMELINE:

2. In December 1955, Rosa Parks, a 42-year-old black seamstress who was also secretary of the Alabama NAACP, sat down in the whites-only front section of a bus. Tired from a hard day's work, she refused orders to move to the back. The bus driver called the police at the next stop, and Parks was arrested and ordered to stand trial for violating the segregation laws. In Montgomery, fifty black civil rights leaders decided to organize a massive boycott of the bus system. Martin Luther King, Jr., the 27-year-old minister of the Baptist church where the meeting was held, soon emerged as the spokesman of the protest.

Although King, like others, was arrested on a trumped-up speeding charge and jailed, grassroots support arose. In Montgomery, 50,000 African Americans walked or formed car pools to avoid the transit system. Their actions cut gross revenue on city buses by 65 percent. Almost a year later, the Supreme Court ruled that bus segregation violated the Constitution and the boycott ended. But, for many blacks, peaceful protest became a way of life. (Nash et al. 776)

Topic: _____

Events: _____

_____

_____

_____

_____

TIMELINE:

3. Data from the government's annual National Household Survey on Drug Abuse (NHSDA) show that the use of most drugs increased from the early to late 1970s, peaked in 1985 when some 37 million people acknowledged using an illegal substance, and then declined. By 1988, that number had fallen to 28 million and remained low until 1992 when slight increases in marijuana and LSD use were reported by eighth graders and college students. A 1993 nation-wide survey of 50,000 junior and senior high school students revealed a marked increase in marijuana use (and smaller rises in the use of other drugs) among high school students. Data from the 1997 NHSDA revealed that drug abuse among individuals 12 to 17 years of age was up as 11.4 percent of those surveyed stated they had used an illicit drug within the past month. Although marijuana was the preferred drug in the age group, a total of 3.9 million teenagers used heroin for the first time in 1996, this later number being a significant increase over the 2.2 million who used that narcotic for the first time in 1995. (Bryjak and Soroka 186)

Topic: _____

Events: _____

_____

_____

_____

_____

TIMELINE:

4. The fact that rain is often acidic (acid rain) was first discovered in 1852 by a British chemist named Angus Smith. Twenty years later, he published a book entitled *Air and Rain*, but the book and Smith's ideas were soon forgotten. Then, in the 1950s, the effects of acid rain were rediscovered by scientists working in the northeastern United States, Scandinavia, and the English Lake District. Reports of damage attributed to acidic precipitation grew dramatically over the next three decades. Dozens of books, scientific papers, and popular articles were written describing the effects already observed and making predictions of more devastating damage yet to come. During the 1980s acid rain received much attention from the media. However, since the 1990s, very little attention has been paid to this problem, even though it has not been solved. (Stanitski et al. 230)

Topic: _____

Events: _____

_____

_____

_____

_____

TIMELINE:

5. Facing reelection in 1964, Kennedy wanted not only to win the presidency for a second term but also to increase liberal Democratic strength in Congress! In November 1963, he went to Texas, hoping to unite the state's Democratic Party for the upcoming election. Dallas, one of the stops on the trip, was said to be hostile to the administration? Now on November 22, Kennedy had a chance to see the city himself. Arriving at the airport, Henry Gonzalez, a congressman accompanying the president in Texas, remarked jokingly, "Well, I'm taking my risks. I haven't got my steel vest yet." As the party entered the city in an open car, the president encountered friendly crowds. Suddenly shots rang out, and Kennedy slumped forward as bullets ripped through his head and throat, and died a short time later. Lee Harvey Oswald, the accused assassin, was himself killed a few days later by a minor underworld figure as he was being moved within the jail. Americans were stunned. For days people stayed at home and watched endless television replays of the assassination and its aftermath. These images were indelibly imprinted on people's minds. United around the event, members of an entire generation remembered where they had been when Kennedy was shot, just as an earlier generation recalled Pearl Harbor. (Nash et al. 755)

Topic: _____ JFK _____

Events: _____

_____

_____

_____

_____

TIMELINE:

MIXED PATTERNS

In more complex writings, an author may use several textbook patterns on the same page or even in the same paragraph. Because introductory college textbooks introduce a great many new words, the term, definition, and example pattern is commonly found within all of the other patterns. A new term may be introduced (highlighted, underlined, _italicized_, or placed in **boldface** print) within a numbered or bulleted list of items or it may be introduced within one of the steps in a process pattern.

A list of items may be found within a process pattern. Let's say that we are reading the directions for baking a cake. We are following a step-by-step process that must follow a specific order, but within this process we find a list of ingredients. The ingredients may even be listed in two or more different groups, as in wet ingredients (water, milk, vanilla) and dry ingredients (flour, oatmeal, sugar).

Authors may define words, list important points, and explain procedures within a selection that introduces events in the order they occur. Thus, there is no limit to the combinations of patterns that authors may use in their textbooks. The following exercise will test your ability to recognize the pattern when combinations of definition, time order, process, and simple listing are used in textbooks.

EXERCISE
6-5

Identifying the Paragraph Pattern

Read the paragraphs below and decide which paragraph pattern applies. Choose from the following patterns: (a) term, definition, and example, (b) topic and list, (c) process, and (d) chronological order. If a paragraph has more than one pattern, indicate an answer for both patterns. The first pattern has been done for you.

_____d_____ **1.** The racial question was dramatized in 1947 when Jackie Robinson broke the color line and began playing major league baseball with the Brooklyn Dodgers. Sometimes teammates were hostile, sometimes runners slid into him with spikes high, but Robinson kept his frustrations to himself. A splendid first season helped ease the way, and after Robinson's trailblazing effort, other blacks, formerly confined to the old Negro leagues, started to move into the major leagues. Next came professional football and basketball. (Nash et al. 744)

_____ **2.** Geologists define three major types of rock: igneous, sedimentary, and metamorphic. **Igneous rocks** are formed by the cooling of volcanic flows, surface or subterranean. **Sedimentary rocks** are formed by the deposits of mineral particles (sediments). **Metamorphic rocks** are either igneous or sedimentary rocks that have been altered by heat and the pressure of overlying rock. (Smith and Smith 97)

_____ **3.** Empowering Others

An important function of leadership (though not limited to leadership positions) is to empower others, to help others (say, group members, your relational partner, co-workers, employees, other students, or siblings) to gain increased power over themselves and their environment. Here are a few ways to empower others:

   ■ Raise the person's self-esteem. Compliment. Resist fault-finding.

- Share skills and share decision-making power and authority.

- Be constructively critical. React honestly to suggestions from all group members.

- Encourage growth in all forms—academic, relational, and professional. This growth and empowerment of the other person enhances your own growth and power. (DeVito 282)

_____ **4.** A cesarean delivery is a surgical birth; the doctor makes an incision in the mother's abdomen and lifts the baby out of the uterus. Thirty years ago, the cesarean delivery was rare in the United States, performed in only 3 percent of births. Since then, the cesarean rate has climbed, reaching 24 percent in 1993 and dropping slightly to 21 percent in 1998. Still it is the highest rate in the world. (Berk 101)

_____ **5. Deviance**, broadly defined, is behavior that violates the norms of a particular society. Deviance can be something as simple as dyeing one's hair purple or wearing outrageous clothing or becoming tipsy at an office party. Or it may be behavior over which the individual has little control, such as being homeless and living on the street, or it may consist of more strongly sanctioned departures from the society's norms—acts such as rape, mugging, and murder. Not all deviance is considered socially wrong, yet it can have negative effects for the individual. For example, "whistle blowers" who publicize illegal or harmful actions by their employers deviate from the norms of bureaucratic organizations and are often threatened with the loss of their jobs. Yet at the same time these employees benefit the public by calling attention to dangerous or illegal activities. As in the case of whistle blowers who are fired for reporting inconvenient truths, many deviant acts are defined as wrong simply because they offend people with enough power to define what is normative and what is deviant. (Kornblum and Smith 125)

OTHER TEXT PATTERNS

As stated earlier, there are over 100 different types of text patterns. Listed below are some others that are common to college textbooks:

- Description
- Comparison/contrast
- Cause/effect
- Problem/solution
- Classification

Description

The descriptive pattern is often found in literature and narratives. Direction words often signal the descriptive pattern, as do words that help us imagine things that we can see, hear, touch, taste, or smell. Some words that signal the description pattern include:

Clue Words for Description	Example
near to far from above the below the next to beside from a distance at the top toward the bottom	*From the distance*, we could see the water flowing from the mountain top. As we came *near to* it, we could hear the loud roar of the rushing water. Standing *beside* the falls, we could feel the soft mist as the water crashed onto the rocks.

Comparison/Contrast

The comparison/contrast pattern is used in almost every type of writing. When we compare two or more people, places, things, or ideas, we look for what is the same and what is different. When we contrast two or more items, we look only for their differences. An author can use this pattern in three ways: to show how two or more items are (1) the same, (2) different, or (3) both the same and different.

Comparison Words	Contrast Words	Example
like	on the other hand	Reading class is a lot *like* English composition class because we read and discuss literature. *However*, reading class is *different from* English composition class because we don't write essays in the reading class.
as	unlike	
similar to	but	
both	however	
just as	although	
the same as	different from	

Cause/Effect

Cause/effect paragraph patterns are common in many textbooks, especially history, business, ecology, psychology, and sociology. Since scientists and scholars look for reasons why something happened the way it did, cause/effect relationships also make up the backbone of research reports.

Words That Signal Cause	Words That Signal Effect	Example
cause	therefore	The country experienced a food shortage because of the three-year drought.
because	thus	
reasons	then	
since	so	Cause (drought)
if, then	effect	↓
react to	as a result	Effect (food shortage)

Problem/Solution   The problem/solution pattern is common among most textbooks because every discipline is seeking answers to problems. A problem is an undesirable condition that creates difficulties. The solution is the action or series of actions that will cure or solve the problem.

Words That Signal Problems	Words That Signal Solutions	Example
problem the problem is the issue is	solution one solution is some strategies include to solve this problem	Volunteers for "Habitat for Humanity" help solve the problem of homelessness by building homes for those who are without a place to live.

Classification

Whenever we identify different types, classes, or groups, we are using the classification pattern. We are putting items into categories so that we can better understand them. When we make a grocery list, for example, we may divide our list into four categories—the four major food groups. Under each group, we may write the foods that are in each category:

Words That Signal Classification		
kinds of	types of	includes
categories	categorized as	elements of
groups of	characteristics of	characterized by
classify	classification	

Example

Every day we should eat foods from each of the four major food groups.

meat	bread	dairy	vegetables
beef	cereal	milk	carrots
ham	bread	yogurt	lettuce
turkey	muffin	eggs	tomatoes
chicken	pancakes	butter	onions
steak	waffles	cheese	peppers

EXERCISE
6-6

Identifying More Paragraph Patterns

Read the paragraphs below and decide which paragraph pattern applies. Choose from the following patterns: (a) description, (b) comparison/contrast (c) cause/effect, (d) problem/solution, or (e) classification. The first pattern has been identified for you.

_____c_____ **1.** The use of inhalants (especially aerosol cans of cleaning products and spray paints as well as glue) in the 12-to-17-year-old age category has also increased in the first half of the 1990s. Users spray the contents of these products into plastic bags and then inhale the fumes, a process called "huffing" or "sniffing." Because of the toxicity of these chemicals, huffing is estimated to result in more brain damage than the effects of all other drugs combined. In spite of the health risks that inhalants pose, only 40 percent of high school students view these substances as dangerous. (Bryjak and Soroka 186)

_____ **2.** To empathize with someone is to feel as that person feels. When you feel empathy for another, you're able to experience what the other is experiencing from that person's point of view. To sympathize, on the other hand, is to feel for the individual—to feel sorry for the person, for example. To empathize is to feel the same feelings in the same way as the other person does. Empathy, then, enables you to understand, emotionally and intellectually, what another person is experiencing. (DeVito 160)

_____ **3.** One of the most useful analyses of human motives is Abraham Maslow's hierarchy of needs, fivefold classification. One of Maslow's assumptions is that you seek to fulfill the need at the lowest level first and only when those needs are satisfied do you progress to fulfill the need at the next higher level. Thus, according to Maslow, you would not concern yourself with the need for security if your need for food had not been fulfilled. Similarly, you would not be concerned with friendship if your need for protection and security had not been fulfilled. (DeVito 397–98)

_____ **4.** In an effort to remedy what has been called the worst air pollution in the United States, a tentative plan has been adopted that would require by 2007 that all cars in the Los Angeles basin be converted to electric power or other clean fuel. Fuel cell research and rapidly developing new automobile battery technologies may permit manufacturers to meet the 2007 deadline. (Stanitski et al. 318)

_____ 5. The typical Iranian extended household lives in a dwelling that features a courtyard surrounded by a high wall, with rooms around the parameter and an open area, often with a pool, in the center. (Farr and Hammers 69–70)

Visual Literacy Box 6.4 ● ● ● ● ● ● ● ● ● ● ● ● ● ● ●

Graphic Organizers: Description

Use graphic organizers to display the information from your textbook in a way that will help you visualize and remember it. One way to organize information in the "description" pattern is to draw a picture of what the author is describing.

Read the sentence below and label the various parts according to the author's description.

The typical Iranian extended household lives in a dwelling that features a courtyard surrounded by a high wall, with rooms around the parameter and an open area, often with a pool, in the center.

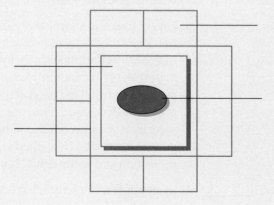

A Reading in Human Communications

Do you live in the past, present, or future? Read the following selection to find out how people can have different perspectives of time.

Vocabulary in Context

Complete the vocabulary exercise before reading the selection to learn the new terms. The first term has been identified for you.

a. orientation—adjustment to a particular situation

b. reverence—great love, respect, or admiration for something

c. socioeconomic—social class based on how much money a person makes

d. fatalism—belief that no one can control his or her fate or the way things turn out

e. hedonism—practice of pleasure seeking, self-satisfaction, self-gratification

_____b_____ **1.** With a future orientation, you have a great _____ for the future in that you look toward and live for the future.

_____ **2.** Those who have a present orientation believe that fate controls what happens to them in life. Their belief in _____ causes them to live for today and not worry about tomorrow.

_____ **3.** Researchers can tell which type of orientation a person will develop by his or her _____ class.

_____ **4.** With a past _____, you have a particular love and respect for the past.

_____ **5.** Children with parents in professional occupations are socialized in a way that does not encourage fatalism and pleasure seeking, or _____.

Psychological Time

[1]   Psychological time refers to the importance placed on the past, present, and future. With a past **orientation**, you have a particular

reverence for the past. You relive old times and regard the old methods as the best. You see events as circular and recurring and find that the wisdom of yesterday is applicable also to today and tomorrow. With a present orientation, you live in the present—without planning for tomorrow. With a future orientation, you look toward and live for the future. You save today, work hard in college, and deny yourselves luxuries because you are preparing for the future.

[2]   Future income is positively related to future orientation; the more future oriented you are, the greater your income is likely to be. Present orientation is strongest among lowest income males.

[3]   The time orientation you develop depends on your **socioeconomic** class and your personal experiences. Researchers have observed that "a child with parents in unskilled and semiskilled occupations is usually socialized in a way that promotes a present-oriented **fatalism** and **hedonism**. A child of parents who are managers, teachers, or other professionals learns future-oriented values and strategies designed to promote achievement." Similarly, the future-oriented person who works for tomorrow's goals will frequently look down on the present-oriented person as lazy and poorly motivated for enjoying today and not planning for tomorrow. In turn, the present-oriented person may see those with strong future orientations as obsessed with amassing wealth or rising in status.

[4]   Different time perspectives also account for much intercultural misunderstanding since different cultures often teach their members drastically different time orientations. For example, members from some Latin cultures would rather be late for an appointment than end a conversation abruptly. While the Latin sees this behavior as politeness toward the person with whom he or she is conversing, others may see this as impolite to the person with whom he or she had the appointment. (DeVito 144–46)

Term: _____

Definition: _____

Examples: _____

_____

_____

Comprehension Questions

Choose the letter of the correct answer and write it in the blank provided. The following questions pertain to all of the skills that you have learned so far. The first one has been completed for you.

_____b_____ 1. The topic of this passage is:
        a. fatalism.

        b. psychological time.

        c. hedonism.

_____ 2. The main point of this selection is:
        a. with a past orientation, you have a particular reverence for the past.

        b. members from some Latin cultures would rather be late for an appointment than end a conversation abruptly.

        c. your culture teaches you a particular time perspective and this influences your actions.

_____ 3. Which of the following text patterns is used in paragraph 1?
        a. term, definition, and example

        b. narration

        c. process

_____ 4. The text pattern used in paragraph 3 is:
        a. comparison/contrast.

        b. term, definition, and example.

        c. chronological order.

_____ 5. The text pattern used in paragraph 4 is:
        a. topic with a list.

        b. comparison/contrast.

        c. chronological order.

A Reading in Physical Science

Did you know that the atmosphere in which we are able to exist is only about 2 miles or 20 city blocks high? Read the following selection to find out more about the atmosphere that surrounds the earth.

Vocabulary in Context

Complete the vocabulary exercise before reading the selection to learn the new terms. The first term has been identified for you.

a. **troposphere**—the lowest layer of the atmosphere; layer in which weather occurs

b. **stratosphere**—the second layer of the atmosphere; contains the ozone layer

c. **mesosphere**—third layer of the atmosphere; has low temperatures at the top ($-90°C$)

d. **thermosphere**—fourth layer of the atmosphere; has very high temperatures ($2000°C$)

e. **ionosphere**—ion-rich section of the atmosphere that lies within the highest layer of the mesosphere and the thermosphere

_____a_____ **1.** The _____ extends 8 kilometers over the polar regions and is the lowest layer of the atmosphere.

_____ **2.** The _____ can be as cold as $-90°C$ at the top and is the third layer of the atmosphere.

_____ **3.** The _____ contains very little air and can get to be $2000°C$.

_____ **4.** The _____ is the part of the atmosphere that contains the ozone layer.

_____ **5.** The _____ is the part of the atmosphere that lies within both the mesosphere and the thermosphere.

The Vertical Structure of the Atmosphere

[1]   If you have ever gone mountain climbing you probably noticed that the air grows cooler and thinner with increasing elevation. At sea level, the air is generally warmer and denser. The greater density near the Earth's surface is due to gravity. Like a deep pile of feathers, the density is greatest at the bottom and least at the top. More than half the atmosphere's mass lies below an altitude of 5.6 kilometers (a kilo-

meter is equal to 5/8 of a mile), and about 99 percent lies below an altitude of 30 kilometers. Unlike a pile of feathers, the atmosphere doesn't have a distinct top. It gradually thins to the near vacuum of outer space.

[2]   We classify the atmosphere in layers, each distinct in its characteristics. The lowest layer, the troposphere, is where weather occurs. The **troposphere** extends to a height of 16 kilometers over the equatorial region and 8 kilometers over the polar regions. Commercial jets generally fly at the top of the troposphere to minimize the buffeting and jostling caused by weather disturbances. Even though the troposphere is the thinnest atmosphere layer, it contains 90 percent of the atmosphere's mass and essentially all of the atmosphere's water vapor and clouds. Temperature in the troposphere decreases steadily

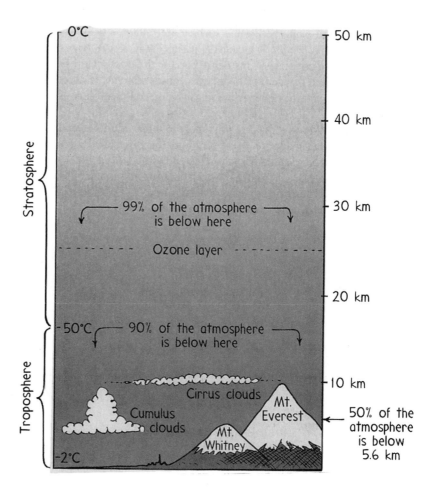

(6°C per kilometer) with increasing altitude. At the top of the troposphere, temperature averages about –50°C.

[3]   Above the troposphere is the **stratosphere**, which reaches a height of 50 kilometers. Ultraviolet radiation from the Sun is absorbed by the ozone layer in the stratosphere. Because of this absorption of energy, temperature in the stratosphere rises from about –50°C at the bottom to about 0°C at the top.

[4]   Above the stratosphere, the **mesosphere** extends upward to about 80 kilometers. The gases that make up the mesosphere absorb very little of the Sun's radiation. As a result, temperature decreases from about 0°C at the bottom of the layer to about –90°C at the top.

[5]   The situation is just the opposite in the layer above the mesosphere, the **thermosphere**. Extending upward to 500 kilometers, this layer contains very little air. What air there is absorbs enough solar radiation to bring about a 2000°C temperature! Because of the low air density, however, this extreme temperature has little significance. Very little heat would be transferred to a slowly moving body in this region.

[6]   The **ionosphere** is an ion-rich region within the thermosphere and uppermost mesosphere. The ions in it are produced from the interaction between high-frequency solar radiation and atmospheric atoms. The incoming solar rays strip electrons from nitrogen and oxygen atoms, producing a large concentration of free electrons and positive ions in this layer. The degree of ionization in the ionosphere depends on air density and on the amount of solar radiation. Because ions are more prevalent where air density is low and solar radiation high, the number of ions increases with altitude and is greatest in the upper part of the ionosphere.

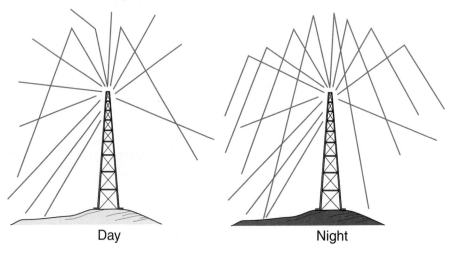

Day   Night

[7]   During the day, solar radiation increases ionization and energized
ions move throughout the ionosphere. This scattered distribution of
ions hinders AM radio-wave reception, because most of the AM radio-
waves are greatly weakened by collisions with the ions as they travel
through the ionosphere. At night, ionization decreases and the remaining ions tend to concentrate in a thick band at the top of the ionosphere. With fewer ionic collisions in the lower ionosphere, AM
radio-waves are able to travel to the upper ionosphere where, because
of the concentrated band of ions, they are reflected back to the Earth's
surface. That's why long distance AM radio reception is better at night.
(Hewitt, Suchocki and Hewitt 645–46)

Comprehension Questions

Choose the letter of the correct answer and write it in the blank provided. The
following questions pertain to all of the skills that you have learned so far. The
first one has been completed for you.

_____b_____ 1. The topic of this passage is the:
    a. thermosphere.

    b. atmosphere.

    c. stratosphere.

_____ 2. Fewer ionic collisions in the lower atmosphere make long distance AM radio reception better:
    a. during the morning.

    b. during the afternoon.

    c. at night.

_____ 3. Which of the following text patterns is used in paragraph 2?
    a. classification

    b. narration

    c. process

_____ 4. According to the illustration, the top of Mt. Everest reaches
into the:
    a. stratosphere.

    b. thermosphere.

    c. troposphere.

_____ **5.** The text pattern used in paragraph 6 is:
 a. topic with a list.
 b. definition.
 c. chronological order.

Getting Ahead in College Box 6.1

SENTENCE COMBINING: CONJUNCTIONS

Combine each group of sentences below into one sentence by using the word "and" to join ideas. Include all ideas without repeating any words. The first one has been done for you.

1. The air is at sea level.

The air is warm.

The air is dense.

The air at sea level is warm and dense.

2. The air grows warmer with increasing elevation.

The air grows thinner with increasing elevation.

_____

_____

3. Like a deep pile of feathers, the density is greatest at the bottom.

Like a deep pile of feathers, the density is least at the top.

_____

_____

4. More than half of the atmosphere's mass lies below an altitude of 5.6 kilometers.

About 99 percent of the atmosphere's mass lies below an altitude of 30 kilometers.

_____

(continued on next page)

5. The troposphere extends to a height of 16 kilometers over the equatorial region.
The troposphere extends to a height of 8 kilometers over the polar regions.

_____

_____

_____

A Reading in Sociology

What makes a marriage fall apart? John Gottman's research explains what makes couples unhappy and how to create a happy relationship.

Vocabulary in Context

Complete the vocabulary exercise before reading the selection to learn the new terms. The first one has been indentified for you.

a. **Apocalypse**—the last book of the Christian bible that describes four horsemen coming to destroy the earth.

b. **significant**—important

c. **engenders**—causes; produces; brings about

d. **contempt**—feeling of disrespect toward someone; looking at the person as though he or she is low or worthless

e. **intimacy**—closeness

_____b_____ 1. Although the phrases "I wish you had taken care of that bill" and "You never get the bills paid on time!" seem to mean the same thing, there is a _____ difference to the person it is said to.

_____ 2. When one person puts down another person, the one put down will become angry and try to say something just as nasty to the person who criticized him. Thus, we can say that criticism _____ criticism.

_____ **3.** The author describes four behaviors that are so deadly to a marriage that he calls these behaviors "The Four Horsemen of the _____."

_____ **4.** In marriage, a couple tries to build _____, but when they get caught up in criticizing each other, they end up destroying what they were trying to build.

_____ **5.** If a couple constantly criticizes each other, eventually they will begin to feel _____ for each other.

The Four Horsemen of the Apocalypse

[1]   Even the most stable marriages of any type can fall apart, and Gottman and company have observed an all-too-predictable pattern in their decline and fall. He likens the process to a cascade—a tumble down the rapids—that starts with the arrival of a dangerous quartet of behaviors. So destructive is their effect on marital happiness, in fact, that he calls these behaviors "The Four Horsemen of the **Apocalypse**."

[2]   The first horseman is "attacking someone's personality or character" rather than making some specific complaint about his or her behavior. The difference between saying, "I wish you had taken care of that bill" (a healthy and specific complaint) and "You never get the bills paid on time!" (a generalizing and blaming attack) is very **significant** to the listener. Criticism often **engenders** criticism in return and sets the stage for the second horseman: **contempt**.

[3]   "What separates contempt from criticism," explains Gottman, "is the intention to insult and psychologically abuse your partner." Negative thoughts about the other come out in subtle put-downs, hostile jokes, mocking facial expressions, and name-calling ("You are such an idiot around money"). By now the positive qualities that attracted you to this person seem long ago and far away, and instead of trying to build **intimacy**, you're ushering in the third horseman.

[4]   Defensiveness comes on the heels of contempt as a seemingly reasonable response to attack—but it only makes things worse.

By denying responsibility, making excuses, whining, tossing back counter-attacks, and other strategies ("How come I'm the one who always pays the bills?!), you just accelerate your speed down river. Gottman also warns that it's possible to skip straight to the third horseman by being oversensitive about legitimate complaints.

[5]   Once stonewalling (the fourth horseman) shows up, things are looking bleak. Stonewallers simply stop communicating, refusing to respond even in self-defense. Of course, all these "horsemen" drop in on couples once in a while. But when a partner habitually shuts down and withdraws, the final rapids of negativity (what Gottman calls the "Distance and Isolation Cascade") can quickly propel the marriage through whirlpools of hopelessness, isolation, and loneliness over the waterfall of divorce. With the arrival of the fourth horseman, one or both partners is thinking negative thoughts about his or her counterpart most of the time, and the couple's minds—as well as their bodies—are in a perpetual state of defensive red alert.

[6]   The stress of conflict eventually sends blood pressure, heart rate, and adrenaline into the red zone—a phenomenon Gottman calls flooding. "The body of someone who feels flooded," he writes, "is a confused jumble of signals. It may be hard to breathe. . . . Muscles tense up and stay tensed. The heart beats fast, and it may seem to beat harder." Emotionally, the flooded person may feel a range of emotions, from fear to anger to confusion.

[7]   Married couples who routinely let the Four Horsemen ransack their living rooms face enormous physical and psychological consequences. Gottman's studies show that chronic flooding and negativity not only make such couples more likely to get sick, they also make it very difficult for couples to change how they relate. When your heart is beating rapidly and your veins are constricting in your arms and legs, it's hard to think fresh, clear thoughts about how you're communicating, nor can the brain process new information very well. Instead, a flooded person relies on "over-learned responses"—old relationship habits that probably just fan the flames.

[8]   Repair attempts are a kind of "meta-communication"—a way of talking about how you're communicating with each other. "Can we please stay on the subject?" "That was a rude thing to say." "We're not talking about your father!" "I don't think you're listening to me." Such statements, even when delivered in grouchy or complaining tone, are efforts to interrupt the cycle of criticism, contempt, defensiveness, and stonewalling and to bring the conversation back on track.

[9] "In stable relationships," explains Gottman, "the other person will respond favorably: 'Alright, alright. Finish.' The agreement isn't made very nicely. But it does stop the person. They listen, they accept the repair attempt, and they actually change" the way they're relating.

[10] Breaking the Four Horsemen cycle is critical, says Gottman, because "the more time [couples] spend in that negative perceptual state, the more likely they are to start making long-lasting attributions about this marriage as being negative." Such couples begin rewriting the story of how they met, fell in love, made commitments. Warm memories about how "we were so crazy about each other" get replaced with "I was crazy to marry him/her." And once the story of the marriage has been infected with negativity, the motivation to work on its repair declines. Divorce becomes much more likely and predictable.

[11] "The hardest thing to do," says Gottman, "is to get back to the fundamentals that really make you happy." Couples who fail to do this allow the Four Horsemen to carry them far from the fundamentals of affection, humor, appreciation, and respect. Couples who succeed cultivate these qualities like gardeners. They also cultivate an affirming story of their lives together, understanding that that is the soil from which everything else grows.

[12] The work may be a continuous challenge, but the harvest, as my long-married friends Bill and Karen would say, is an enormous blessing: the joy in being truly known and loved, and in knowing how to love.

[13] **The Four Keys to a Happy Relationship.** Despite all his sophisticated analysis of how relationships work (and don't work), researcher John Gottman's advice to the love-lorn and fight-torn is really quite simple.

■ Learn to Calm Down. This will cut down on the flooding response that makes further communication so difficult. Once couples are calm enough, suggests Gottman, they can work on three other basic keys to improving their relationship.

■ Learn to Speak and Listen Non-defensively. This is tough, Gottman admits, but defensiveness is a very dangerous response, and it needs to be interrupted. One of the most powerful things you can do—in addition to working toward the ideal of listening with empathy and speaking without blame—is to reintroduce praise and admiration into your relationship. A little appreciation goes a long way toward changing the chemistry between people.

■ Validate Your Partner. Validation involves putting yourself in your partner's <u>shoes</u> and imagining his or her emotional state. Let your partner know that you understand how he or she feels, and why, even if you don't agree. You can also show validation by acknowledging your partner's point of view, accepting appropriate responsibility, and apologizing when you are clearly wrong. If this still seems too much of a stretch, at least let your partner know that you are trying to understand, even if you're finding it hard.

■ Practice, Practice, Practice. Gottman calls this "over-learning," doing something so many times that it becomes second nature. The goal is to be able to calm yourself down, communicate non-defensively, and validate your partner automatically—even in the heat of an argument. (Atkisson Sept./Oct. 1994)

Comprehension Questions

Choose the letter of the correct answer and write it in the blank provided. The following questions pertain to all of the skills that you have learned so far. The first one has been completed for you.

___c___ 1. The topic of this passage is:
a. four keys to a happy relationship.
b. four criticisms to stay away from.
c. learning how to communicate in marriage.

_____ 2. The implied main idea in paragraph 1 is:
a. there are four horsemen in the "Apocalypse."
b. even stable marriages can fall apart.
c. there are four predicable behaviors that can ruin a marriage.

_____ 3. The text pattern for paragraph 2 is:
a. term, definition, and example.
b. topic with a list.

c. chronological order.

_____ **4.** The overall text patterns for this selection are:
  a. topic with a list *and* problem/solution.

  b. comparison/contrast *and* time order.

  c. time order *and* definition.

_____ **5.** Identify the text pattern used in the paragraph below.

  "What separates contempt from criticism," explains Gottman, "is the intention to insult and psychologically abuse your partner." Negative thoughts about the other come out in subtle put-downs, hostile jokes, mocking facial expressions, and name-calling ("You are such an idiot around money").
  a. comparison/contrast

  b. topic and list

  c. chronological order

_____ **6.** The text pattern used in paragraph 4 is:
  a. topic with a list.

  b. term, definition, and example.

  c. cause/effect.

_____ **7.** The "four horsemen" of divorce are:
  a. criticism, contempt, defensiveness, and stonewalling.

  b. calming down, listening, validating, and practice.

  c. blood pressure, heart rate, adrenaline, and confusion.

_____ **8.** Which term is defined in paragraph 6?
  a. stress

  b. conflict

  c. flooding

_____ **9.** The overall paragraph pattern in paragraph 7 is:
  a. topic with a list.

  b. cause/effect.

  c. chronological order.

Getting Ahead in College Box 6.2

THE PRONUNCIATION OF VOCABULARY

When two or three consonants are grouped together, the combination of the letters makes one sound, although each letter can still be heard within that sound. For example, the *s*, the *t*, and the *r* sounds in <u>str</u>ong are blended together to make one sound. Thus, they form a consonant blend. Using the following examples as a pronunciation guide, highlight the words in each sentence that have blends and underline the blend. The first one has been done for you.

st	as in	**st**art
sp	as in	**sp**end
sh	as in	**sh**ut
str	as in	**str**ong

1. Even the most <u>st</u>able marriages of any type can fall apart.

2. The first criticism: "attacking someone's personality or character" rather than making some specific complaint about his or her behavior.

3. Criticism often engenders criticism in return and sets the stage for the second horseman: contempt.

4. By denying responsibility, making excuses, whining, tossing back counter-attacks, and other strategies ("How come I'm the one who always pays the bills?!"),

5. You just accelerate your speed down the river.

6. Once stonewalling (the fourth horseman) shows up, things are looking bleak.

7. Stonewallers simply stop communicating, refusing to respond even in self-defense.

8. Of course, all these "horsemen" drop in on couples once in a while.

9. The stress of conflict eventually sends blood pressure, heart rate, and adrenaline into the red zone.

10. Can we please stay on the subject?

_____ **10.** In paragraph 13, the author presents a list of four items: (1) Learn to Calm Down, (2) Learn to Speak and Listen Non-defensively, (3) Validate Your Partner, and (4) Practice, Practice, Practice. Which topic goes with this list?

a. The Four Horsemen of the Apocalypse

b. The Four Keys to a Happy Relationship

c. Breaking the Four Horsemen Cycle

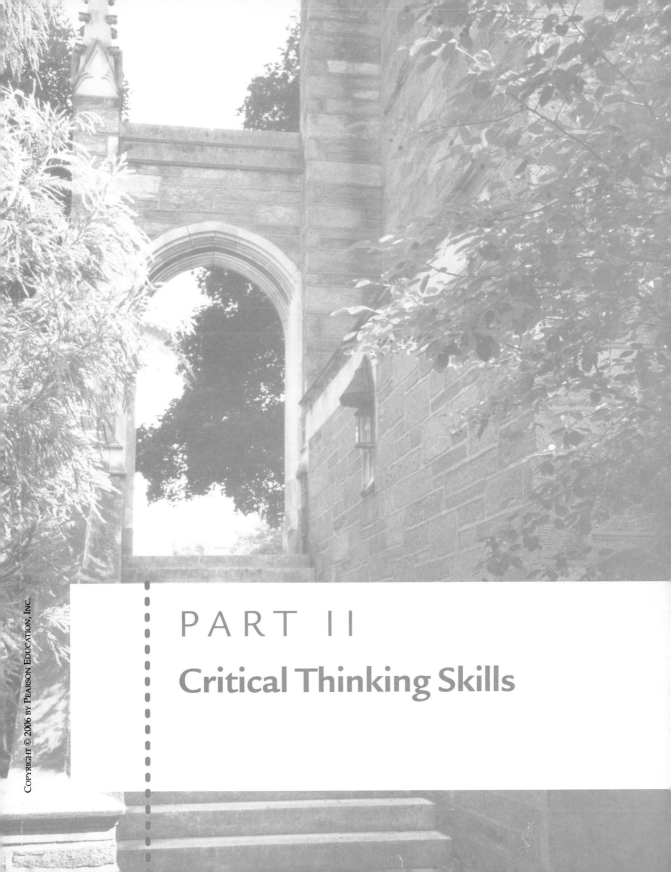

PART II
Critical Thinking Skills

7

Inference

● ●

REVIEWING IMPLIED MAIN IDEA

If you recall our previous discussions on main idea, you will remember that some paragraphs contain only sentences with supporting details. This does *not* mean these paragraphs lack a main idea. It means that *we* must figure out the main idea in our minds based on the details we are given. Let's review the four steps that we follow to do this:

Step 1: Look at the individual details in each sentence.

Step 2: Decide what the details have in common.

Step 3: Think of a general category under which each common detail may fall. In other words, establish a main idea. Then, make up a general statement about the common details; that is, write a main idea statement.

Step 4: Check the details in each sentence against the main idea you have just established. Check to see if the details in each sentence provide more information about the general statement.

If all of the sentences in a paragraph support our main idea, we can say that we understand the author's unstated, or implied, main idea. Let's follow these steps to *create an implied main idea* for the paragraph below. Consider the following example and think about how the above four steps can help us determine the unstated main idea of the paragraph:

Copyright © 2006 by Pearson Education, Inc.

267

Generally, the students who have high grade point averages always attend class. Successful students also go to class prepared to discuss the topic listed on the syllabus. In addition to class preparation and attendance, students who are successful in college have and use good study skills. Finally, high achieving students always create an organized study routine.

We can see that all of the sentences in this example address student success. More specifically, each statement mentions the things students do to become successful in college. A statement that includes all these ideas could look like this:

There are four things that successful students do to get good grades in college.

Each new sentence we write about the above general statement will add more detail. In other words, the sentences will explain the four things that students must do to get good grades.

Now that we have reviewed how to create an implied main idea, we are ready to learn a similar, yet more challenging, element of reading. In this chapter we:

■ practice making inferences;

■ learn about the different types of inferences;

■ practice drawing conclusions.

MAKING INFERENCES

Just as the organization of ideas helps the reader follow the author's train of thought, knowledge of the world helps the reader to interpret the meaning of the author's words. **World knowledge** refers to everything we have learned since we were born—all that we know about the world. When each new fact enters our brains, we immediately begin to classify it. We try to associate it with other information on that same topic—connect it to what we already know. Each time we do this, we create a network of information called a **schema**.

The process of putting pieces of information together so that it makes sense is called **making an inference**. In other words, when we "infer" something, we are drawing a conclusion from information we already have.

What Is an Inference?

While reading, we use our general knowledge of the world to make predictions. As the author presents **facts** (information that can be proved true or false), we connect what we know to the new information and then make an educated guess about what will happen next or about the author's point. In this way we become involved with the text as we try to find out if our guesses are correct.

If our initial guess is incorrect, we review once again all of the clues or evidence provided by the text and make another guess. We continue reading the text this way, making guesses from what we know and from the facts the author presents. These guesses are called **inferences**. The following flowchart illustrates the process of making and evaluating an inference.

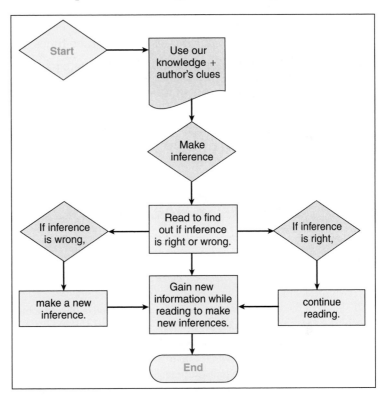

Clues to Meaning

Our success at making guesses, or inferences, all depends on our background knowledge and the facts that we're given. In general, our background knowledge includes everything that we know about the world. **Logical reasoning**, or the use of logic, analysis, and reasoning to make sense of our experiences, allows us to make inferences about ideas or concepts that the author has not directly stated. Thus, while we read, we look at the important details and think of them as clues or evidence that will support our inferences or conclusions. Review the example below to see how we find clues within the facts and how we use these facts to make inferences.

> **Situation:** During the second inning of the baseball game, the batter swings and misses the ball three times. The Red Team members go out onto the field. The Blue Team members come in from the field. One Blue Team member picks up the bat and walks up to the home plate.

What clues help us to infer what is happening in this scene?

- The batter misses the ball three times.
- The Red Team goes out onto the field.
- A Blue Team member has the bat.

Based on these clues, what conclusion can we draw?

Inference: The Red Team batter struck out and the Blue Team is up to bat.

Visual Literacy Box 7.1

Mapping Inferences

What clues help you make an inference about the scene below?

It is a hot summer day and fans have filled the bleachers to watch the game. The bases are loaded and Team Red is up to bat. Members from Team Blue take their places in the field. The pitcher throws the ball over the plate; the batter swings and misses. The umpire calls "Striiiiiike 2!" The pitcher throws a curve ball. Suddenly, the fans hear a loud "crack" as the bat meets the ball. The ball flies past both the pitcher and the short stop. In the bleachers, the Red fans cheer wildly! Three Red Team players cross the home plate. The pitcher finally has the ball and throws it to home plate. The catcher receives the ball just after the batter runs across the home base.

(continued on next page)

The clues or facts provided are:

- Two teams are playing a game that involves a ball.

- A member of Team Red first misses, then hits the ball with a bat.

- The pitcher and short stop are unable to catch the ball.

- Three Red Team players cross the home plate.

- The Red Team fans are excited.

- The pitcher gets the ball, but throws it to home plate after the batter crosses it.

What can you guess or infer about this scene?

Create a map that shows how you would reach an inference about this scene.

If you are familiar with baseball, you can probably guess that the batter made a home run for Team Red. You can also guess that 4 points were made, one for the three players who made it to home base and one for the batter who also crossed home base before the ball reached there. Even if you have never watched a baseball game, based on knowledge of another familiar team sport, such as football or soccer, you could have guessed that the Red team was increasing its score. You can also conclude that the Red fans would *not* cheer if the opposing team (Team Blue) was in the process of scoring.

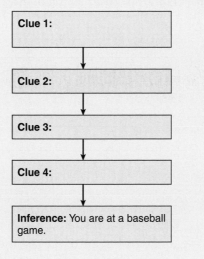

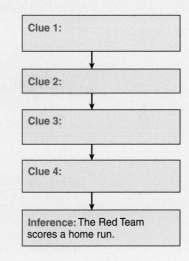

| EXERCISE 7-1 | Locating Inference Clues |

Study the facts from each situation. Locate the clues to help you make a logical inference or draw a reasonable conclusion. For each situation, one clue is already written in for you.

1. **Situation:** Marka is a student in Professor Chu's biology class. Class starts at 9:00 a.m. It is 9:15 a.m. Professor Chu is speaking to the biology class. Marka opens the door and walks into the classroom.

   Clues:

   - ■ Marka is a biology student in Professor Chu's class.
   - ■ Class starts at 9:00 a.m.
   - ■ Marka walks into the classroom at 9:15 a.m.

   Inference: Marka is late for class.

2. **Situation:** In the dining room, the last of the customers paid his bill. The wait staff cleared the tables and put on fresh linens. In the kitchen, the chef put the leftovers in the cooler as the dishwasher put the last set of dishes through the cycle.

   Clues:

   - ■ The last customer paid his bill.

   - ■ _____

   - ■ _____

   Inference: _____

   _____

3. **Situation:** Looking up at the engine of the car, the mechanic tugged one more time on the wrench. This time, the bolt loosened and the hot oil came pouring down into the pan. Unfortunately, the bolt slipped through his fingers and now he would have to wait for the oil to cool before he could finish changing the oil and filter.

Clues:

■ <u>The mechanic loosened a bolt under the engine of the car.</u>

■ <u>THE bold loosend & tht oil pourd out</u>

■ <u>THE bold fell INTO THE oil</u>

Inference: Accidently droped in oil

4. **Situation:** The professor walked into the second-floor classroom above the library. She noticed that only half of her class was in attendance. She had seen the missing students 10 minutes before on the first floor of the library near the elevator. The elevator had a reputation for getting stuck in between floors.

Clues:

■ <u>The classroom was on the second floor.</u>

■ only half the class was there

■ she saw THem at THe Elevator

Inference: The Elevater got stuck

5. **Situation:** In his arrogance, the chef never admitted to making mistakes. When he absentmindedly filled an order twice, the waitress asked the hostess what to do with the extra food. Knowing the chef had the power to fire employees for making mistakes and that he always blamed his mistakes on others, the hostess told the waitress to serve the first order. She then dumped the second order in the garbage can.

Clues:

■ <u>The chef made a mistake.</u>

■ Waitress was Scared to get hired

■ threw away food

Inference: _____

_____

<table>
<tr><td>EXERCISE
7-2</td><td>**Making Logical Inferences**</td></tr>
</table>

Study the facts from each situation. Locate the clues to help you make a logical inference or draw a reasonable conclusion. For each situation, one clue is already written in for you.

1. **Situation:** The ticket line for the flight to Boston was long. Gerd was standing in line ahead of Segrid. The ticket agent sold Gerd the last ticket.

   Clues:

   Gerd was in line before Segrid.

   ■ _____

   ■ _____

   Inference: _____

   _____

2. **Situation:** Segrid stood in the window, watching the flight to Boston depart with Gerd on board. She desperately needed to get to Boston that night. However, there were no more flights available until the next morning. Half an hour passed as she sat in the lobby of the Chicago airport, wondering what to do. Suddenly, Gerd walked down the hall, waving to her.

   Clues:

   ■ Segrid watched the plane leave.

   ■ _____

   ■ _____

Inference: _____

_____

3. **Situation:** Gerd explained that one engine of the plane had caught on fire and they were forced to return to Chicago. The crew was now getting another plane ready to go to Boston. Although the flight to Boston had originally been full, there were many seats available now. Some passengers had missed their connections, while others decided not to fly at all. However, Segrid was not afraid.

Clues:

- The plane to Boston caught fire and returned to Chicago.
- _They were getting another plane_
- _many seats now available_

Inference: _ppl didn't want to take a chance - w/ fire._

4. **Situation:** Some of the passengers who had been flying "first class" changed their travel arrangements. Theirs were the only seats available. Gerd already had a seat in the "passenger" section. Segrid was offered a seat in the "first class" section for the same price as those in the "passenger" section.

Clues:

- The only seats available were in the "first class" section.
- _first class were now in pass._
- _ppl offered first class seats_

Inference: _He flew first class_

_____

5. **Situation:** In the "first class" section, Segrid was offered a wide, comfortable seat while Gerd, in the passenger section, sat in a small, narrow

seat. Segrid had a full-course dinner complete with appetizers, steak, and dessert. Gerd was offered peanuts and soda as a snack and a burrito and chips for dinner.

Clues:

- The "first class" seats were more comfortable than those in the "passenger" section.
- first class has better food
- passengers dnt get food

Inference: _first class better_

TYPES OF INFERENCES

Many different situations in reading require the reader to make inferences. Sometimes a sentence or paragraph does not give us all of the information we need to determine the *implied meaning*. (Remember, *implied* means that hints or clues are given, but the idea is not directly stated.) In this case, we need to read ahead to gain more information before we can identify and understand the inference or make the intended connections.

We make four general types of inferences: (1) instrumental, (2) elaborative, (3) causal, and (4) metonymic.

Instrumental Inferences

Sometimes we read a sentence and it is unclear as to what the author is "getting at," or implying. So we read the sentence over and over again and become frustrated because we still do not understand. In this case we need to read further; we need more information to "get" the author's point. Consider the example below:

Last year Magali took a full load of classes every semester. This year she failed most of them again.

When we read the first sentence in this example, all we know is that Magali went to school every semester and took a full course load each time. It's not until we read the second sentence that we begin to understand that <u>Magali is having difficulty in school.</u> We know from the word "again" that Magali failed most of her classes last year. However, had we stopped reading after the first sentence, we would have been unable to make this connection.

Other times we can read a sentence and pretty much determine the inference right away; as we read further, that inference is confirmed, as in the example below:

> Training for the Olympics, Glenn peddled tirelessly up and down the steep mountain roads each day. His bicycle was specially made for this type of workout.

In the first sentence, we can pretty much infer that Glenn used a bicycle, since people most commonly peddle bicycles on roads. (People don't use the word "peddle" to refer to cars, trucks, or other types of vehicles.) The second sentence tells us that a bicycle was, in fact, the type of vehicle he used to get up and down the mountains. In both cases, a word or phrase in a following sentence helps us, or is *instrumental* to our making the correct inference.

EXERCISE 7-3	Identifying Instrumental Inferences

Read the sentences below and choose the letter that best explains the inference. Then write which words helped you make that inference. The first question has been completed for you.

_____b_____ **1.** Steve taught all of the children how to read. The children's parents were pleased. The principal was also very pleased.
   a. Steve is a principal.
   b. Steve is an elementary school teacher.
   c. Steve is a parent.

   Instrumental word or phrase: <u>taught the children how to read</u>

_____ **2.** Natalia has been studying dance for two years. She has one more year of training before she can try out for the New York City Ballet.

a. It took Natalia two years to train for the New York City Ballet.

b. Natalia will try out for the New York City ballet three years from now.

c. Natalia is in a three-year ballet training program.

Instrumental word or phrase: _____

3. Harris learned a new play yesterday. He really looks forward to football practice every day.

a. Harris learned a new football play.

b. Harris learned a new basketball move.

c. Harris has become interested in theatre.

Instrumental word or phrase: _____

4. We watched the network evening news last night. Even though it was a 30-minute news program, the commercials took 10 minutes away from that time.

a. The news show lasted 30 minutes.

b. The news show lasted 15 minutes.

c. The news show lasted 20 minutes.

Instrumental word or phrase: ___Even though___

5. Guita was recognized again this semester. She has been on the Dean's List for the last two years.

a. Guita was on the Dean's List again this semester.

b. Guita will be on the Dean's List next semester.

c. Guita was recognized for her athletic ability.

Instrumental word or phrase: ___recognized again___

Elaborative Inferences

Another situation that requires inference is when a general term is used first and is then followed by a more specific term, or vice versa. It is called an **elaborative** inference because it adds more information, or elaborates on the subject.

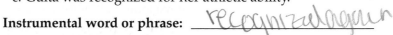

Our neighbor's *dog* would sometimes sit on our doorstep and bark. The *collie* wanted us to give her a snack.

> Our neighbor's *collie* would sometimes sit on our doorstep and bark. The *dog* wanted us to give her a snack.

In the first case, for example, the more general term, "dog," is related to the more specific term, "collie." In the second case, the specific term, "collie," is related to the more general term, "dog." In both cases, the second sentence confirms that a collie is a type of dog. Let's look at another example:

> Only one student in our sophomore class could afford a *car*. The rest of us depended on public transportation or walked if our destination was close enough. After the game on Friday night the temperature really dropped. None of us wanted to walk, so we all piled into Carmen's *car*. Twenty-one altogether. Boy, I don't know how that *Volkswagen Bug* ever got off the ground!

In this case, the more general term, "car," is presented first. From this, we can infer that the "Volkswagen Bug" is a type of car.

<table>
<tr><td>EXERCISE
7-4</td><td>**Identifying Elaborative Inferences**</td></tr>
</table>

Read the sentences below and choose the letter that best explains the elaborative inference. In addition, identify the general and specific terms that lead you to your conclusion. The first question has been completed for you.

_____b_____ **1.** The Metropolitan has many interesting exhibits. Joaquin went to the museum last week to see a French Impressionist exhibit.
  a. The Metropolitan is an exhibit.
  b. The Metropolitan is a museum.
  c. The Metropolitan is an Impressionist painter.

General term: <u>museum</u>

Specific term: <u>Metropolitan</u>

_____ **2.** Cecilia put the Blizzards in her locker along with her boots and poles. She would not need her skis or other equipment until the racing camp started next week.

a. Blizzards are snowstorms.

b. Blizzards are ski boots.

c. Blizzards are skis.

General term: _____

Specific term: _____

_____ 3. Reginald packed to leave for Newport News. He was excited about his opportunity to work in a southern city.

a. Newport News is a southern city.

b. Newport News is a newspaper.

c. Newport News is a news stand.

General term: _____

Specific term: _____

_____ 4. Maribella promised to meet her friends at the Galleria at 6:30 p.m. With its glittering strings of lights over the ice rink, exclusive department stores, glass-ceiling restaurants, and highrise hotels, she thought it was the most glamorous mall she had ever visited.

a. The Galleria is an ice rink.

b. The Galleria is a highrise hotel.

c. The Galleria is a mall.

General term: _____

Specific term: _____

_____ 5. Fredrick loved the DeLorean. Riding in the car made him feel like Michael J. Fox in the movie *Back to the Future*.

a. The DeLorean is a car.

b. The DeLorean is a movie.

c. The DeLorean is the name of an actor in the movie *Back to the Future*.

General term: _____

Specific term: _____

Causal Inferences

We must also make inferences when we read about one event causing another event, or **cause/effect** relationships. Review the sentences below. In order to explain why the dogs had been following the ladies, what two inferences do we need to make?

> The two ladies ran to meet the bus—four shopping bags in each hand. It seemed as though all of the dogs in New York City had been following them. The driver closed the door just in time to keep the dogs out of the bus. As they sat down, they began to recount their purchases—5 loaves of Paska bread, 2 Polish hams, and 12 rings of garlic kilbasa (sausage). What a feast they would have during the Ukrainian Easter holidays.

First, we would make the connection between the shopping bags and the purchase of the meat and draw the conclusion that the shopping bags were filled with meat. We could also draw the conclusion that the dogs were following the shopping bags because dogs love meat.

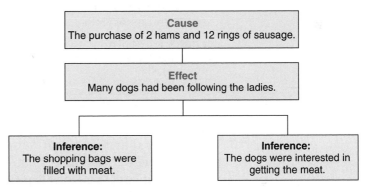

| **Cause** |
| The purchase of 2 hams and 12 rings of sausage. |

| **Effect** |
| Many dogs had been following the ladies. |

| **Inference:** | **Inference:** |
| The shopping bags were filled with meat. | The dogs were interested in getting the meat. |

EXERCISE
7-5

Identifying Causal Inferences

Read the sentences below and choose the letter that best explains the causal inference. The first one has been done for you.

   b   **1.** Although he was very intelligent, Tylor failed all of the biology exams. He had developed a streamlined method for studying. He never felt the need to read the biology textbook. Instead he memorized the answers from old biology exams found on file in the library.

  a. Tylor is failing biology because he is not very intelligent.

  b. Tylor is failing biology because he does not read the text-book.

  c. Tylor is failing biology because he is unfamiliar with the biology exam format.

Cause: <u>Tylor never felt the need to read the textbook</u>

Event: <u>Failure</u>

_____ 2. Lemar, a full-time student in Atlanta, studies twice as many hours as his friend Summer, who is a full-time student in Los Angeles. Although Summer would like to study more hours to get higher grades, she works a full-time job.

  a. Summer doesn't study as much as Lemar because she doesn't have as much free time (she works a full-time job).

  b. Summer doesn't study as much as Lemar because she lives in Los Angeles.

  c. Summer doesn't study as much as Lemar because Lemar is a full-time student.

Cause: _____

Event: _____

_____ 3. Wilkie charged that Roosevelt wanted to take the United States into the war (World War II). "If you reelect him," he told one audience, "you may expect war in April 1941," to which Roosevelt replied, "I have said this before, but I shall say it again and again and again: Your boys are not going to be sent into any foreign wars." In November Roosevelt won the election with the electoral count 449 to 82. (Garraty and Carnes 775)

  a. Wilkie wanted to help Roosevelt get reelected because Roosevelt promised to lead the country into the war.

  b. Wilkie told one audience that Roosevelt would lead the country into war because he was trying to help Roosevelt get reelected.

c. Roosevelt won the election because he promised not to get the United States involved in the war.

Cause: _____

Event: _____

4. Vitamins A, D, E, and K dissolve in fat, but not in water. They are stored in fat cells where they are available on demand. It also means that these vitamins can build up to toxic (poisonous or deadly) levels if taken well beyond normal requirements. For example, high doses of vitamin A can result in fatigue, headache, dizziness, blurred vision, dry skin, nausea, and liver damage. Vitamin D toxicity occurs at just four to five times its RDA, making vitamin D the most toxic vitamin. Such high levels of the vitamin are reached using vitamin supplements, not through a normal diet. Cardiac (heart) and kidney damage can result. (Stanitski et al. 444)

   a. Fat soluble vitamins need not be taken daily because they can build up to toxic levels.

   b. High doses of vitamin D are safe because toxicity occurs at just four to five times its RDA.

   c. A normal diet can cause kidney damage because vitamin D is stored in fat cells.

Cause: _____

Event: _____

5. Modern waste disposal facilities (trash dumps) are covered and lined to prevent waste from leaking into the surrounding ground. Landfill linings and coverings create oxygen-free conditions that slow down bacterial and fungal action. Recent excavations (digging out) of old landfills have found 37-year-old newspapers that are still readable and five-year-old hotdogs that, while hardly edible (not able to be eaten), are at least recognizable. (Stanitski et al. 363)

   a. Many substances break down slowly or not at all when buried and covered with landfill linings.

   b. Newspapers are made of substances that do not break down.

   c. Hotdogs never rot.

Cause: _____

Event: _____

—

Metonymy: Inferences About People

Often we make inferences without even realizing it. We use what linguists call **metonymy**, or the use of symbols to simplify communication. We take a part of something we know very well and use it to symbolize something else with which it is associated. For example,

> As she collected the papers from the 500 students in the auditorium, the professor told the Dean, "*The red cap* snored through the entire exam."

The inference here is that a student who was wearing a red cap snored during the exam. To the professor, it is easier to describe what the student is wearing than to sort through a list of 500 names to try to identify the student.

| EXERCISE 7-6 | **Identifying Metonymy: Inferences About People** |

Read the sentences below and explain what the italicized word or phrase stands for. The first one has been explained for you.

1. Monique Carbeau and Mitchell Armelle headed to the registration table as the man with the bullhorn shouted out "*A through D* come to this table."

   "A through D" refers to: <u>all of the people whose last names begin with letters A, B, C, or D, including Monique Carbeau and Mitchell Armelle.</u>

2. The bartender told the waiter, "No more drinks for *the blonde*; she's had enough!"

"The blonde" refers to: _____

_____

3. The ticket officer told his partner, "*The Chevy* has to pay a fine for parking next to the fire hydrant."

"The Chevy" refers to: ~~are~~ The person

_____

4. The sports announcer called out to the football fans, "Once again, *the Blue and White* wins the game!"

"The blue and white" refers to: The Colts

_____

5. The waitress said to the cook, "*The ham and cheese* wants another order of chips."

"The ham and cheese" stands for: The customer

_____

Metonymy: Inferences About Places

We also use inferences to let a place stand for events that occurred there. Look at the example below:

This is becoming another *Watergate*.

This sentence implies that people are illegally gathering information just as aides to President Nixon did when they bugged the Hotel Watergate.

A place can also stand for an organization that is located at that place. Read the example below and note the inference.

The White House said today that the economy was improving.

Here "The White House" refers to the president and the members of his cabinet.

Finally, the date of an event can symbolize what happened on that day.

Nine-eleven has changed the world.

"Nine-eleven" stands for the terrorist attacks on the World Trade Center in New York City and the Pentagon in Washington, D.C., that took place on September 11, 2001.

EXERCISE 7-7	Identifying Metonymy: Inferences About Places

Read the sentences below and explain what the italicized word or phrase stands for. The first one has been done for you.

1. Yesterday *Wall Street* reported an upswing in the economy.

Wall Street refers to: <u>the entire U.S. investing network that is located in New York. The meaning implied is that the financial institutions in the United States will soon start making a profit again.</u>

2. *North Korea* said today that they had no weapons of mass destruction.

North Korea refers to: _____

_____

3. *Hollywood* made millions when the latest film turned out to be a smash hit.

Hollywood refers to: ___MOVIES_____

_____

4. All week, summer heat waves caused *L.A.* to suffer rolling black-outs as temperatures climbed into the high 90s.

L.A. refers to: ___People of L.A._____

_____

5. *Houston* was back in the swing today as the Astros played their first game in the Astrodome.

Houston refers to: ̲A̲S̲T̲R̲O̲S̲ ̲̲̲̲̲̲̲̲̲̲̲̲̲̲̲̲̲̲̲̲̲̲̲̲

̲̲

TYPES OF REASONING

Two types of reasoning are connected with making an inference and drawing a conclusion: deductive reasoning and inductive reasoning.

Deductive reasoning starts with a statement and provides reasons, examples, or data to support the statement.

Example:

Statement: Secondary smoke is harmful to non-smokers.

Reason 1: Over thirty thousand non-smokers die each year from passive smoke.

Reason 2: Being exposed to secondary smoke for one hour per week does 20% as much damage to a person's arteries as smoking does.

Inductive reasoning starts with reasons, examples, or data and then draws a conclusion based on the information.

Example:

Reason 1: Over thirty thousand non-smokers die each year from passive smoke.

Reason 2: Being exposed to secondary smoke for one hour per week does 20% as much damage to a person's arteries as smoking does.

Conclusion: Therefore, researchers have concluded that secondary smoke is harmful to non-smokers.

DRAWING CONCLUSIONS

When we make an inference, we start with a guess and then we read or gather more information that confirms or verifies our guess. If the information checks out, our inference is correct. If later information or clues do not make sense in light of our first guess, we must rethink the situation and make a new guess.

Drawing a conclusion is different from making an inference. Instead of starting with a guess and looking for facts to verify our thoughts, we look at the facts first. Then we create a logical explanation based on the facts. Thus, we can define drawing a conclusion as putting together an explanation based on facts. Look at the paragraph below. How do we know that both Olivia and Luke passed the exam?

> All of the students in Professor Young's class passed the final exam. Olivia and Luke were in Professor Young's class. Therefore, we can conclude that Olivia and Luke passed the final exam.

First we look at the information provided:

Fact 1: All of the students in Professor Young's class passed the final exam.

Fact 2: Olivia and Luke were in Professor Young's class.

And then, we make an inference based on that information.

Inference: Since we know that Olivia and Luke were in Professor's Young's class and that all of the students in Professor Young's class passed the final exam, we have no reason to believe that Olivia and Luke were exceptions. From this, we draw the logical conclusion that Olivia and Luke passed the final exam.

Conclusion: <u>Olivia and Luke passed the final exam.</u>

EXERCISE
7-8

Drawing Reasonable Conclusions

Draw a reasonable conclusion from the facts provided. Follow the steps as described above. The first conclusion has been done for you.

1. All Galveston residents must evacuate one day before a hurricane strikes. The hurricane is predicted to strike tomorrow.

   Fact 1: All Galveston residents must evacuate one day before a hurricane strikes.

   Fact 2: The hurricane is predicted to strike tomorrow.

Inference: Today is one day before the hurricane strikes.

Conclusion: <u>All Galveston residents must evacuate today.</u>

2. In Texas, teenagers can get a learner's permit to drive a car at age fourteen if they have no one to drive them to school. Carlos is age fifteen and has no one to drive him to school.

Fact 1: In Texas, teenagers can get a learner's permit to drive a car at age fourteen if they have no one to drive them to school.

Fact 2: Carlos is age fifteen and has no one to drive him to school.

Inference: Carlos's situation satisfies state requirements.

Conclusion: _____

_____

3. The M & D Moving Company requires a two-week notice to move a load of furniture. Katrina wants to move her furniture to a new apartment but can only give M & D's Moving Company one week's notice.

Fact 1: M & D requires a two-week notice.

Fact 2: Katrina can give only one week's notice.

Inference: Katrina does not have enough time to give the M & D Moving Company notice.

Conclusion: *She will give one week notice.*

4. The Mad Magic Band only hires drummers with five years of stage experience.

Fact 1: Mad Magic Band requires drummers to have five years of stage experience.

Fact 2: Ryan has ten years of stage experience.

Inference: Ryan has more experience than required.

Conclusion: _He will get in_

5. Takemoney University requires 130 credits to graduate with a four-year degree. Antoine has 128 credits.

Fact 1: Takemoney University requires 130 credits to graduate with a four-year degree.

Fact 2: Antoine has 128 credits.

Inference: Antoine needs two more credits to graduate.

Conclusion: _Needs one more class_

Getting Ahead in College Box 7.1

CAN YOU TELL THE DIFFERENCE BETWEEN FACTS AND INFERENCES?

Carefully read the following report developed by William Haney (1973) and the observations based on it. Indicate whether you think the observations are true, false, or doubtful on the basis of the information presented in the report. Write **T** if the observation is definitely true, **F** if the observation is definitely false, and **?** if the observation may be either true or false. Judge each observation in order. Do not reread the observations after you have indicated your judgment, and do not change any of your answers.

A well-liked college teacher had just completed making up the final examinations and had turned off the lights in the office. Just then a tall, broad figure appeared and demanded the examination. The professor opened the

(continued on next page)

drawer. Everything in the drawer was picked up and the individual ran down the corridor. The dean was notified immediately.

_____ **1.** The thief was tall and broad.

_____ **2.** The professor turned off the lights.

_____ **3.** A tall figure demanded the examination.

_____ **4.** The examination was picked up by someone.

_____ **5.** The examination was picked up by the professor.

_____ **6.** A tall figure appeared after the professor turned off the lights in the office.

_____ **7.** The man who opened the drawer was the professor.

_____ **8.** The professor ran down the corridor.

_____ **9.** The drawer was never actually opened.

_____ **10.** Three persons are referred to in this report.

Thinking Critically About Facts and Inferences

This test is designed to trap you into making inferences and treating them as facts. Statement 3 is true (it's in the report). Statement 9 is false (the drawer was opened), but all other statements are inferences and should have been marked with a question mark (?). Review these eight statements to see why you cannot be certain that any of them are either true or false. (DeVito 216)

SITUATIONS THAT REQUIRE INFERENCE

Much of our daily communication depends heavily on inferences. Very few forms of writing, such as legal contracts and technical information, are written in a straightforward precise manner. In most situations it is assumed that people have a certain amount of world knowledge and that every detail does not need to be spelled out. Take, for example, the statement "I missed the boat on that one." Even though the phrase "missed the boat" does not make much sense literally, everyone would understand what you meant. It is not necessary to explain that you misunderstood something that others knew about.

Imagery

Imagery is the process by which an author's description helps the reader to create mental images—we try to create a picture of the author's experiences in our minds. When authors use imagery, we, as readers, interpret the mood or the meaning by making inferences based on the images or descriptions the author presents. Let's look at some images that S. E. Hinton provides in her novel *The Outsiders*. How can we tell that the character in this story is very frightened?

> I was sweating something fierce, although I was cold. I could feel my palms getting clammy and the perspiration running down my back. I get like that when I'm real scared. I glanced around for a pop bottle or a stick or something—Steve Randle, Soda's best buddy, had once held off four guys with a busted pop bottle—but there was nothing.

Through the use of imagery the writer shows us that the character is terribly frightened. The clues that help us to experience this perspective lie in the descriptive details in the passage. The main character, Ponyboy, is so frightened that he:

- is sweating,

- feels cold,

- has clammy palms, and

- can feel the perspiration running down his neck.

We can also infer from the passage that the character is frightened because he describes himself as experiencing these conditions when he is afraid. Also, we know how dangerous broken glass is and we can imagine how frightened someone must be if they wanted to use it in self-defense. "I glanced around for a pop bottle . . . —Steve . . . once held off four guys with a busted pop bottle."

 ## A Reading in Narrative

Read the following excerpts from *The Outsiders* by S. E. Hinton and decide what inference we should make based on the images the author projects. The first one has been done for you.

_____b_____ **1.** I like walking. I about decided I didn't like it so much, though, when I spotted that red Corvair trailing me. I was almost two blocks from home then, so I started walking a little faster. I had never been jumped, but I had seen Johnny after four Socs got hold of him, and it wasn't pretty. Johnny was scared of his own shadow after that. Johnny was sixteen then.

    a. Ponyboy was not afraid because he was only two blocks from home.

    b. The Socs were trailing Ponyboy for the purpose of hurting him.

    c. Ponyboy was a little scared, but he didn't think the Socs would hurt him as they had hurt Johnny.

_____ **2.** "Need a haircut, greaser?" The medium-sized blond pulled a knife out of his back pocket and flipped the blade open. I finally thought of something to say.

    "No." I was backing up, away from that knife. Of course I backed right into one of them. They had me down in a second. They had my arms and legs pinned down and one of them was sitting on my chest with his knees on my elbows, and if you don't think that hurts, you're crazy. I could smell English Leather shaving lotion and stale tobacco, and I wondered foolishly if I would suffocate before they did anything. I was scared so bad I was wishing I would. I fought to get loose, and almost did for a second; then they tightened up on me and the one on my chest slugged me a couple of times. So I lay still, swearing at them between gasps. A blade was held against my throat.

    "How'd you like that haircut to begin just below the chin?"

    a. The Socs intended to cut off Ponyboy's hair.

    b. The Socs intended to beat up Ponyboy.

    c. The Socs intended to slit Ponyboy's throat.

_____ **3.** It occurred to me then that they could kill me. I went wild. I started screaming for Soda, Darry, anyone. Someone put his hand over my mouth, and I bit it as hard as I could, tasting the blood running through my teeth. I heard a muttered curse and got slugged again, and they were stuffing a handkerchief in my mouth. One of them kept saying, "Shut him up, for Pete's sake, shut him up!"

    a. Ponyboy's cries for help had no effect on the Socs.

    b. The Socs had complete control now.

    c. Ponyboy's cries for help alarmed the Socs.

_____ 4. Then there were shouts and the pounding of feet, and the Socs jumped up and left me lying there, gasping. I lay there and wondered what in the world was happening—people were jumping over me and running by me and I was too dazed to figure it out. Then someone had me under the armpits and was hauling me to my feet. It was Darry.

    a. Ponyboy knew immediately that Darry had come to help him.

    b. The Socs were not afraid of Darry.

    c. Ponyboy was too confused to understand what was happening.

_____ 5. "Are you alright, Ponyboy?"

He was shaking me and I wished he'd stop.

Darry jammed his fists in his pockets.

"They didn't hurt you too bad, did they?"

They did. I was smarting and aching and my chest was sore and I was so nervous my hands were shaking and I wanted to start bawling, but you just don't say that to Darry.

"I'm okay."

    a. Ponyboy lied to Darry by saying he was okay.

    b. The Socs didn't hurt Ponyboy.

    c. Ponyboy felt calm after the Socs ran away.

Metaphor

Authors require us to make inferences when they use metaphors in their writing. A **metaphor** is a comparison of two unlike things without using the words "like" or "as." The metaphor simply states that one thing *is* another. We have to use our inference skills to figure out the implied comparison. For example, look at the two sentences below. The first uses "like" to make a comparison while the second does not.

Abby can swim like a fish!

We know that a human being does not have a tail and cannot breathe under water, or even dart around as fast as a fish. But the inference is that Abby can swim better than many people.

When it comes to swimming, Abby is a real fish!

We know, of course, that a human being is a human being and not a fish. However, by saying that a human being *is* a fish, we imply that compared with other human beings, Abby swims better.

EXERCISE 7-9

Explaining Metaphor

Read each metaphor and explain its implied meaning. The first one has been done for you.

1. The lake was sheer glass in its stillness.

   Implied Meaning: The lake looked like glass because nothing was disturbing the water.

2. This place is a real ghost town.

   Implied Meaning: _____

   _____

3. Although he said he would stand up for his rights, Rashawn was a mouse at the meeting.

   Implied Meaning: He was shy

   _____

4. The Dean was a real grizzly when the budget didn't balance.

   Implied Meaning: He was mean

   _____

5. Olga and Boris get along so well; they are two peas in a pod.

Implied Meaning: _They are_ _____

~~of a kind~~ _____

Getting Ahead in College Box 7.2

THE PRONUNCIATION OF VOCABULARY

Groups of two or three consonants that make one sound are called digraphs. The letters that create the digraph combine to make a new sound—we don't hear every letter pronounced. Some examples of digraphs are:

ch as in **ch**urch   **thr** as in **thr**ough

ph as in **ph**oto   **wh** as in **wh**at

sh as in **sh**oe   **wh** as in **wh**o

th as in **th**ought   **th** as in **th**ing

Fill in a digraph to complete the word in each sentence.

1. I like walking. I about decided I didn't like it so much, th_____ when I spotted th_____ red Corvair trailing me.

2. Johnny was scared of his own sh_____ after that.

3. Johnny was sixteen th_____.

4. Then th_____ were sh_____ and the pounding of feet, and the Socs jumped up and left me lying there, gasping.

5. I lay th_____ and wondered wh_____ in the world was happening.

6. I was smarting and aching and my ch_____ was sore and I was so nervous my hands were sh_____.

Idioms

Sometimes authors use idioms to emphasize a point. **Idioms** are colorful expressions that project an image of a common situation. Idioms require inference skills especially if we are unfamiliar with the expression. Let's look at some common expressions:

This test will be a *piece of cake.*

Most people eat cake when they are relaxed and taking it easy, as at a party. This expression implies that the test taker can relax because the test will be easy. Look at the idiom below and decide which of the following inferences best explains it.

Juanita is really *walking on eggshells* by telling her employer she is too ill to work while she is really going to the beach.

a. There are eggshells along the beach.

b. Juanita cannot go to work because she stepped on some eggshells.

c. Juanita's untrue excuse for skipping work could cause her problems.

The idiom is not literal. In other words, it does not mean exactly what it says but projects a picture that emphasizes a point. In this case, "c" is the correct answer. The phrase "walking on eggshells" is meant to emphasize the point that her relationship with her employer could fall apart as easily as eggshells crumble if someone found out that she was giving a false reason for not being at work.

| EXERCISE 7-10 | **Explaining Idioms** |

Choose the letter for the answer that best explains the idiom. The first one has been done for you.

_____b_____ **1.** It's *raining cats and dogs.*

a. A lot of cats go outside when it rains.

b. It is raining extremely hard.

c. Cats and dogs are falling from the sky.

_____ 2. *Time flies* when you are having fun.
    a. When people are having a good time, they throw their clocks into the air.
    b. Clocks can sometimes fly through the air.
    c. The time passes quickly when you are enjoying yourself.

_____ 3. Finding your contact lens in the dark movie theater will be like *finding a needle in a haystack.*
    a. People often find needles in haystacks.
    b. It will be almost impossible to find.
    c. It will be easy to find.

_____ 4. Joanna has a *green thumb* for gardening.
    a. Joanna's thumb is green.
    b. Working in a garden stains Joanna's hands, including her thumbs, green.
    c. Joanna is good at gardening.

_____ 5. As soon as Clifford realized that he had *bought a lemon*, he drove it straight back to the showroom floor.
    a. Clifford's car has many problems that need to be fixed before it will work properly.
    b. Clifford's car is shaped like a lemon.
    c. Clifford's car is painted yellow.

Analogy

Analogies are word comparisons that are used to help us understand the relationship between two ideas. For example, if you want to make the point that going to reading class without a book defeats the whole purpose for being in class, you might draw up a relationship like this:

> Going to class without a book is like a nearsighted person going to a movie without his glasses.

The similarity in the two situations is that a student without a book and a nearsighted movie-goer without eyeglasses will both miss a great deal of information and might get very little out of the experience.

Usually, when people begin working with analogies, they practice first with words before trying to find similarities in statements. Words can have many different relationships, but it is helpful to start with like-meaning words and opposite words. Look at the example below:

Chalk is to a chalkboard   just as   a pen is to paper.

The similarity is that both chalk and a pen are utensils to write with and are matched with the things that they are used to write on.

Often, the analogy is written out like this:

chalk: chalkboard   just as   pen: paper

EXERCISE
7-11
Explaining Analogies

Word puzzles. Find the missing word by drawing an analogy.

1. driver: car   just as   pilot: _____

2. shoe: foot   just as   glove: _____

3. sun: daytime   just as   moon: _night_

4. library: studying just as   dining hall: _eat_

5. athlete: sport   just as   musician: _music_

A Reading in American History

Did you know that in the 1960s, the United States and the former Soviet Union came very close to starting a nuclear war? Read the following selection to gain an understanding of this historical event. Comprehension questions follow each paragraph and are meant to be completed as you read through the selection.

Vocabulary in Context

Complete the vocabulary exercise before reading the selection to learn the new terms. The first one has been done for you.

    a. Bay of Pigs Invasion—the American CIA's unsuccessful attempt to get Cubans who were against the Cuban leader Castro to overthrow the Cuban government

    b. Castro—president of Cuba

    c. Kennedy—president of the United States during the early 1960s.

    d. aerial photographs—pictures taken from above the earth by airplanes

    e. Khrushchev—president of the former Soviet Union (now Russia and surrounding states)

_____d_____ **1.** The spy planes took _____ of Cuba so they could determine if the country had nuclear weapons.

_____ **2.** _____ wanted to increase the Soviet Union's stockpile of nuclear weapons so the Soviet Union would not be seen as weaker than the United States.

_____ **3.** The president of Cuba, _____, wanted the Soviet Union to bring nuclear weapons to Cuba to stop the Americans from trying to overthrow his government.

_____ **4.** During the _____, the American government tried to get Cubans who were against Castro to overthrow the Cuban government.

_____ **5.** Since Cuba is only 90 miles from the southernmost part of Florida, _____ (the president of the United States in 1962) wanted to keep Cuba from having nuclear weapons.

The Cuban Missile Face-off

Using your logical reasoning skills, decide from the choices which conclusion makes the most sense. First read the paragraph and the breakdown of the facts. Then finish the inference and decide on the best conclusion.

    1. In 1962 a new crisis arose. Fearful of the American threat after the Bay of Pigs invasion, Castro asked for Soviet assistance. American aerial photographs taken in October 1962 revealed that the USSR had begun to place what Kennedy considered offensive missiles (missiles to attack another country) on Cuban soil, although Cuba insisted they were defensive (missiles to defend against an attack).

Fact 1: Fearful of the American threat, Castro asked for Soviet assistance.

Fact 2: The USSR began to place missiles in Cuba.

Inference: Castro wanted missiles in Cuba because <u>he was fearful of the American threat.</u>

_____ **Conclusion:** The missiles were:

    a. offensive.

    b. defensive.

2. With Russian weapons installed just 90 miles from American shores, Kennedy was this time determined to win a confrontation with the Soviet Union over Cuba.

Fact 1: Russian weapons were installed 90 miles from American shores.

Fact 2: Kennedy was this time determined to win a confrontation with the Soviet Union.

Inference: The adjective "Russian" refers to: _____.

_____ **Conclusion:** The country that installed the weapons was:

    a. Cuba.

    b. The Soviet Union.

3. Kennedy went on nationwide TV to tell the American people about the missiles and to demand their removal. He declared that the United States would not shrink from the risk of nuclear war and announced a naval "quarantine" around Cuba to prevent Soviet ships from bringing in additional missiles.

Fact 1: Kennedy went on nationwide TV to demand the removal of the weapons.

Fact 2: Kennedy declared that the United States would not shrink from risk of nuclear war.

Inference: Kennedy would risk a nuclear war for: _____.

_____ **Conclusion:** Kennedy was going to:

    a. get the Soviet missiles out of Cuba even if it meant nuclear war.

    b. negotiate with the Soviet Union to prevent nuclear war.

4. As Soviet ships steamed toward the island and the nations stood "eyeball to eyeball" at the brink, the world held its breath. After several days, the tension broke when **Khrushchev** called the Soviet ships back. Khrushchev then sent Kennedy a long letter pledging to remove the missiles if the United States lifted the quarantine and promised to stay out of Cuba altogether. A second letter demanded that America remove its missiles from Turkey as well. The United States agreed to the first letter, ignored the second, and said nothing about its intention, already voiced, of removing its own missiles from Turkey. With that, the crisis ended.

    Fact 1: Khrushchev then sent Kennedy a long letter pledging to remove the missiles.

    Fact 2: The United States agreed to the first letter and the crisis ended.

    Inference: Khrushchev removed the:_____.

    _____ **Conclusion:** The United States and the Soviet Union

        a. went to war.

        b. avoided war.

5. The Cuban missile crisis was the most terrifying confrontation of the Cold War. One consequence of the crisis was the installation of a Soviet-American hotline to avoid similar episodes in the future. Another consequence was the USSR's determination to increase its nuclear arsenal so that it would never again be exposed as inferior to the United States.

    Statement 1: The Cuban missile crisis was the most terrifying confrontation of the Cold War.

Statement 2: One consequence of the crisis was the installation of a Soviet-American hot line to avoid similar episodes in the future.

Inference: The Cuban M.issile crisis was terrifying to: _____.

_____ **Conclusion:** A Soviet-American hotline would:

   a. decrease nuclear weapons.

   b. lessen the fear of nuclear war.

(Nash et al. 733–34)

Getting Ahead in College Box 7.3

IDIOMS: CUBAN MISSILE CRISIS

Reread the sentences below. Choose the letter that best explains what the idiom in each sentence means.

_____ **1.** He declared that <u>the United States would not shrink</u> from the risk of nuclear war.

   a. The United States would become smaller.

   b. The United States would be willing to go to war with another country.

_____ **2.** As Soviet ships steamed toward the island and <u>the nations stood "eyeball to eyeball"</u> at the brink, the world held its breath.

   a. The two presidents stared each other in the eyes.

   b. The military ships of the two nations were positioned very near each other.

_____ **3.** As Soviet ships steamed toward the island and the nations stood "eyeball to eyeball" at the brink, <u>the world held its breath</u>.

   a. All the people in the world held their breath.

   b. All the people in the world were very nervous about a possible nuclear war.

A Reading in Interpersonal Communications

Read the following selection to gain an understanding about the differences in the way that men and women listen. Decide from the choices which conclusion makes the most sense. Then, list facts from the passage that support the conclusion you've made. Comprehension questions follow each paragraph and are meant to be completed as you read through the selection.

Vocabulary in Context

Complete the vocabulary exercise before reading the selection to learn the new terms. The first one has been identified for you.

a. rapport—an understanding relationship

b. subsequent—following or next

c. empathic—sensitive to what another person is going through

d. posture—stand; attitude

e. ingratiate—to try to please others so they will like you

_____b_____ 1. _____ research studies confirmed what the first researcher discovered.

_____ 2. Women who called counselors were helped by a listener who provided _____ support.

_____ 3. Men take an argumentative _____ while listening; it seems as though they are thinking of ways to make others adopt their point of view.

_____ 4. Women use listening to build _____ with others for the purpose of establishing a closer relationship.

_____ 5. Women do not intentionally _____ themselves, while men do not intentionally try to prove that they are superior.

Gender and Listening

_____a_____ **1.** Men and women learn different styles of listening just as they learn different styles of using verbal and nonverbal messages. Not surprisingly, these different styles can create major difficulties in opposite sex interpersonal communication. According to Deborah Tannen (1990) in her best-selling *You Just Don't Understand: Women and Men in Conversation*, women seek to build **rapport** and establish a closer relationship and use listening to achieve these ends. Men, on the other hand, will play up their expertise, emphasize it, and use it in dominating the interaction. Women play down their expertise and are more interested in communication supportiveness. Tannen argues that the goal of a man in conversation is to be given respect and so he seeks to show his knowledge and expertise. A woman, on the other hand, seeks to be liked and so she expresses agreement.

   a. Women have different listening styles than men.

   b. Both men and women express agreement in conversation in order to be liked.

   c. Men try to build rapport and establish a closer relationship through conversation.

What facts support your conclusion? _____

_____

_____

_____ **2.** Men and women also show that they are listening in different ways. In conversation, a woman is more apt to give lots of listening cues such as interjecting "yeah, uh-uh," nodding in agreement, and smiling. A man is more likely to listen quietly, without giving lots of listening cues as feedback. **Subsequent** research seems to confirm Tannen's position. For example, an analysis of calls to a crisis center in Finland revealed that calls received by a female counselor were significantly longer for both men and women callers. It is likely that the greater number of listening cues given by the women encouraged the callers to keep talking. This same study also found that male callers were helped by "just listening" whereas women callers were helped by "**empathic** understanding."

  a. Males give less feedback when they listen than do females.

  b. Females in crisis are helped more by listening then by understanding.

  c. Males are more likely to encourage others to talk longer by giving listening cues.

What facts support your conclusion? _____

_____

_____

_____ 3. Tannen argues, however, that men do listen less to women than women listen to men. The reason, says Tannen, is that listening places the person in an inferior position whereas speaking places the person in a superior position. Men may seem to assume a more argumentative **posture** while listening, as if getting ready to argue. They may also appear to ask questions that are more argumentative or that seek to puncture holes in your position as a way to play up their own expertise.

  a. Women listen more to men than men listen to women.

  b. Men listen more to women than women listen to men.

  c. Women listen less to men than men listen to women.

What facts support your conclusion? _____

_____

_____

_____ **4.** Women are more likely to ask supportive questions and per-haps offer criticism that is more positive than men. Women let the speaker see that they are listening. Men, on the other hand, use fewer listening cues in conversation. Men and women act this way to both men and women; their custom-ary ways of talking do not seem to change depending on whether the listener is male or female.

    a. Men are more likely to ask supportive questions than women.

    b. Men are more likely to offer criticism that is more positive than women.

    c. Women use the same ways of talking to both males and females.

What facts support your conclusion? _____

_____

_____

_____ **5.** There is no evidence to show that these differences represent any negative motives on the part of men to prove themselves superior or of women to **ingratiate** themselves. (DeVito 140–41)

    a. Men and women are socialized to have different listening styles.

    b. Both men and women try to prove themselves superior while listening.

    c. Men _intentionally_ try to speak more to prove themselves superior in conversation.

What facts support your conclusion? _____

_____

_____

Getting Ahead in College Box 7.4

PARTS OF SPEECH: CONJUNCTIONS

"And" is a common connecting word. Read the groups of sentences below and connect them with the word "and."

Example

Men learn different styles of listening.

Women learn different styles of listening.

Men and women learn different styles of listening

1. They learn different styles of using verbal messages.

    They learn different styles of using nonverbal messages.

    _____

2. Women play down their expertise.

    Women are more interested in communication supportiveness.

    _____

3. Women are more likely to ask supportive questions.

    Women offer criticism that is more positive than men.

    _____

 **A Reading in Chemistry**

Read the following selection to find when vitamins can be helpful or harmful. Comprehension questions follow each paragraph and are meant to be completed as you read through the selection.

Vocabulary in Context

Complete the vocabulary exercise before reading the selection to learn the new terms. The first one has been identified for you.

a. adequate—enough; plenty

b. malnourished—not having proper nutrition

c. implications—inferences; suggestions

d. toxic—poisonous; deadly; lethal

e. cardiac—of the heart

_____b_____ **1.** It's possible to be _____ but still have eaten a lot of calories.

_____ **2.** The fact that some vitamins are not soluble has important _____ for people who take vitamins.

_____ **3.** Along with calories, your daily diet should have an _____ supply of vitamins.

_____ **4.** High doses of vitamin A can result in fatigue, headache, dizziness, blurred vision, dry skin, nausea, and liver damage. Too much vitamin D can also build up to _____ levels.

_____ **5.** Too much vitamin D can result in kidney damage and _____ damage.

Vitamins

1. Your daily diet should supply an **adequate** number of calories, but calories alone are not enough. You have already read about the essential fatty acids and amino acids that must be ingested for good health, and you are well aware that a balanced diet must also provide certain vitamins and minerals. Unfortunately, many popular foods that are high in sugars and fats are lacking in these essential micro-nutrients. It

is thus possible that a person can be overfed with excess calories but **malnourished** through a diet lacking adequate vitamins and minerals.

Fact 1: Many popular foods that are high in sugars and fats are lacking essential vitamins.

Fact 2: It's possible that a person can have an excess of calories but be malnourished because of a lack of vitamins.

Conclusion: <u>You could be malnourished if your diet is high in sugars and fats.</u>

2. Vitamins are often classified on the basis of solubilities; they either dissolve in water or in fat. Vitamins A, D, E, and K dissolve in fat, but not in water. These solubility differences among vitamins have significant **implications** for nutrition and health. Because of their fat solubility, vitamins A, D, E, and K are stored in cells rich in lipids where they are available on biological demand. This means that the fat-soluble vitamins need not be taken daily. This means that the fat-soluble vitamins can build up to **toxic** levels if taken far in excess of normal requirements. For example, high doses of vitamin A can result in fatigue, headache, dizziness, blurred vision, dry skin, nausea, and liver damage. Vitamin D toxicity occurs at just four to five times its RDA, making vitamin D the most toxic vitamin. Such high levels of the vitamin are reached using vitamin supplements, not through a normal diet. **Cardiac** and kidney damage can result.

Fact 1: The fat-soluble vitamins can build up to toxic levels if taken far in excess of normal requirements.

Fact 2: Vitamin D toxicity occurs at just four to five times its RDA, making vitamin D the most toxic vitamin.

Fact 3: High levels of vitamin D are reached by using vitamin supplements, not through a normal diet.

Conclusion: _____

_____

3. Water soluble vitamins, by contrast, are not generally stored; any unused excess is excreted in urine. Thus, they must be consumed frequently and in small doses. Unfortunately, when taken in very large doses, water-soluble vitamins can also accumulate until they reach toxic levels, although such

cases are rare. For example, there are reports that vitamin B6, taken at 10 to 30 times the recommended dose per day for extended periods, results in nerve damage, including paralysis. Even higher doses of vitamin B6 supplements, up to 1000 times the recommended dosage, have been consumed to alleviate the symptoms of pre-menstrual syndrome (PMS), again causing abnormal neurological symptoms. For most people, a balanced diet should provide all the necessary vitamins and minerals in appropriate amounts, making vitamin supplements unnecessary.

Fact 1: When taken in very large doses, water-soluble vitamins can also accumulate until they reach toxic levels.

Fact 2: Vitamin B6, taken at 10 to 30 times the recommended dose per day for extended periods, results in nerve damage, including paralysis.

Conclusion: _____

_____

4. Vitamin C must also be supplied in the diet via citrus fruits and green vegetables. An insufficient supply of the vitamin leads to scurvy, a disease in which collagen, an important structural protein, is broken down. The link between citrus fruits and scurvy was discovered more than 200 years ago when it was found that feeding British sailors limes or lime juice on long sea voyages prevented the disease. Ascorbic acid is also required for the uptake, use, and storage of iron, important in the prevention of anemia. The claims that high doses of vitamin C can prevent colds and ward off certain cancers remain largely unsubstantiated.

Fact 1: An insufficient supply of vitamin C leads to scurvy.

Fact 2: Vitamin C is supplied in the diet via citrus fruits and green vegetables.

Conclusion: _____

_____

5. The last vitamin in this overview is vitamin E, important in the maintenance of cell membranes and as protection against high concentrations of oxygen, such as those that occur in the lungs. Vitamin E is so widely distributed in foods that it is difficult to create a diet deficient in it,

although people who eat very little fat may need supplements. Vitamin E deficiency in humans has been linked with nocturnal cramping in the calves and fibrocystic breast disease. (Stanitski et al. 443–44)

Fact 1: Vitamin E is widely distributed in foods.

Fact 2: It is difficult to create a diet deficient in Vitamin E.

Conclusion: _____

_____

Visual Literacy Box 7.2 ● ● ● ● ● ● ● ● ● ● ● ● ● ● ● ● ●

Comparison Charts

Use a comparison chart to help you organize information when more than two items are being compared. To create a comparison chart:

1. Count how many items you are comparing and make that number of rows.

2. Count how many points you will be comparing and make that number of columns.

Use the reading on vitamins to finish the chart below.

	Vitamin A	Vitamin B	Vitamin C	Vitamin D	Vitamin E
Toxic level				D toxicity occurs at just four to five times its RDA.	
Dangers				Cardiac and kidney damage can result.	
Source				Sun Dairy	

Purpose and Tone

Authors write because they have something to say to a certain audience. In other words, they have a **purpose** for their writing. Mistakes in comprehension can easily happen if the reader does not recognize the author's purpose. Consider the excerpt below:

> I remember the day I started school. Me and the kids in the neighborhood, walking along with our little lunch pails, looking like we was going off to tiny jobs. 'Course, we had our mothers with us. Two blocks was a long way to go. (Mac 6)

If we understand that the author's purpose is to entertain, we accept the language errors because we know the author needs to make them in order to create the right effect. However, if we mistakenly think the author's purpose is to teach us proper English, we will be very confused.

This purpose generally directs the author's **tone** of voice or the way he feels about a chosen subject. How can you tell from the language used that the author had fond memories of his first day of school? What specific words help you understand that he felt a sense of pride in this situation? In this chapter, you learn how an author uses both purpose and tone to communicate specific messages to his audiences.

AUTHOR'S PURPOSE

The three common purposes for writing are:

■ to inform.

■ to entertain.

■ to persuade.

As readers, it is important for us to be able to distinguish between facts that are presented in an informative way and those that are presented in a persuasive way. We need to be able to recognize when the author is being serious and when he or she is being humorous. Understanding the author's purpose also helps us to identify the *main idea* of the writing. Let's look more closely at these three types of purpose.

To Inform

If the author's purpose is *to inform*, we can expect to find factual information on a given subject. College textbooks, for example, provide information on specific topics. These facts may be used to explain an idea, compare or contrast two things, show cause-and-effect relationships, define a term, illustrate a process, demonstrate solutions to problems, and so forth. The paragraph below, for example, is informative. What information does it provide? Is the author's purpose to explain an idea or compare or contrast two things? Does the author define a term or provide solutions to problems?

> Being *assertive* means recognizing your feelings and making your needs and desires clear to others. Unlike *aggression*, a far less healthy means of expression, assertiveness usually works. You can change a situation you don't like by communicating your feelings and thoughts with words that are not offensive, by focusing on specifics, and by making sure you're talking with the person who is directly responsible. (Hales 45)

This excerpt is *informative* because it provides information or facts about assertiveness. The term "assertiveness" is defined as "recognizing your feelings and making your needs and desires clear to others." The author further explains the term by giving three actions that show what it means to be assertive.

To Entertain

If the author's purpose is *to entertain*, you may read humorous, dramatic, or historical accounts. They may be either fictional (such as a mystery novel) or nonfictional (such as an autobiography). The paragraphs below are excerpts from an autobiographical novel by Bernie Mac.

> My grandma was the mayor of the neighborhood. Everybody knew my grandma. When somebody was sick, she was the first one there. Bringing soup, cleaning up. If somebody couldn't pay the rent, she organized a rent party. Other times, I got sent out to help the neighbors—even if they didn't need it.
>
> "Grandma says for you to go help Mr. Willis wash his car," my grandpa would tell me.
>
> "What for? He got a boy of his own."
>
> WHAM! Right across the back of the head. No warning. "I'll knock your eyeball out, boy! Then s*tep* on it."
>
> No idle hands in our house. Busy busy busy. We was church people, and we were there to set an example. (Mac 10)

Humor, drama, mystery, biography, autobiography, and current news stories are among the many types of writing that authors may use to entertain. The excerpt above is an autobiography that is written with much humor; therefore, it **entertains**.

To Persuade

If the author's purpose is *to persuade*, he or she will offer information that supports a certain position. When authors write to persuade, they intend to convince their audience to share their views, adopt their positions, or take a particular course of action. Sometimes an author may have plenty of factual support for an issue, but for only one side of it. Although an author may strongly favor one side of a case over another, he or she should present both sides. In order to convince the audience to see his or her **point of view** (position from which we look at a problem), the author will use persuasive strategies. The paragraph below, for example, is persuasive. What is the author's point of view? What position does he want his readers to adopt?

> Food should never be *irradiated*. Just because corporate meat executives are too lazy to have a clean *sterile* environment for packaging food doesn't mean that we should suffer high doses of radiation

every time we eat. The sterilization of unclean beef through the irradiation process causes health problems such as cancer. Scientists have known for decades that exposing red meat to high doses of radiation creates a host of known *carcinogens*, including deadly chemicals such as benzene. The public needs to write letters to congressmen and senators letting them know they will not eat dangerous food.

Although the piece is informative, we can tell the author's purpose is **to persuade**. In the first sentence, the author tells us what idea to adopt—food should never be irradiated. The author also tries to persuade us to adopt his stand by providing facts about the deadly chemicals that are created by this process. The author's final point of persuasion urges us to take action by telling our government officials that this process is dangerous and that we do not approve of it.

| EXERCISE 8-1 | **Identifying the Author's Purpose Through Titles** |

Read each of the following article and book titles and decide whether the author's purpose is to inform, to entertain, or to persuade. Explain your answer below. The first one has been done for you.

_____b_____ 1. "The Mystery of the Devil's Triangle"
   a. to inform
   b. to entertain
   c. to persuade

   Explanation: _____

   _____

_____ 2. "How to Create a PowerPoint Presentation"
   a. to inform
   b. to entertain
   c. to persuade

   Explanation: _____

   _____

_____ 3. "Why You Should Exercise Daily"
   a. to inform
   b. to entertain
   c. to persuade

   Explanation: _____

   _____

_____ 4. "Building Your Own Home"
   a. to inform
   b. to entertain
   c. to persuade

   Explanation: _____

   _____

_____ 5. "Dramatic Adventures in the Hawaiian Surf!"
   a. to inform
   b. to entertain
   c. to persuade

   Explanation: _____

   _____

_____ 6. "Laugh Yourself Silly and Other Short Stories"
   a. to inform
   b. to entertain
   c. to persuade

   Explanation: _____

   _____

_____ 7. "The Fundamentals of College Algebra"
   a. to inform
   b. to entertain
   c. to persuade

   Explanation: _____

   _____

_____ 8. "The Human Genome Project"

    a. to inform

    b. to entertain

    c. to persuade

Explanation: _____

_____

_____ 9. "Introduction to Sociology"

    a. to inform

    b. to entertain

    c. to persuade

Explanation: _____

_____

_____ 10. "The Dangers of Smoking and Why You Must Quit!"

    a. to inform

    b. to entertain

    c. to persuade

Explanation: _____

_____

EXERCISE	
8-2	**Identifying the Author's Purpose Through Sentences**

Read each of the following topic sentences and decide what the author's purpose is. Explain your answer. The first one has been done for you.

___a___ 1. There are three types of rocks: igneous, metamorphic, and sedimentary.

    a. to inform

    b. to entertain

    c. to persuade

Explanation: _____

_____

_____ C _____ 2. Astro-biologists question if there is water on the planet Mars.
    a. to inform

    b. to entertain

    c. to persuade

Explanation: _____

_____

_____ A _____ 3. There are ten good reasons why you should avoid eating junk food.
    a. to inform

    b. to entertain

    c. to persuade

Explanation: _____

_____

_____ B _____ 4. All acts of violence should be banned from the television and from the Internet.
    a. to inform

    b. to entertain

    c. to persuade

Explanation: _____

_____

_____ A _____ 5. In the United States, a president is elected to a term of four years.
    a. to inform

    b. to entertain

    c. to persuade

Explanation: _____

_____

_____ A _____ 6. Bode Miller smoked the mountain and came in first to win the race.
    a. to inform

    b. to entertain

    c. to persuade

Explanation: _____

_____

_____ 7. "Everything happens for the best," my mother said whenever
I faced disappointment.
   a. to inform

   b. to entertain

   c. to persuade

Explanation: _____

_____

_____ 8. Nuclear fuel should not be used unless scientists can determine a safe way to get rid of the waste products.
   a. to inform

   b. to entertain

   c. to persuade

Explanation: _____

_____

_____ 9. Seafaring people have always known there is a connection
between the ocean tides and the Moon.
   a. to inform

   b. to entertain

   c. to persuade

Explanation: _____

_____

_____ 10. The lawn chair pilot said that "One flight is enough!"
   a. to inform

   b. to entertain

   c. to persuade

Explanation: _____

_____

EXERCISE
8-3

Identifying the Author's Purpose Through Paragraphs

Read each of the following paragraphs and identify the author's purpose. Explain your answer. The fiirst one has been done for you.

_____a_____ 1. As rain hits the ground, it loosens soil and washes it away. As more and more rain falls and the ground continues to lose soil, a gully forms. Once water and soil particles funnel into such a gully, a stream channel is created. This erosive action may be extremely rapid, as in the erosion of sediments, or very slow, as in the erosion of solid rock. (Hewitt, Suchocki and Hewitt 603)

   a. to inform

   b. to entertain

   c. to persuade

   Explanation: _____

   _____

2. Teachers' salaries should be equal to those of the other professionals—executives, lawyers and doctors. Although often perceived as having part-time jobs, teachers spend just as many, if not more, hours at work as the other professionals. Corporate executive officers (CEOs), lawyers and doctors can hide behind their secretaries, but teachers are "on stage" all day making 500 decisions every hour that impact 30 to 150 children. Other professionals leave their work at the end of the day. However, for teachers, the end of the day with the children signals just the beginning of their workday. Papers need to be corrected; parents need to be contacted; lessons must be created—not to mention the tons of materials that must be found, sought after, or created for the next day's work. Although teachers manage large numbers of people and make countless numbers of important decisions each day, their $30,000 salaries are no match to average $700,000 corporate executive salaries.

a. to inform

b. to entertain

c. to persuade

Explanation: _____

_____

3. "The soul needs an intense, full-bodied spiritual life as much as and in the same way that the body needs food," observes psychologist Thomas Moore in *Care of the Soul.* "Just as the mind digests ideas and produces intelligence, the soul feeds on life and digests it, creating wisdom and character out of the fodder of experience."

For years, spiritual matters were rarely recognized or discussed by mental health professionals. Until 1982, fewer than 3 percent of the articles published in leading psychiatry journals focused on spirituality or religiosity. Since then dozens of scientific studies have found that spiritual beliefs and activities—such as prayer or mediation—positively affect psychological well-being and may even speed recovery from medical illness. How? "Faith provides a support community, a sense of life's meaning, a reason to focus beyond self, and a timeless perspective on life's temporary ups and downs," observes psychologist David Meyers. (Hales 54)

a. to inform

b. to entertain

c. to persuade

Explanation: _____

_____

4. Both Mike and Reese walked out of genetics class carrying their new experiments—glass jars with two fruit flies. After a few weeks the fruit flies would multiply; they were to count the number of flies with red eyes and the number with blue eyes to determine dominant characteristics. Each day they stared into their glass jars, counted red and blue, and

recorded their findings into notebooks. On the last day of the experiment, Mike wanted to get a more accurate count, but his fruit flies had all gathered at the bottom of the jar.

"Tip the jar upside down," Reese said. "Force 'em to move so you can count."

As Mike did this, the lid slipped and most of the fruit flies escaped.

"Oh, look," Reese cried. "There goes your experiment! Now you have to tell the prof that your work just flew away!"

a. to inform

b. to entertain

c. to persuade

Explanation: _____

_____

5. You go to the pantry to get ingredients for a cake. You select sugar, flour, eggs, milk, baking soda plus an assortment of other ingredients, all of which you will measure and mix in some particular fashion. If you change your measurements or alter your procedure, however, you can create any of a large number of different products—pancakes, muffins, biscuits, or who knows what—instead of a cake.

Nature is a bit like a baker. The ingredients in nature's pantry are the chemical elements. Different combinations of the elements give rise to the diversity of materials in our environment. Cotton, for instance, is made of carbon, hydrogen, and oxygen, but the same elements combined in a different way make sugar. Arranged still differently, we have a potato. (Hewitt, Suchocki and Hewitt 380)

a. to inform

b. to entertain

c. to persuade

Explanation: _____

_____

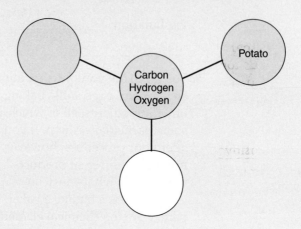

Visual Literacy Box 8.1 ● ● ● ● ● ● ● ● ● ● ● ● ● ● ●

Visualization in Chemistry

Read the paragraph below. Use the following diagram to help you form a picture of its meaning. Fill in the two blank circles.

Nature is a bit like a baker. The ingredients in nature's pantry are the chemical elements. Different combinations of the elements give rise to the diversity of materials in our environment. Cotton, for instance, is made of carbon, hydrogen, and oxygen, but the same elements combined in a different way make sugar. Arranged still differently, we have a potato.

AUTHOR'S TONE

When authors write, they voice their thoughts and feelings on paper. These thoughts can be as varied as our human emotions. As we read, it is important to recognize the author's feelings or *attitude* toward the subject so that we can understand his or her intended meaning. We call this the author's **tone of voice** or, simply, **tone**. The author gives us clues to interpret his or her mood through the words in the text. In order to identify the author's tone, imagine that the author is speaking directly to you. Ask yourself the following questions:

■ How does the author sound?

■ Does the author's or character's tone of voice sound cheerful, depressed, fearful, or worried?

■ Is the author being **objective** (sticking to the facts) or **subjective** (giving his or her opinion of the facts)?

- Is the manner of expression **formal** (following exact rules for language) or **informal** (using everyday language)?

- Does the author show excitement toward the subject or does he or she display anger?

- Is the author's mood **optimistic** (hopeful) or **pessimistic** (doubting)?

- Does the mood appear **nonchalant** (unconcerned) or **nostalgic** (homesick for things that happened in the past)?

Below is a list of words that clue us in to the author's tone. For example, if the author's tone is joyous, lighthearted, or hopeful, we sense an overall positive feeling as we read. On the other hand, if the author's tone is angry, hostile, or fearful, the overall tone becomes negative. Sometimes, the author's tone is neutral, meaning it is neither positive nor negative. Other times, tone depends on the situation presented. For example, a serious tone can be positive, as in a description of a graduation ceremony. However, it could be negative if the description is of a terrorist attack. Or a serious tone could be just plain neutral, as in a description of writing an essay.

Positive	Negative	Neutral	Contextual
amused	disappointed	informal	ironic
humorous	angry	authoritative	sarcastic
optimistic	doubtful	formal	serious
encouraging	pessimistic	nonchalant	subjective
respectful	anxious	curious	
enthusiastic	sad	nostalgic	
joyous	fearful	objective	
cheerful	critical		
lighthearted	helpless		
concerned	depressed		
loving	hostile		
hopeful			
sympathetic			
thoughtful			

Now read the following sentences and note the differences in the author's tone in each.

- **objective**: "Restaurants in the resort areas generally hire college students during the summers and holidays."

- **subjective**: "Our wait staff is made up of the most energetic and enthusiastic college-age youth."

- **formal**: "Our dining staff includes several youth who are in the process of obtaining an education from some very impressive institutions."

- **informal**: "College kids work in those dives all summer."

- **optimistic**: "College students can earn quite a bit of tuition money by working in restaurants during their summer vacations."

- **pessimistic**: "Although the students work really hard, it costs more for them to live in a seaside resort town than they can earn by working in a restaurant."

Getting Ahead in College Box 8.1

AUTHOR'S TONE

Read the passage below and place an "X" in the box next to the adjectives that describe the author's tone.

❏ lighthearted *(Positive)* ❏ sympathetic *(Positive)*   ❏ encouraging *(Positive)*

❏ helpless *(Negative)*   ❏ optimistic *(Positive)*   ❏ authoritative *(Neutral)*

❏ hopeful *(Positive)*   ❏ fearful *(Negative)*   ❏ angry *(Negative)*

❏ hostile *(Negative)*   ❏ serious *(Contextual)*   ❏ cheerful *(Positive)*

❏ joyous *(Positive)*   ❏ critical *(Negative)*   ❏ concerned *(Positive)*

❏ pessimistic *(Negative)* ❏ sarcastic *(Contextual)*   ❏ enthusiastic *(Positive)*

Feeling in Control

Although no one has absolute control over destiny, there is a great deal that we can do to control how we think, feel, and behave. By assessing our life situations realistically, we can make plans and preparations that allow us to make the most of our circumstances. By doing so, we gain a sense of mastery. In nationwide surveys, Americans who feel in control of their lives report greater psychological well-being than those who do not, as well as "extraordinarily positive feelings of happiness." (Hales 45)

| EXERCISE 8-4 | **Identifying the Author's Mood** |

Practice recognizing the author's mood by reading each sentence or paragraph below and identifying the overall tone. Determine whether each statement or paragraph is **positive**, **negative**, or **neutral**. The first one has been done for you.

___b___ 1. Angry consumers are complaining about their increasing telephone bills. They are also outraged by the many incidents in which they have been overcharged.
   a. Positive
   b. Negative
   c. Neutral

 2. The automobile industry has always recommended the use of high-grade gasoline. Although the low-grade gas shortens the life of your car, the sneaky oil industry is trying to persuade the public to buy it instead. The less efficient low-grade gas is cheaper to manufacture and brings in almost as much money as the high-grade gas.
   a. Positive
   b. Negative
   c. Neutral

___A___ 3. Although Lance Armstrong crashed his bicycle during the Tour de France, his optimistic attitude helped him win his fifth consecutive victory.
   a. Positive
   b. Negative
   c. Neutral

___C___ 4. The Newport Jazz Festival takes place every July 4th holiday at the amphitheater in Saratoga Springs, New York.
   a. Positive
   b. Negative
   c. Neutral

 5. Although the Federal Reserve is cutting interest rates, the stock market continues to go down. That means the economy

is still in the dumps and will not improve for a long, long time.
   a. Positive
   b. Negative
   c. Neutral

 6. At the end of the graduation ceremony, students whooped and tossed their caps into the air in cheerful celebration.
   a. Positive
   b. Negative
   c. Neutral

 7. Tiger Woods seems determined to use his old golf clubs again. After little success on the greens with the new clubs, Tiger cancelled his contracts with Nike in spite of the million dollar losses.
   a. Positive
   b. Negative
   c. Neutral

 8. The Eagles high-spirited quarterback, McNabb, said that this *will* be the year for the Eagles and for him to win the national title.
   a. Positive
   b. Negative
   c. Neutral

9. Fall semester will begin on August the 15th and end on December the 15th. Registration for classes will take place during the first three days of the semester.
   a. Positive
   b. Negative
   c. Neutral

10. The nine rescued coal miners emerged from the shafts smiling as the crowd greeted them joyfully.
   a. Positive
   b. Negative
   c. Neutral

Irony

Whether writing fiction or nonfiction, sometimes an author may attempt to amuse the audience through the use of humor or **irony**. Irony is when the opposite of what we normally expect to happen, happens. Usually, our knowledge of the world guides our expectations for how a situation or an event will unfold. When the opposite of what we expect to happen occurs instead, we refer to the situation as *ironic*. When authors purposely write one thing while actually meaning another, they are writing with an *ironic* tone. They do this to get the reader's attention.

Study the examples of irony below and then complete Exercise 8.5.

Example 1: Drenched from the sudden downpour, Jim finally found his umbrella in the car as the rain stopped.

Example 2: The football player was six feet tall and weighed over 200 lbs. Because of his loud boisterous voice, his team members nicknamed him "The Mouse."

EXERCISE 8-5

Identifying Irony

Read the sentences below and place a check mark next to those that describe an ironic situation or an ironic statement.

_____ 1. Juan made the Dean's list seven times.

_____ 2. "Juan made the Dean's list seven times in a row. He's not too bright, is he?"

_____ 3. If Anika had known there was a job offer on her voice mail, she would not have spent all morning searching for a job.

_____ 4. Anika spent all morning searching for a job.

_____ 5. After the boat tipped over and the tackle was lost, Zakaria exclaimed, "What a wonderful idea it was to go fishing!"

A Reading in Anthropology

Often the author's tone or mood of a story can be described by more than one adjective. Read the story below and complete the comprehension exercises that follow it. The first term has been done identified for you.

Vocabulary in Context

Complete the vocabulary exercise before reading the selection to learn the new terms.

a. **mucus**—the thick slimy substance given off by mucous membranes

b. **saturated**—soaked; filled completely

c. **anthropology**—study of the origin, development, and culture of human beings

d. **pigment**—color, tint

e. **ensuing**—following

_____e_____   1. Often Chagnon could hardly believe what he saw, and his _____ months of fieldwork brought him more and more surprises.

_____   2. A green slime always ran from the Indians' noses. This _____ was always green and disgusting.

_____   3. The disgusting green slime that ran from their noses was _____ with green powder.

_____   4. The author was disgusted with the Indians' hygiene, but soon he, too, was covered with _____

_____   5. Chagnon was depressed when he realized that he had switched into the field of _____.

The Yanomamo

[1] In just a few moments I was to meet my first Yanomamo, my first primitive man. What would it be like? . . . I looked up (from my canoe) and gasped when I saw a dozen burly, naked, filthy, hideous men staring at us down the shafts of their drawn arrows. Immense wads of green tobacco were stuck between their lower teeth and lips, making them look even more hideous, and strands of dark-green slime dripped or hung from their noses. We arrived at the village while the men were blowing a hallucinogenic drug up their noses. One of the side effects of the drug is a runny nose. The **mucus** is always **saturated** with the green powder, and the Indians usually let it run freely from their nostrils. . . . I just sat there holding my notebook, helpless and pathetic. . . .

[2] The whole situation was depressing, and I wondered why I ever decided to switch from civil engineering to **anthropology** in the first place. . . . [Soon] I was covered with red **pigment**, the result of a dozen or so complete examinations. . . . These examinations capped an otherwise grim day. The Indians would blow their noses into their hands, flick as much of the mucus off that would separate in a snap of the wrist, wipe the residue into their hair, and then carefully examine my face, arms, legs, hair, and the contents of my pockets. I said (in their language), "Your hands are dirty"; my comments were met by the Indians in the following way: they would "clean" their hands by spitting a quantity of slimy tobacco juice into them, rub them together, and then proceed with the examination.

[3] So went Napoleon Chagnon's eye-opening introduction to the Yanomamo tribe of the rain forests of Brazil. His **ensuing** months of fieldwork continued to bring surprise after surprise, and often Chagnon could hardly believe his eyes—or his nose. (Henslin 129)

Comprehension Questions

Read each sentence or paragraph and determine which word below best describes the author's tone. The first one has been done for you.

_____ c _____ **1.** I looked up (from my canoe) and gasped when I saw a dozen burly, naked, filthy, hideous men staring at us down the shafts of their drawn arrows. Immense wads of green tobacco were stuck between their lower teeth and lips, making them look even more hideous, and strands of dark-green slime dripped or hung from their noses.

    a. anxious

    b. optimistic

    c. disgusted

    d. cheerful

    e. concerned

_____ **2.** I just sat there holding my notebook, helpless and pathetic.

    a. amused

    b. useless

    c. lighthearted

    d. respectful

    e. doubtful

_____ **3.** I was covered with red pigment, the result of a dozen or so complete examinations. . . . These examinations capped an otherwise grim day.

    a. angry

    b. depressed

    c. lighthearted

    d. amused

    e. nostalgic

_____ **4.** "Your hands are dirty"; my comments were met by the Indians in the following way: they would "clean" their hands by spitting a quantity of slimy tobacco juice into them, rub them together, and then proceed with the examination.

    a. hostile

    b. disgusted

    c. joyous

    d. curious

    e. responsible

_____ **5.** So went Napoleon Chagnon's eye-opening introduction to the Yanomamo tribe of the rain forests of Brazil. His ensuing months of fieldwork continued to bring surprise after surprise, and often Chagnon could hardly believe his eyes—or his nose.

   a. hostile

   b. humorous

   c. joyous

   d. curious

   e. subjective

Questions for Discussion

Answer the following questions concerning the Yanomamo. Use complete sentences for your answers.

1. Why did the author wish he had not changed his line of work from civil engineering to anthropology?

_____

_____

2. What is the irony with regard to who was studying whom?

_____

_____

Getting Ahead in College Box 8.2

THE PRONUNCIATION OF VOCABULARY

Every word has to have a vowel because the vowel carries most of the sound in a word. The English vowels are:

a, e, i, o, u

(continued on next page)

(continued from previous page)

Any letters that are not vowels are consonants. Every vowel has two sounds: a long sound and a short sound. This lesson covers only the long sounds. Pronounce the following words and listen for the sound of the vowel:

Long	**a**	as in	g**a**me
Long	**e**	as in	sh**e**
Long	**i**	as in	s**i**gn
Long	**o**	as in	t**o**ne
Long	**u**	as in	**u**niform

Read the paragraph below and underline all of the words that contain long vowel sounds. Then highlight the letter that has the long vowel sound.

I looked up [from my canoe] and gasped when I saw a dozen burly, <u>na</u>ked, filthy, hideous men staring at us down the shafts of their drawn arrows. Immense wads of green tobacco were stuck between their lower teeth and lips, making them look even more hideous, and strands of dark-green slime dripped or hung from their noses. We arrived at the village while the men were blowing a hallucinogenic drug up their noses. One of the side effects of the drug is a runny nose. The mucus is always saturated with the green powder, and the Indians usually let it run freely from their nostrils. . . . I just sat there holding my notebook, helpless and pathetic.

A Reading in Humanities

Read the article below to find out why some people believe that television violence is not the real cause of violence in America. After reading the selection, complete the comprehension exercises that follow it.

Vocabulary in Context

Complete the vocabulary exercise before reading the selection to learn the new terms. The first term has been identified for you

a. **imitate**—copy; try to be like

b. **exploitative**—manipulative; using in a selfish or unfair way

c. **assault**—physical attack

d. **inflicted**—caused by hitting

e. **elicited**—drew out; brought out

_____b_____ 1. Influenced by an _____ media, the public thinks of teens as a robot-like generation.

_____ 2. Children _____ adults because they want to be like them.

_____ 3. In October 1996, the Department of Health and Human Services reported 565,000 serious injuries that abusive parents _____ on children and teenagers in 1993.

_____ 4. Although television is blamed for violence, 40,000 children die each year from parental _____.

_____ 5. Although it was reported that large numbers of children are injured or killed by abusive parents, this report _____ no comment from government officials.

Stop Blaming Kids and TV

[1] "Children have never been very good at listening to their elders," James Baldwin wrote in *Nobody Knows My Name*. "But they have never failed to **imitate** them." This basic truth has all but disappeared as the public increasingly treats teenagers as a robot-like population under sway of an **exploitative** media. White House officials lecture film, music, Internet, fashion, and pop-culture moguls and accuse them of programming kids to smoke, drink, shoot up, have sex, and kill.

[2] So do conservatives, led by William Bennett and Dan Quayle. Professional organizations are also into media bashing. In its famous report on youth risks, the Carnegie Corporation devoted a full chapter to media influences.

[3]   Progressives are no exception. *Mother Jones* claims it has "proof that TV makes kids violent." And the Institute for Alternative Media emphasizes, "the average American child will witness . . . 200,000 acts of [TV] violence by the time that child graduates from high school."

[4]   None of these varied interests note that during the eighteen years between a child's birth and graduation from high school, there will be fifteen million cases of real violence in American homes grave enough to require hospital emergency treatment. These **assaults** will cause ten million serious injuries and 40,000 deaths to children. In October 1996, the Department of Health and Human Services reported 565,000 serious injuries that abusive parents **inflicted** on children and youths in 1993. The number is up fourfold since 1986.

[5]   The Department of Health report disappeared from the news in one day. It **elicited** virtually no comment from the White House, Republicans, or law-enforcement officials. Nor from Carnegie scholars, whose 150-page study, "Great Transitions: Preparing Adolescents for a New Century," devotes two sentences to household violence. The left press took no particular interest in the story, either.

[6]   All sides seem to agree that fictional violence, sex on the screen, Joe Camel, beer-drinking frogs, or naked bodies on the Internet pose a bigger threat to children than do actual beatings, rape, or parental addictions! (Males)

Comprehension Questions

Choose the best answer that completes each sentence below. The first one has been done for you.

_____c_____ 1. The author's purpose is:
       a. to inform.
       b. to entertain.
       c. to persuade.

_____ 2. The tone of this article is:
       a. serious.
       b. humorous.
       c. nostalgic.

_____ **3.** The author believes that:

    a. television makes kids violent.

    b. actual beatings, rape, or parental addictions have less impact on children than television violence.

    c. household violence makes kids violent.

_____ **4.** According to the author, authorities

    a. are very interested in solving the problem of household violence.

    b. hardly recognize that household violence exists.

    c. devote much time and effort into identifying the problem of household violence.

_____ **5.** By the time a child graduates from high school, how many acts of TV violence will he or she witness?

    a. 200,000

    b. 565,000

    c. 40,000

Visual Literacy Box 8.2 ● ■ ■ ■ ■ ■ ■ ■ ■ ■ ■ ■ ■ ■ ●

Making Graphic Organizers for Statistics

If, as we read, we organize statistical information, it will be easier to draw the conclusions that the numbers suggest. Read the paragraphs below and fill in the table with the correct numbers. Then fill in these numbers on the pie chart to make a visual comparison.

> Progressives are no exception. _Mother Jones_ claims it has "proof that TV makes kids violent." And the Institute for Alternative Media emphasizes, "the average American child will witness . . . 200,000 acts of [TV] violence by the time that child graduates from high school."
>
> None of these varied interests note that during the eighteen years between a child's birth and graduation from high school, there will be fifteen million cases of real violence in American homes grave enough to require hospital emergency treatment. These assaults will cause ten million

(continued on next page)

(continued from previous page)

serious injuries and 40,000 deaths to children. In October 1996, the Department of Health and Human Services reported 565,000 serious injuries that abusive parents inflicted on children and youths in 1993. The number is up four-fold since 1986.

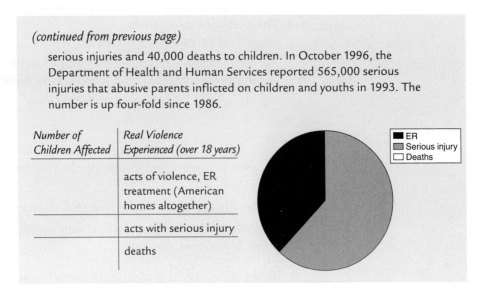

Number of Children Affected	Real Violence Experienced (over 18 years)
	acts of violence, ER treatment (American homes altogether)
	acts with serious injury
	deaths

A Reading in Political Science

Read the passage below to find out how Bushmen prevent violence in their society. After reading the selection, complete the comprehension exercises that follow it.

Vocabulary in Context

Complete the vocabulary exercise before reading the selection to learn the new terms. The first term has been identified for you.

a. **destructive conflict**—violence and fighting that kills people and destroys property

b. **entails**—involves, includes

c. **suppression**—restraint, control

d. **feasible**—possible, realistic, workable, doable

e. **cooperative management**—a way of living in which people share and get along with each other without fighting ___a___ **1.** To avoid _____, the Bushmen teach their people how to share and how to talk out their problems.

_____ **2.** Since American society is based on competition, the prevention of conflict _____ control of fighting instead of teaching people how to share and accept their differences.

_____ **3.** The _____ of conflict is not the best way to deal with differences because it does not lead to any understanding or get rid of a problem—it only keeps it under control.

_____ **4.** The Bushmen teach their people how to share and get along with each other without fighting. Prevention means looking at what causes fights and conflict and includes the _____ of their differences.

_____ **5.** Suppression is not _____ because it does not teach people how to share and get along with each other.

Why We Fight and How We Can Stop

[1] "The greatest lesson my father taught me," the Bushman elder Korakoradue told me, "was, 'Never cause a problem, so that it won't have to be settled. Try to live in harmony.'" Every day in such horizontal societies becomes an exercise in prevention.

[2] We are learning in our modern societies that prevention is the best cure when it comes to fighting disease. The best way to deal with heart attack, for example, better than the most sophisticated bypass operations, is to prevent them through good nutrition, regular exercise, and medication. As the Bushmen demonstrate, the priority of prevention holds in the arena of **destructive conflict** too.

[3] Prevention in vertically organized societies generally **entails suppression** of conflict. In horizontally organized societies, however, suppression is neither **feasible** nor desirable. Prevention means addressing the root causes of conflict and laying the foundation for the **cooperative management** of differences.

[4] Conflict usually arises in the first place from frustrated needs. This helps explain why the Bushmen go to such lengths to share food and

other resources. Anthropologist Lorna Marshall once studied what happens when Bushman hunters come back to camp with an eland, a large antelope. To her amazement, the eland was divided, in successive waves of gifts to kin and friends, at least sixty-three times before it was even cooked, after which the meat was distributed widely yet again. In a Bushman camp no one is allowed to go hungry. The idea of eating alone and not sharing shocks them. "Lions could do that," they say, "but not human beings!" Sharing helps everyone meet their basic needs, thus preventing conflict.

[5]   Tensions over conflicting needs can easily escalate when people lack the proper skills or attitudes to defuse them. The Bushmen refrain from violence. Children learn to tolerate and respect others, and to avoid giving offense. They are also taught to share what they have. When two little girls were quarreling over a blanket, Purana, an elder I interviewed, explained how he told the one with the blanket that "she is very lucky that Bise [the good god] gave it to her and, to show her happiness, she should share the blanket with her friend." He was teaching them how to find ways in which both could "win."

[6]   Children learn mainly from watching what adults do. The adults place great value on talking as a way to handle problems; indeed, the Bushmen call themselves "the people who talk too much." Go into a Bushman camp and you will hear the steady stream of chatter and joking. The sounds of human voices seem to rise from the very desert, from the early hours of the morning to the late hours of the evening. The constant talk lets people know how everyone is feeling and whether any frictions need to be smoothed or problems hashed out. Listeners continually respond to people's stories, often echoing what they hear. In effect, they are practicing what modern psychologists call "active listening," a technique to defuse negative emotions. (Ury 115)

Comprehension Questions

Choose the best answer that completes each sentence below. The first one has been done for you.

_____a_____ **1.** The author's purpose is:
     a. to inform.

     b. to entertain.

     c. to persuade.

_____ **2.** The tone of this article is:

     a. angry and hostile.

     b. serious and formal.

     c. humorous and informal.

_____ **3.** The Bushmen go to great lengths to share food and other resources because they believe that:

     a. conflict starts when people let their feelings be known.

     b. conflict starts when people talk too much.

     c. conflict starts when people do not have what they need.

_____ **4.** The Bushmen teach their children to:

     a. ignore differences.

     b. use talking as a way to handle problems.

     c. suppress feelings.

_____ **5.** Which of the following is an example of "active listening"?

     a. Listeners continually respond to people's stories, often echoing what they hear.

     b. Listeners find ways in which both parties can win.

     c. Listeners avoid giving offense.

Getting Ahead in College Box 8.3

PARTS OF SPEECH:
PREPOSITIONAL PHRASES

Authors can use two or more prepositional phrases in one sentence. Read the groups of sentences below and write a sentence that adds in the prepositional phrases.

Example

Conflict usually arises.

Conflict arises <u>in the first place</u>.

Conflict arises <u>from frustrated needs</u>.

<u>Conflict usually arises in the first place from frustrated needs.</u>

(continued on next page)

(continued from previous page)

1. The land was divided.

It was divided <u>for gifts</u>.

The gifts were <u>for their kin</u>.

_____

_____

2. Two little girls were quarreling.

They were quarreling <u>over a blanket</u>.

The blanket was <u>on the floor</u>.

_____

_____

3. Adults place a great deal of value.

The value is placed <u>on talking</u>.

The talking is done as a way <u>of handling problems</u>.

_____

_____

A Reading in Autobiography

Read the article below to see how Bernie Mac discovered his gift for comedy. As you read, think about the author's purpose and tone of voice. After reading the selection, complete the comprehension exercises that follow it.

Vocabulary in Context

Complete the vocabulary exercise before reading the selection to learn the new terms. The first one has been identified for you.

a. **deacon**—church officer who helps the minister or priest

b. **gestures**—signs or signals made with the hands to show an idea or feeling

c. **aisles**—places to walk in between chairs or benches

d. **pulpit**—platform, stage, podium, stand

e. **shuffles**—drags one's feet

---

   d   **1.** The church officer wanted Bernie to go up to the _____ so that he could speak in front of all the people in the church.

_____ **2.** When someone drags his feet on the ground walking very slowly, we say that he _____ his feet.

_____ **3.** Bernie imitated his grandpa making all the same type of _____ that his grandpa would make with his hands.

_____ **4.** When Bernie spoke in front of the church, he had them laughing so hard his grandma said "they were rolling in the _____."

_____ **5.** One of the church _____ wanted Bernie to speak in front of the congregation.

Maybe You Never Cry Again

[1] One day we had a little banquet after church, and one of the guest **deacon** said to me, "Bernie, I hear you think you're funny?"

[2]   "Pretty funny," I said.

[3]   Eight years old and I already had a reputation. This was 1966. Cosby was going strong. Richard Pryor was a rising star. And Bernie Mac was about to test the waters.

[4]   "Ladies and gentleman," the man said. "We have some entertainment for you this afternoon. I think you all know little Bernie. Little Bernie is a regular comedian."

[5]   He made me go stand up front, where everyone could see me, and I looked out at their stony faces. Tell you something I learned early on: Black people are tough; they want to be entertained. And I could see it in their eyes: *We don't think you're funny, boy. Nothin' funny*

about kids. I waited for them to quiet down, then I got started: My family—you don't want to mess with my family. My grandpa, he says everything four times—four times he says it—four!" They're laughing already, looking over at Grandpa, who's not laughing. They know what I'm talking about, though. I do his voice, make it go all deep, and I snort and breathe heavy and do all his **gestures** just right: "Pass me that gravy, woman. Don't be hoggin' that gravy. How many times I got to ask for that gravy? I'll bonk the top of your head you don't pass me that gravy *now."*

[6]   Those two, Thurman and Lorraine, they were bickering all the time. She says black, he says white.

[7]   So then I do my grandma, giving it back: "Thurman, you ain't bonkin' nobody. And you calm down about the gravy. Boat'll get to you. You start on 'em potatoes." I squint my eyes the way she does, and it's clear from the laughter that they got grandmas that squint, too. I tell 'em how she **shuffles** up behind you, scares you half to death. "And when she gives you a bath, man—she rub you til you bleed." They're really laughin' now.

[8]   But my grandma's not laughin'. She grabs me by the ear and takes me out back and smacks my [butt] hard. "You making fun of my family, Bernie? In front of all these people!"

[9]   "No, ma'am."

[10]   "You think it's right to tell the family business?"

[11]   "No ma'am. I'm sorry, ma'am. I was just jokin'."

[12]   "Ain't no joke. You go out there and apologize right now!"

[13]   She follows me out, and I can't help myself. I'm doing it again—in my grandpa's deep snort: "Who done ate up all the corn bread? How many times I got to tell you, woman—you never make enough corn bread!"

[14   Yank! She's got me by the ear again. Drags me outside and up the stairs. It hurts like [crazy], but I don't care because everybody's laughin'. They're laughin' so hard I can hear them all the way up in my room. Pull on my ear all you want, Grandma—it's worth it.

[15]   "So," my grandpa asked me later in that evening, circling me, "you think I say things four times? I don't say things four times. Have I ever said anything four times?"

[16]   "Never, sir," I said, bowing my head. "I was just makin' up stories."

[17]   He told me he was gonna whup my [butt]—four times he told me—but he didn't whup my [butt]. He thought it was funny, too. He didn't say so, of course, but I heard them talking about it later that night in

the kitchen. My grandma's laughin' as she tells it again, saying, "That Bern, he too funny! Had 'em rolling in the **aisles**."

[18] My mama sayin', "Boy told me he wanted to be a comedian. He gonna do it, too. Bernie gonna surprise everyone. Big things in store for my son."

[19] Following Sunday, people still talking about it. Visitin' deacon takes me aside, says, "You got the power of speech, Bern. Ought to sign up for Young Deacon Night. Lord Almighty's callin' you to the **pulpit**, he be callin' you, and he be callin' *loud.*"

[20] When I get old, if I say things four times, please shoot me.

[21] I tell the deacon: "I don't think I got time, sir, Mama wants me to do better in school. I'm near the bottom of my class."

[22] The deacon thinks on this for a moment. "Maybe she got a point Bern. Maybe you ain't smart enough to serve the Lord."

[23] Black people: They tell it like it is.

[24] School, I was funny too. I couldn't help myself. I like making people laugh. Teachers call my mama to complain. Principal talks to me. Minister. Coach. School *janitor*, even. Everybody tryin' to talk sense into Bernard, but Bernard ain't listenin'.

[25] Miss Ford says, "Why you accept failure, Bernie? Are you afraid to succeed? You're better than this. You got smarts to spare."

[26] "I'm sorry," I say.

[27] "You want to be funny?" she says.

[28] "I guess," I say.

[29] "Okay," she says. "Friday afternoon, you can be funny. You get up in front of the class and be funny."

[30] I thought she was kidding, but she wasn't kidding. She wanted to see me fail. She wanted to embarrass me so I'd fly right. "Everybody, put up your books," she said. "Bernie gonna tell a story."

[31] And that's what I did. I got up there and told a story, and everybody listened. It was about a man who had all the water in the world, and it was hot, like maybe a thousand degrees, and he wouldn't give anyone even a little sip. Not all my stories were funny. Some of them were just stories.

[32] When I was done, the teacher couldn't believe it. "Bernie," she asked me—and the class was listening, everybody nice and quiet, "where'd that story come from?"

[33] "I don't know," I said. "Inside."

[34] "You made that story up?"

[35] "Yes, ma'am."

[36] "By yourself?"

[37] "Yes, ma'am."

[38] "I want you to write it down for me."

[39] I went home that night and tried to write it down, but I couldn't do it. It didn't work that way. Stories came out of me when I opened my mouth, not when I was sitting in front of my blue notebook.

[40] I told my teacher how it was.

[41] "Okay," she said. "Never mind about the writing. If you behave yourself, you can tell stories every Friday."

[42] And that's what I did. Every Friday I'd get up in front of the class and tell stories. Kids lived for that. I ain't lyin. I'd be up there tellin' crazy stories, anything that popped into my head. I'd tell them stories I made up, like the one about the man who lived right outside my window, only an inch tall, named Li'l Bit. Or I'd tell them things from real life: the way my grandpa made up words, say, or the way my grandma's feet spilled out of her shoes like big fat sausages. I told them about all the beans at our house—seventeen kinda beans—and I said our house was fulla gas.

[43] Got to a point where the teacher's using me to keep order. "You kids keep making noise, Bernie won't be telling his Friday story." That made them toe the line. It was magic. I was just a kid, but I felt the power in stories.

[44] In the schoolyard big kids comin' at me now. "You think you funny, spooky juice? I don't think you funny."

[45] I'd tell the big kids the story about the visiting deacon: "Lord be callin' you to the pulpit, Bern!" Voice rolling like thunder. "He be callin' you *loud.*"

[46] *Hear them laughin'.* Feels good. Better than getting beat up. Feels good to be popular. We all want to be loved. And some people, well—they need it more than others. Some people *hungry* for it. And I might as well admit it here and now: I used to be one of those people. At home, phone would ring, I'd jump to my feet: "That for me?" Mail come, I'd run over to see if anyone's writin' little Bern. Someone knockin' out front, I'd race my big brother to the door.

[47] Grandma says, "Bern, there's gonna come a day when the phone rings and you won't want to answer it. The doorbell rings and you'll look through the peephole and creep off and hide. Mail comes and you'll let it pile up.

[48]   "By the time you die," she went on, "two million people will have passed through your life. And maybe three or four of them will still be by your side."

[49]   I didn't have a clue what she was talking about. But I do now. (Mac 11–15)

Comprehension Questions

Choose the best answer that completes each sentence below.

_____b_____ **1.** The author's purpose is:
   a. to inform.
   b. to entertain.
   c. to persuade.

_____ **2.** The tone of this article is:
   a. humorous.
   b. serious.
   c. disapproving.

_____ **3.** Read the excerpt below. Which phrase tells you that the people of the congregation didn't expect Bernie to be funny?

> He made me go stand up front, where everyone could see me, and I looked out at their stony faces. Tell you something I learned early on: Black people are tough; they want to be entertained. And I could see it in their eyes: *We don't think you're funny, boy. Nothin' funny about kids. I waited for them to quiet down, then I got started:*

   a. Black people are tough.
   b. They want to be entertained.
   c. I looked out at their stony faces.

_____ **4.** Bernie was:
   a. a 35-year-old comedian.
   b. an eight-year-old child.
   c. a 50-year-old deacon.

_____ **5.** Why did the teacher let Bernie tell stories *every* Friday afternoon?

    a. She used Bernie's talent as a reward for good behavior.

    b. She wanted to see him fail at being a comic so that he
would give up on being the class clown.

    c. She wanted him to teach the other children how to tell
stories.

Questions for Discussion

Answer the following questions in complete sentences.

1. Why do you think Bernie wants to be a comedian?

_____

_____

_____

2. What does his grandma mean when she tells him, "By the time you die,
two million people will have passed through your life. And maybe three
or four of them will still be by your side?"

_____

_____

_____

3. Do you think Bernie's grandma and grandpa were angry when he got
up in front of the congregation and made fun of them?

_____

_____

_____

4. At first, why did the teacher want Bernie to go in front of the class and tell a story?

_____

_____

_____

5. What did the visiting deacon want Bernie to do? How did he get out of doing it?

_____

_____

_____

Getting Ahead in College Box 8.4

PURPOSE AND TONE:
MAYBE YOU NEVER CRY AGAIN

The tone of an article helps us determine the author's overall purpose. Place an "X" in the box next to the adjectives that describe the author's tone in the reading "Maybe You Never Cry Again."

❏ lighthearted *(Positive)*   ❏ informal *(Neutral)*   ❏ encouraging *(Positive)*

❏ helpless *(Negative)*   ❏ optimistic *(Positive)*   ❏ authoritative *(Neutral)*

❏ hopeful *(Positive)*   ❏ fearful *(Negative)*   ❏ angry *(Negative)*

❏ hostile *(Negative)*   ❏ serious *(Contextual)*   ❏ cheerful *(Positive)*

❏ playful *(Positive)*   ❏ critical *(Negative)*   ❏ humorous *(Positive)*

❏ pessimistic *(Negative)*   ❏ determined *(Positive)*   ❏ enthusiastic *(Positive)*

❏ formal *(Contextual)*   ❏ objective *(Contextual)*   ❏ subjective *(Contextual)*

(continued on next page)

(continued from previous page)

After assessing the various adjectives that describe the author's tone, determine the author's overall purpose for writing this article.

The author's overall purpose is:

_____a. to inform.

_____b. to persuade.

_____c. to entertain.

9

Logical Reasoning

● ●

*L*ogical reasoning is a skill used to understand complex relationships in logic. In this chapter you learn how to:

■ interpret cause and effect statements;

■ draw reasonable conclusions.

To illustrate these processes, read the paragraph below and think about what it means for college students who find themselves drinking five beers within a very short period of time.

> A Harvard University study of the drinking habits of 17,000 college students revealed that 84 percent of the respondents reported drinking alcohol on a regular basis during the academic year. Almost 44 percent of students said they engaged in "binge drinking," that is, downing five or more drinks for a male and four or more for a female in a short period of time. The study also found that 23 percent of male students and 17 percent of female students are frequent binge drinkers, chugging alcoholic drinks in rapid succession on three or more occasions in a two-week period. An estimated 50 college students die as a result of binge drinking each year. (Bryjak and Soroka 185–89)

Copyright © 2006 by Pearson Education, Inc.

Let's analyze the information in the above paragraph. Almost half of the students surveyed said that they engaged in "binge drinking." Binge drinking sometimes causes death. In terms of logical reasoning, we can call binge drinking the "cause," and we can say that death is the "effect." Binge drinking can cause death, or people can die from binge drinking. If we diagram it out, it will look like this:

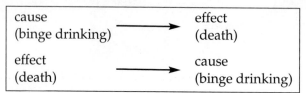

We can carry this a step further by making an inference from the cause-effect relationship. We could reason that:

- **Cause:** binge drinking

- **Effect:** death for 50 college students each year

- **Fact:** I am a college student who drinks five or more drinks in a short period of time.

- **Conclusion:** I could die from binge drinking.

CAUSE-EFFECT PATTERNS

Cause-effect paragraph patterns are common in many textbooks, literature, newspaper articles, and just about everything we read. Our daily lives are often filled with cause-effect patterns. We may wonder, "What caused me to get a C on the exam?" or "What would be the effect of sending out this résumé?" or "Will this aspirin cause my headache to go away?"

Although the idea that a certain action produces an effect does not seem hard to understand, cause and effect relationships can often be very tricky. This happens because there are many different ways cause-effect relationships can be stated and many different combinations of causes and effects:

- One cause may lead to one effect.

■ Two or more causes may lead to one effect.

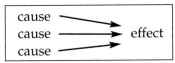

■ One cause may lead to two or more effects.

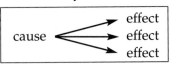

■ Two or more causes may lead to two or more effects.

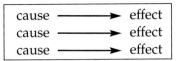

Another reason cause-effect can be tricky is that sometimes the effect becomes a new cause that, in turn, creates a new effect. We call these sequences "chains of reasoning."

A third reason cause-effect relationships are tricky is that the cause may be mentioned first, followed by the effect. Or the effect may be mentioned first, followed by the cause. We must be careful not to assume that the first part of a cause-effect statement is always the cause.

I was caught in traffic; therefore, I missed my first class.

cause ——————▶ effect

I missed my first class because I was caught in traffic.

effect ◀—————— cause

A way to make this easier is to look at the cause as being an action and the effect as being a result of that action.

I was caught in traffic (action); therefore, I missed my first class (result).

I missed my first class (result) because I was caught in traffic (action).

Getting Ahead in College Box 9.1

SIGNALS TO CAUSE AND EFFECT RELATIONSHIPS

If we are familiar with the words that signal cause and effect relationships, we will not be stumped by the various arrangements of cause and effect statements.

Words That Signal Cause		Words That Signal Effect	
cause	reason	therefore	thus
since	many factors	resulting in	is the result of
due to	if . . . then	so	consequently
because	this prompted	effect	then
			affect

Activity

Read the excerpt below and underline the signal words related to cause and effect. Then finish the cause-effect statements that follow the excerpt.

The Effects of Radiation on Humans

Cosmic radiation is reduced at sea level <u>because</u> of the protective blanket of the atmosphere. Thus, at higher altitudes cosmic radiation is more intense. For instance, in Denver, the "mile-high city," a person receives more than twice as much cosmic radiation as at sea level. A couple of round-trip flights between New York and San Francisco cause us to be exposed to as much radiation as we receive in a chest X ray. The air time of airline personnel is limited because of this extra radiation. (Hewitt, Suchocki and Hewitt 334)

1. **Cause:** the protective blanket of the atmosphere

   Effect: _____

2. **Cause:** two round-trip flights between New York and San Francisco

   Effect: _____

3. **Cause:** extra radiation in air travel

   Effect: _____

EXERCISE
9-1

Identifying Cause and Effect in Sentences

Identify the cause and the effect for each of the following sentences. The cause and effect of the first sentence have been identified for you.

1. Juan wanted to become a doctor, so he majored in biology.

   cause: <u>Juan wanted to become a doctor.</u>

   effect: <u>He studied biology.</u>

2. Juan studied biology because he wanted to become a doctor.

   cause: _____

   effect: _____

3. Shianne worked in the bakery because she needed money to support her family.

   cause: _____

   effect: _____

4. Shianne needed money to support her family, so she worked in the bakery.

   cause: _____

   effect: _____

5. Zakaria told funny stories; therefore, his friends enjoyed listening to them.

   cause: _____

   effect: _____

6. Zakaria's friends enjoyed listening to his stories because they were funny.

   cause: _____

   effect: _____

7. Because she had work to do, Zoe went to the library.

cause: _____

effect: _____

8. The hot, dry weather is causing fires.

cause: _____

effect: _____

9. Fires are starting because the weather is hot and dry.

cause: _____

effect: _____

10. Because of the hot dry weather, fires are starting.

cause: _____

effect: _____

Cause and Effect Chains

Some cause-effect relationships are complicated. A cause can create an effect that becomes the cause of another effect. The pattern looks like this:

A caused B and B caused C.

Example
Hassan studied every night so he could make the Dean's List, which made him feel quite proud.

A caused B:

■ cause: Hassan studied every night.

- effect: Hassan made the Dean's List.

B caused C:

- cause: Hassan made the Dean's List.

- effect: Hassan felt proud.

EXERCISE 9-2	**Identifying Cause and Effect Chains**

Identify the cause and effect chains for each of the following sentences. The first one has been done for you.

1. Anita missed breakfast, which made her hungry, so she stopped at the coffee shop for a donut.

   A caused B

   - **cause:** Anita <u>missed breakfast.</u>

   - **effect:** Anita <u>felt hungry.</u>

   B caused C

   - **cause:** Anita <u>felt hungry.</u>

   - **effect:** <u>She stopped at the coffee shop for a donut.</u>

2. Katia caught the flu, which made her feel feverish, so she took some aspirin.

   A caused B

   - **cause:** _____

   - **effect:** _____

   B caused C

   - **cause:** _____

   - **effect:** _____

3. Maurice qualified to be a semi-pro because he was good at pitching due to constant practice.

<u>A</u> caused <u>B</u>

■ **cause:** _____

■ **effect:** _____

<u>B</u> caused <u>C</u>

■ **cause:** _____

■ **effect:** _____

4. Due to heavy traffic the old stone bridge was weakened and so became dangerous to drive over.

<u>A</u> caused <u>B</u>

■ **cause:** _____

■ **effect:** _____

<u>B</u> caused <u>C</u>

■ **cause:** _____

■ **effect:** _____

5. The relationship between the two countries became strained because of differences in opinion; therefore, an agreement could not be made.

<u>A</u> caused <u>B</u>

■ **cause:** _____

■ **effect:** _____

<u>B</u> caused <u>C</u>

■ **cause:** _____

■ **effect:** _____

6. Tired from working overtime, Raul took a nap.

<u>A</u> caused <u>B</u>

■ **cause:** _____

■ **effect:** _____

<u>B</u> caused <u>C</u>

- **cause:** _____

- **effect:** _____

7. Because she was happy about getting a new car, Kioko called all of her friends on the telephone.

<u>A</u> caused <u>B</u>

- **cause:** _____

- **effect:** _____

<u>B</u> caused <u>C</u>

- **cause:** _____

- **effect:** _____

8. After reading the article on solar power, Matthew was interested in finding out more information, which led him to install solar panels on his house.

<u>A</u> caused <u>B</u>

- **cause:** _____

- **effect:** _____

<u>B</u> caused <u>C</u>

- **cause:** _____

- **effect:** _____

9. The groundwater table was very low from the drought; therefore, water restrictions were placed on residents.

<u>A</u> caused <u>B</u>

- **cause:** _____

- **effect:** _____

<u>B</u> caused <u>C</u>

- **cause:** _____

- **effect:** _____

10. The switch from leaded to unleaded gasoline introduced hydrocarbons into the air, and this resulted in an increased risk of cancer.

<u>A</u> caused <u>B</u>

- ■ **cause:** _____

- ■ **effect:** _____

<u>B</u> caused <u>C</u>

- ■ **cause:** _____

- ■ **effect:** _____

Multiple Causes

Sometimes, two or more causes create one effect. Look at the example below.

It was snowing and school was canceled, so Shawn went snow-boarding.

Cause 1: It was snowing.
Cause 2: School was cancelled.
Effect: Shawn went snowboarding.

It makes sense that Shawn went snowboarding because of the information that we have been given. People generally go snowboarding when it is snowing. The fact that school was cancelled is also encouraging because we know Shawn would be free that day. Therefore, the conclusion that "Shawn went snowboarding" makes sense according to the facts that were given.

EXERCISE
9-2

Identifying More Than One Cause

Identify the multiple causes and the effect for each of the following sentences. The first one has been done for you.

1. Elena liked working with numbers, and she was accepted into the accounting program, so she changed her major to accounting.

Cause 1: <u>Elena liked working with numbers.</u>

Cause 2: <u>She was accepted into the accounting program.</u>

Effect: <u>She changed her major to accounting.</u>

2. Kusun loved flowers, and she enjoyed being her own boss, so she bought a florist shop.

Cause 1: _____

Cause 2: _____

Effect: _____

3. Tyrone fixed the car quickly because he was behind with his work and didn't want customers to complain.

Cause 1: _____

Cause 2: _____

Effect: _____

4. Mei studied the homeland security documents thoroughly because she wanted to stop terrorism and she knew she had to understand the information before she could make any decisions.

Cause 1: _____

Cause 2: _____

Effect: _____

5. Upon finding the sales down, and because he wanted to make more money, the manager told his sales people to make more telephone calls.

Cause 1: _____

Cause 2: _____

Effect: _____

Visual Literacy Box 9.1 ● ● ● ● ● ● ● ● ● ● ● ● ● ● ● ●

FISHBONE MAPS: CAUSE AND EFFECT

Fishbone maps are used to show cause and effect relationships.

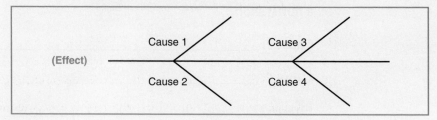

The following sentence shows how the information would look on a map.

Tyrone fixed the car quickly because he was behind with his work and didn't want customers to complain.

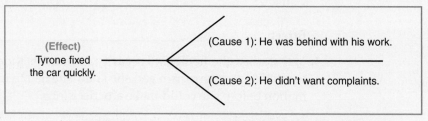

Practice making a fishbone map by mapping out the sentence below.

Anjali liked working with computers, and she was accepted into the computer programming department, so she changed her major to computer programming.

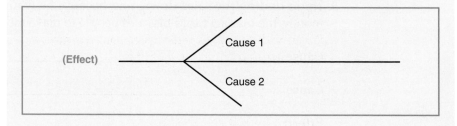

Implied Cause

Sometimes when there are two causes and one effect, one cause is stated and the other cause is implied. In that case, we have to connect the gap between the stated cause and the effect. Look at the example below.

> The cheerleading squad was holding tryouts, so Anjelica went to the gym to join the competition.

Stated Cause: Tryouts were being held in the gym.

Implied Cause: Anjelica wanted to be a cheerleader.

Effect: Anjelica went to the gym to join the competition.

The sentence does not tell us why Anjelica decided to participate in the competition. We have to read between the lines to fill in that information. We are given the information that tryouts were being held in the gym and that Anjelica went to join in the competition. Therefore, we would be safe in assuming she did so because she wanted to be a cheerleader.

EXERCISE 9-4	**Identifying the Implied Cause**

For each of the following sentences, identify the cause, the effect, and the implied cause.

1. When Clifford finished his paper, he invited all of his friends to his house for a party.

   Stated Cause: <u>Clifford finished his paper.</u>

   Implied Cause: <u>Clifford was very happy.</u>

   Effect: <u>He invited all of his friends to his house for a party.</u>

2. When Celena's painting was chosen for display at the art show, she called her mom on the telephone.

   Stated Cause: _____

   Implied Cause: _____

   Effect: _____

3. Every weekend after his divorce, Josh drove from New York to Michigan to pick up his son because his son wanted to spend time with him.

Stated Cause: _____

Implied Cause: _____

Effect: _____

4. When the temperature reached 110, everyone went to the swimming pool.

Stated Cause: _____

Implied Cause: _____

Effect: _____

5. When the summer was over, everything at the mall was half price.

Stated Cause: _____

Implied Cause: _____

Effect: _____

6. In Iran, marriages are viewed as important to the entire family, and are therefore usually arranged by the parents. (Farr and Hammers 70)

Stated Cause: _____

Implied Cause: _____

Effect: _____

7. Japanese values stress the group needs over the individual wants, and therefore these values lead to strong family and company loyalties. (Farr and Hammers 8)

Stated Cause: _____

Implied Cause: _____

Effect: _____

8. Because of large populations and high property values in the cities, workers must either commute great distances or live in tiny apartments in the city.

Stated Cause: _____

Implied Cause: _____

Effect: _____

9. Japanese people live longer on average than the people of any other nation. By 2015, Japan will have a higher percentage of people over 65 than any country in the world. (Farr and Hammers 8)

Stated Cause: _____

Implied Cause: _____

Effect: _____

10. Many people in South Africa have the AIDS virus and, therefore, are not expected to live very long lives.

Stated Cause: _____

Implied Cause: _____

Effect: _____

DRAWING CONCLUSIONS

Drawing a conclusion is similar to figuring out cause-effect relationships. Facts are presented, and from these facts the reader draws a logical conclusion. The conclusion must make sense based on the given facts.

Example

It rained today in Baltimore. Samuel lives in Baltimore. We can conclude that it rained at Samuel's house.

Fact 1: It rained today in Baltimore.

Fact 2: Samuel lives in Baltimore.

Conclusion: It rained at Samuel's house.

Identifying Reasonable Conclusions

Identify a reasonable conclusion from the facts provided. The first conclusion has been done for you.

1. Flu shots are free to all students and faculty at the campus medical center. I am a student. I do not have to pay for my flu shot.

   Fact 1: <u>Flu shots are free to all students and faculty.</u>

   Fact 2: <u>I am a student.</u>

   Conclusion: <u>I do not have to pay for my flu shot.</u>

2. You must be age 16 or over to be eligible for a driver's license in Vermont. Nina is 22. Nina is eligible for a driver's license.

   Fact 1: _____

   Fact 2: _____

   Conclusion: _____

3. The governor of Vermont said he would like to run for president in the next election. Howard Dean is the governor of Vermont. Howard Dean would like to be a presidential candidate.

   Fact 1: _____

   Fact 2: _____

   Conclusion: _____

4. We can conclude that Howard Dean would like to be a presidential candidate because the governor of Vermont said he would like to run for president and Howard Dean is the governor of Vermont.

Fact 1: _____

Fact 2: _____

Conclusion: _____

5. Thomas must have gone to work today because he said he would either go to work or go to school, and we know he is not at school.

Fact 1: _____

Fact 2: _____

Conclusion: _____

6. Celeste was either going to major in English or journalism. Since she didn't declare a major in English, we can conclude that she majored in journalism.

Fact 1: _____

Fact 2: _____

Conclusion: _____

7. The teachers will probably ask Niru to read the poem, since they were looking for people to either read poetry or short stories. Niru is very good at reading poetry.

Fact 1: _____

Fact 2: _____

Conclusion: _____

8. We can conclude that the entire student body of 10,000 registered for the new semester since this morning. The director said he wanted all of the students to be registered by the end of the day and it is now 6:00 p.m.

Fact 1: _____

Fact 2: _____

Fact 3: _____

Conclusion: _____

9. People became ill if certain foods were missing from their diets. Since vitamins are present in the foods that made them well, vitamins must be important to good health.

Fact 1: _____

Fact 2: _____

Conclusion: _____

10. If the cost of renting a one-bedroom apartment was $250/month twenty-five years ago and the cost today is $1,000, then we can expect the cost of a one-bedroom apartment to be $4,000/month twenty-five years from now.

Fact 1: _____

Fact 2: _____

Conclusion: _____

Visual Literacy Box 9.2 ● ● ● ● ● ● ● ● ● ● ● ● ●

Conclusion Maps

Conclusion maps are used to show the relationship between the facts and the conclusion. Read the sentence below and look at the outline.

(continued on next page)

Thomas must have gone to work today because he said he would either go to work or go to school, and we know he is not at school.

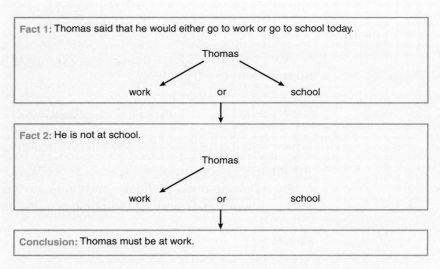

Fact 1: Thomas said that he would either go to work or go to school today.

Thomas

work   or   school

Fact 2: He is not at school.

Thomas

work   or   school

Conclusion: Thomas must be at work.

Practice making a conclusion map by using the sentence below.

Molina was either going to major in chemistry or architecture. Since she didn't declare a major in chemistry, we can conclude that she majored in architecture.

Fact 1: Molina was going to major in chemistry or architecture.

Molina

chemistry   or   architecture

Fact 2: She didn't declare a major in chemistry.

Molina

chemistry   or   architecture

Conclusion:

Identifying Cause and Effect in Paragraphs

Identify the cause and the effect relationships for each group of sentences. The first set of relationships has been identified for you.

1. Each day our dreams, fears, desires, and concerns are analyzed by advertisers anxious to sell products.

   Cause: Advertisers are anxious to sell products.

   Effect: Our dreams, fears, desires, and concerns are analyzed.

2. Advertising's chief purpose is to persuade people to buy, and to continue to buy, certain products. Radio, TV, and online advertisements are geared to the particular audiences that will tune in or log on.

   Cause: _____

   Effect: _____

3. During a weekday afternoon, soap operas that attract millions of viewers are interrupted with commercials featuring laundry, cleansing, and beauty products. Football games are sprinkled with commercials for beer, sturdy trucks, and men's underwear. Saturday morning TV is filled with advertisements for sugar-coated cereals and the latest action figures and toys of the future. Through various means of measuring audiences, companies have learned about the types of people comprising their target audiences and what products they would be most interested in buying.

   Cause: _____

   Effect: _____

   Cause: _____

   Effect 1: _____

   Effect 2: _____

Effect 3: _____

4. Many of you can easily recall certain advertising slogans or commercials. These advertising messages must do more than keep attention to be successful. No matter how interesting an advertisement may be, if it fails to influence consumer buying habits, it fails.

Cause: _____

Effect: _____

5. Advertising has been widely accepted in the print and broadcast media. Commercials now invade local movie theaters and rental videotapes before you can see the feature presentation.

Cause: _____

Effect: _____

6. But many people still view television and online advertising as an invasion of privacy. They resent their lack of control over the type and length of commercials. For this reason, many TV viewers are turning to cable television or remote-control devices to turn off advertising.

Cause: _____

Effect: _____

7. Consumers can have a voice in methods of advertising. Because of consumer complaints about exaggerated claims, broadcast regulations now govern the content of advertisements.

Cause: _____

Effect: _____

8. One medium can be more successful than another for certain products. Radio is most effective in announcing items where the visual appeal is not as important as the information.

Cause: _____

Effect: _____

9. Television and the Internet are highly successful where both visual and verbal content is important. Seeing how a drop of super-strength glue suspends a 500-pound weight is more effective than just hearing about it. So is viewing a product and reading its specifications, as is possible on may web sites.

Cause: _____

Effect 1: _____

Effect 2: _____

10. Very often consumers are unaware of the widespread influence of the mass media. A consumer may buy a product without realizing that the seed for that purchase was planted by a TV commercial, newspaper ad, or web site. (Barker and Gaut 330–31)

Cause: _____

Effect: _____

Drawing a Reasonable Conclusion from Facts

Draw a reasonable conclusion from the facts provided.

1. Architecture and objects. Have you ever walked into a room and immediately felt at home, calm and relaxed? Or avoided a building that made you feel nervous and insecure? Nonverbal messages from architectural structures and other objects around us indeed can influence our behavior. For this reason dentists have comfortable chairs and pleasant decors in their waiting rooms—all to make us worry a little less. Night-club, bar, and restaurant owners have also learned that interiors can greatly influence their customers. They realize that dim lighting, a quiet atmosphere, and soft music lead to greater intimacy, which encourages their patrons to stay longer. (Barker and Gaut 74)

Cause 1: <u>Dentists have comfortable chairs and pleasant decors in their waiting rooms.</u>

Effect 1: <u>This makes us worry less.</u>

Cause 2: <u>Night-club, bar, and restaurant owners have dim lighting, quiet atmosphere, and soft music.</u>

Effect 2: <u>This makes patrons stay longer.</u>

Conclusion: <u>Non-verbal messages from architectural structures and other objects around us can influence our behavior.</u>

2. These informal observations are supported by scientific studies. One classic experiment, for example, used three rooms: an "ugly" room, designed like a janitor's storeroom; a "beautiful" room, with carpeting, draperies, and other decorations; and an "average" room, decorated like a professor's office. While located in these different rooms, subjects were asked to rate a series of photographs of faces. Those in the beautiful room gave higher ratings to the faces than did those in the ugly room. While the beautiful room was found to stimulate feelings of pleasure, comfort, enjoyment, and the desire to continue the activity, the ugly room caused fatigue, headaches, discontent, sleepiness, irritability, and hostility. Subsequent measures of recall and problem solving in these rooms showed better performance in the beautiful surroundings. (Barker and Gaut 74)

Cause 1: _____

Effect 1: _____

Cause 2: _____

Effect 2: _____

Conclusion (refer to the above paragraph): _____

3. In reasoning from causes and effects, you can go in either of two directions. First, you can reason from a cause to an effect; you can draw the conclusion that a specific cause is producing a specific effect. Second, you

can reason from effect to cause; you can draw the conclusion that a specific effect was produced by a specific cause. Causal reasoning goes like
this:

> X results from Y. Since X is undesirable, Y should be eliminated.

All the available evidence shows unmistakably that cancer [X] results
from smoking [Y]. Smoking is personally destructive [X]; we have no
choice but to do everything we can to eliminate smoking entirely [Y].
    Alternatively, of course, you might argue that X results from Y; since
X is desirable, Y should be encouraged. In a speech, you might say:
    We know that general self-confidence [X] results from positively rein-
forcing experiences [Y]. Therefore, if you want to encourage the development of self-confidence in your children [X], give them positively
reinforcing experiences [Y]. (DeVito 395–96)

Cause 1: _____

Effect 1: _____

Conclusion 1: _____

Cause 2: _____

Effect 2: _____

Conclusion 2: _____

4. Alcohols affect living things profoundly, partly because they act as lipid
solvents. Their ability to dissolve lipids out of cell membranes allows
alcohols to penetrate rapidly into cells, destroying cell structures and
thereby killing the cells. For this reason, most alcohols are toxic in relatively small amounts; by the same token, because they kill microbial
cells, they are useful as disinfectants. (Whitney and Rolfes 230)

Cause: _____

Effect: _____

Conclusion 1: _____

Conclusion 2: _____

5. Ethanol is less toxic than the other alcohols. Sufficiently diluted and taken in small enough doses, its action in the brain produces an effect that people seek—not with zero risk, but with a low enough risk (if the doses are low enough) to be tolerable. Used in this way, alcohol is a drug—that is, a substance that modifies body functions. Like all drugs, alcohol offers both benefits and hazards. It must be used with caution, if used at all. (Whitney and Rolfes 230)

Cause: _____

Effect 1: _____

Effect 2: _____

Conclusion: _____

A Reading in Communications

Read the article below to find out how people communicate while under stress. As you read, think about the effects that these reactions can have on relationships. Comprehension questions follow each paragraph and are meant to be completed as you read through the selection. Decide from the choices which conclusion makes the most sense.

Vocabulary in Context

Complete the vocabulary exercise before reading the selection to learn the new terms. The first term has been defined for you.

  a. placater—peacemaker; one who calms

  b. ingratiating—trying to please so that one is liked

    c. prone—likely to do something; likely to have something happen

    d. relentlessly—persistently; not stopping

    e. anticipation—expectation that something will happen

_____a_____ 1. A _____ is someone who wants to keep all interactions peaceful and calm.

_____ 2. The placater can be _____ or eager to please, saying things like "whatever you want" or "never mind about me, it's okay."

_____ 3. People who blame others become angry because of their _____ that they will not be getting something that they want.

_____ 4. The blamer continuously and _____ criticizes others.

_____ 5. The placater is _____ to become ill or depressed because he holds all of his feelings inside without expressing them.

Getting Ahead in College Box 9.2

THE PRONUNCIATION OF VOCABULARY

Every word has to have a vowel because the vowel carries most of the sound in a word. The English vowels are:

a, e, i, o, u

    Any letters that are not vowels are consonants. Every vowel has two sounds: a long sound and a short sound. This lesson covers only the short sounds. Pronounce the following words and listen for the sound of the vowel:

Short	a	as in	sat
Short	e	as in	men
Short	i	as in	ill
Short	o	as in	got
Short	u	as in	up

(continued on next page)

Read the paragraph below and highlight all of the short vowel sounds in the underlined words.

Each style <u>is</u> a unique <u>response</u> to pain, <u>anger</u>, or fear, which keeps <u>us</u> from <u>understanding</u> each other.

- Placaters need to know <u>it</u> is okay to <u>express</u> anger.

- Blamers need to be able to speak <u>on</u> their own behalf <u>without</u> indicting others in the <u>process</u>.

- Computers need someone to <u>ask</u> how they feel about specific <u>things</u>.

- Distracters need to know that they are safe, not <u>helpless</u>, that problems <u>can</u> be solved and conflicts resolved.

On Communication Styles in Marriage and Family

[1] Most people tend to react to stress with one or more of four communication styles:

[2] *Placating.* The placater is **ingratiating**, eager to please, apologetic, and a "yes" man or woman. The placater says things like "whatever you want" or "never mind about me, it's okay." It's a case of peace at any price. The price, for the placater, is worthlessness. Because the placater has difficulty expressing anger and holds so many feelings inside, he or she tends toward depression and, as studies show, may be **prone** to illness. Placaters need to know it is okay to express anger.

_____b_____ **1.** One of the effects of reacting to stress by placating is:

  a. the person knows it is okay to express anger.

  b. the person feels worthless.

  c. the person feels healthy.

[3] *Blaming.* The blamer is a fault finder who criticizes **relentlessly** and speaks in generalizations: "You never do anything right." "You're just like your mother/father." Inside, the blamer feels unworthy or unlovable, angry at the **anticipation** he or she will not be getting what is wanted. Given a problem, the best defense is a good offense. The blamer is unable to deal with or express pain or fear. Blamers need to be able to speak on their own behalf without indicting others in the process.

_____ 2. One reason a person blames others when problems arise is:

    a. the person feels unworthy or unlovable.

    b. the person likes to speak in generalizations.

    c. the person is good at dealing with pain and fear.

[4]   *Computing.* The computer is super-reasonable, calm and collected, never admits mistakes, and expects people to conform and perform. The computer says things like, "Upset? I'm not upset. Why do you say I'm upset?" Afraid of emotion, he or she prefers facts and statistics. "I don't reveal my emotions and I'm not interested in anyone else's." Computers need someone to ask how they feel about specific things.

_____ 3. When a person reacts to stress as if he or she were a computer the cause is:

    a. the person is afraid of emotion.

    b. the person expects people to conform and perform.

    c. the person prefers facts and statistics.

[5]   *Distracting.* The distracter resorts to irrelevancies under stress, avoids direct eye contact and direct answers. Quick to change the subject, he or she will say, "What problem? Let's have Sam and Bridget over." Confronting the problem might lead to a fight, which could be dangerous. Distracters need to know that they are safe, not helpless, that problems can be solved and conflicts resolved.

_____ 4. When a person reacts to stress by becoming a distracter, the cause is:

    a. the person feels she or he is safe.

    b. the person feels that her or his problems can be solved.

    c. the person feels helpless and endangered.

[6]   Each style is a unique response to pain, anger, or fear, which keeps us from understanding each other. Knowing that, the next time you find yourself resorting to blame, you can conclude there is something painful or scary bothering you and try to figure out what it is. If it's your partner who is blaming, you can conclude he or she is possibly not intending to be aggressive or mean but probably afraid of some development. What's needed is to find a way to make it safe to talk about the worry; find out what is bothering him or her. (Gordon)

_____ **5.** One conclusion that you can draw when you find yourself resorting to blame is:

    a. your partner is at fault.

    b. there is something scary or painful bothering you.

    c. your partner is unable to deal with something painful or scary.

A Reading in Health Sciences

Read the article below to gain an understanding of how our actions can have a positive effect on others. Comprehension questions follow each paragraph and are meant to be completed as you read through the selection. Decide from the choices which conclusion makes the most sense.

Vocabulary in Context

Complete the vocabulary exercise before reading the selection to learn the new terms. The first term has been defined for you.

a. minute—tiny, little, small

b. elevate—lift up; raise up

c. profoundly—deeply, intensely, greatly

d. impact—influence, impression, effect

e. insignificant—so small and unimportant that no one would notice

___e___ **1.** Even though it may seem that smiling to others is an _____ act that no on notices, it can have a very positive effect on their lives.

_____ **2.** With one smile, you can _____ or lift up another person's mood.

_____ **3.** According to "The Chaos Theory," the tiny flaps of a butterfly's wings could create _____, or very small, disturbances in the atmosphere that grow and grow until they create an effect on weather patterns elsewhere in the world.

_____ **4.** Great changes can come from small and gentle acts. We can make a positive _____ on other people's lives with simple acts of kindness.

_____ **5.** Wishing for someone's good and sending positive thoughts his or her way can have a _____ positive effect on his or her life.

The Butterfly Effect

[1] We have no idea of the **impact** we can have on other people's lives. The Chaos Theory, a branch of mathematics, has a principle called the Butterfly Effect that says you can't predict outcomes in nature, that a butterfly flapping its wings in Brazil can cause a tornado in Texas. Imagine that: the tiny flaps of a butterfly's wings could create **minute** disturbances in the atmosphere that grow and grow until they can affect entire weather patterns. Think of that seemingly **insignificant** smile, the one you flash to a perfect stranger. It can have the same effect. With one smile, you have a chance to **elevate** another person's mood in a second. You have created an opening for the person to pass on that positive feeling to another, and another, and another. Like the butterfly, you have started a chain reaction with limitless possibilities.

_a_ _____ **1.** According to the author, smiling:

    a. can create a chain of positive causes and effects.

    b. has no effect on others.

    c. has no impact on other people's lives.

[2] The effects of our actions may not be immediately clear to us, but the way we act always affects our environment and the people in it. A kind word or a thoughtful gesture can go farther than we know. Even something as seemingly insignificant as exchanging a smile or holding a door open for someone can profoundly affect another person. In fact, wishing for someone's good, sending positive thoughts his or her way, praying for someone, whether the person knows it or not, can have a **profoundly** positive effect on his or her life. A study published in *The Archive of Internal Medicine* (October 25, 1999) showed that praying for patients, even without their knowledge, is linked to their improved health.

_____ **2.** According to the author, wishing for someone's good or sending positive thoughts his or her way:

  a. has no effect on others' lives.

  b. has a positive effect on others' lives.

  c. has a negative effect on others' lives.

[3] One day while in a taxi in New York City, I happened to ask the driver to roll up the window because it was getting a bit chilly. He became agitated, muttering angrily under his breath. Like any New Yorker, my first reaction was to ignore him. Then a sudden impulse changed my mind and I decided to press forward.

[4] "Did it bother you that I asked you to roll up the window?"

[5] He snapped back, "Of course it didn't bother me."

[6] I persisted, "Well, it sounds like you've had a really rough day."

[7] He responded that he had been having a really rough *year*. I asked him what had happened, and finding a friendly ear, he proceeded to tell me about the difficulties in his life. He had had a really rough year. His wife had been hospitalized and after a long, painful illness had passed away. He had lost a son as well and was struggling with finances when he was recently robbed. Now he was alone, trying to pick up the pieces of his life. By the time we reached my destination, he had finished his story. The simple and direct way he related his hardships moved me. Not really knowing how I could help, I offered him my sympathy for all he had experienced. He thanked me and we said good-bye. As I started to walk away, he remained there, leaning out his cab window, watching me go.

_____ **3.** What caused the taxi driver's grouchiness?

  a. He didn't like the woman who got into his taxi.

  b. He didn't want to roll up the window.

  c. His wife and son had died, finances were tight, and he had been robbed.

[8] Suddenly, he called out, "Lady, will you do something for me?" I looked back at his open face, so earnest at that moment.

[9] "If I can," I responded.

[10] And cautiously, as though afraid of my response, he gently asked, "Will you pray for me?"

[11] "Of course." Touched by the intimacy of the connection between us I responded without hesitation. It was this moment that was so simple, yet so human.

[12]   With a nod of satisfaction, as if a deal had been brokered between us, he drove off, leaving me stunned on the sidewalk staring as his cab disappeared in the distance. I knew I was holding a treasure in my heart. A moment so true, so real, had happened, with a perfect stranger. I realized that it was the decision to reach out and connect that allowed me to receive so much back in return. The giver is always the receiver.

_____ **4.** What did the author mean when she said: "The giver is always the receiver"?

   a. At first, she acted as "the giver" by reaching out to the taxi driver and the she became the "receiver" because she received a good feeling from their interaction.

   b. The taxi driver was "the giver" when he reached out to her and asked her to pray for him and he also became the "receiver" because she agreed to pray for him.

   c. Both "a" and "b" are correct.

[13]   We want to give. We want to connect. We want to do something extraordinary and make a difference. Often when we have that impulse we think we must be part of some grand, global effort: ending starvation in Sudan, wiping out AIDS in Africa, freeing women in Afghanistan. Each of these causes is urgent and worthwhile. But no kindness is wasted, no consideration is unimportant or frivolous, and the simple truth is that great changes can come from small and gentle acts. A hello to the cashier in your grocery store, a thank-you to a salesperson who waited on you, a wave to the newsstand vendor as you grab your daily paper—all these simple actions can have life changing effects. These small, seemingly inconsequential acts can uplift and shift a person's view of life in an instant. (Haddon 268–72)

_____ **5.** According to the author, small acts of kindness are:

   a. just as important as grand global efforts to change the world.

   b. unimportant and probably go unnoticed.

   c. not as important as ending starvation in Sudan or wiping out AIDS in Africa.

A Reading in Literature

Read the article below to gain an understanding of what it was like to be a young male adult in the 1960s. As you read, think about the cause and effect relationships that directed Miguel Melendez's life. After reading the selection, complete the comprehension exercises that follow it.

Vocabulary in Context

Complete the vocabulary exercise before reading the selection to learn the new terms. The first term has been defined for you.

a. interlude—break, rest, pause

b. escalating—rising, growing, increasing, getting bigger

c. postpone—put off, delay, push back

d. induction—entrance process; initiation

e. remote—distant; far off

_____b_____ 1. With the war effort growing and _____ more and more every day, the possibility of becoming drafted into the armed forces was increasing.

_____ 2. I did not want to go to war and so I did everything I could to _____ being drafted.

_____ 3. I tried to put off the _____ into the Air Force by going for a physical six times.

_____ 4. Even though the shantytowns in Vietnam were _____, they looked very much like the town in Puerto Rico where I came from.

_____ 5. After graduating from college, I worked at a clothing store with my friends for a short time—it was just an _____.

Opening My Eyes

[1] ...I would graduate from high school in June 1966.

[2]   I went to work full-time that summer at Ripley's clothing store, joining my friends Walter Bosque and Joe Perez. But it was just a short **interlude**. Adulthood had arrived, and along with it, the war. It stopped being a distant problem and became a very personal one. With the war effort **escalating**, the draft was breathing down hard on all our backs. In an effort to **postpone induction** until I could figure something out, I went to Whitehall Street and Fort Hamilton for a preinduction physical six times.

[3]   Eddie went to the Marines, Mikey to the Air Force, Bobby to the Army, while Augie attended St. Frances College. My neighbor, Pedro, came back in a body bag with his tags on his big toe.

[4]   It just didn't make sense. Was there any reason for him to die? The news on the TV, the radio, or the papers did not provide a good answer to that question. War was not popular. Neither was defeat.

[5]   So much has been written about the Vietnam War and the anti-war movement in the States during those years, it seems unnecessary for me to revisit that entire history. But certain things about that time ought to be remembered in order to understand the development of the Young Lords.

[6]   Nobody knew when the war started. Tons of paper were wasted trying to explain the difference between a "war" and a "conflict." There was not a war in Vietnam, but a conflict. Then how come Pedro was dead in a war that was not taking place? Human beings are the only animals that know the names of things. Maybe that is the reason why when the politicians in power fail to name things correctly, the people feel their intelligence is being assaulted and suspect a plot by the government. The suspicion was so widespread, that the mayor of New York, John V. Lindsay, was among the voices against that war, and claimed it was draining the city of badly needed lives and funds just to please the military-industrial complex.

[7]   There was another aspect to it. The "enemy" looked too much like us—Puerto Ricans. American troops were destroying shantytowns in a **remote** country, which had an eerily similar appearance of the tropical country of our fathers. Either through the press or by the stories brought back home by the friends who survived their tours of duty, instead of tales of heroism we heard horrific and obscene recounts of mass murders, senseless destruction, and hell. The way in which the Viet Cong, a Southeast Asian David, armed with little and using bam-

boo booby-traps, were able to foil the high-tech American Goliath was not encouraging.

[8]   There was also a very subjective matter: Respect. The war in Vietnam was not only considered a failure in itself but, unlike World War Two, those who were sent there did not have the respect or the praise of the community. To leave the Bronx clad in a military uniform was not a badge of honor.

[9]   The only way to stay out of the Armed Forces was to escape to Canada or become a student and receive a "2S deferment" which was granted by your local draft board. I did apply to a couple of universities when I finished high school, but I didn't get into any local colleges, and almost gave up the idea. I was scared . . . to come home from the war like Pedro.

[10]   Still, I had a crazy scheme, if it would only work. I'd joined the U.S. Air Force and didn't have to report to active duty for ninety days. This would give me enough time to take the Search for Education, Excellence, and Knowledge (SEEK) program entrance exam, a program aimed at helping students in need of remedial academic work, or in a low economic bracket, get into college. If all went well, I would receive my acceptance letter to the program, and to a college, before my ninety days were up. It came nail-bitingly close. After the sixty-day mark passed, I started to really panic at the possibility of spending four years in the Air Force. Finally, the letter arrived that would determine my future. I took a deep breath, asked Saint Jude to do what he knows best (which is the impossible), and opened the envelope: I had been accepted to the City University of New York (CUNY) at Queens College, the least integrated of all CUNY institutions in "lily-white" Kew Gardens, Queens. I can't even describe how relieved I was. I had been given another life and I knew deep inside me that this was a turning point.

[11]   As the summer went on and September approached, my relief became overshadowed by my growing anxiety as the reality of attending college sank in. I'd never read a book cover to cover, and now college classes and professors loomed. I was going to have to work hard and take some non-credit remedial courses as well as classes for credit, but I believed in myself enough to know that I would do well. It seemed like heaven when compared to the alternative, and a necessary step toward gaining the respect of my family and community that I so wanted.

[12]   On campus, I felt self-conscious, but I knew I had to get through this academic plunge somehow. Black and Latino students were an obvious

minority; we were for sure a new sight in the student lounge and cafe-teria. We stuck together. . . . We knew we had as much right to be there as anyone else, and we were just beginning to understand our rights and stand up for them. We reclaimed our right to have access to higher education, and eventually demanded and received black and Puerto Rican studies programs in every single CUNY institution. (Melendez 67–70)

Comprehension Questions

Select the best choice from the answers provided below. The first answer has been provided for you.

_____c____ **1.** Miguel Melendez thought the war in Vietnam was not logical because the cause-effect relationships did not make sense. Which statement best shows this?

   a. Nobody knew when the war started.

   b. Tons of paper were wasted trying to explain the difference between a "war" and a "conflict."

   c. There was not a war in Vietnam, but a conflict. Then how come Pedro was dead in a war that was not taking place?

_____ **2.** Miguel Melendez had several reasons for not wanting to fight in the Vietnam War. Along with not wanting to return in a body bag, he wrote that:

   a. the Vietnamese and their country reminded him of his ancestors and their country.

   b. furthering his college education was more important.

   c. he was not interested in becoming a hero.

_____ **3.** With which of the following statements would the author agree?

   a. There were many tales of heroism during the Vietnam War.

   b. During the Vietnam War it was an honor to leave the Bronx clad in a military uniform.

   c. Those who were sent to the Vietnam War did not have the respect or the praise of the community.

_____ **4.** The author said that he was afraid to "come home from the war like Pedro." This caused him to do all of the following except:

    a. escape to Canada.

    b. apply to the SEEK program.

    c. join the Air Force.

_____ **5.** Which of the following was not an outcome of Melendez's acceptance into the Search for Education, Excellence, and Knowledge (SEEK) program?

    a. He became a college student.

    b. He avoided the draft.

    c. He went to Canada.

_____ **6.** How do we know that Melendez was a minority at CUNY?

    a. The author stated that CUNY was the least integrated of all CUNY institutions in "lily-white" Kew Gardens, Queens.

    b. The author described himself as being from Puerto Rican descent.

    c. The author said that he "had been given another life and knew deep inside that this was a tuning point."

_____ **7.** At first Melendez felt relief from escaping the Vietnam War. Why did that relief then turn into worry and fear?

    a. He could be drafted again in 90 days.

    b. He didn't want to be a minority in a mostly white school.

    c. He'd never read a book cover to cover and now he was enrolled in college-level classes.

_____ **8.** All of the following are reasons Melendez felt he would do well in college except:

    a. he was motivated because he believed it was a necessary step toward gaining the respect of his family and community.

    b. he could take remedial courses.

    c. he had mentors who believed in him.

_____ **9.** On campus Melendez
  a. felt welcomed by the non-minority students.
  b. felt self-conscious because black and Latino students were an obvious minority.
  c. felt no need to fight for black and Puerto Rican studies programs on campus.

_____ **10.** From the author's statement "We reclaimed our right to have access to higher education, and eventually demanded and received black and Puerto Rican studies programs in every single CUNY institution," we can conclude that:
  a. the mainstream culture had little interaction with and understanding of blacks and Puerto Ricans.
  b. the mainstream culture was well informed with respect to black and Puerto Rican studies.
  c. black and Puerto Rican studies programs had already been included in New York's University system before Melendez went to college.

Getting Ahead in College Box 9.3

GRAMMAR: COMMAS AND NAMES

In literature, when authors introduce a new character and explain something about him or her, they may place the name or information about the person between two commas. Look at the example below.

Example 1: The author of the book, Miguel Melendez, enrolled in college to keep from being drafted into the Air Force.

The author's name is placed between two commas. We could take his name completely out of the sentence and it would still make sense.

The author of the book enrolled in college to keep from being drafted into the Air Force.

The same is true if the name is given first, with the details between the commas.

(continued on next page)

Example 2: Miguel Melendez, the author of the book, enrolled in college to keep from being drafted into the Air Force.

The sentence would also make sense without the phrase "the author of the book."

Miguel Melendez enrolled in college to keep from being drafted into the Air Force.

Combine the sentences below into one sentence without repeating any words. Then add the author's name.

Example
The author of the book enrolled in college.
He enrolled in college to keep from being drafted.
He would be drafted into the Air Force.
The author's name is Miguel Melendez.

<u>The author of the book, Miguel Melendez, enrolled in college to keep from being drafted into the Air Force.</u>

1. My neighbor came back in a body bag.
His tags were on his big toe.
His name was Pedro.

_____

_____

2. The mayor of New York was among the voices against the war.
The mayor was John V. Lindsay.

_____

_____

3. I went to work that summer.
I went to work full-time.
The work was at Ripley's clothing store.
I joined my friends.
My friends were Walter Bosque and Joe Perez.

_____

_____

PART III
Strategies for Staying Ahead

CHAPTER

10

The Best Way to Use Your Textbook

From this chapter you learn the following skills for taking notes from textbooks:

- marking;
- highlighting;
- annotating;
- note-taking;
- outlining;
- paraphrasing;
- summarizing.

In interviews, twelve professors made clear that they all expected students to do a thorough reading of the textbook, extract the main ideas, and record the main points before coming to class. Some of their comments are listed below:

PROFESSOR HALLAN: Students should read it once before they come to class and highlight it. For some others, maybe they have to outline it.

PROFESSOR ARVILLA: They should read it through two times. The first just to familiarize themselves with the context. . . . Then they ought to read through a second time, looking for major ideas. Underlining the major ideas is important.

Professor Cooper: Probably a [careful] reading once is sufficient *if* the student is able to identify the main issues.

Professor Michaels: Students should either write in the margins of the book or write in a notebook, taking down questions that occur to them as they are reading.

Professor Cecilias: Students should give a rough survey and get the general ideas that the author is trying to make. Quick surveying and *then read more carefully*. Take notes in the margins of the book . . . underlining the main points in the book is very important.

Taking notes from a textbook involves reading and organizing new information *before hearing it for the first time* in a lecture. In order to do this, you must create a system that helps you to "see" the important ideas and how these ideas are connected with the details that explain them.

MARKING

When you read a section of a textbook and discover the main points or the answers to important questions, you should mark them. By doing so, you will be able to find them later without reading the entire section again. Also, when you mark the text, you will be able to see exactly what to "lift" from the page and write into your notes.

It is best to read, or at least skim, the selection once through before marking. It is necessary to be exposed to all of the information so that you can judge which is most important and how all of it fits together. After reading the selection, while it is still fresh in your mind, you should go back to the beginning and go through the selection, circling and underlining the main points and support.

It is also a good idea to mark with a pencil, so that you can erase if you find you have marked more than is necessary. Let's take a look at the way the following excerpt is marked:

From the Boston Tea Party, to burning draft cards, Americans have engaged in countless political protests. **Protest** is a form of political participation designed to achieve policy change through dramatic and unusual tactics. The media's willingness to cover the unusual can make protest worthwhile, drawing attention to a point of view that many Americans might otherwise never encounter. **Ex:** For example, when an 89-year-old woman decided to try to walk across the country to draw attention to the need for campaign finance reform, she put this issue onto the front page of newspapers most everywhere she traveled. (Edwards, Wattenberg and Lineberry 207)

The text pattern is "term, definition, and example." Therefore, we drew a circle around the term, underlined the definition, and wrote the abbreviation "Ex:" next to the phrase that gave an example of the term.

<table>
<tr><td>EXERCISE
10-1</td><td>Identifying the Main Points</td></tr>
</table>

Read the following passage and mark the main points.

Throughout American history, individuals and groups have sometimes used **civil disobedience** as a form of protest; that is, they have consciously broken a law that they thought was unjust. In the 1840s, Henry David Thoreau refused to pay his taxes as a protest against the Mexican War and went to jail; he stayed only overnight because his friend Ralph Waldo Emerson paid the taxes. Influenced by India's Mahatma Gandhi, the Reverend Martin Luther King Jr. won a Nobel Peace Prize for his civil disobedience against segregationist laws in the 1950s and 1960s. His "Letter from a Birmingham Jail" is a classic defense of civil disobedience. (Edwards, Wattenberg and Lineberry 208)

HIGHLIGHTING

Highlighting does the same thing as marking, but it is faster and easier. However, if you highlight before you read the entire selection, you can end up with more highlighted areas than not. When almost everything is highlighted, you cannot see "the forest from the trees." Unlike marking with a pencil, you cannot erase the highlighting.

There are two things you can do to avoid highlighting too much. One is to mark the text in pencil first and then highlight only the main points. The other is to read the text first and carefully consider what to mark. In either case, it is wise to read the text before marking and/or highlighting. Let's take a look at the way the following excerpt is highlighted.

Researchers study peer acceptance by asking children's classmates to judge one another's likeability. Children responses reveal four different categories: ①**popular children**, who get many positive votes; ②**rejected children**, who are actively disliked; ③**controversial children**, who get a large number of positive and negative votes; and ④**neglected children**, who are seldom chosen, either positively or negatively. About two-thirds of pupils in a typical elementary school classroom fit one of these categories. The rest are average in peer acceptance; they do not receive extreme scores. (Berk 329)

The text pattern is "topic with a list." The "peer acceptance" is the topic and the numbered items present a list of characteristics of the topic. Definitions are also included. When highlighting, we would emphasize only the topic and main points. If we tried to highlight the examples or any additional information, we would end up highlighting the entire paragraph and thus defeat our purpose for making some information stand out.

| EXERCISE 10-2 | Identifying the Main Points in a Paragraph |

Read the following passage and highlight the main points.

What causes one child to be liked and another to be rejected? A wealth of research shows that social behavior plays a powerful role. Popular children communicate with peers in sensitive, friendly, and cooperative ways. When they do not understand another child's reaction, they ask for an explanation. If they disagree with a play partner in a game, they go beyond voicing their displeasure and suggest what the other child could do instead. When they want to enter an ongoing play group, they adapt their behavior to the flow of activity.

Rejected children, in contrast, display a wide range of negative social behaviors. At least two subtypes exist. **Rejected-aggressive children** . . . show high rates of conflict, unfriendliness, and overexcited, distracted, and impulsive behavior. They also have little social understanding. For example, they are more likely than other children to blame others for their social difficulties and to act on their angry feelings. In contrast, **rejected-withdrawn children** are willing to give in to the demands of other children and are socially awkward. These children, especially, feel lonely, hold negative expectations for how peers will treat them, and are very concerned about being scorned and attacked. Because of their clumsy, obedient style of interaction, they are at risk for abuse by bullies. (Berk 329)

ANNOTATING

Once we mark a text and know the main points and support, we can take this information and write it in the margin of the page. We can later review the main points and supporting information at a glance without rereading the page or turning to other notebooks.

Let's take a look at the way the following excerpt is annotated. *Situational non-assertiveness— lack assertive behavior only in certain situations Ex: situations that create much anxiety or situations requiring the use of authority.* *Generalized non-assertiveness—typical non-assertive behavior.* *Ex:* *(1) timid and reserved* *(2) unable to assert rights* *(3) do what others say* *(4) do nothing when rights are infringed upon* *(5) ask permission from others when w/in rights*	**Non-assertiveness**. **Non-assertiveness** comes in two forms: situational and generalized. **Situational non-assertiveness** refers to a lack of assertiveness only in certain kinds of situations—Ex: for example, those that create a great deal of anxiety or those in which authority must be exercised. **Generalized non-assertiveness**, as the term implies, is nonassertive behavior that is typically demonstrated. People Ex: who exhibit this behavior are timid and reserved and are unable to assert their rights regardless of the situation. These people do what others tell them to do—parents, employers, and the like—without questioning and without concern for what is best for them. When these persons' rights are infringed upon, they do nothing about it and sometimes accuse themselves of being non-accepting. Generalized non-assertive persons often ask permission from others to do what it is their perfect right to do. (DeVito 101)

Annotating Passages

Read and annotate the following passage.

Aggressiveness. Aggressiveness also comes in two forms. **Situationally aggressive** people are aggressive only under certain conditions or in certain situations. For example, they may become aggressive after being taken advantage of over a long period or by someone for whom they have done a great deal. These people are normally not aggressive; only in certain situations do they behave aggressively.

Generally aggressive people, however, meet all or at least most situations with aggressive behavior. These people seem in charge of almost all situations; regardless of what is going on, they take over. They appear to think little of the opinions, values, or beliefs of others, and yet they are extremely sensitive to criticisms of their own behavior. Consequently, they frequently get into arguments with others and find that they have few friends. They think little of others, and others think little of them.

Assertive Communication. Assertive communication—communication that enables you to act in your own best interests without denying or infringing upon the rights of others—is the desired alternative. Assertive individuals are willing to assert their own rights, but unlike their aggressive counterparts, they do not hurt others in the process. Assertive individuals speak their minds and welcome others doing likewise. (DeVito 101)

NOTE-TAKING

Note-taking is just like annotating, except that you write the main points and support into a separate notebook instead of writing in the textbook. You also put this information into some type of organized form. There are many systems of note-taking. *The Cornell Method* is very popular among college students. With this system, you divide your notebook page into three sections, as shown in the following example. In the right-hand column you write your main points and support in outline form. Then, you look at the information you have written in the right-hand column and ask yourself what questions it answers. You write the questions in the left-hand column. (If the information consists mainly of terms and definitions, a simple question and answer format may work better than an outline format.) Finally, at the bottom of the page you write, in paragraph form, a summary of that page's notes.

Let's look at an excerpt from a psychology text and the notes taken from it in Cornell form:

Newton's Third Law

Newton's third law—the law of action and reaction, is often stated thus: "To every action there is always opposed an equal reaction." In any interaction, there is an action and reaction pair of forces that are equal in magnitude and opposite in direction. Neither force exists without the other—forces always come in *pairs*, one action and the other reaction. The action and reaction pair of forces make up one interaction between two things.

You interact with the floor when you walk on it. Your push against the floor is coupled to the floor's push against you. The pair of forces occur simultaneously. Likewise, the tires of a car push against the road while the road pushes back on the tires— the tires and road push against each other. In swimming you interact with the water: You push it backward while it pushes you forward—you and the water push against each other. In each case, there is a pair of forces, one action and the other reaction, that make up an interaction. Which force we call *action* and which we call *reaction* doesn't matter. The point is that neither exists without the other. (Hewitt, Suchocki and Hewitt 44)

Questions	Notes
What is Newton's 3rd Law?	To every action there is always opposed an equal reaction.
What happens in any interaction?	In any interaction, the action and reaction forces are equal in magnitude and opposite in direction.
What are some examples of action and reaction?	Ex: You push against the floor when you walk and the floor pushes against you.
	Ex: Car tires push back against a road and the road pushes the car forward.
	Ex: In swimming, you push water back and water pushes you forward.

Summary: Newton's third law states that "to every action there is always opposed an equal reaction." In other words, forces come in pairs—an action and a reaction that are equal in magnitude and opposite in direction. For example, when you swim, the pair of forces is you and the water. However hard you push, the water will push that hard back on you. The two forces will go in opposite directions—you push back on the water and the water pushes you ahead.

EXERCISE
10-4

Note-Taking with the Cornell Method

Read and take notes from the following excerpt using the Cornell Method.

Imprinting is learning that is limited to a specific time period in an animal's life and that is irreversible. One result of imprinting is the formation of a strong bond between two animals, often a hatchling or other newborn animal and its parent. The specific time during which imprinting occurs is called the **critical period**.

In perhaps his most famous study, Konrad Lorenz used the graylag goose to demonstrate imprinting. He divided a batch of eggs from a nest, leaving some with the mother and putting the rest in an incubator. The young reared by the mother served as the control group. They showed normal behavior, following the mother about as goslings and eventually growing up to mate and interact with other geese. The geese from the artificially incubated eggs formed the experimental group. These geese spent their first few hours after hatching with Lorenz, rather than with their mother. From that day on, they steadfastly followed Lorenz and showed no recognition of their mother or other adults of their own species. This early imprinting lingered into adulthood: The birds continued to prefer the company of Lorenz and other humans to that of their own species. The critical period for imprinting varies with the species. Lorenz found it to be the first two days after hatching for the graylag goose. During that time, the hatchlings apparently have no innate sense of their species (what we might think of as "mother" or "I am a goose, you are a goose"). Instead, they simply respond to and identify with the first object they encounter that has certain simple characteristics. Imprinting has both innate and learned components. Its innate component is the ability or tendency to imprint during a critical period. The actual imprinting itself is a form of learning. (Campbell, Mitchell, and Reece 742)

Questions	Notes

Summary

OUTLINING

Outlining is important. The outline is a visual display of the main ideas and supporting details. When we look at an outline, we can tell instantly which ideas are the main points and which ideas support them. Outlines also put information into categories and make recall much easier. For example, the list of words is the same in each column below. Which arrangement would you rather try to memorize?

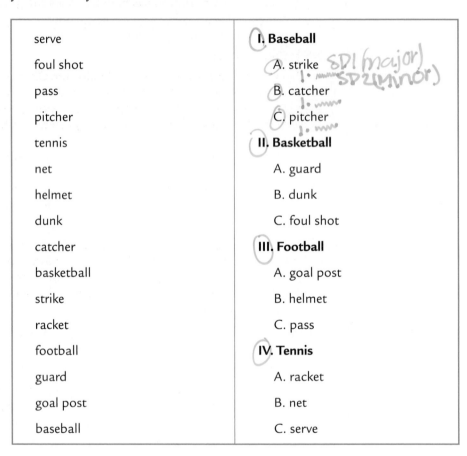

serve	**I. Baseball**
foul shot	A. strike _SD1 (major)_
pass	_1. ~~~ SD2 (minor)_
pitcher	B. catcher
tennis	_1. ~~~_
net	C. pitcher
helmet	_1. ~~~_
dunk	**II. Basketball**
catcher	A. guard
basketball	B. dunk
strike	C. foul shot
racket	**III. Football**
football	A. goal post
guard	B. helmet
goal post	C. pass
baseball	**IV. Tennis**
	A. racket
	B. net
	C. serve

Most people would choose the arrangement on the right because it is organized into categories. Once you have looked over the list, it is easy to remember the four sports and the equipment and movements that are used for each game. The arrangement on the left side is more taxing for our memories because it is presented as a list of random items and we cannot tell the difference between the main points and subpoints or details.

EXERCISE 10-5	Completing an Outline

Read the excerpt from a communications text and finish the partial outline that follows by providing the subpoints or details.

Initiating Conversations

Opening a conversation is especially difficult. Often you may not be sure what to say or how to say it. You may fear being rejected or having someone misunderstand your meaning. Several approaches to opening a conversation can be derived from the elements of the interpersonal communication process:

- *Self-references* say something about yourself. Such references may be of the name-rank-and-serial-number type—for example: "My name is Joe. I'm from Omaha." On the first day of class, students might say, "I'm worried about this class" or "I took this instructor last semester; she was excellent."

- *Other-references* say something about the other person or ask a question: "I like that sweater." "Didn't we meet at Charlie's?" Of course, there are pitfalls here as well. Generally, it is best not to comment on the person's race ("My uncle married a Korean"), the person's affectional orientation ("Nice to meet you; I have a gay brother"), or physical disability ("It must be awful to be confined to a wheelchair").

- *Relational references* say something about the two of you: for example, "May I buy you a drink?" "Would you like to dance?" or simply "May I join you?"

- *Context references* say something about the physical, social-psychological, cultural, or temporal context. The familiar "Do you have the time?" is a reference of this type. But you can be more creative and say, for example, "This place seems very friendly" or "That painting is just great."

Keep in mind two general rules. First, be positive. Lead off with something positive rather than negative. Say, for example, "I really enjoy coming here" instead of "Don't you just hate this place?" Second, do not be too revealing; don't self-disclose too early in an interaction. If you do, you risk making the other person feel uncomfortable. (DeVito 271–72)

Initiating Conversations

I Approaches to Opening Conversations

    A. Self-references (say something about yourself)

        1. _____

        2. _____

        3. _____

    B. Other-references

        1. Say something about the person or ask a question

            a. _____

            b. _____

        2. Don't comment on:

            a. _____

            b. _____

            c. _____

    C. Relational references (say something about the two of you)

        1. _____

        2. _____

        3. _____

    D. Context references (say something about the context)

        1. _____

        2. _____

        3. _____

        4. _____

II Two General Rules

    A. _____

    B. _____

EXERCISE
10-6

Adding Details to an Outline

Read the excerpt from a communications text and add the subpoints or details to the outline.

The Opening Line. Another way of looking at the process of initiating conversations is to examine the infamous "opening line," the opener designed to begin a romantic-type relationship. Interpersonal researcher Chris Kleinke (1986) finds that opening lines are of three basic types:

■ *Cute-flippant openers* are humorous, indirect, and ambiguous as to whether the one opening the conversation actually wants an extended encounter. Examples include "Is that really your hair?" "Bet I can out drink you," "Bet the cherry jubilee isn't as sweet as you are."

■ *Innocuous openers* are highly ambiguous as to whether they are simple comments that might be made to just anyone or whether they are in fact openers designed to initiate an extended encounter. Examples include "What do you think of the band?" "I haven't been there before," "What's good on the menu?" "Could you show me how to work this machine?"

■ *Direct openers* clearly demonstrate the speaker's interest in meeting the other person. Examples include: "I feel a little embarrassed about this, but I'd like to meet you." "Would you like to have a drink after dinner?" "Since we're both eating alone, would you like to join me?"

The opening lines most preferred by both men and women are generally those that are direct or innocuous (Kleinke, 1986). The least preferred lines by both men and women are those that are cute-flippant; women dislike these openers even more than men do. Men generally underestimate how much women dislike the cute-flippant openers but probably continue to use them because they are indirect enough to cushion any rejection. Men also underestimate how much women actually like innocuous openers.

Women prefer men to use openers that are relatively modest and to avoid coming on too strong. Women generally underestimate how much men like direct openers. Most men prefer openers that are very clear in meaning, possibly because men are not used to having a woman initiate a meeting. Women also overestimate how much men like innocuous lines. (DeVito 271–72)

The Opening Line

I Types of Lines

    A. Cute-Flippant

        1. Definition

        2. Examples

    B. Innocuous

        1. Definition

        2. Examples

    C. Direct

        1. Definition

        2. Examples

II Line Preferences

    A. Most Preferred

        1. Men

        2. Women

    B. Least preferred

        1. Men

        2. Women

PARAPHRASING AND SUMMARIZING

Paraphrasing involves finding the main ideas in a paragraph and putting them into your own words. You should mentally paraphrase the meaning of every paragraph while reading information that you will be tested on. If you can put the information into your own words, then you know you understand it. Also, you have a better chance of remembering the information that you understand.

Visual Literacy Box 10.1

MAPPING: THE OPENING LINE

Use the outline that you created for Exercise 10.6 to map the main points and supporting details in the reading "The Opening Line."

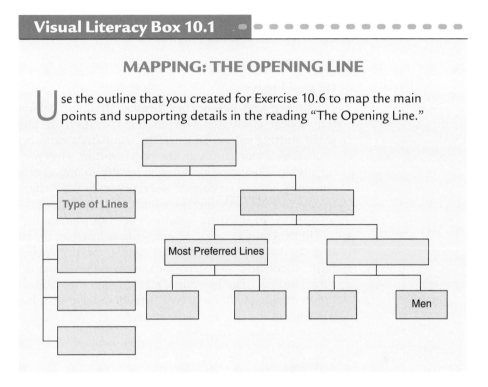

Example 1:

Original Version

How were the Japanese able to arise from the defeat of World War II—including the nuclear destruction of two of their main cities—to become such a giant in today's global economy? Some analysts trace part of the answer to how their corporations are organized. One of these analysts, William Ouchi (1981), pinpointed five ways in which Japanese corporations differ from those of the United States. You will be surprised at how different they are. But, are these differences myth or reality? (Henslin 117)

Paraphrase

In order to explain how Japan became a giant in today's global economy, analysts pinpointed five ways in which the organization of Japanese corporations are different from those of the United States.

Summarizing condenses or shortens the amount of text by one-third its overall length. We take only the main points and most important support and write it in paragraph form. Summarizing is another important part of the Cornell Method for taking notes.

Example 2:

Original Version

> **Hiring and Promoting Teams.** In Japan, teamwork is essential. College graduates who join a corporation are all paid about the same starting salary. To learn the company's various levels, they are rotated as a team through the organization. They are also promoted as a team. They develop intense loyalty to one another and to their company, for the welfare of one represents the welfare of all. Only in later years are individuals singled out for recognition. When there is an opening in the firm, outsiders are not even considered.
>
> In the United States, an employee is hired on the basis of what the firm thinks that individual can contribute. Employees try to outperform others, and they strive for raises and promotions as signs of personal success. The individual's loyalty is to himself or herself, not to the company. Outsiders are considered for openings in the firm. (Henslin 117)

Summary

> In Japan, loyalty for team members and the company is great because people are hired and promoted as teams. In contrast, people who work for American companies are loyal to themselves because they are hired and promoted on an individual basis. They try to outperform each other because they must compete for raises and promotions.

EXERCISE
10-7
Paraphrasing and Summarizing Sources

1. Read and paraphrase the following selection.

> **Lifetime Security.** In Japan, lifetime security is taken for granted. Employees can expect to work for the same firm for the rest of their lives. In return for not being laid off or fired, the firm expects them to be loyal to the company. In the United States, companies lay off workers in slow times. To become competitive, they even reorganize and fire entire divisions. Workers, too, "look out for number one." Job shopping and job hopping are common. (Henslin 117)

Paraphrase: _____

_____

_____

2. Read and summarize the following selection.

> **Almost Total Involvement.** In Japan, work is like a marriage: The employee and the company are committed to each other. The employee supports the company with loyalty and long hours at work, while the company supports its workers with lifetime security, health services, recreation, sports and social events, even a home mortgage. Involvement with the company does not stop when the workers leave the building. They join company study and exercise groups, and are likely to spend evenings socializing with co-workers in bars and restaurants.
>
> In the United States, work is a specific, often temporary contract. Employees are hired to do a certain job. When they have done that job, they have fulfilled their obligation to the company. Their after-work hours are their own. They go home to their private lives, which are separate from the firm.
>
> **Broad Training.** In Japan, employees move from one job to another within the company. Not only are they not stuck doing the same thing for years on end, but also they gain a broader picture of the corporation and how the specific jobs they are assigned fit into the bigger picture.
>
> In the United States, employees are expected to perform one job, to do it well, and then to be promoted upward to a job with more responsibility. Their understanding of the company is largely tied to the particular corner they occupy, often making it difficult for them to see how their job fits into the overall picture.
>
> **Decision Making by Consensus.** In Japan, decision making is a lengthy process. Each person who will be affected by a decision is consulted. After lengthy deliberations, a consensus emerges, and everyone agrees on which suggestion is superior. This makes workers feel that they are an essential part of the organization, not simply cogs in a giant wheel.
>
> In the United States, the person in charge of the unit to be affected does as much consulting with others as he or she thinks necessary and then makes the decision.

Summary: _____

_____

_____

_____

_____

_____

Visual Literacy Box 10.2   ● ■ ● ● ● ● ● ● ● ● ● ● ● ●

Venn Diagrams: Hiring and Promoting Teams

We can draw a Venn diagram when trying to discover the likenesses and differences between two items. Read, for example, the paragraph below about the business practices of Japanese and American corporations.

> In Japan, loyalty for team members and the company is great because people are hired and promoted as teams. In contrast, people who work for American companies are loyal to themselves because they are hired and promoted on an individual basis. They try to outperform each other because they must compete for raises and promotions.

First, we sort through the information point-by-point to decide whether the information contains likenesses, difference, or both. We start by drawing two circles to represent both groups— Japanese and American. In the blue circle where there is no common area, we list only the Japanese business practices. In the green circle where there is no shared area, we list only the American business practices. The separate areas represent their differences. We make the circles overlap if there is any information that is common to both. In the example below, there are no similarities, and so the overlapping space is empty.

Japan
Loyalty for team members
Loyalty for company
People are hired as teams
People are promoted as teams

United States
Loyalty to self
People are hired as individuals
People are promoted as individuals
People compete for raises
People compete for promotions

Read the paragraph below and decide where to place the main points on the Venn diagram.

Lifetime Security. In Japan, lifetime security is taken for granted. Employees can expect to work for the same firm for the rest of their lives. In return for not being laid off or fired, the firm expects them to be loyal to the company.

(continued on next page)

In the United States, companies lay off workers in slow times. To become competitive, they even reorganize and fire entire divisions. Workers, too, "look out for number one." Job shopping and job hopping are common.

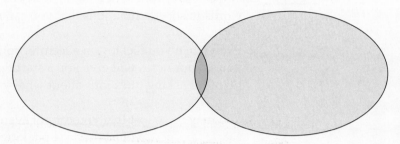

A Reading in Mathematics

Have you ever felt lost during math class? Read the following article for advice from the experts on what to do when you are lost and how to get help. It all starts with good notes. After reading, summarize the selection and answer the comprehension questions that follow.

Vocabulary in Context

Answer the vocabulary questions first to become familiar with the new terms.

a. nevertheless—even so; however

b. reference—source to consult

c. precise—exact; accurate; clear-cut

d. abbreviation—short form

e. reducing—decreasing, cutting, lowering

_____ c   **1.** This is not necessarily a good note-taking system, since it is very difficult to take _____, specific notes while trying to understand the instructor.

_____   2. You should use an _____ system to reduce the amount of written notes that you take in class.

_____   3. You can save time when taking notes by _____ long words to shorter notations that you can understand.

_____   4. Even when you feel lost in a lecture, you should still take notes. Your notes will give you a starting place or _____ point for asking questions about what you don't understand.

_____   5. You may be so lost that you cannot even think of a question to ask; _____, you should keep taking notes so that you can show your professor where it was that you became confused.

How to Become a Good Notetaker

[1] Becoming a good notetaker requires two basic strategies. One strategy is to be specific in detail. In other words, copy the problems down, step by step. The second strategy is to understand the general principles, general concepts, and general ideas.

[2]   **Copying from the Board** While taking math notes, you need to copy each and every step of the problem even though you may already know every step of the problem. While in the classroom, you might understand each step, but a week later you might not remember how to do the problem unless all the steps were written down. In addition, as you write down each step, you are memorizing it. Make sure to copy every step for each problem written on the board.

[3]   There will be times when you will get lost while listening to the lecture. **Nevertheless**, you should keep taking notes, even though you do not understand the problem. This will provide you with a **reference** point for further study. Put a question mark (?) by those steps that you do not understand; then, after class, review the steps you did not understand with the instructor, your tutor, or another student.

[4]   **Taking Notes** The goal of note-taking is to take the least amount of notes and get the greatest amount of information on your paper. This could be the opposite of what most instructors have told you. Some instructors tell you to take down everything. This is not neces-

sarily a good note-taking system, since it is very difficult to take **precise**, specific notes while trying to understand the instructor. What you need to develop is a note-taking system in which you write the least amount possible and get the most information down while still understanding what the instructor is saying.

[5]   **Develop an Abbreviation List** [1]To reduce the amount of written notes, an **abbreviation** system is needed. [2]An abbreviation system is your own system of **reducing** long words to shorter versions that you still can understand. [3]By writing less, you can listen more and have a better understanding of the material.

[4]Example: When the instructor starts explaining the commutative property, you need to write "commutative property" out the first time. After that, use "COM."

[5]You should develop abbreviations for all the most commonly used words in math. [6]By using abbreviations as much as possible you can obtain the same meaning from your notes and have more time to listen to the instructor.

Summarizing Practice

Summarize the excerpt above using the following prompts.

Copying from the board _____

_____

_____

Taking notes _____

_____

_____

Developing an abbreviation list _____

_____

_____

Comprehension Questions

Answer the following questions with the best response below. The first one has been answered for you.

_____c_____ **1.** Which of the following is *not* a good strategy for taking notes?
    a. Copy the problems down step by step.
    b. Gain an understanding of the general principles, concepts, and ideas.
    c. Copy only the steps that you don't have memorized.

_____ **2.** Why does the author suggest that you continue taking notes in situations when you do not understand a problem?
    a. If you have the information in your notes, you will be able to memorize it and pass the test.
    b. After class, you will be able to review what you did not understand with the instructor, your tutor, or another student.
    c. Later, you will be able to review it as many times as it takes to understand it.

_____ **3.** According to the author, the goal of note-taking is to:
    a. take the greatest amount of notes so that you don't miss anything.
    b. take the least amount of notes and get the greatest amount of information on your paper.
    c. Take the least amount of notes and information, so there is less to study.

_____ **4.** The main idea of paragraph 5 is contained in:
    a. sentence 4.
    b. sentence 5.
    c. sentence 6.

_____ **5.** The text pattern used in paragraph 5 is:
    a. term, definition, and example.
    b. topic and list.
    c. time order.

Getting Ahead in College Box 10.1

SEQUENCING: THE BROADCAST MEDIA

Below is a paragraph from the reading "The Broadcast Media." It doesn't make much sense because the sentences are scrambled. Unscramble the sentences by numbering them in the correct order, then answer the questions below.

___5___ His homey appeal brought a flood of sympathetic telegrams to the Republican National Committee, and party leaders had little choice but to leave him on the ticket.

_____ Noting that his daughters loved the dog, Nixon said that regardless of his political future, they would keep it.

_____ In 1952, while running as Dwight Eisenhower's vice-presidential candidate, Nixon made a famous speech denying that he took under-the-table gifts and payments.

_____ During those years, the political career of Richard Nixon was made and unmade by television.

_____ He did admit accepting one gift—his dog Checkers.

1. What was the name of the Nixon's dog?

2. How did Nixon's family get the dog?

3. Nixon was accused of accepting gifts that might, once he was in office, sway his decisions toward the gift givers. Do you think the practice of accepting gifts is a fair practice?

4. Why wouldn't Nixon give the dog back once it was made known that it was illegal to accept this gift?

5. Why were voters not angry that Nixon kept the dog?

A Reading in Political Science

If you had to choose a president by listening to debates on radio rather than on television, do you think you would make the same choice? Read the following article to find out how the different media affect voters' judgment. After reading, summarize the selection and answer the comprehension questions that follow.

Vocabulary in Context

Answer the vocabulary questions first to become familiar with the new terms. The first term has been defined for you.

a. predisposed—likely to be; willing to

b. skeptical—distrustful

c. naiveté—lack of awareness or knowledge

d. memoirs—autobiography; life story

e. denying—saying that something is not true

_____e_____ 1. When Nixon ran for vice president in 1952, he gave a speech _____ that he had broken the law by accepting money and gifts while running for political office.

_____ 2. Generally, people are more likely or _____ to be distrustful about what they read in a newspaper.

_____ 3. People are more suspicious or _____ about what they read in newspapers than television because they feel they can see what is happening for themselves on TV.

_____ 4. Every night, Americans watched the horrors of the Vietnam War through television. In this way, TV exposed the government's _____ or lack of awareness about the war.

_____ 5. When judged by television watchers, Kennedy won a debate over Nixon because they could see his clean-cut appearance. When judged by radio listeners, Nixon was thought to be the winner. Russell Baker wrote about this event in his _____. "Television replaced newspapers as the most important communications medium in American politics" that very night.

The Broadcast Media

[1] Gradually, the broadcast media have displaced the print media as Americans' principal source of news and information. By the middle of the 1930s, radio ownership had become almost universal in America, and during World War II, radio went into the news business in earnest. The 1950s and early 1960s were the adolescent years for American television. During those years, the political career of Richard Nixon was made and unmade by television. In 1952, while running as Dwight Eisenhower's vice-presidential candidate, Nixon made a famous speech **denying** that he took under-the-table gifts and payments. He did admit accepting one gift—his dog Checkers. Noting that his daughters loved the dog, Nixon said that regardless of his political future, they would keep it. His homey appeal brought a flood of sympathetic telegrams to the Republican National Committee, and party leaders had little choice but to leave him on the ticket.

[2] In 1960, Nixon was again on television's center stage, this time in the first televised presidential debate against Senator John F. Kennedy. Nixon blamed his poor appearance in the first of the four debates for his narrow defeat in the election. Haggard from a week in the hospital and with his five o'clock shadow and perspiration clearly visible, Nixon looked awful compared to the crisp, clean, attractive Kennedy. The poll results from this debate illustrate the visual power of television in American politics; people listening on the radio gave the edge to Nixon, but those who saw the debate on television thought Kennedy won. Russell Baker, who covered the event for the *New York Times*, writes in his **memoirs** that "television replaced newspapers as the most important communications medium in American politics" that very night.

[3] Just as radio had taken the nation to the war in Europe and the Pacific during the 1940s, television took the nation to the war in Vietnam during the 1960s. TV exposed governmental **naiveté** (some said it was outright lying) about the progress of the war. . . . Every night, in living color, Americans watched the horrors of war through television. President Johnson soon had two wars on his hands, one in faraway Vietnam and the other at home with antiwar protesters—both covered in detail by the media. In 1968, CBS anchor Walter Cronkite journeyed to Vietnam for a firsthand look at the state of the war. In an extraordinary TV special, Cronkite reported that the war was not being won, nor was it likely to be. Watching from the White House,

Johnson sadly remarked that if he had lost Cronkite, he had lost the support of the American people.

[4]　With the growth of cable TV, particularly the Cable News Network (CNN), television has recently entered a new era of bringing the news to people—and political leaders—as it happens. President [George H. W.] Bush and his aides regularly watched CNN during the Gulf War, as did the Iraqi leadership. Marlin Fitzwater, Bush's press secretary, stated that "CNN has opened up a whole new communications system between governments in terms of immediacy and directness. In many cases it's the first communication we have." A frequent response from U.S. officials to reporters' questions during the Gulf War was "I don't know any more than what you saw on CNN."

[5]　Since 1963, surveys have consistently shown that more people rely on TV for the news than any other medium. Furthermore, by a regular two-to-one margin, people think the television reports are more believable than newspaper stories. (Consider the old sayings "Don't believe everything you read" and "I'll believe it when I see it.") Whereas people are **predisposed** to be **skeptical** about what they read in a newspaper, with television seeing is believing. Young people are particularly likely to rely on television as opposed to newspapers for news. (Edwards, Wattenberg and Lineberry 224–25)

Paraphrasing Practice

Paraphrase each paragraph of the selection above.

Paragraph 1: _____

_____

Paragraph 2: _____

_____

Paragraph 3: _____

_____

Paragraph 4: _____

_____

Paragraph 5: _____

_____

Comprehension Questions

Select the best answer for each question below. The first one has been selected for you.

___c___ **1.** What event made it clear that television had become the principal source of news and information in America?
   a. Nixon's 1952 speech denying that he had accepted gifts and money illegally.
   b. Cronkite's 1968 report on the Vietnam War.
   c. The 1960 presidential debate between Richard Nixon and John F. Kennedy.

_____ **2.** Why did Nixon admit to accepting one gift?
   a. He wanted to be honest with the American people by admitting that he took under-the-table gifts.
   b. He wanted to be honest with the American people by admitting that he took under-the-table payments.
   c. He wanted to gain public sympathy by appearing honest and homey by admitting that he had accepted a pet for his children.

_____ **3.** Why did Nixon lose the debate with Kennedy according to the television watchers?
   a. Unlike radio, television displayed physical appearance.
   b. Nixon's physical appearance made a better impression than Kennedy's.
   c. Kennedy was able to speak more effectively over the radio than Nixon.

_____ **4.** In 1968, CBS anchor Walter Cronkite journeyed to Vietnam for a firsthand look at the state of the war. In a TV special, Cronkite reported that
   a. the war was being won.
   b. the war was likely to be won in the future.
   c. the war was not being won, nor was it likely to be.

_____ **5.** Read the sentence below and decide which paragraph pattern it represents:

> Haggard from a week in the hospital and with his five o'clock shadow and perspiration clearly visible, Nixon looked awful compared to the crisp, clean, attractive Kennedy.

  a. comparison

  b. contrast

  c. comparison and contrast

Getting Ahead in College Box 10.2

GRAMMAR: USING THE SEMICOLON TO JOIN SENTENCES

Sometimes authors have two complete thoughts that are so closely related they want to join them into one sentence. They can do this without creating a sentence that is long and awkward by placing a semicolon between the two sentences. This signals the reader to look for the connection between the two thoughts.

Look at the example below.

Manic love is obsessive; the manic lover has to possess the beloved completely.

There are two complete sentences, with the second explaining the first. The idea that the manic lover has to completely possess the beloved explains what "obsessive love" means. Look at the sentences below. Make one sentence out of each set of sentences by joining them with a semicolon.

1. The manic lover's poor self-image seems capable of being improved only by being loved.

Self-worth comes from being loved rather than from any sense of inner satisfaction.

_____

_____

(continued on next page)

2. Because love is so important, danger signs in a relationship are often ignored.

The manic lover believes that if there is love, then nothing else matters.

_____

_____

A Reading in Interpersonal Communications

Do all people look at "love" in the same way? Read the following article to learn about the different types of love. After reading, outline and summarize the selection and answer the comprehension questions that follow.

Vocabulary in Context

Answer the vocabulary questions first to become familiar with the new terms. The first term has been defined for you.

 a. compassionate—wanting to help others based on sympathy

 b. deteriorate—to get worse

 c. compatibility—ability to get along or work well together

 d. reciprocate—to give back; to give in return for something

 e. provoke—to stir up

_____a_____ **1.** The agapic lovers are _____; they have a desire to help people with whom they have no close ties.

_____ **2.** The agapic lovers love the stranger on the road even though they will probably never meet again. They give without expecting others to _____ or give anything in return.

_____ **3.** The manic lover may become extremely jealous even if the other person did very little to _____ the jealous feelings.

_____ **4.** Pragma lovers' relationships rarely fall apart or _____ because pragma lovers choose their mates carefully, emphasize similarities, and have realistic romantic expectations.

_____ **5.** Pragma lovers want to be well-matched—they want _____ in their relationships.

Types of Love

[1] Although there are many theories about love, the one that has captured the attention of interpersonal researchers was the proposal that there is not one, but six types of love (Lee, 1976). View the descriptions of each type that follow as broad characterizations that are generally *but not always true.*

[2] **Eros: Beauty and Sexuality.** Like Narcissus, who fell in love with the beauty of his own image, the **erotic** lover focuses on beauty and physical attractiveness, sometimes to the exclusion of qualities you might consider more important and more lasting. Also like Narcissus, the erotic lover has an idealized image of beauty that is unattainable in reality. Consequently, the erotic lover often feels unfulfilled. Not surprisingly, erotic lovers are particularly sensitive to physical imperfections in the ones they love.

[3] **Ludus: Entertainment and Excitement. Ludus** love is experienced as a game, as fun. The better he or she can play the game, the greater the enjoyment. Love is not to be taken too seriously; emotions are to be held in check lest they get out of hand and make trouble; passions never rise to the point where they get out of control. A ludic lover is self-controlled, always aware of the need to manage love rather than allow it to be in control. Perhaps because of this need to control love, some researchers have proposed that ludic love tendencies may reveal tendencies to sexual aggression (Sarwer, Kalichman, Johnson, Earl, et al., 1993). Not surprisingly, the ludic lover retains a partner only as long as he or she is interesting and amusing. When interest fades, it is time to change partners. Perhaps because love is a game, sexual fidelity is of little importance.

[4] **Storge: Peaceful and Slow.** Storge lacks passion and intensity. Storgic lovers do not set out to find lovers but to establish a companionable relationship with someone they know and with whom they can share interests and activities. Storgic love is a gradual process of unfolding thoughts and feelings; the changes seem to

come so slowly and so gradually that it is often difficult to define exactly where the relationship is at any point in time. Sex in storgic relationships comes late, and when it comes it assumes no great importance.

[5] **Pragma: Practical and Traditional.** The pragma lover is practical and seeks a relationship that will work. Pragma lovers want **compatibility** and a relationship in which their important needs and desires will be satisfied. They are concerned with the social qualifications of a potential mate even more than with personal qualities; family and background are extremely important to the pragma lover, who relies not so much on feelings as on logic. The pragma lover views love as a useful relationship, one that makes the rest of life easier. So the pragma lovers ask such questions of a potential mate as "Will this person earn a good living?" "Can this person cook?" "Will this person help me advance in my career?" Pragma lovers' relationships rarely **deteriorate.** This is partly because pragma lovers choose their mates carefully and emphasize similarities. Another reason is that they have realistic romantic expectations.

[6] **Mania: Elation and Depression.** Mania is characterized by extreme highs and extreme lows. The manic lover loves intensely and at the same time intensely worries about the loss of the love. This fear often prevents the manic lover from deriving as much pleasure as possible from the relationship. With little **provocation**, the manic lover may experience extreme jealousy. Manic love is obsessive; the manic lover has to possess the beloved completely. In return, the manic lover wishes to be possessed, to be loved intensely. The manic lover's poor self-image seems capable of being improved only by being loved; self-worth comes from being loved rather than from any sense of inner satisfaction. Because love is so important, danger signs in a relationship are often ignored; the manic lover believes that if there is love, then nothing else matters.

[7] **Agape: Compassionate and Selfless.** Agape (ah-guh-pay) is a **compassionate**, egoless, self-giving love. The agapic lover loves even people with whom he or she has no close ties. This lover loves the stranger on the road even though they will probably never meet again. Agape is a spiritual love, offered without concern for personal reward or gain. This lover loves without expecting that the love will be **reciprocated**. Jesus, Buddha, and Gandhi practiced and preached this unqualified love, agape (Lee 1976). In one sense, agape is more a philosophical kind of love than a love that most people have the strength to achieve.

[8]   **Love Styles and Personality.** In reading about the love styles, you may have felt that there are certain personality types who are likely to favor one type of love over another. Here are personality traits that research finds people assign to each love style. Try identifying which personality traits people think go with each of the six love styles: eros, ludus, storge, pragma, mania, and agape.

1. _____ inconsiderate, secretive, dishonest, selfish, and dangerous

2. _____ honest, loyal, mature, caring, loving, and understanding

3. _____ jealous, possessive, obsessed, emotional, and dependent

4. _____ sexual, exciting, loving, happy, optimistic

5. _____ committed, giving, caring, self-sacrificing, and loving

6. _____ family-oriented, planning, careful, hard-working, and concerned

[9]   Very likely you perceived these personality factors in the same way as did the participants in research from which these traits were drawn (Taraban and Hendrick, 1995): 1 = ludus, 2 = storge, 3 = mania, 4 = eros, 5 = agape, 6 = pragma. Note, of course, that these results do not imply that ludus lovers are inconsiderate, secretive, and dishonest. They merely mean that people *think* of ludus lovers as inconsiderate, secretive, and dishonest.

[10]   **Love Styles in Combination.** Each of these varieties of love can combine with others to form new and different patterns (for example, manic and ludic or storge and pragma). These six, however, identify the major types of love and illustrate that different people want different things, that each person seeks satisfaction in a unique way. The love that may seem lifeless or crazy or boring to you may be ideal for someone else. At the same time, another person may see these same negative qualities in the love you are seeking. (DeVito 408–11)

Practice Highlighting and Outlining

Mark and highlight the reading above. Then outline it and write a summary from your outline.

Six Types of Love

I. _____: Beauty and Sexuality

    A. Erotic lover focuses on

        1. _____

        2. _____

    B. Also the erotic lover has

    C. Consequently

II. _____: Entertainment and Excitement—not serious.

    A. Characteristics of ludus lover

        1. Needs to control love

        2. _____

        3. _____

III. Storge:

    A. Storge love

        1. Lacks passion and intensity

        2. Is a gradual process of unfolding thoughts and feelings

    B. Storgic lovers set out to establish a companionable relationship with

        1. _____

        2. _____

IV. Pragma:

    A. The pragma lover

        1. _____

        2. _____

        3. _____

(continued on next page)

B. Pragma lovers' relationships rarely deteriorate because:

    1. _____

    2. _____

V. Mania: Elation and Depression

  A. Mania is characterized by

    1. _____

      a. Loves intensely

      b. Wants to be loved intensely and possessed

      c. Self-image improved by being loved

    2. _____

      a. Worries about loss of love

      b. May experience extreme jealousy/has to possess the beloved

      c. Self-worth comes from being loved

VI. _____

  A. Agape love is

    1. _____

    2. _____

    3. _____

    4. _____

    5. A philosophical kind of love

      a. Jesus

      b. Buddha

      c. Gandhi

Comprehension Questions

Select the best answer for each question below. The first answer has been selected for you.

_____c_____ **1.** With respect to love, the author concludes that:

    a. each person fits into only one of six types of love.

    b. there is really only one major type of love.

    c. different people want different things from relationships.

_____ **2.** Which type of lover focuses on beauty and physical attractiveness?

    a. eros

    b. storge

    c. mania

_____ **3.** Which type of lover is most likely to keep a partner only as long as he or she is interesting and amusing?

    a. ludus

    b. pragma

    c. agape

_____ **4.** Storgic lovers are looking for

    a. someone they can share interests and activities with.

    b. beauty and physical attractiveness.

    c. fun and entertainment.

_____ **5.** Agape is

    a. an obsessive type of love.

    b. a spiritual type of love.

    c. a practical type of love.

Getting Ahead in College Box 10.3

THE PRONUNCIATION OF VOCABULARY

A syllable is a word or part of a word that is spoken as one unit. A word can have one, two, or many sounds, depending on the combination of vowels and consonants. Therefore, we can say that words are made up of one or more syllables. Look at the examples below.

"I"   is a one-syllable word. It has one vowel sound.

(continued on next page)

(continued from previous page)

"it"   is a one-syllable word. It has one vowel and one consonant.

"sit"   is a one-syllable word. It has one vowel and two consonant sounds.

"transit"   is a two-syllable word. It has two vowels (the "a" and the "i").

Say the words in bold print and listen for the number of sounds you hear. Then write that number in the blank next to the word.

The love (1) **that** __1__ may seem lifeless (2) **or** _____ crazy or (3)

boring_____ to you may be ideal for someone else. At the same time, (4)

another_____ (5) **person**_____ may see these same negative qualities in

the love you are seeking.

CHAPTER

11

Preparing for Exams

In this chapter you learn how to best prepare for exams by:

- developing good academic habits (class preparation, attendance, and participation);
- gathering information and organizing information from class;
- organizing and combining your textbook and classroom notes;
- studying and reviewing your notes.

Sometimes students believe they are well prepared for an exam and then fail it. They will say, "I studied six hours for that exam!" or "I stayed up all night studying for that exam!" What these students do not understand is that studying for a test or an exam starts on the very first day of classes. Studying for an exam involves:

1. attending every class.

2. listening with concentration and asking questions about what you do not understand during class.

3. taking good notes in class and integrating them with the notes that you take from your textbook.

4. learning review techniques to remember the information.

ATTEND YOUR CLASSES

Do you believe you can skip classes and still get good grades? The student interview responses below show that it's a common habit among some college students to skip classes if they have not finished writing a paper that is due.

LYNN: I skip the class and hand [my paper] in late.
TONI: [If my paper is not finished] I don't go; I skip the class.
LUKE: I probably won't go to class. I [would] hand it in later.
GENE: If it [the paper] is really bad and I know I am going to be called on, I probably wouldn't go [to class].

Yes. It is a common practice for some students to skip class. However, it is a common practice among students who do *not* have good grades in college. One student explains why he changed his attendance habits.

JODY: I used to think, in freshman year and sophomore year, that if you don't have your homework in, don't go to class. . . . I did that, but that just gives you an absentee problem on top of your homework missing.

Most college and university policies give students three chances to miss class without it hurting their grade. Does this mean you automatically have three days off from every class?

No!!! This means it is possible for a person to have several emergencies in one semester and that the person will not be punished with a bad grade for having an emergency. You should try very hard to attend *all* classes for the following reasons:

■ You will gain a greater understanding of the material through the professor's explanations and examples than you will from trying to follow another classmate's notes.

■ You will strengthen and make your understanding of the material clearer by discussing it with other students.

■ You will have the opportunity to ask questions about material that you don't understand.

For these reasons, you put yourself at a tremendous disadvantage and risk lower grades if you skip classes.

<table>
<tr><td>EXERCISE
11-1</td><td>**Creating an Emergency Contact Chart**</td></tr>
</table>

Sometimes unfortunate things happen and you may have to miss class. If you miss a class, you will need to find out what you missed. (1) Make a contact chart with the phone numbers and email addresses of your professors and several students who are in your classes. (2) Fill in the names of your courses. (3) Leave spaces to write in assignments missed and any explanations for how to complete them. (4) Photocopy the chart several times and keep the copies in your notebook.

Emergency Contact Chart **Course:**
Professor's Name
Office Phone
Email
Classmate's Name
Email
Assignments Missed
Explanation of Assignment

Listen Carefully

Often it is easier to follow a textbook than a lecture because the reader can reread the book as many times as needed while a listener will hear the information only once. Here are a few suggestions to make listening easier.

1. Never go to a class without first reading the assignment. Always read and take notes on the information in the textbook that matches the lecture. By doing this, you will get to know the new terms and their spellings and recognize them in the lecture.

2. Make note of anything you do not understand so that you can ask the professor to explain it when you go to class.

3. Write down any questions that you may think of during the lecture. Ask the professor your questions either during the class discussion or at the end of the lecture. *It is extremely important to ask* about what you do not understand or your notes will not make sense to you. Once this happens, it will be difficult to study from them.

There are four roadblocks to good listening:

■ lack of interest in the topic.

■ lack of knowledge about the topic.

■ lack of vocabulary knowledge.

■ difficulty in following the speaker's thoughts.

How do we go around these roadblocks? We can become good listeners by finding an interest in the subject being discussed, by getting to know more about the topic, by increasing listening vocabulary, and by identifying the speaker's outline.

EXERCISE
11-2

Making a List of New Terms

Choose one course syllabus and find the topic of your next lecture. Next, read the assigned readings that go with that lecture. Then, make a list of any new terms introduced in the reading assignment. Write the definitions next to these terms and leave a blank space for additional information. Listen carefully during the next class meeting and write down any additional information the professor may give about each particular term.

New Term	Definition	Professor's definition or additional information

FIND AN INTEREST

When a topic is important to us, we immediately listen to what people have to say about it. For example, let's say we turn on our radio and hear that a traffic accident is blocking Highway 31. We suddenly become very interested because Highway 31 is our main route in traveling home from work. We want to know exactly where the accident took place and how this will affect our plans to get home.

Make It Interesting!

The information that your professors give you in lectures may not always hold your interest. However, you can make this information more interesting by relating it to your life:

■ Put yourself in the circumstances that you are hearing about. How can this information be applied to your life?

■ Think about how you can use this information in the future (can you use this information in conversation? to earn more money? to become skillful at a certain type of work?)

■ Think about how this information could benefit others. How would you explain this information to them?

■ Think about cases, situations, or examples in which this information has played a role in the lives of people you know. How were their lives affected? What would you do in similar circumstances?

Relating Information to Your Own Life

Read the following excerpt from a communications textbook. Then think of the information in terms of how it relates to your life and answer the discussion questions that follow.

> You develop and maintain friendships to satisfy those needs that can only be satisfied by certain people. On the basis of your experiences or your predictions, you select as friends those who will help to satisfy your basic growth needs. Selecting friends on the basis of need satisfaction is similar to choosing a marriage partner, an employee, or any person who may be in a position to satisfy your needs. Thus, if you need to be the center of attention or to be popular, you might select friends who allow you, and even encourage you, to be the center of attention or who tell you, verbally and nonverbally, that you are popular.
>
> As your needs change, the qualities you look for in friendships also change. In many instances, old friends are dropped from your close circle to be replaced by new friends who better serve these new needs. (DeVito 401)

1. What are some of your own basic growth needs (e.g., being the center of attention; being exposed to new ideas; being able to see your good points and abilities)? How do your friends allow and encourage you to fulfill these needs?

2. What qualities did you look for in the friendships you made before you started college? What qualities do you look for in the friendships that you have made in college?

3. Have you ever experienced the replacing of old friends from your close circle with new friends who better serve new needs?

Learn More About the Subject

The more we know about a subject the more interesting it becomes to us. Therefore, to develop an interest, you need to learn more about the topic! For example, if you are taking a theater class but have never seen a play, it may seem boring to read a critique of a play. However, if you see the play and then read the critique, you may become very interested. You may find that the critic had the same thoughts and opinions about the play that you did. Or the critique may lead you to see the play from a completely different point of view. Your interest would increase more if you watched other students auditioning for this play on campus, helped paint the set, or even auditioned for a part in a play yourself!

EXERCISE 11-4	**Expanding Your Knowledge of a Subject**

Engage in an activity on campus that provides more information about a subject that you are studying. Some examples include: (1) attending a lecture on the environment if you are studying earth science, (2) writing an article for the school newspaper if you are studying composition, (3) going to the language lab if you are studying Spanish or another foreign language, (4) attending a debate if you are studying political science, (5) attending an art show if you are studying art, (6) observing at a school if you are taking an education class.

Increase Your Listening Vocabulary

When speakers use sophisticated terms with an audience whose vocabulary is not on the same level, the listeners can become very bored. Although it takes effort and determination to bring ourselves up to advanced levels of speech, it is also very exciting to know that we are able to increase our vocabulary. There are several ways to learn new vocabulary from class lectures. As discussed earlier in this chapter, reading the textbook and learning the new terms before hearing the lecture provides a solid base for understanding the words used in the speech.

A second way to learn vocabulary from a lecture is to keep a journal for new terms. During every lecture, write down all unfamiliar words along with the sentence or phrase in which the terms were used—this provides the necessary context you will need later. After the class, look up these words in the dictionary and choose the meaning that makes the most sense. Write the meanings under their terms in your notes. Listen for these words to be used again in the following lectures. Try using these words in their proper context during class discussions. And ask the professor about any words that you are unsure of.

Starting a Vocabulary Journal

Start a vocabulary journal. Write down any unfamiliar terms from a textbook reading assignment along with their definitions. Listen for these words during your lectures and write down how they were used. During class, ask your professor if you are unsure about any terms, definitions, or use of these terms.

Vocabulary Journal		
New term & definition	Sentence or phrase using new term	Professor's explanation

TAKE NOTES FROM LECTURES

It is easier to take notes from a textbook than it is to take notes from a lecture. While we are reading a textbook we are able to stop at any point, think about the information, and then choose what to write in our notes. We lose this advantage when listening to a lecture because the speaker has control of the pace and the words vanish into thin air as quickly as they are spoken.

Also, textbook information is more organized than lectures because the writer can write and rewrite the information until the meaning is very clear. A speaker cannot revise spoken words in this way. A speaker may forget a point and then later remember and mention it out of the planned sequence of ideas. A speaker may also drift away from the original outline or insert a long-winded example to further explain a point. Questions from the listeners may further drive the speaker from the intended organization. Therefore, our notes may end up a little jumbled at the end of a talk.

There are a few things we can do to help organize our lecture notes:

1. Read or skim the textbook chapter before going to class. The more background information we gather on a subject, the easier it is to understand and remember what we hear.

2. Ask questions when something in a lecture is not understood. It is much easier later to study notes that make sense to us than to try to memorize notes that we don't understand.

3. Rewrite lecture notes immediately after class is over; fill in any missing information before it is forgotten. Be sure you are able to answer the question "What is the speaker's purpose for giving the lecture: to inform, entertain, or persuade?"

Identifying the Speaker's Outline

Every speaker follows (or should follow) an outline. Be ready to listen for the speaker's outline. How do we listen for the outline? First, identify the topic, the important main ideas, and the organization of the *supporting details* (information that explains the main ideas). To do this, you need to recognize if the speaker is providing a solution to a problem or comparing two things. You must realize when the speaker is presenting examples to support an idea and when he or she is presenting evidence to support an argument. Ask yourself the following questions:

1. What is the speaker's organizational pattern: term, definition, and example; topic and list; process; time order; or argument?

2. If directions are being given, what exactly are we required to do? What are the steps of the process and in what order should we complete them?

3. Is the speaker's information true to our own experiences? Will this new information change what we believe to be true?

4. Does the speaker have good support for his or her statements/arguments? Is the speaker giving us facts, statistics, or personal experiences? Is the support logical? Does the support contain any fallacies?

Several types of clues can help you recognize the speaker's main points. The speaker may provide:

■ An outline of the lecture on a chalkboard, transparency, or PowerPoint presentation.

■ A summary of important points at the end of the lecture.

■ Key words and phrases that introduce the main points:

Above all	The most important ideas are
This is the problem	The main point is
Statistics indicate	The solution to this is
The most important thing to remember is	

■ Key words and phrases that help us recognize when supporting details fall into a topic and list, process, or example pattern:

Topic and List	Sequence	Example
first	the first step is	to illustrate
second	first	a demonstration
third	the process is	for example
also	next	
in addition	after that	
furthermore	finally	

■ Key words and phrases that show us the speaker is changing direction:

nevertheless	whereas	this is not always true
but	on the contrary	different from this
however		

■ Key words and phrases that indicate uncertainty or show that a statement has not been proven to be true:

perhaps	probable causes	sometimes
possible	may or may not	

Other types of clues that can help you identify a speaker's main points include a particular tone of voice and body language. For example, the sentence "This is too much" could mean many things depending on the speaker's intonation and expressions:

"This is too much!" (excited, enthusiastic)

"This is too much?" (unsure, questioning)

"This is too much." (sarcastic)

EXERCISE
11-6

Identifying Key Words to Organization

Key words provide clues to the organization of a presentation. Select the appropriate key words for the following actions. The first one has been done for you.

___c___ 1. Which of the following key words help us to recognize the speaker's main point?
   a. perhaps
   b. however
   c. above all
   d. after that

_____ 2. Which of the following key words help us recognize when supporting details fall into a process pattern?
   a. to illustrate
   b. after that
   c. a demonstration of this is
   d. for example

_____ 3. Which of the following key words help us recognize that the speaker is changing the direction of his or her idea?
   a. sometimes
   b. perhaps
   c. the main point is
   d. however

_____ 4. Which of the following key words help us recognize when supporting details fall into a topic and list pattern?

a. first

b. to illustrate this

c. for example

d. the main point is

_____ **5.** Which of the following key words help us recognize when supporting details fall into an example pattern?

a. furthermore

b. after that

c. to illustrate this

d. the first step is

Getting Ahead in College Box 11.1

ABBREVIATIONS FOR NOTE-TAKING

Develop a system of abbreviations to write information as quickly as possible. Since it takes so long to write entire sentences, your notes should include only the important points, supporting information, and examples. You can especially leave out words that carry little meaning such as "the" or "a."

Sample Abbreviations for Note-Taking

and	+
equals	=
number	#
therefore	∴

Create your own system for abbreviating words for note-taking purposes. Practice abbreviating the following words and symbols. Then look at your abbreviations while covering the words. Can you tell what your abbreviation means? If not, choose another abbreviation that will quickly remind you of the word.

Word	Abbreviation	Word	Abbreviation
within		first	
with		for example	
without		information	
because		political science	

| EXERCISE 11-7 | Identifying Organizational Patterns in a Lecture |

Go to a lecture given on your campus. Listen for the speaker's outline. Identify the organizational patterns that he or she uses. (Review Chapter 6.) Some common organizational patterns are: (1) term, definition, and example, (2) topic and list, (3) time order, and (4) process.

The Cornell Method

There are many systems of note-taking. The Cornell Method is very popular among college students. With this system you take the following steps:

1. Divide your notebook page into three sections as shown in the example below.

2. Label the right-hand column "Notes," and write your main points and support in outline form.

3. Label the left-hand column "Questions," and review the information that you wrote in the right-hand column. Determine what questions get answered by each piece of information. Write those questions in the left-hand column. (If the information consists mainly of terms and definitions, a simple question and answer format may work better than an outline format.)

4. Label the bottom of the page "Summary" and write a summary of that page's notes in paragraph form.

Let's look at an excerpt from a biology text and the notes taken from it in the Cornell form:

More commonly used than any other depressant, alcohol can be a very dangerous drug. Habitual heavy drinking (three or more drinks a day at least three times a week) can cause liver and brain damage and may be associated with cardiovascular disease and several forms of cancer. When a woman drinks during pregnancy, alcohol enters the fetus's bloodstream and causes serious birth defects. (Campbell, Mitchell and Reece 571)

Questions	Notes
What is heavy drinking?	3 + drinks/day for 3 + times/week
What are the effects of heavy drinking?	■ liver damage ■ brain damage ■ cardiovascular disease ■ cancer
What happens when pregnant women drink?	child born with serious birth defects

Summary: Heavy drinking can cause liver and brain damage, cardiovascular disease, and cancer. Any amount of alcohol can cause serious birth defects if a woman drinks when she is pregnant.

Getting Ahead in College Box 11.2

PARTS OF SPEECH: USING THE CONJUNCTION "AND"

The conjunction "and" can be used to join two complete thoughts or two similar ideas. Combine the following sentences by inserting the word "and."

1. Alcohol is more commonly used than any other depressant.

It can be a very dangerous drug.

Alcohol is more commonly used than any other depressant and it can be a very dangerous drug.

2. Habitual heavy drinking can cause liver and brain damage.

It may be associated with cardiovascular disease and cancer.

_____

_____

(continued on next page)

3. When a woman drinks during pregnancy, alcohol enters the fetus's bloodstream.

It causes serious birth defects.

_____

_____

EXERCISE
11-8

Reading and Taking Notes with the Cornell Method

Read and take notes from the following excerpt using the Cornell Method.

Bacteria

All organisms, humans included, are almost constantly exposed to bacteria, some of which are potentially harmful. In fact, most of us are well most of the time only because our body defenses check the growth of bacterial pathogens, disease-causing agents. Occasionally, the balance shifts in favor of a pathogen, and we become ill. Even some of the bacteria that are normal residents of the human body can make us ill when our defenses have been weakened by poor nutrition or by a viral infection.

Pathogenic bacteria cause about half of all human diseases. Most cause disease by producing poisons, which are of two types: exotoxins and endotoxins. Exotoxins, toxic proteins secreted by bacterial cells, include some of the most potent poisons known. A single gram of the exotoxin that causes botulism, for instance, could kill a million people.

Bacterial species that are generally harmless can also develop strains that cause illness. In the past decade there have been a number of outbreaks of severe illness and several thousand deaths caused by a pathogenic, exotoxin-producing strain E. coli. Commonly found in cattle, these bacteria do not hurt the cattle, but in infected humans, the exotoxin selectively enters the cells that line blood vessels and kills them. Bloody diarrhea ensues and, in extreme cases, kidney failure. Vaccines for both people and cattle are being developed, but the best preventive measure at present is to avoid eating undercooked meat. (Campbell, Mitchell and Reece 330)

BACTERIA	
QUESTIONS	NOTES

SUMMARY:

Reading and Taking Lecture Notes with the Cornell Method

Apply the Cornell Method of taking notes to one of your lecture classes. Follow these steps:

1. Read the chapters that the speaker will talk about.

2. Organize your notebook to include areas on one side of the page for questions, notes, and summaries.

3. Take notes from the lecture.

4. Write questions in the margin and a summary of each page if you have time during the lecture or immediately after the lecture.

STUDY! STUDY! STUDY! USING THE R2D2 SYSTEM

It is easier to learn information that is organized instead of information that is jumbled together. The **R2D2 System** helps you un-jumble your notes and decide what to study. **R2D2** stands for:

■ **Review** class notes.

■ **Review** text notes.

■ **Draw** them together.

■ **Determine** what to study.

You first start by reviewing your lecture notes and deciding what is important enough to be on an exam. Then, you review your textbook notes and do the same. Next, you draw together or combine the important information from both your lecture and textbook notes. Finally, you determine what you don't know and concentrate on learning it. This method keeps you from wasting time going over information that you already understand and remember. It also reminds you to study both text and class notes.

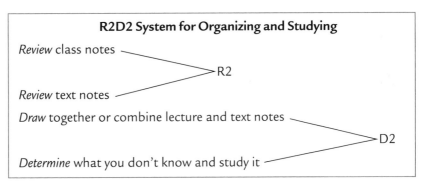

Combine Your Text and Study Notes

Studying is an ongoing process that starts the first day of classes and ends after the last final exam has been taken. Begin by buying a three-ring binder, and write only on one side of the page. Label each day's notes with the topic of the lecture and the date. This enables you to rewrite notes and replace them in the best order. Leave the first page blank. Write your notes from the textbook chapter on the right-hand side of your notebook. This leaves the back of the first page to write lecture notes.

Topic Leave this side blank until you go to class. If the professor has anything to add to your text notes, write it here.	Topic Your textbook notes should be written here. During class, you can check the professor's notes against these notes. If they are the same, there is no need to add new notes.	Topic **Class notes** (back of 1st page)	Topic **Text notes**
page 2	page 3	page 2	page 3

In class, you can check your text notes against the information provided by the speaker. If the information is already in your textbook notes, there is no need to write it a second time. If the speaker adds information that is different from what you have in your notes, you can jot it down on the side that you left blank. If you skip every other page in your notebook when you are taking notes from your textbook, you will always have room to add new information during class lectures.

The information from the speaker may fill in the gaps that you have from your textbook reading. The speaker may also provide additional information that is not in your textbook. By setting up your notebook in this way, you are sure to get all of the information from both the lecture and the textbook without writing notes twice or writing information on the same topic in different areas of your notebook.

EXERCISE
11-10

Using the R2D2 System

Use the R2D2 system to combine the information from the following textbook and lecture excerpts. The textbook provides a detailed definition of "love." However, the textbook author mentions information about "clusters" that he assumes the reader should know. During the lecture the professor explains what the clusters are. Read both the lecture and text information.

1. Take notes on the textbook excerpt.

2. Take notes on the lecture information.

3. Combine the information from both notes.

Textbook Excerpt

Love is a combination of intimacy, passion, and commitment (Sternberg, 1986, 1988). **Intimacy** (corresponding to part of Davis's caring cluster) is the emotional aspect of love and includes sharing, communicating, and mutual support; it is a sense of closeness and connection. **Passion** (corresponding to the passion cluster) is the motivational aspect and consists of physical attraction and romantic passion. **Commitment** (corresponding to part of Davis's caring cluster) is the cognitive aspect and consists of the decisions you make concerning your lover. When you have a relationship characterized by intimacy only, you have essentially a liking relationship. When you have only passion, you have a relationship of infatuation. When you have only commitment, you have empty love. When you have all three components to about equal degrees, you have complete or consummate love. (DeVito 406)

Lecture Excerpt

Your textbook explains Sternberg's definition of love. Another researcher, named Davis, looks at love a little differently. He thinks love is a combination of passion and caring. Both of these emotions are looked at as clusters consisting of more specific emotions. The passion cluster, for example, consists of fascination (seen in the lovers' preoccupation with each other), exclusiveness (seen in their mutual commitment), and sexual desire (seen in their desire to touch). The caring cluster consists of giving the utmost (seen in sacrifice for the lover) and serving as the lover's champion or advocate (seen in support for the lover's interest and success). (DeVito 408)

	Textbook Notes (Page 3 of Notebook)

What is love?	I. Love =
	    A.
	    B.
	    C.
	 <div align="right">*(continued on next page)*</div>

What is intimacy?	II. Intimacy =
What cluster does it correspond to?	A. It corresponds to
What is passion?	III. Passion =
What cluster does it correspond to?	A. It corresponds to
What is commit-ment?	IV. Commitment =
	A. It corresponds to
What cluster does it correspond to?	
What is a liking rela-tionship?	V. A liking relationship is
What is infatuation?	VI. Infatuation is
What is empty love?	VII. Empty love is
What is consum-mate love?	VIII. Consummate love is

Summary
Sternberg's definition of love is:

	Lecture Notes (Page 2 of Notebook)
What is love?	I. Love =
What is the passion cluster?	II. Passion cluster
	A.
	B.
	C.
What is the caring cluster?	III. Caring cluster
	A.
	B.

Summary
According to Davis, love is:

	Rewritten Combined Lecture and Text Notes
What is love?	I. Love is
	A. Sternberg's Definition:
	B. Davis's Definition:
What is intimacy?	II. Intimacy is
What cluster does it correspond to?	A. Sternberg's Definition:
	B. Davis's Definition:
What is passion?	III. Passion is
What cluster does it correspond to?	A. Sternberg's Definition:
	B. Davis's Definition:
What is commitment?	VI. Commitment is
	A. Sternberg's Definition:
What cluster does it correspond to?	B. Davis's Definition:
What is a liking relationship?	V. Liking is:
What is infatuation?	VI. Infatuation is:
What is empty love?	VII. Empty love is:
What is consummate love?	VIII. Consummate love is:

Summary

Sternberg and Davis's definitions of love are similar because each includes:

Sternberg and Davis's definitions of love are different because:

KEY WORDS AND CONCEPTS FOR NOTES

Once you have your notes in perfect order, you should use a study technique such as the "recite and review" step of the PQ4R method (see Chapter 2) to help you memorize your notes. At this point you will think of one key word to remind you of each main idea and its supporting details. Memorizing these key words will help you to recall the information in your notes when you are taking an exam. You can number the key words and place them in the left-hand column across from the information they represent.

As in the review step of the PQ4R method, you should quiz yourself on the content of the notes by looking at the key word clues and reciting the corresponding information several different times during the week before an exam. You can also use the key words to make up possible test questions. If you have trouble remembering the information that is connected with any of the key words, you need to study the information some more and quiz yourself again on the weak areas.

Key Word	Term or Concept	Definition	Example
emotional	**Intimacy**	emotional aspect of love that provides a sense of closeness and connection	sharing, communicating, and giving support
physical	**Passion**	motivational aspect of love; consists of physical attraction and romantic passion	two people fascinated with each other
mental	**Commitment**	the mental aspect; consists of the decisions you make concerning your lover	giving and supporting

EXERCISE
11-11

Creating Short-Answer and Multiple-Choice Questions for Study

Let's say that you are in a communications course and tomorrow's daily quiz will include the information from the text and lecture notes about love. Create two short-answer questions and two multiple-choice questions to use in studying for the quiz. Follow the example below.

Example
Question: What is intimacy? Define the term and give an example.

Answer: Intimacy is the emotional part of love that makes people feel close and connected. For example, they communicate, share, and give support to each other.

Question: What is the term for the emotional aspect of love that provides a sense of closeness and connection?
  a. commitment
  b. passion
  c. intimacy

Short-Answer Questions

1. Question: _____

  Answer: _____

2. Question: _____

  Answer: _____

Multiple-Choice Questions

1. Question: _____

  a. _____

  b. _____

  c. _____

2. Question: _____

  a. _____

  b. _____

  c. _____

HINTS FOR TEST-TAKING

Professors realize that students may not do well on the first exam simply because they do not know what to expect. Many professors will keep old exams and copies of lecture notes on file in the library. This is so students can look over an exam similar to the one that will be given and plan how to study for it. Therefore, it is a good idea to study the format of old exams. You should not confuse this advice with studying an old exam as a shortcut for learning the information without reading the textbook and going to class. *You will surely fail* if you take this shortcut. A three-page exam cannot possibly teach you how to understand all the information in a 600-page textbook or replace the 45 hours of lecture/discussion that goes on in a classroom.

Begin your exam preparation by recognizing possible test questions. There are not many places where test questions can come from. Most instructors test only on items that are covered in the assigned readings or from class discussions/lectures. Therefore, you can try to guess the questions that will be on the exam, and you can prepare the answers and memorize them before the exam.

The exam format (multiple choice, essay, short answer) will direct your decision on how to study for the exam. For example, rereading a chapter is a good strategy for a multiple-choice exam. You read the chapter once through to gain an understanding of the information. Then, you should read it a second time and create multiple-choice questions and distracters (incorrect choices) from the information as you read.

When you study for an essay exam, you should look for lists of items that can be defined, explained, or discussed. Because the grading of essay exams can become very subjective, professors look for answers containing lists of items that can be counted. In this way, they will be able to say that Tyrone's paper deserved an "A" because he included "all six types of love." However, Hanif received a "B" because he left out one of the types in his explanation.

Guessing the test questions from lectures is not any more difficult. However, you must always be on your toes or the clues could slip past you unnoticed. You should pay particular attention to questions the professor asks the class, writes on the board, includes on pop quizzes, or repeats in one or more lectures. If the questions are important enough to bring up in class, they will be important enough to include on an exam. You should ask questions about information you did not understand. Chances are that other students did not understand the same issue either and they will be glad that you brought it up. You should also pay attention to questions that other students ask the professor. They may bring up questions or problems that may have gone completely unnoticed by you. Chances are that if others did not understand a point, you may not have understood it either. Finally, you should watch for class discussion of information from your reading assignments. If it is discussed in depth, then there is a good chance it will appear on the exam.

What do you do with all of these possible exam questions? You should write questions in the left-hand column of your notebook and answers to these questions in the right-hand column of your notebook **after every textbook reading** *and* **after every lecture**. If you keep up with this system throughout the semester, you should have many of the test questions and answers to the test before you start to study. If you don't keep up with this question/answer system, you may end up using all of your study time searching for and organizing information. You may spend all of your time getting ready to study and actually run out of time to memorize and learn the material.

| EXERCISE 11-12 | **Creating Essay Questions for Study** |

Choose one subject that you are studying and use one of the four clue words below to create an essay question for an upcoming exam. Use the information in your textbook and your lecture notes to predict the question. After predicting the question, write out the answer. Use the information in your textbook and in your notes to formulate your answer.

1. **Define:** In your answer, provide the term, its definition or meaning, and an example that illustrates or shows the meaning of the term.

2. **List:** In your answer, mention a list of facts, reasons, ideas, or events. These items should be written in sentence and paragraph form—not as a numbered or bulleted list of short phrases.

3. **Compare:** In your answer, show similarities (how they are alike) and differences of two or more concepts, persons, events, or things.

4. **Contrast:** In your answer, show the differences between two or more concepts, persons, events, or things.

THE WEEK BEFORE

Follow the plan below and you will never have to cram for an exam again!

Plan spaced reviews a week before a major exam. Use the R2D2 system to organize your notes and decide what is important to study. Then determine a study schedule. After organizing your notes, you should study and review every other day for a period of about a week. This means you will need to look at your syllabus ahead of time to find out when your exams are given and plan special study and review sessions up until the day of the exam.

On the first review day, you should organize and combine your class and textbook notes and determine what you need to study. On the second day, you should make up key words that will help you remember important information. You should memorize the key words and then review using your key words. Next, you should repeat your review every other day until the day of the exam. Be sure to review the day of the exam and immediately before the exam. This will help you recall the information more quickly and accurately.

You give yourself a huge advantage when you complete this type of study and review because with it, you will remember at least 80 percent of the information. Without the study and review, you will recall only 20 percent of the information. In other words, you will forget 80 percent.

Study and Review Schedule						
Day 1	Day 2	Day 3	Day 4	Day 5	Day 6	Day 7
Use R2D2 system to determine what to study.	Make up key words. Quiz yourself until you make no mistakes.		Review key words. Study notes for items forgotten.		Review key words. Study notes for items forgotten. Rest Get 8 hours of sleep	Review key words. Exam

THE NIGHT BEFORE

There are two things you should do the night before an exam: rest and sleep. It is not good to stay up all night before an exam. You will only tire yourself out and make it more difficult to think during the exam. Lack of sleep impairs both long-term and short-term memory and will *most certainly work against you.*

It is best to start preparation early in the week and space reviews throughout the week. You should review the day before and then give yourself time to rest and get your mind off the exam the night before. Also, because of the relationship between sleep and memory, you should get eight hours of sleep before the exam. You should, however, review the material once more before the exam to keep the material fresh in your mind.

Getting Ahead in College Box 11.3

THE PRONUNCIATION OF VOCABULARY

A single vowel appearing in a one-syllable word is usually short. For example, in the word "bat," the "a" is short because it is a single vowel in a one-syllable word. The word "rate" has two vowels in a one-syllable word; therefore, the "a" carries a long sound.

Underline all of the one-syllable words in the following paragraph that contain a single short vowel.

All organisms, humans included, are almost constantly exposed to bacteria, some of which are potentially harmful. In fact, most of us are well most of the time only because our body defenses check the growth of bacterial pathogens, disease-causing agents. Occasionally, the balance shifts in favor of a pathogen, and we become ill. Even some of the bacteria that are normal residents of the human body can make us ill when our defenses have been weakened by poor nutrition or by a viral infection.

A Reading in Political Science

Do the media give us enough information to make important political decisions? Read the following excerpt from a political science textbook to find out how much information we are receiving from the television news. After reading, mark and annotate the passage. Then, answer the comprehension questions that follow.

Vocabulary in Context

Answer the vocabulary questions first to become familiar with the new terms. The first term has been identified for you.

a. precipitously—sharply

b. threshold—maximum, upper limit, ceiling

c. peripheral—minor, unimportant, not the main point

d. essence—real meaning

e. significance—importance

_____b_____ **1.** CBS tried to give presidential candidates at least 30 seconds to talk on the television news without being interrupted, but CBS soon dropped this upper limit or _____ to 20 seconds.

_____ **2.** While he was president of the United States, Jimmy Carter told a news reporter that the unimportant or _____ parts of his speech were reported by the news.

_____ **3.** Carter felt that the reporters always missed the real meaning or _____ of what he had said.

_____ **4.** Politicians are generally given seven-second sound-bites. Many people believe that it is impossible to say anything important or of any _____ in that short period of time.

_____ **5.** Since the late 1960s, the amount of time that a presidential candidate can talk on the TV news without interruption has dropped _____.

Presenting the News

[1] Strangely enough, as technology has enabled the media to pass along information with greater speed, news coverage has become less thorough. Newspapers once routinely reprinted the entire text of important political speeches; now the *New York Times* is virtually the only paper that does so—and even the *Times* has cut back sharply on this practice. In place of speeches, Americans now hear sound bites of 15 seconds or less on TV. The average length of time that a presidential candidate has been given to talk uninterrupted on the TV news has declined **precipitously** since the late 1960s. Responding to criticism of sound-bite journalism, in 1992 CBS News briefly vowed that it

would let a candidate speak for at least 30 seconds at a time. However, CBS found this to be unworkable and soon dropped the **threshold** to 20 seconds, noting that even this was flexible. In 1996, the average sound bite of a candidate shown talking on the nightly news once again averaged less than 10 seconds.

[2]   Even successful politicians sometimes feel frustrated by sound-bite journalism. A year after his election to the presidency, Jimmy Carter told a reporter that

> It's a strange thing that you can go through your campaign for president, and you have a basic theme that you express in a 15- or 20-minute standard speech . . . but the traveling press—sometimes exceeding 100 people—will never report that speech to the public. The **peripheral** aspects become the headlines, but the basic **essence** of what you stand for and what you hope to accomplish is never reported.

Rather than presenting their audience with the whole chicken, the media typically give just a McNugget. Why should politicians work to build a carefully crafted case for their point of view when a catchy line will do just as well? As former CBS anchor Walter Cronkite writes, "Naturally, nothing of any **significance** is going to be said in seven seconds, but this seems to work to the advantage of many politicians. They are not required to say anything of significance, and issues can be avoided rather than confronted." Cronkite and others have proposed that in order to force candidates to go beyond sound bites they should be given blocks of free air time for a series of nights to discuss their opposing views. (Edwards, Wattenberg and Lineberry 230–31)

Comprehension Questions

Select the best answer that completes each sentence below. The first has been completed for you.

_____ c _____ **1.** The main point of this selection is:

  a. sound bites of political candidates are less than 10 seconds.

  b. Jimmy Carter felt that the press missed the main points of his speeches.

  c. news coverage has become less thorough.

_____ 2. Today most Americans learn about a candidate's political ideas:

    a. by reading a candidate's entire political speech in a newspaper.

    b. by reading part of a candidate's political speech in the *New York Times*.

    c. by hearing 15-second sound-bites of their political positions on TV.

_____ 3. What is the text pattern of the following sentence?

Responding to criticism of sound-bite journalism, in 1992 CBS News briefly vowed that it would let a candidate speak for at least 30 seconds at a time.

    a. topic and list

    b. cause and effect

    c. time order

_____ 4. One inference the author wants us to make in paragraph 2 is:

    a. the media provide Chicken McNuggets for their audiences.

    b. Jimmy Carter felt that sound-bite technology helped him get his main points across to audiences during his campaign.

    c. politicians will stop trying to support their opinions with logical evidence because they will never need to speak on their views for any length of time.

_____ 5. Walter Cronkite believes that political candidates will avoid issues rather than debate them

    a. if the candidates are given more than 20-second sound bites to explain their views.

    b. if the entire text of important political speeches is not printed in newspapers.

    c. if the candidates are not given blocks of free air time for discussion.

Visual Literacy Box 11.1

Bar Graphs: Presenting the News

When the numbers in the paragraph below are displayed in a bar graph, it is easier to see the author's point. The horizontal axis (going across on the bottom of the chart) represents the year, while the vertical axis (going up and down on the left-hand side of the chart) represents the number of seconds a political candidate could speak on television. Did the number of seconds that a candidate could speak on television increase or decrease between 1992 and 1996?

❏Increase   ❏Decrease

In 1992 CBS News briefly vowed that it would let a candidate speak for at least 30 seconds at a time. However, CBS found this to be unworkable and soon dropped the threshold to 20 seconds, noting that even this was flexible. In 1996, the average sound bite of a candidate shown talking on the nightly news once again averaged less than 10 seconds.

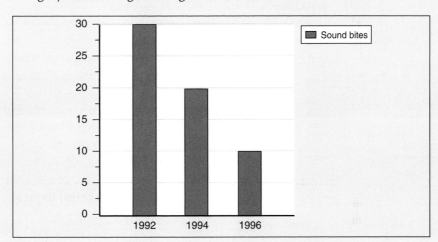

A Reading in Math Study Skills

Have you ever had math anxiety? Read the following passage to find out what happens when people become anxious about taking a math exam. Then, answer the comprehension questions that follow the reading.

Vocabulary in Context

Answer the vocabulary questions first to become familiar with the new terms. The first term has been identified for you.

a. intensify—increase

b. anxiety—worry, fear

c. persists—continues

d. inconveniences—troubles, problems, bothers

e. nausea—unsettled stomach, sickness

_____a_____ **1.** Some students become physically ill when their worries and fears over an exam increase or _____.

_____ **2.** The worry and fear that some students feel causes them to experience sweaty palms, high blood pressure, nervousness, and _____ or stomach upset.

_____ **3.** These bothers or physical _____ that students feel affect their concentration and can cause them to "draw a blank."

_____ **4.** Some students cannot recall the needed math information when worry or fear _____ throughout the test.

_____ **5.** Students with high test _____ have two basic types of troubled feelings—emotional distress and worry.

The Different Types of Test Anxiety

[1] The two basic types of test **anxiety** are emotional and worry. Students with high test anxiety have both emotional and worry anxiety.

[2]   Signs of emotional anxiety are upset stomach, **nausea**, sweaty palms, pain in the neck, still shoulders, high blood pressure, rapid shallow breathing, rapid heartbeat, or general feelings of nervousness. As anxiety increases, these feelings **intensify**. Some students even run to the bathroom to throw up or have diarrhea.

[3]   Even though these *feelings* are caused by anxiety, the physical response is real. These feelings and physical **inconveniences** can affect your concentration and your testing speed, and they can cause you to completely "draw a blank."

[4]   Worry anxiety causes the student to think about failing the test. These negative thoughts can happen either before or during the test. This negative "self-talk" causes students to focus on their anxiety instead of recalling math concepts.

[5]   The effects of test anxiety range from a "mental block" on a test to avoiding homework. One of the most common side effects of test anxiety is getting the test and immediately forgetting information that you know. Some students describe this event as having a "mental block," "going blank," or finding that the test "looks like Greek."

[6]   After five or ten minutes into the test, some of these students can refocus on the test and start working the problems. They have, however, lost valuable time. For other students, anxiety **persists** throughout the test and they cannot recall the needed math information. It is only after they walk out the door that they can remember how to work the problems.

[7]   Sometimes math anxiety does not cause students to "go blank" but slows down their mental processing speed. This means it takes longer to recall formulas and concepts and to work problems. The result is frustration and loss of time, leading to *more* anxiety. (Nolting 48)

Comprehension Questions

Select the best answer that completes each sentence below. The first has been completed for you.

_____c_____ 1. According to the author, a "slow down of mental processing speed" means:

a. students will remember more information at a slower rate.

b. it takes students less time to remember formulas and work problems because they are able to blank out all distractions.

       c. it takes longer to remember formulas and to work problems.

_____ 2. If someone tells you that a "test looks like Greek," the person means that:

       a. the test contains Greek and Latin word parts.

       b. the person immediately forgot all the information he or she knew about the subject.

       c. the person is studying Greek and therefore knows all of the answers.

_____ 3. Worry anxiety causes the student to think about:

       a. other projects that are due.

       b. getting an "A" on the math text.

       c. failing the math test.

_____ 4. The overall text pattern in this selection is:

       a. cause and effect

       b. term, definition, and example

       c. process

_____ 5. Emotional anxiety can cause:

       a. negative "self-talk"

       b. a mental block

       c. an upset stomach

Visual Literacy Box 11.2

Contrast Charts: The Excuse

When we read a paragraph that is written in a contrast pattern, it is easier to understand the information if it is put into a contrast chart. To make a contrast chart, you simply list all of the points connected

(continued on next page)

with one idea on one side of the page and all points connected with the opposite idea on the other side of the page. Read "The Excuse" (the Reading in Interpersonal Communications in this chapter), and finish the contrast chart below.

Contrast Chart: The Excuse

Good Excuse Makers	Bad Excuse Makers
■ make excuses in moderation	■ make excuses too often
■	■
■	■
■	■
■	**Worst Excuses**
Best Excuses	■
■	■ no request for forgiveness
■ a request for forgiveness	■
■	■

A Reading in Interpersonal Communications

Why do people make excuses for their behavior? Read the article below to find out which excuses are considered good and which ones are considered bad. After reading, answer the comprehension questions and follow the directions to complete an outline of the ideas presented in this selection.

Vocabulary in Context

Answer the vocabulary questions first to become familiar with the new terms. The first term has been identified for you.

a. pervade—touch every part of

b. justify—give a good reason for; give an explanation for; defend

c. implications—associations; suggestions

d. counter—opposite

e. subsequent—following, later, resulting

_____

_____a_____ **1.** Excuses _____ all interactions and behaviors.

_____ **2.** We must always give excuses to _____ why we have done something that others view negatively.

_____ **3.** A good excuse will lessen the negative reaction and _____ or resulting stress of an action viewed negatively by others.

_____ **4.** A good excuse will help us keep a positive image and reduce the negative suggestions or _____ that our performance was not good.

_____ **5.** We must be especially prepared with an excuse when we say something that is against or _____ to what others expect.

The Excuse

[1] At times you may say the wrong thing, but because you can't erase the message, you may try to account for it. Perhaps the most common method for doing so is the **excuse**. Excuses **pervade** all forms of communication and behavior.

[2]   You learn early in life that when you do something that others will view negatively, an excuse is in order to **justify** your performance. The excuse, as C. R. Snyder (1984) notes, "plays a central role in how we get along in life, both with yourself and with other people." Snyder (1984; Snyder, Higgins, and Stucky, 1983) defines excuses as "explanations or actions that lessen the negative **implications** of an actor's performance, thereby maintaining a positive image for oneself and others."

[3]   Excuses seem especially in order when we say or are accused of saying something that runs **counter** to what is expected or considered "right" by the people involved or by society in general. The excuse, ideally, lessens the negative impact, or effect, of the message.

[4]   **Some Motives for Excuse Making**. The major motive, or reason, for excuse making seems to be to maintain our self-esteem, to project a positive image to ourselves and to others. Excuses are also offered to reduce the stress that may be created by a bad performance. We feel that if we can offer an excuse—especially a good one that is accepted by those around us—it will reduce the negative reaction and the **subsequent** stress that accompanies a poor performance.

[5]   Excuses enable you to take risks and engage in behavior that may be unsuccessful; you may offer an anticipatory excuse (anticipating or expecting a negative reaction, you offer the excuse ahead of time): "My throat's a bit sore, but I'll give the speech a try." The excuse is designed to lessen the criticism should you fail to deliver an acceptable speech.

[6]   Excuses also enable us to maintain effective interpersonal relationships even after some negative behavior. For example, after criticizing a friend's behavior and observing the negative reaction to our criticism, we might offer an excuse such as, "Please forgive me; I'm really exhausted. I'm just not thinking straight." Excuses enable us to place our messages—even our possible failures—in a more favorable light.

[7]   **Good and Bad Excuses.** The most important question to most people is what makes a good excuse and what makes a bad excuse (Snyder 1984; Slade 1995). How can you make good excuses and thus get out of problems, and how can you avoid bad excuses and thus only make matters worse? Good excuse makers use excuses in moderation; bad excuse makers rely on excuses too often. Good excuse makers avoid using excuses in the presence of those who know what really happened; bad excuse makers will make excuses even in these inappropriate situations. Good excuse makers avoid blaming others, especially those they work with; bad excuse makers blame even their work colleagues. In a similar way, good excuse makers do not blame others or the company for their failures; bad excuse makers do. Good excuse makers acknowledge their own responsibility for the failure by noting that they did something wrong (not that they lack competence); bad excuse makers refuse to accept any responsibility for their failure.

[8]   The best excuses are apologies because they contain three essential elements for a good excuse. (Slade)

- ■ an acknowledgment of the responsibility;

- ■ a request for forgiveness;

- ■ the suggestion that things will be done better in the future.

The worst excuses are the "I didn't do it" type because they fail to acknowledge responsibility and also because they offer no assurance that this failure will not happen again. (DeVito 281–83)

Comprehension Questions

Select the best answer that completes each sentence below. The first has been completed for you.

_____a_____ 1. The *main* reason for making an excuse is:
  a. to present a positive image to ourselves and to others.
  b. to continue important relationships after a negative behavior.
  c. to allow us to risk trying a new activity in which we may fail.

_____ 2. An anticipatory excuse is:
  a. an excuse offered after a negative behavior to save our self-esteem.
  b. an excuse that is offered before we try to do something so that it will lessen the negative reaction of others if we fail.
  c. an excuse offered after a failed attempt to do something to lessen the negative reaction of others.

_____ 3. An excuse is expected:
  a. when we have given a good performance.
  b. when we say something that is generally expected by society.
  c. when we say something that runs opposite to what is considered "right."

_____ 4. Good excuse makers:
  a. use excuses in moderation.
  b. blame others.
  c. fail to acknowledge responsibility.

_____ 5. The worst excuses:
  a. contain a request for forgiveness.
  b. suggest that things will be done better in the future.
  c. make no assurance that this failure will not happen again.

Taking Notes

Use the Cornell Method to take notes from this reading. Write your questions in the left-hand margin and the answers to your questions in the right margin. Below summarize the passage. The summary will highlight only the main points.

Questions	Notes
Questions	**Notes**
What is an excuse?	I. An excuse is:
Why do people make excuses?	II. Motives for Excuses
	A.
	B.
	C.
	D.
How do you make good excuses?	III. Good and Bad Excuse Makers
	A. Good Excuse Makers
How do you make bad excuses?	1.
	2.
	3.
	B. Bad Excuse Makers
	1.
	2.
	3.
What are 3 essential elements for good excuses?	IV. Three essential elements for good excuses:
	A.
	B.
	C.

Summary

CHAPTER
12

Reading Speed

● ●

In this chapter we learn about:

■ reading comprehension and how to improve it;

■ reading speed and how to calculate it;

■ reading rate and how to increase it.

WHAT IS SPEED READING?

Many commercial speed-reading programs boast high reading rates (2,500 words per minute) and teach people to move their eyes down the page quickly in zigzag or sweeping motions. The problem with these programs is that we can all move our eyes down the page very fast—even more quickly than we can turn the pages. However, there is a big difference between moving our eyes quickly and "reading." Reading requires understanding, or comprehending.

READING COMPREHENSION

As we read, we use all of the skills presented in this book:

■ finding the stated or implied main ideas.

- connecting the details to the main idea.

- recognizing the author's purpose or point of view.

- recognizing the text patterns.

- understanding inferences.

- drawing conclusions.

- understanding figurative language, idioms, and imagery.

- recognizing issues and arguments.

Comprehension, or understanding what we read, is a complex process with all of these connected activities happening at once in our brains. It takes a certain amount of time for our brains to think through all of these processes. Moving our hands along quickly or darting our eyes faster and faster down the page does not in any way help us to think faster. Therefore, *we can only read as quickly as we can think.*

How fast can we think? This depends on *what* we are reading. Research shows that we read faster when:

- we *know a lot* about the subject we are reading.

- we *know the meanings* of all of the words we are reading.

- we *are highly interested* in what we are reading.

- we *want to have only a general idea* without remembering details.

When all of these conditions that help us to read faster are present, we can calculate a general reading speed.

CALCULATING YOUR READING SPEED

There are two scores that we can calculate associated with reading speed: our **reading speed** and our **comprehension speed**. Our reading speed means how fast we read the words. The comprehension speed refers to how much we understand while reading the words. Use three simple math procedures (subtracting, dividing, and multiplying) to find your reading comprehension speed.

Step 1: Write down the time you begin reading the passage.

Example: 10:00:00 a.m. (hour: minutes: seconds)

Step 2: Write down the time you finish reading the passage.

Example: 10:02:30 (hour: minutes: seconds)

Step 3: Answer the comprehension questions at the end of the selection and correct your answers. If there are 10 questions, each question is worth 10 percentage points. For each question missed, subtract 10 percentage points. For example, if you miss one question, your score would be 90%. If you miss two questions, your score would be a 80%, and so on.

Step 4: Subtract your start time from your finish time. This gives you the number of minutes it took you to read the selection.

Example: Finish   10:02:30
Start   − 10:00:00
                 2:30   (2 minutes and 30 seconds)

Step 5: Change your reading time into seconds.

Example: If you read this passage in 2 minutes and 30 seconds, your reading rate would be calculated as follows.

Multiply the number of minutes in which you read the passage by 60 (seconds) and add any remaining seconds.

1 minute = 60 seconds

2 minutes = 2 × 60 seconds = 120 seconds

2 minutes and 30 seconds = 120 seconds + 30 seconds = 150 seconds

Step 6: Then divide the number of words in the passage by your time (150 seconds) and multiply that answer by 60 seconds to get your words per minute.

600 words ÷ 150 seconds = 4

4 × 60 seconds = 240 wpm

Step 7: Multiply your percentage correct on the comprehension questions times your words per minute.

Example: If you missed one question, your percentage correct would be 90% or .90.

.90 × 240 = 216 words per minute comprehension rate

In this case, you would have read 240 words per minute but understood what you were reading at a speed of 216 words per minute.

EXERCISE
12-1

Calculating Your Reading Speed and Comprehension Level

What is your reading speed and comprehension of college-level material? To find your reading rate, first record your starting time. Then read the passage below at a comfortable pace. In other words, read fast enough to stay interested in the passage, but at the same time read slowly enough to understand what you are reading. When you are finished, record your ending time. Then, answer the comprehension questions at the end of the passage. Finally, calculate your reading rate by using the formula described above.

UFO True Believer Sure the Truth Is out There

[1] Stanton Friedman has no doubts that some UFOs are alien spacecraft. No doubts that alien wreckage and bodies were retrieved in the "Roswell incident" of July 1947, near Roswell, N.M. No doubts the government has engaged in a kind of cosmic Watergate for decades, hiding the truth about UFOs from the American public.

[2] Friedman worked for 14 years as an industrial nuclear physicist spending "a lot of time on far-out, advanced, highly classified, eventually canceled research and development programs." He developed an interest in UFOs in the 1950s and has lectured on the subject since 1967, speaking at hundreds of colleges and on radio and television. He has published more than 70 papers on UFOs and is co-author of "Crash at Corona: The Definitive Story of the Roswell Incident." Born in New Jersey, he moved to Canada in 1980 and holds dual U.S. and Canadian citizenship.

[3] Despite decades of research, he has never seen a UFO. But then he has never seen Tokyo, he observes, yet it seems a safe bet that it exists.

[4] The most common question he gets is why: Why would aliens visit our planet and why would the government cover it up?

[5] The answer to the first is self-preservation, Friedman said.

[6] "I make one assumption about every advanced civilization, namely that it is concerned about its own security and survival. That means you've got to keep tabs on the primitives in the neighborhood, particularly those who show signs of being able to bother you."

[7] As for a government cover-up, there are plenty of reasons, Friedman said. For one, the government wants to study and adopt alien technology without other countries catching on.

[8] If the presence of intelligent life elsewhere were confirmed, the announcement would lead to a view of ourselves as Earthlings instead

of Americans and Russians and so on, Friedman said. And no govern-ment wants that, he adds. "*Nationalism* is the only game in town."

[9]   Friedman's convictions are clear from the title of a talk the well-known UFO researcher is scheduled to give in Denver today: "Flying Saucers ARE Real." The talk is sponsored by the Colorado arm of the Mutual UFO Network.

[10]   *UFO Watchtower.* Is Colorado's San Luis Valley a top vacation spot for visitors from other worlds? The valley has long been a hot spot for the unexplained, from cattle mutilations to whispers of secret bases to lights zigzagging across the sky. And for three years, it has been home to the UFO Watchtower, which welcomes humans and aliens alike.

[11]   Unable to make a go of her ranch, Judy Messoline opened the UFO Watchtower on Memorial Day 2000. An igloo-shaped, UFO-themed gift shop sits partly under the 10-foot tower.

[12]   The site draws UFO buffs as well as the merely curious. "This year, we've had large buses come in, which has been really nice," Messo-line said.

[13]   There have been about two-dozen sightings from the tower, from a long, narrow object that zipped across the sky to an object that resembled the bottom of a roulette wheel.

[14]   "I don't know if they're little green men or not," Messoline said of the sightings, "but, they're strange."

[15]   We are not alone. According to the Roper poll commissioned last year by the Sci-Fi channel two-thirds of Americans think there are other forms of intelligent life in the universe. Nearly half of those sur-veyed believe UFOs have visited the Earth in some form over the years; 45 percent believe intelligent life from other worlds has moni-tored life on Earth. Roughly seven in 10 people believe the govern-ment does not tell us everything it knows about *extra-terrestrial* life and UFOs. (Ridder C-1)

Number of words in this selection: 600 words

Starting Time: _____

Ending Time: _____

1. Multiply the number of minutes in which you read the passage by 60 (seconds) and add any remaining seconds.

2. Then divide the number of words from the passage by your time (_____ seconds) and multiply that answer by 60 seconds to get your words per minute.

600 words ÷ _____ seconds = _____

_____ × 60 seconds = _____ wpm

3. Answer the questions below and then multiply your percentage correct on the comprehension questions times your words per minute.

_____ (% correct) × _____ (wpm) = _____ words per minute comprehension rate

Comprehension Questions

_____c_____ **1.** The topic of this passage is:
   a. Roswell.
   b. Sci Fi.
   c. UFOs.

_____ **2.** The implied main idea of paragraph 1 is:
   a. Friedman is an expert on UFOs.
   b. Friedman worked for 14 years as an industrial nuclear physicist.
   c. Friedman has published more than 70 papers on UFOs.

_____ **3.** The author's purpose for writing this passage is:
   a. to inform.
   b. to persuade.
   c. to entertain.

_____ **4.** What percentage of people surveyed by the Roper poll believe UFOs have visited the Earth in some form over the years?
   a. 10%
   b. 45%
   c. 50%

_____ **5.** The organizational pattern used in paragraph 2 is:
   a. time order.

   b. topic and list.

   c. term, definition, and example.

_____ **6.** The author's tone is:
   a. critical.

   b. doubtful.

   c. objective.

_____ **7.** From the information provided in the passage, we can infer that the author:
   a. believes that alien wreckage and bodies were retrieved in the "Roswell incident."

   b. does not believe that some UFOs are alien spacecraft.

   c. thinks Stanton Friedman believes the government is hiding the truth about UFOs from the American public.

_____ **8.** From the UFO Watchtower, Judy Messoline saw:
   a. little green men.

   b. an object that resembled the bottom of a roulette wheel in the sky.

   c. an igloo-shaped UFO.

_____ **9.** As used in paragraph 15, the term *Nationalism* refers to:
   a. the wish to keep one's country from being controlled by other countries.

   b. the game of politics.

   c. agreement between Americans and Russians.

_____ **10.** Stanton Friedman has published more than 70 papers and has lectured on the topic of UFOs since 1967. Why has his topic gained so much attention over the years?
   a. He is one of the few persons that has actually seen a UFO.

   b. Seventy percent of the American public believes the government does not tell us everything it knows about extraterrestrial life and UFOs.

   c. Most people doubt the government has engaged in any kind of cover-up but find the topic interesting.

WHAT IS READING RATE?

It is important to know your reading rate and to try to increase your reading speed and comprehension. However, you should not have one single rate but several different rates.

You should be able to shift from one rate to another according to (1) your purpose, (2) the difficulty level of the material, and (3) your familiarity with the topic. For example, you should have varying reading rates to accomplish different tasks, and you should change your reading rate for different types of materials.

How fast should you read? Sometimes fast, sometimes at a medium rate, and sometimes very slowly. The factor that affects your reading rate the most is your purpose and the type of material that you are reading.

Levels of Reading Rate

There are six different reading rates. Some are true reading rates, but others are not. When we talk about reading 800 or more words per minute, we are talking about skimming and scanning, not reading. Many freshmen start out having one reading speed that is between 150 to 250 words per minute. The average graduate student (who has been in college for over five years) has a rapid reading rate of about 400 to 500 words per minute. Most people don't read over 500 words per minute unless they are skimming or scanning. Below is a list of reading rates with their approximate reading speeds.

- Slow and Careful Reading Rate: 50–250 wpm
- Average Reading Rate: 251–350 wpm
- Rapid Reading Rate: 351–400 wpm
- Very Rapid Reading Rate: 401–500+ wpm
- Skimming: 801–1000 wpm
- Scanning: 1001–1500 wpm

Slow and Careful Reading Rate: 50–250 wpm This is the rate at which a lot of academic material should be read, especially if the subject is new or completely unfamiliar to you. You will need to stop and look up new terms that are unfamiliar to you so that the passage will make sense. Even if new terms are introduced with definitions and examples, it takes time to read the definition, study the example, and then relate your understanding of it back to the term. When reading textbooks, you may need to reflect on the information in each paragraph and mentally summarize and digest it before going on to the next paragraph. Some situations in which it is beneficial to read slowly include:

■ reading about ideas that are new to you.

■ reading about ideas that are difficult to understand.

■ reading that has vocabulary that you don't know.

■ reading technical material, such as a computer science textbook.

■ reading to remember every detail.

■ reading that requires your judgment of difficult ideas (critical reading).

■ reading to memorize classification systems (e.g., the Periodic Table in chemistry; classifications of plants in biology).

■ reading for exams that require you to know many details.

2 *Average Reading Rate: 251–350 wpm*   The average person speaks at a rate of about 150 wpm. Since we can think faster than we can talk, the average reading rate is 250 wpm—clearly much faster. We generally read at an average rate when:

■ reading newspaper or magazine articles to keep informed about what is happening in the news.

■ reading social studies or social science textbooks to gain an understanding of the topics discussed.

■ reading literary novels and short stories to prepare for class discussions.

■ reading articles and book chapters to gain background information for a research paper.

3 *Rapid Reading Rate: 351–400 wpm*   A reading rate of 350 wpm is very fast and should be used only when you want to get the main ideas and important facts. At this rate, you are not stopping to reflect, paraphrase, or sum-

marize what you have just read. You are only thinking about the main points and finding the facts that support them.

Read at this rate when you:

■ want only important facts and ideas.

■ are very familiar with the topic.

■ have a good understanding of all of the vocabulary and terms used.

■ have a good understanding of all of the concepts discussed.

Very Rapid Reading Rate: 401–500 wpm   The last true reading rate is approximately 400 wpm. The average reading rate of most graduate students is about 300 wpm, so 400 wpm is truly a fast pace. Read this fast when you:

■ read light, easy, fast-moving fiction.

■ read only for entertainment.

■ just want a general idea of what the material is about.

■ are very familiar with and interested in the material.

Skimming: 801–1000 wpm   *Skimming* is not a true reading rate. It involves previewing or overviewing. You skim just to get a general idea and find the main points. You will not completely understand the details of the article, but you will know what the article is about.

You should skim:

■ chapters of textbooks before reading to find the author's outline.

■ articles or books to find related information on a research topic.

■ to decide if you would like to read a book or article.

■ an editorial to learn an author's opinion on a particular topic.

■ as a review (assuming that you have read the material at least once).

■ to bypass unrelated parts of a book or an article.

■ newspapers to get a summary of the day's events.

SKIMMING CHAPTERS AND BOOKS

Part I

Borrow a textbook for a class that you have never taken before. Follow the instructions below to skim the textbook. Then answer the questions.

Instructions

Skim a book by reading the:

- title.

- print on the back or inside cover of the publisher's jacket.

- preface and/or introduction.

- table of contents.

- first chapter.

- first and last paragraphs of the other chapters.

- last chapter.

Questions

1. What is the topic of the book?

2. What subtopics does it cover?

3. Would you be interested in taking a course on this subject based on what you found out from skimming this book? Why or why not?

Part II

Using the same book that you used for part one, follow the instructions below to skim a chapter of this textbook. Then answer the questions.

Instructions

Skim a chapter in a book by reading the:

- title.

- introduction.

(continued on next page)

■ headings within the chapter.

■ first and last sentence of each paragraph for key ideas.

■ diagrams, pictures, charts, and graphs.

■ summary or concluding paragraphs.

Questions

1. What is the topic of the chapter?

2. What subtopics does it cover?

3. Did the introduction and summary contain similar information?

4. Would you be interested in reading this chapter? Why or why not?

Skimming is an effective tool to use when trying to identify a selection's organizational pattern. Recognizing the author's outline helps you establish a framework for understanding the information. For example, if an author uses a problem-and-solution outline, you will know to look for the problem as you read and also pinpoint any solutions that are given. If the pattern is comparison/contrast, you will begin to look for the pros and cons instead of searching for solutions to a problem. If you do not recognize the author's organizational pattern, it will be more difficult for you to pick up on what you mentally need to do with the information in order for it to make sense.

Visual Literacy Box 12.1 ● ▪ ● ● ● ● ● ● ● ● ● ● ● ● ● ● ●

What Does Skimming Look Like?

When we skim, we cover a large amount of material, but we do not read every word. That is why we can claim such high reading rates. Look at the diagram below to get an idea of what you should read and what you should skip when skimming. The marks (""""""") indicate what we would most likely skip.

(continued on next page)

(continued from previous page)

Read the Title
The title either spells out the topc in specific terms or provides clues to the topic. Then, **read the introduction.** ″″″″″″″″″″″ ″″″″″″″″″″″″ The author explains his or her purpose and plan for the article in the introduction.

Read headings
Read the headings within the chapter ″″″″″″″″″″″″ ″″″″″″″″″″″″″″″″″″″″″″″″″ ″″″″″″″″″″″″″″″″″″″″″″″″″ ″″″″″″″″″″″″″″″″″″″″″″″″″ ″″″″″″″″″″″ The headings show you the author's outline.

Read the first sentence
″″″″″″″″″″″″″″″″″″″″″″″″″ ″″″″″″″″″″″″″″″″″″″″″″″″″ ″″″″″″″″″″″″″″″″″″″″″″″″″ ″″″″″″″″″″″″″″″″″″″″″″″″″ ″″″″″″″″″″″″″″″″″″″″″″″″″ ″″″″″″″″″″″″″″″″″″″″″″″″″

″″″″″″″″″″″″″″″″″″″″″″″″″ ″″″″″″″″″″″″ **and the last sentence** of each paragraph for key ideas.

Read headings
Read the first sentence ″″″″″″″″″″″″″″″″″″″″″″″″″ ″″″″″″″″″″″″″″″″″″″″″″″″″ ″″″″″″″″″″″″″″″″″″″″″ ″″″″″″″″″″″″″″″″″″″″″″″″″ ″″″″″″″″″″″″″″″″″″″″″″″″″ ″″″″″″ and the last sentence.

Study any visual aids and read the captions, keys, or other information that is provided for their interpretations. ″″″″″″″″″″″″″ ″″″″″″″″″″″″″″″″″″″″″″″″″ ″″″″″″″″″″″″″″″″″″″″″″″″″ ″″″″″″″″″″″″″″″″″″″″″″″″″ ″″″″″″″″″″″″″″″″″″″″″″″″″ ″″″″″″″″″ Often it is easier to read the words that describe a concept once you have a visual image of the concept.

Read headings
Read the first sentence ″″ ″″″″″″″″″″″″″″″″″″″″″″″″″ ″″″″″″″″″″″″″″″″″″″″″″″″″ ″″″″″″″″″″″″″″″″″″″″″ ″″″″″″″″″″″″″″″″″″″″″″″″″ ″″″″″ and the last sentence.

The main idea is usually stated in the first sentence ″″″″″″″″″″″″″″″″″″″″″″″″″ ″″″″″″″″″″″″″″″″″″″″″″″″″ ″″″″″″″″″″″″″″″″″″″″″″″″″ ″″″″″″″″″ while the last sentence provides a transition from paragraph to paragraph.

Summary
Read the summary or concluding paragraphs. Here the author pulls together all of the main points covered in the chapter. ″″″″″″″″″″″ ″″″″″″″″″″″″″″″″″″″″″″″″″ ″″″″″

Go to one of your textbooks and choose a passage. Skim it in the same way that you skimmed the example above.

1. Write down the general idea of the passage.

2. Read the entire passage. Then write your new understanding of the general idea.

3. Compare what you wrote before skimming to what you wrote after skimming. Is it the same or different? If different, what changes did you make?

Scanning: 1001–1500 wpm Have you ever heard about people who can read at fantastic and unbelievable rates? Impressive as their claims may

get examples
make chart

sound, they are probably not truly reading, but **scanning** for bits and pieces of information that provide answers to certain questions they may have. Scanning is not a true reading rate; you simply look through the reading to find a single piece of information.

There are three levels of scanning. At the **first level,** you're scanning for a piece of information that stands out easily, such as a number, date, or name. In this case, you know exactly what you are searching for and in which form it will appear. You start with your question and look for the answer. In the example below, you are looking for a number (either numerical or spelled out), the word "percent," or a percent sign (%).

First-Level Example

What percentage of the U.S. population is composed of Hispanic Americans?

Reading

Hispanic Americans—chiefly from Mexico, Puerto Rico, and Cuba but also from El Salvador, Honduras, and other countries in Central America—will soon displace African Americans as the largest minority group. Today they compose about *10 percent* of the U.S. population. (Edwards, Wattenberg and Lineberry 157)

Answer: 10%.

At the **second level** of scanning, you look for an *answer that is worded exactly like the question.* In this case you are expecting the fact to stand out from the rest of the page because you know the exact words to look for. Again, you do not actually read word for word but look quickly over the pages, lists, or columns for these specific words.

Second-Level Example

Which minority group will soon displace African Americans as the largest minority group?

Reading

Hispanic Americans—chiefly from Mexico, Puerto Rico, and Cuba but also from El Salvador, Honduras, and other countries in Central America—*will soon displace African Americans as the largest minority group.* Today they compose about 10 percent of the U.S. population.

Answer: Hispanic Americans

At **the third level** of scanning, you are thinking about an idea. The wording may not be written exactly like the question even though the idea is the same. Because the answer may be worded differently from the question, you must brainstorm words that are related to the idea. Then, you must hold them in memory while you look quickly over the pages for all possibilities.

Third-Level Example

From which countries have the Latinos emigrated?
   In this example, the word "Latinos" may not appear on the pages at all. Therefore, you would think to yourself that Latinos are also referred to as "Hispanic Americans." Then you would scan for the word "Hispanic Americans" to answer your question.

Question

From which countries have the Latinos emigrated?

   Reading

   Hispanic Americans—*chiefly from Mexico, Puerto Rico,* and *Cuba but also from El Salvador, Honduras, and other countries in Central America*—will soon displace African Americans as the largest minority group. Today they compose about 10 percent of the U.S. population.

Answer: Mexico, Puerto Rico, and Cuba but also from El Salvador, Honduras, and other countries in Central America.

EXERCISE 12-2	**Scanning at Level I**

Level I Scanning: Scan the table for the information given in the questions. Then use that information to answer the questions. The first question has been answered for you.

   1. The number of calories consumed per hour by running the 7-minute mile is

   865

2. We don't use any calories when we are

_____

3. The average person can use up 599 calories doing what activity?

_____

4. Do we use more calories playing chess or writing?

_____

5. Does it take more calories to swim or to walk?

_____

6. Which two activities require 28 calories an hour to accomplish?

_____

7. How many calories would it take to play the piano for two hours?

_____

8. How many calories do you use while driving a car for one hour?

_____

9. What activity could you engage in to use up 321 calories in one hour?

_____

10. Which activity requires fewer calories—eating or sleeping?

_____

| Energy Consumed by Various Activities (in Kcal) | |
Activity	Kcal Consumed per Hour by a 67.5-kg (150-lb) Person
Bicycling (racing)	514
Bicycling (slowly)	170
Dancing (slow)	202
Dancing (fast)	599
Driving a car	61
Eating	28

(continued on next page)

Activity	Kcal Consumed per Hour by a 67.5-kg (150-lb) Person
Gymnastics	186
Laboratory work	73
Piano playing	73
Running (7 min/mi)	865
Sitting (writing)	28
Sitting (playing chess)	30
Sleeping or lying still	0
Standing (relaxed)	32
Swimming (2 mph)	535
Walking (3 mph)	158
Walking (4 mph)	231

From *Biology: Concepts and Connections*, 3/e, by Neil A. Campbell, Lawrence G. Mitchell, and Jane B. Reece (San Francisco: Benjamin/Cummings, 2000), p. 91.

EXERCISE
12-3

Scanning at Level II

The second level of scanning requires you to look for an answer that is worded exactly like the question. In this case you are expecting the fact to stand out from the rest of the page because you know the exact words to look for. Scan the document below (the first 10 articles of the Universal Declaration of Human Rights) to find the answers to these Level II scanning questions. The first answer has been provided for you.

Level II Scanning Questions

1. Which article states that everyone has the right of life, liberty, and the security of person?

   In Article 3, it is stated that "Everyone has the right of life, liberty and the security of person."

2. According to Article 1, in what respect are all human beings born free and equal?

3. According to this document, who is entitled to equal protection of the law and protection against any discrimination?

_____

4. In Article 4, what is prohibited in all its forms?

_____

5. How should people act toward one another?

_____

The Universal Declaration of Human Rights

(first 10 of 27 articles)

Article 1

All human beings are born free and equal in dignity and rights. They are endowed with reason and conscience and should act towards one another in a spirit of brotherhood.

Article 2

Everyone is entitled to all the rights and freedoms set forth in this Declaration, without distinction of any kind, such as race, colour, sex, language, religion, political or other opinion, national or social origin, property, birth or other status.

Furthermore, no distinction shall be made on the basis of the political jurisdictional or international status of the country or territory to which a person belongs, whether it be independent, trust, non self-governing or under any other limitation of sovereignty.

Article 3

Everyone has the right of life, liberty and the security of person.

Article 4

No one shall be held in slavery or servitude; slavery and the slave trade shall be prohibited in all their forms.

Article 5

No one shall be subjected to torture or to cruel, inhuman or degrading treatment or punishment.

Article 6

Everyone has the right to recognition everywhere as a person before the law.

Article 7

All are equal before the law and are entitled without any discrimination to equal protection of the law. All are entitled to equal protection against any discrimination in violation of this Declaration and against any incitement to such discrimination.

Article 8

Everyone has the right to an effective remedy by the competent national tribunals for acts violating the fundamental rights granted him by the constitution or by law.

Article 9

No one shall be subjected to arbitrary arrest, detention or exile.

Article 10

Everyone is entitled in full equality to a fair and public hearing by an independent and impartial tribunal, in the determination of his rights and obligations and of any criminal charge against him.

EXERCISE
12-4

Scanning at Level III

The third level of scanning is looking for an answer to a question that is worded differently than the question. Instead of looking for one particular word, you must think of related words that you are most likely to find. Then, hold them in memory while you look quickly over the pages for all possibilities. Scan the following document to find the answers to the questions below. The first answer has been provided for you.

Level III Scanning Questions

1. Which group is more likely to have an extended family: Caucasians or African Americans?

   <u>African Americans</u>

2. How do African Americans feel about their extended families?

   _____

3. How do aging African Americans feel about their family lives?

   _____

4. From whom do African American children learn their ethics and beliefs?

   _____

5. How are the elderly in African American society regarded by their kin?

   _____

The African-American Extended Family

[1] The African-American extended family can be traced to the African heritage of most black Americans. In many African societies, newly married couples do not start their own households. Instead, they marry into a large extended family that assists its members with all aspects of daily life. This tradition of a broad network of kin ties traveled to the United States during the period of slavery. Since then, it has served as a protective shield against the destructive impact of poverty and racial prejudice on African-American family life (McAdoo, 1993). Today, more black than white adults have relatives other than their own children living in the same household. African-American parents also see more kin during the week and perceive them as more important figures in their lives, respecting the advice of relatives and caring deeply about what they think is important (Wilson et al., 1995).

[2]   By providing emotional support and sharing income and essential resources, the African-American extended family helps reduce the stress of poverty and single parenthood. In addition, extended-family members often help with the rearing of children (Pearson et al., 1990). The presence of grandmothers in the households of many African-American teenagers and their infants protects babies from the negative influence of an overwhelmed and inexperienced mother. Furthermore, black adolescent mothers living in extended families are more likely to complete high school and get a job and less likely to be on welfare than are mothers living on their own—factors that return to benefit children's well-being (Trent & Harlan, 1994).

[3]   For single mothers who were very young at the time of their child's birth, extended family living is associated with more positive adult-child interaction during infancy and the pre-school years. Otherwise, establishing an independent household with the help of nearby relatives is related to improved child rearing. Perhaps this arrangement permits the more mature mother who has developed effective parenting skills to implement them (Chase-Lansdale, Brooks-Gunn, & Zamsky, 1994). In families rearing adolescents, kinship support increases the likelihood of effective parenting, which is related to adolescents' self-reliance, emotional well-being, and reduced delinquency (Taylor & Roberts, 1995).

[4]   Finally, African-American elderly report a very high degree of satisfaction from family life. Compared with their white counterparts, black grandmothers are more likely to provide child-rearing assistance and financial help to their children and grandchildren. Relatives hold them in high esteem, describing them as sources of love, strength, and stability. And grandmothers play a central role in transmitting African-American culture by teaching moral and religious values, encouraging cooperation and mutual support, and teaching children about their African heritage (Tolson & Wilson, 1990). These influences strengthen family bonds, protect children's development, and increase the chances that the extended-family lifestyle will carry over to the next generation. (Berk 67)

| EXERCISE 12-5 | Assessing Your Reading Speed |

Look at each of the situations below and mark the speed with which you think each task should be approached. Use an "F" to indicate "Fast," an "M" to indicate "Moderate," and an "S" to indicate "Slow." The first one has been done for you.

_____S_____ **1.** studying for a chemistry exam

_____ **2.** reading a sociology chapter that has vocabulary and concepts that are new to you

_____ **3.** learning an updated version of PowerPoint by following printed directions

_____ **4.** finding the name and address of a particular person in a telephone book

_____ **5.** reading a newspaper article on a topic that you know well

_____ **6.** reading a travel magazine

_____ **7.** reading a history textbook

_____ **8.** reading to solve a math problem

_____ **9.** reading a novel to understand the plot

_____ **10.** skimming to find the answer to a question

EXERCISE 12-6

Reviewing Reading Rates

Answer the questions below concerning the information that you learned about reading rates. The first question has been answered for you.

1. Name the three reasons you would shift from one reading rate to another.

purpose, difficulty of material, familiarity with subject matter

2. Describe the three levels of scanning.

_____

_____

3. Name the six steps in skimming.

_____

_____

4. How fast should you read technical material?

_____

5. How fast should you read to get a general impression of an article or book?

_____

6. How fast should you read a social studies textbook?

_____

7. How fast should you read a novel for entertainment?

_____

8. How fast should you read to remember every detail?

_____

9. How fast should you read magazine articles?

_____

10. What is a good reading rate when you are scanning for a piece of information that stands out easily, such as a name or a date?

_____

INCREASING READING SPEED

Most speed-reading programs focus on increasing eye movements and reducing the number of times our eyes stop to look at words on the page. These techniques may increase the speed with which we move our eyes, but they do not increase the speed at which we understand the meaning of the print. Reading is a complex process that cannot be reduced to just moving our eyes faster. Just as we said before, _you can only read as fast as you can think._

If it's not moving our eyes faster, then how can we learn to read faster? The following are factors that support fast reading:

- recognizing or being able to pronounce the words

- knowing what the words mean

- understanding the author's purpose

- knowing about the topic (having background knowledge)

- recognizing the author's outline (organizational patterns)

How to Increase Your Reading Speed

Before concentrating on rapid eye movements and timed readings, you need to establish habits for thinking faster. There are five types of exercises that you can do to increase thinking speed and, in turn, increase reading speed. They include:

- building word recognition speed

- building vocabulary

- building thinking speed

- building background knowledge

- previewing/recognizing the author's outline

Building Rapid Word Recognition   The ability to recognize words accurately is called *visual discrimination*. For example, let's say that you are reading the following paragraph:

> Jim hired a man to clean the ducts. They had not been cleaned since the house had been built twenty years ago. Jim thought it would eliminate a lot of dust from the air.

Let's suppose that while reading very quickly, we made a mistake in visual discrimination. At first glance, we thought it said "ducks" instead of "ducts." In other words, we are under the wrong impression that the sentence reads:

> Jim hired a man to clean the *ducks*.

Although there is only a one letter difference between "ducts" and "ducks," suddenly the meaning of the word *and* the meaning of the sentence has changed. We begin to imagine a man coming with a wash bin to soap up some dirty animals. Unless it is a silly children's book, we realize that it doesn't make sense. This slows us down because we must go back and reread the sentence to find our mistake.

A second glance at the sentence shows us that the word is "ducts." Since the word "ducts" refers to vents in the floor that are connected to the furnace, suddenly the sentence and the paragraph make perfect sense. However, the mistake cost us time. We had to go back and double check the sentence to find our mistake. Then we had to rethink the meaning of the paragraph in light of the correction. If we train our minds to read each word carefully, we will actually save time in the long run. The following exercise is designed to help you discriminate between similar words and, thus, increase rapid word recognition.

EXERCISE
12-7

Testing Your Visual Discrimination

The word in the left-hand column is repeated in the string of words on the right. Find and circle the word at the right that is exactly the same as the key word. Then go on to the next key word. Work as quickly as you are able to without making mistakes in visual discrimination.

1. regular	regard, regular, relay, relegate, relate
2. disease	decease, dissect, direct, disease, disuse
3. vital	vibrant, veto, vitality, vicious, vital
4. relieve	relieve, relive, receive, reward, relinquish
5. depression	recession, depression, deepen, decision, deprive
6. tension	tennis, tense, tenure, tension, tenacious
7. stress	street, stream, stress, stigma, duress, success
8. benefits	been, benefits, benevolent, befriend, benign
9. convincing	convincing, convene, convenient, constant, convivial
10. populations	polite, regulations, propel, popular, populations
11. prevention	prevent, convention, invention, premature, prevention
12. consider	considerate, consider, concern, consulate, consign
13. intensity	intensity, density, internship, insensitive, insistent

14. meditative   mediate, meditative, creative, medicinal, meditate

15. attributed   attribution, attractive, distributed, attributed, attrition

16. resistance   restrain, assistance, resistance, recitation, resistive

17. inactivity   interact, inactivity, activate, nativity, inaccessible

18. significantly   signify, magnificently, sufficiently, significantly, slightly

19. endorphins   endodermic, dolphins, endorphins, endoplasmic, endemic

20. maintain   mainstay, mountain, remain, maintain, maintenance

Time: _____   Errors: _____

Building Vocabulary

Knowledge of vocabulary is absolutely essential to speed up comprehension. Sometimes not knowing the meaning of one word can stop you from understanding a sentence, a paragraph, or even a whole passage. While you are previewing a selection, highlight or underline all of the vocabulary that you are unfamiliar with. Then stop to read the sentence that contains each unknown word. If you can guess the word's meaning from the context, move on. If you cannot guess at the meaning of the unknown word from the context or from its word parts, then look it up in the dictionary. Merriam/ Webster's electronic dictionary is especially quick and easy to use (http://www.m-w.com).

EXERCISE
12-8

Identifying Words Closest in Meaning

The word in the left-hand column is defined within the string of words on the right. Find and circle the word at the right that is closest in meaning to the key word at the left. Then go on to the next key word. Look up the meanings of any words that you miss.

1. virtually   really, likely, seemingly, apparently, nearly

2. literally   nearly, falsely, timely, repeatedly, actually

3. embarked   began, ended, required, assured, reminded

4. sedentary   energetic, lively, vigorous, inactive, assuming

5. contemporary   traditional, conservative, usual, modern, established

6. aspects   restrictions, features, considerations, reactions, reflections

7. significantly   considerably, slightly, realistically, somewhat, unimportantly

8. anxious   quiet, peaceful, worried, calm, interested

9. fatigue   energy, tiredness, sympathy, livelihood, vigor

10. incidence   occurrence, reflection, resistance, maintenance, recurrence

Time: _____   Errors: _____

Building Thinking Speed

As we said earlier, you can read only as fast as you can think. If you read the words without thinking, then you have only pronounced the words either aloud or silently, but you have not read them. Reading requires a certain amount of reflection on the meaning of the words and understanding of the combination of words that make up a sentence. Questioning and searching for answers to our questions helps us think about the words we are looking at. Below is an exercise that will help you to think about the words you are reading and to push yourself to think quickly.

EXERCISE
12-9

Perceiving with Your Five Senses

No matter how fast you move your eyes, your speed of comprehension is dependent on your ability to understand one idea and pass on to the next. As you look at the following phrases, ask yourself if any word in the phase is *concrete* or *abstract*. Place a checkmark in front of each group of words that is concrete. To determine if it is concrete, ask yourself if it can be perceived by the five senses. **Can you see it, taste it, smell it, hear it, or touch it?**

_____ 1. cancerous tumors

_____ 2. inactive people

_____ **3.** muscles of the body

_____ **4.** too stressful

_____ **5.** require a concentration

_____ **6.** millions of adults

_____ **7.** since high school or college

_____ **8.** to be happy and healthy

_____ **9.** Centers for Disease Control

_____ **10.** individuals of similar age

_____ **11.** three times a week

_____ **12.** the exercise program

_____ **13.** less tension, fatigue, and depression

_____ **14.** the risk of colds or flu

_____ **15.** life satisfaction

_____ **16.** strengthening the heart muscle

_____ **17.** exercise contributes to good health

_____ **18.** on a regular basis

_____ **19.** activities that you enjoy

_____ **20.** your outlook on life

Time: _____   Errors: _____

Building Background Knowledge

Another type of exercise you can do to increase speed of comprehension is building background knowledge. The best way to do this is to read information on the same topic that has been written on a lower reading level. In other words, if you are reading a history assignment on the Watergate Affair from a college textbook, you should go to the library and check out a junior high school history textbook and read the same information on an easier level first. You will be able to read with less effort and gain an understanding of this event. You will then be able to read the more detailed version from the college-level book with more ease.

490 508
503

A Reading in Developmental Psychology

The following passage is on the health benefits of exercise. It is written in simple terms and provides a more detailed account than you will find in some other books. The accounts that follow in later exercises (in this chapter) are more difficult to read because they assume that you are already familiar with this information. Read the passage. Then, answer the comprehension questions that follow the reading.

Vocabulary in Context

First complete the vocabulary exercise to become familiar with the new terms. The first term has been defined for you.

a. **vital**—very important; necessary

b. **impediment**—barrier, obstacle, burden

c. **endorphins**—hormones produced by the brain that give one a pleasurable feeling

d. **aerobic**—making the body take in and use oxygen more efficiently (aerobic sport)

e. **aquatic**—done in or on the water (aquatic sport)

+ /5

_____A___ 1. It is _____ to good health to get regular exercise.

_____b___ 2. The attitude that we just can't be bothered to exercise is the biggest _____ to getting started on a healthful exercise routine.

_____d___ 3. A mini-trampoline not only makes you feel like a kid again, but it is as vigorous as _____ sports.

_____c___ 4. Regular exercise keeps you flexible, strong, and lean. It also releases hormones called _____, which give you a strong feeling of well-being.

_____e___ 5. Swimming and other _____ exercises give you a total workout, making them a great choice for all-over body tone.

Health and Fitness

[1] [1]Regular exercise is **vital** to honoring your body. [2]And the key word here is _regular._ [3]You cannot have a strong, healthy body without regular activity. [4]The good news is that simply by exercising thirty minutes at least three times a week, you can improve your health, reduce body fat, fight disease, and relieve depression, tension, and stress. [5]The benefits are endless.

[2] Need further convincing? Consider this: According to the Centers for Disease Control and Prevention (CDC) some 60 percent of the U.S. population is overweight. And 250,000 to 300,000 deaths are attributed to inactivity every year. So listen to what the doctor says and try to fit in at least one half hour of low-intensity exercise three times a week. Even a small amount of exercise can help you to greatly reduce your risk of heart disease. Don't wait until you have a health issue. Exercise now to prevent one. Keep moving and . . .

- **Improve Your Outlook on Life**: Regular exercise can significantly improve mental outlook and help keep depression at bay.

- **Build Muscle:** Our bodies burn an extra fifty calories a day for each pound of muscle gained. Muscle also protects our bones.

- **Maintain a Healthy Weight:** Regular exercise has been proven to help long-term weight loss. Good news for the 60 percent of American adults who are overweight.

- **Build Stronger Bones:** Weight-bearing activities create strong bones, protecting against fractures.

- **Lower Your Risk of Heart Disease:** Exercising three times a week for only thirty minutes reduces the risk of heart disease.

[3] For those of you who feel you have failed at exercise attempts, take heart. It's important to remember that research shows us that it takes about eight weeks to break a habit no matter what that habit might be. So be patient with yourself and just keep on moving.

[4] And make it fun. You may need a couple of sessions with a trainer to get you started. You may need the encouragement of exercising with a friend or a group to keep you going. That's fine. If working out with others will help keep you committed, then that's what you should do. Find out what motivates you and follow through. But whatever you do, don't forget the willpower element. Willpower is an

important factor in exercising. And we all need a dose of it. You have to make a commitment and you have to have a goal. There will be moments when you won't feel like it.

[5]   Sometimes attitude can be the biggest **impediment** to exercise—that old can't-be-bothered tape can play pretty loudly sometimes. When that happens, I find that the easiest way to recharge myself and to change my attitude is to go for a walk. If I'm feeling a little sluggish, or perhaps I'm at a bit of a loose end—not sure what I want to do and not in the mood for the things I need to do—then I lace up my Nikes and head to the park. I may not feel like it at the time, and it may take a little discipline to get me going, but I have enough experience to know how great I'll feel later, and it's that thought that pushes me forward. Besides keeping you flexible, strong, and lean, exercise releases **endorphins**, which give you the great feeling that life is wonderful! What better motivator do you need?

[6]   Two types of exercise are particularly important for building and maintaining bone mass and density—weight-bearing exercises and resistance exercises. Weight-bearing exercises make your bones and muscles work against gravity. This group of exercises contains any activity in which your feet and legs bear your own weight, such as jogging, walking, stair climbing, dancing, and playing soccer. Resistance exercises involve moving objects (including our own body weight) to create resistance and strengthen our bones. Free weights, weight-training machines, and exercise bands are some ways to do resistance exercise. You should try to get in both resistance and weight-bearing exercise to keep your body strong and healthy. The good news is, there is no shortage of creative and interesting ways to get exercises. Here are a few to start you off:

- *Trampolines:* A mini-trampoline is great fun! It offers the same benefits as **aerobic** sports and the best thing is that it brings out the kid in you.

- *Swimming:* Swimming gives you a total workout, making it a great choice for all-over body tone. It strengthens your back muscles, all your major muscle groups, as well as your lungs and heart. Certain **aquatic** exercises can create resistance, especially when you use paddles or fins.

- *Dance:* Dance is more than aerobic exercise—it is a complete mind-body workout and an amazing way to de-stress from a challenging day.

■ *Tai Chi:* Tai chi is a slow, controlled series of poses, all weight-bearing movements. The poses require a concentration that is almost meditative. Tai chi makes you calmer and more centered while making you more physically fit.

■ *Hiking:* Hiking is an active form of relaxation, and a great weight-bearing exercise. It can be as challenging as you want and a great way to bond with family and friends.

[7] The secrets to keeping up an exercise routine are:

1. Weave it into your life on a regular basis.

2. Vary the routine so you don't burn out.

3. Find activities that you enjoy so you look forward to them.

4. Sneak exercise into your day whenever—and wherever—you can. (Haddon 183–91)

Comprehension Questions

 1. A good title for this selection would be:
   a. Aquatic Exercises for Everyone
   b. The Importance of Weight-Bearing Exercise
   c. The Benefits of Regular Exercise

 2. According to the Centers for Disease Control and Prevention, how many deaths are attributed to inactivity each year?
   a. 60 to 100,000
   b. 100,000 to 250,000
   c. 250,000 to 300,000

 3. The author's purpose for writing this article is:
   a. to inform.
   b. to persuade.
   c. to entertain.

 4. The main idea of the first paragraph is found in:
   a. sentence 1.
   b. sentence 3.
   c. sentence 4.

_____ B **5.** The overall paragraph pattern found in paragraph 4 is:
    a. time order.

    b. process.

    c. topic and list.

_____ B **6.** Dancing and jogging are examples of:
    a. resistance exercises.

    b. weight-bearing exercises.

    c. aquatic exercises.

_____ B **7.** We can reduce the risk of heart disease by:
    a. exercising once a week for a couple of hours.

    b. exercising twice a week for thirty minutes.

    c. exercising three times a week for thirty minutes.

_____ C **8.** An example of a resistance exercise is:
    a. stair climbing.

    b. playing soccer.

    c. weight-training.

_____ A **9.** The author implies that it is easier to have the willpower to exercise when you have:
    a. commitment and a goal.

    b. strong muscles and bones.

    c. good concentration.

_____ C **10.** The overall paragraph pattern for paragraph 2 is:
    a. definition.

    b. topic and list.

    c. process.

Visual Literacy Box 12.2 ● ● ● ● ● ● ● ● ● ● ● ● ● ● ●

Schedules

We create schedules to organize the things that we need to accomplish every day. According to the information provided in the "Health and Fitness" reading, exercising **30 minutes** at least **three times a week** can improve your health, reduce body fat, fight disease, and relieve depression, tension, and stress. Create a schedule that would allow you to follow this exercise plan.

1. Fill in your work time in the appropriate blocks.

2. Fill in the times that you would normally spend eating your meals.

3. Fill in times that you would spend studying and going to school.

4. Find **three 30-minute blocks** of time for an exercise routine.

Time	Monday	Tuesday	Wednesday	Thursday	Friday	Saturday	Sunday
8:00 a.m.							
8:30 a.m.							
9:00 a.m.							
9:30 a.m.							
10:00 a.m.							
10:30 a.m.							
11:00 a.m.							
11:30 a.m.							
12:00 p.m.							
12:30 p.m.							
1:00 p.m.							
1:30 p.m.							
2:00 p.m.							

(continued on next page)

(continued from previous page)

Time	Monday	Tuesday	Wednesday	Thursday	Friday	Saturday	Sunday
2:30 p.m.							
3:00 p.m.							
3:30 p.m.							
4:00 p.m.							
4:30 p.m.							
5:00 p.m.							
5:30 p.m.							
6:00 p.m.							
6:30 p.m.							
7:00 p.m.							
7:30 p.m.							
8:00 p.m.							

Previewing   In order to think quickly, you need to know what to expect. You would never go to a social function without first asking what type of gathering you will be attending. You would want to know the type of gathering, the length of time it would last, how many people would be there, what type of food would be available, and what you would need to bring with you. For example, you would prepare differently for a basketball game than you would for a formal wedding dinner or a trip to the beach. If you were not prepared, you would not have essential accessories with you such as a bathing suit and casual summer clothes for a beach trip or formal wear for a wedding event.

It is the same with reading. In order to read more efficiently, you must prepare to read. We do this by previewing the topic, the vocabulary, and the author's outline. You use the same steps for previewing that you do when you skim a chapter.

- Read the title.

- Read the introduction.

- Read headings within the chapter.

- Read the first and last sentence of each paragraph for key ideas.

- Read the diagrams, pictures, charts, graphs.
- Read the summary or concluding paragraphs.

However, you want to be sure to look for the author's outline or the organizational pattern of the text. Is the paragraph comparison/contrast, problem/solution, topic and list, or some other pattern?

Once you know the author's outline, you know how the main ideas are arranged. In other words, you know what the author's main ideas are and where they are. Once you know this, you can read much faster.

 A Reading in Developmental Psychology

The following article is also on the health benefits of exercise. It is a little more difficult to read because the author assumes that you are already knowledgeable on this topic. Preview the selection by completing the outline below and answer the comprehension questions at the end of the reading.

Vocabulary in Context

First complete the vocabulary exercise to become familiar with the new terms. The first term has been defined for you.

   a. literally—factually; in fact; actually

   b. virtually—almost, nearly, practically

   c. embarked—began; started out

   d. contemporary—modern, current, up to date

   e. sedentary—inactive, sitting

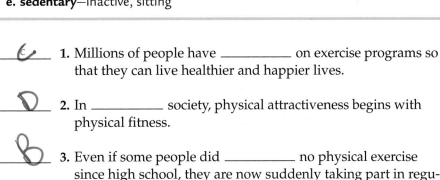

_____ *c* ___ **1.** Millions of people have _____ on exercise programs so that they can live healthier and happier lives.

_____ *D* ___ **2.** In _____ society, physical attractiveness begins with physical fitness.

_____ *B* ___ **3.** Even if some people did _____ no physical exercise since high school, they are now suddenly taking part in regular exercise programs.

_____ *e*   **4.** Time after time, researchers in numerous studies of cardiovascular fitness have found that people who exercise regularly have less chance of heart disease than people who have _____ lives.

_____ *A*   **5.** We are not exaggerating when we say that _____ millions of adults are now starting exercise programs.

Previewing "Exercise"

Preview the selection and then finish filling in the outline below.

I. <u>Ways to Exercise</u>

II. _Participate_ _____

III. _Play_ _____

    A. _be active_ _____

    B. <u>exercise reduces body fat</u>

    C. _Contemporary_ _____

IV. <u>both control and experimental groups were administered three psychological tests</u>

    A. _Sedentary_ _____

    B. _____

    C. <u>general aspects of everyday functioning</u>

        1. _____

        2. _____

V. _____

    A. _____

    B. _____

VI. _____

    A. _____

        1. _____

2. _____

3. _____

4. confusion

5. _____

VII. Through exercise, adults can increase:

A. their well-being

B. their sense of well-being

Exercise

[1] Participate! Play tennis! Racquetball! Squash! Dance! Join a spa! An exercise class! Skate! Ski! Swim! Run! Jog! At least walk.

[2] [1]**Literally** millions of adults, many of whom had engaged in **virtually** no unnecessary physical activity since high school or college—and perhaps not even then—have now **embarked** on exercise programs. [2]And many undertake these programs with the same dedication and serious determination that they bring to their careers—and perhaps to other aspects of their lives. [3]Why? [4]Simply, to be happy and healthy. [5]That is, after all, what most of us want. [6]Exercise, we are told, will make us healthier, may enable us to live longer, and should make us trimmer, more fit, and perhaps even more attractive, given our **contemporary** cultural standards of physical attractiveness.

[3] How valid are these claims? Research leaves little doubt that exercise contributes significantly to good health. Numerous studies of cardiovascular fitness have repeatedly found higher levels of fitness and lower incidence of coronary heart disease among those who exercise regularly than among those whose lives are more **sedentary** (for example, Blumenthal et al., 1982; Fox & Haskell, 1978). In addition, it has been clearly established that exercise is importantly involved in reducing the percentage of body fat and in increasing muscle and bone density.

[4] But does exercise make us happier? Does it affect us psychologically? Blumenthal et al. (1982) provide some answers, following an investigation of the effects of exercise on a group of 16 subjects who had registered for a 10-week adult fitness program. The average age of this group was 45 years; the youngest subject was 25 and the oldest

61. At the very beginning of the program, all subjects were administered a battery of three psychological tests to assess mood, anxiety, and some general aspects of everyday functioning such as sleep patterns and social habits. A control group, consisting of healthy but sedentary individuals of similar age, was also administered these same tests.

[5]   The exercise program that the 16 experimental subjects then undertook consisted of a 10-minute routine of stretching exercises, followed by 45 minutes of walking or running, 3 times a week over a period of 10 weeks. All exercise periods were under medical supervision. Control-group members continued as before, without any regular exercise program.

[6]   At the end of the 10-week period, individuals in both the experimental and the control groups were again administered the three psychological instruments. The results are clear and striking. Whereas the groups had initially been similar on each of these instruments, the experimental group now felt less tension, fatigue, depression, and confusion and experienced significant reductions in immediate and general anxiety. And, as expected, physiological measures indicated significant improvements in the experimental groups.

[7]   It appears that adults that are inactive but basically healthy can increase their well-being, as well as their sense of well-being, through exercise. (Lefrancois 511)

Comprehension Questions

 1. In this article, the author's tone of voice is:
   a. positive.
   b. negative.
   c. neutral.

 2. The author's purpose for writing this article is:
   a. to inform.
   b. to persuade.
   c. to entertain.

 3. The main idea of the second paragraph is found in:
   a. sentence 2.
   b. sentence 4.
   c. sentence 6.

_____A___ **4.** The overall paragraph pattern found in paragraph 3 is:
    a. cause/effect.

    b. process.

    c. topic and list.

_____C___ **5.** How many people participated in Blumenthal's study that explained how exercise affects people?
    a. 10

    b. 16

    c. 45

_____C___ **6.** All of the people who took part in Blumenthal's research study were given three psychological tests for the purpose of measuring:
    a. their opinions of physical attractiveness.

    b. how sedentary their lifestyles were.

    c. mood, anxiety, sleep patterns, and social habits.

_____B___ **7.** Millions of people are beginning exercise programs for all of the following reasons except:
    a. to be healthier and live longer.

    b. to socialize at health clubs.

    c. to be more fit and more attractive.

_____C___ **8.** The author's tone in the first paragraph is:
    a. angry.

    b. bored.

    c. encouraging.

_____B___ **9.** The author concludes that:
    a. exercise cannot improve the health of adults who have been inactive for many years.

    b. healthy inactive adults can improve their health and sense of well-being by exercising.

    c. adults who have been inactive for many years cannot improve their sense of well-being by suddenly beginning an exercise program.

_____ **10.** In Blumenthal's research study, the control group:

    a. had no regular exercise routine.

    b. participated in an exercise program for 10 weeks.

    c. did only stretching exercises for 10 weeks.

A Reading in Developmental Psychology

Now that you are familiar with the topic "the health benefits of exercise," test your speed of comprehension by reading yet another article on this same topic. By reading the two previous articles, you have built vocabulary and background knowledge on this topic and are at the point where you can begin to push yourself to read faster. Calculate your reading rate and your comprehension rate according to the directions given earlier in this chapter. Your reading rate is computed by dividing the number of words in the article (650) by your reading time. Your comprehension rate is computed by multiplying your reading rate by your percentage correct on the multiple-choice questions. Take 30 seconds to preview the article before you start your timed reading.

Vocabulary in Context

First complete the vocabulary exercise to become familiar with the new terms. The first term has been defined for you.

    a. moderate—mild; not strenuous *(adj)*

    b. bouts—sessions

    c. longitudinal—observed over several or many years

    d. impact—influence, effect

    e. inhibits—slows up, holds back, restrains

_____d_____ **1.** Exercise has a direct _____ on health because it helps prevent diseases.

_____U_____ **2.** In _____ research studies that lasted 10 to 20 years, it was found that people who exercised were less likely to have cancer than people who did not exercise.

A   **3.** Even though most Americans know that exercise makes them healthy, less than one- fourth of the population actually does _____ exercise at least five times a week.

B   **4.** Frequent _____ of exercise that is not strenuous can lower the risk of colds or flu.

C   **5.** In their experiments with animals, researchers found that exercise _____, or slows down, the growth of cancerous tumors.

More Benefits to Exercise

[1] Three times a week, over the noon hour, Sharese delighted in running, making her way to a wooded trail that cut through a picturesque part of the city. Regular exercise kept her fit and slim. Compared to earlier days when she had been sedentary and overweight, it also limited the number of respiratory illnesses she caught. And as Sharese explained to a friend one day, "Exercise gives me a positive outlook. It calms me down—takes the edge off. Afterward, I feel a burst of energy that gets me through the day. If I don't do it, I get tired in the afternoon." Although most Americans are aware of the health benefits of exercise, only 23 percent engage in **moderate** physical activity for 20 minutes or more at least five times a week (U.S. Department of Health and Human Services, 1999c).

[2]   Besides reducing body fat and building muscle, exercise fosters resistance to disease. Frequent **bouts** of moderate-intensity exercise enhance the immune response, thereby lowering the risk of colds or flu and, when these illnesses do strike, promoting faster recovery (Nieman, 1994). Furthermore, in several **longitudinal** studies extending over 10 to 20 years, physical activity was linked to reduced incidence of cancer at all body sites except the skin, with the strongest findings for cancer in the rectum and colon (Albanes, Blair, & Taylor, 1989; Wannamethee, Shaper, & Macfarlane, 1993). Exercise also helps prevent adult-onset diabetes (Kriska, Blair, & Pereira, 1994). Finally, physically active people are less likely to develop cardiovascular disease. If they do, it typically occurs at a later age and is less severe than among their inactive age-mates (Bokovoy & Blair, 1994).

[3]   Just how does exercise prevent the serious illnesses just mentioned? It may do so by reducing the incidence of obesity—a risk factor for heart disease, diabetes, and several forms of cancer. In addition, people who exercise probably adopt other healthful behaviors, thereby lowering the risk of diseases associated with high-fat diets, alcohol consumption, and smoking. Exercise can also have a direct **impact** on disease prevention. For example, in animal research, it **inhibits** growth of cancerous tumors beyond the impact of diet, body fat, and the immune response (Mackinnon, 1992). And it promotes cardiovascular functioning by strengthening the heart muscle, producing a form of "good cholesterol" (high-density lipoproteins) from the artery walls, and decreasing blood pressure (Donatelle & Davis, 2000).

[4]   Yet another way that exercise may guard against illness is through its mental health benefits. Many studies show that physical activity reduces anxiety and depression, improves mood, and enhances alertness and energy (Kirkby & Lindner, 1998; Weyerer & Kupfer, 1994). The impact of exercise on a "positive outlook," as Sharese expressed it, is most obvious just after a workout and can last for several hours (Chollar, 1995). The stress-reducing properties of exercise undoubtedly strengthen immunity to disease. And as physical activity enhances psychological well-being, it promotes self-esteem, ability to cope with stress, on-the-job productivity, and life satisfaction.

[5]   When we consider the evidence as a whole, it is not surprising that physical activity is associated with substantially lower death rates from all causes (Blair et al., 1989). The contribution of exercise to longevity cannot be accounted for by preexisting illness in inactive people, since sedentary individuals who start to exercise live longer than those who remain inactive (Paffenbarger et al., 1993).

[6]   How much exercise is recommended for a healthier, happier, and longer life? The usual prescription is 20 minutes, three to five times a week, of relatively vigorous use of the large muscles of the body in which heart rate is elevated to 60 to 90 percent of its maximum—through rowing, cycling, dancing, cross-country skiing, swimming, running, or brisk walking (American College of Sports Medicine, 1998). At the same time, exercise should be pleasurable, not a chore. If the exercise program is too stressful, its health benefits will be reduced. (Berk 431–32)

Reading Rate (based on 650 words): _____

Reading Comprehension Rate: _____

Comprehension Questions

___a___ **1.** What percentage of Americans engage in moderate physical activity for 20 minutes or more at least five times a week?
   a. 23%
   b. 60%
   c. 90%

___B___ **2.** Exercise does all of the following except:
   a. reduce body fat.
   b. reduce muscle.
   c. foster resistance to disease.

___C___ **3.** Frequent exercise of moderate intensity:
   a. increases the risk of colds.
   b. increases the risk of flu.
   c. promotes faster recovery from colds.

___D___ **4.** Which of the following is false?
   a. Physical activity was linked to cancer at all body sites except the skin.
   b. Physically active people are less likely to develop cardio-vascular disease.
   c. Exercise also helps prevent adult-onset diabetes.

___B___ **5.** Which of the following is false?
   a. Obesity is a risk factor for heart disease, diabetes, and several forms of cancer.
   b. People who exercise probably drink alcohol, eat fatty foods, and smoke.
   c. Exercise strengthens the heart muscle, produces a "good" cholesterol, and decreases blood pressure.

6. With regard to mental health, exercise:
   a. increases anxiety and depression.
   b. improves mood.
   c. decreases alertness and energy.

 7. Physical activity:
   a. interferes with self-esteem.
   b. increases ability to cope with stress.
   c. decreases life satisfaction.

 8. If people who never exercised before suddenly started and continued to exercise on a regular basis, they would:
   a. live longer than those who do not exercise on a regular basis.
   b. harm themselves from the sudden change in lifestyle.
   c. live the same length of time as those who never exercised before.

 9. The author's purpose is:
   a. to inform.
   b. to entertain.
   c. to persuade.

 10. Why should exercise be pleasurable?

   a. If the exercise program is too stressful, its health benefits will be reduced.
   b. If the exercise program is not fun, people will not continue the program.
   c. If the exercise program is too stressful, people will drink and smoke afterwards to unwind from the stress.

Multiply the number correct by 10 to find your percentage score. For example, if you missed one question, you would multiply 9 correct by 10 to get 90% or .90.

Number of words in this selection: 650 words

Starting Time: _____

Ending Time: _____

_____ 1. Multiply the number of minutes in which you read the passage by 60 (seconds) and add any remaining seconds.

_____ 2. Then divide the number of words from the passage by your time (_____ seconds) and multiply that answer by 60 seconds to get your words per minute.

650 words ÷ _____ seconds = _____

_____ × 60 seconds = _____ wpm

_____ 3. Multiply your percentage correct on the comprehension questions by your words per minute.

_____ (% correct) × _____ (wpm) = _____ words per minute comprehension rate

Getting Ahead in College Box 12.2

GRAMMAR: COMMAS FOR ITEMS IN A SERIES

Sometimes we can say the same thing about several different items. When we write, we don't want to repeat the same thought. Instead, we can simply attach all items to the related thought with commas. Study the example below. What do all of the sentences have in common? Which words or phrases are different?

Example

By exercising 30 minutes at least three times a week, you can improve your health.

By exercising 30 minutes at least three times a week, you can reduce body fat.

By exercising 30 minutes at least three times a week, you can fight disease.

(continued on next page)

(continued from previous page)

By exercising 30 minutes at least three times a week, you can relieve depression.

By exercising 30 minutes at least three times a week, you can relieve tension.

By exercising 30 minutes at least three times a week, you can relieve stress.

<u>By exercising 30 minutes at least three times a week, you can improve your health, reduce body fat, fight disease, and relieve depression, tension, and stress.</u>

Combine the sentences below into one sentence by using commas to join the items in a series.

1. Obesity is a risk factor for heart disease.

Obesity is a risk factor for diabetes.

Obesity is a risk factor for several forms of cancer.

_____

_____

2. Many studies show that physical activity reduces anxiety and depression.

Many studies show that physical activity improves mood.

Many studies show that physical activity enhances alertness and energy.

_____

_____

3. Physical activity enhances psychological well-being.

Physical activity promotes self-esteem.

Physical activity promotes the ability to cope with stress.

Physical activity promotes on-the-job-productivity.

Physical activity promotes life satisfaction.

_____

_____

APPENDIX

Sentence Structure and Patterns

When interviewed, professors at a small private college said they did not think the majority of their students were good readers. One professor thought it was because students generally don't spend much time reading:

> I consider them to be non-readers. Really. I don't think they read fiction. I don't think they read nonfiction. I don't think they read newspapers, magazines. I don't think they read.

When this professor labeled his students "non-readers," he didn't mean that his students couldn't read. He meant that his students chose to do other things with their free time rather than read for pleasure. Like top tennis players and singers, readers spend a lot of time practicing to gain the high level of skill that makes others take notice.

The first step to becoming a highly skilled reader is recognizing sentence structure. Sentence structure consists of (1) parts of speech and (2) sentence patterns. Each word in a sentence plays a specific part in carrying the meaning. We call these roles **parts of speech**. Also, there are seven ways that the words in a sentence can be arranged or ordered. We call these **sentence patterns**. You need to have a very clear understanding of the parts of speech before the sentence patterns will make sense. Therefore, in this appendix we will learn:

- How to recognize the parts of speech in sentences.
- How to identify the subject and the predicate.
- How to recognize three basic sentence patterns.

PARTS OF SPEECH

Every word in a sentence plays a role in making meaning. The most basic parts of speech include:

- nouns (person, place, thing, or idea)
- pronouns (replace nouns)
- verbs (action and being)
- adjectives (describe nouns)
- adverbs (describe verbs, adjectives, and adverbs)
- prepositions (position words)

Many words can act as more than one part of speech depending upon how they are used in a sentence. For example, the word *race* can be a noun if we say "The canoe *race* is on Saturday." But it becomes a verb if we say "Don't *race* your car down the highway." In this section we will describe the parts of speech and give examples of each in sentences. Then, we will practice recognizing each part of speech in sentences. After that, we will look at the sentence patterns these parts of speech can make when put together into predictable combinations.

NOUNS

A **noun** is a person, place, thing, or idea. A noun can be anywhere in a sentence. Look at the following sentence:

The *books* were in the *office*.

The words "books" and "office" are both nouns. A book is a thing and an office is a place. Let's look at another sentence:

Martina studied *biology* at the *university*.

"Martina" is a noun because it is the name of a person; "biology" is a noun because it is an idea; "university" is a noun because it is a place.

Getting Ahead in College Box A.1

SINGULAR AND PLURAL NOUNS

The endings of nouns show how many persons, places, things, or ideas are being discussed. **Singular** means there is only one, while **plural**

(continued on next page)

means there are two or more. Most often, to make a noun plural, we **add** **-s** to the end of the word. If the word ends in –s, –sh, –ch, or –x, then we would **add -es** to the end of the word.

Look at the examples below.

Singular	Plural
one student	two or more students
one building	two or more buildings
one book	two or more books

Add –s or –es to the endings of the numbered words to make them plural.

The 1999 California Work and Health Survey found that only one-third of (1) workers held traditional work (2) schedule___ in which they worked eight-hour (3) day___] five (4) day___ per week. California is often the place where national (5) trend___ begin. If this study is a prediction of the future, a quarter of the people did not work year-round, and 12 percent held multiple (6) job___.

EXERCISE A-1

Identifying the Noun Type

Read each sentence. Identify the word that is a noun from the choices. Then indicate whether it is a person, place, thing, or idea. The first noun and noun type have been identified for you.

___a___ **1.** Your *friendships* and the way you
look at friendships will be *influenced* by your culture.
   a. friendships
   b. look
   c. influenced

   Noun type: "Friendships" is an idea.

_____ **2.** For example, in the *United States* you *can* be friends with someone, yet not really be *expected* to go much out of your way for this person.

   a. go

   b. United States

   c. expected

   Noun type: _____

_____ **3.** Many Middle Easterners, *Asians*, and Latin Americans would *consider* going out of their way (significantly) an absolute *essential* ingredient in friendship.

   a. Asians

   b. essential

   c. consider

   Noun type: _____

_____ **4.** If you *are* not willing to sacrifice *for* your friend, then this *person* is really not your friend.

   a. are

   b. for

   c. person

   Noun type: _____

_____ **5.** *Generally*, friendships are closer in collectivist *cultures* than in *individualistic* cultures. (DeVito 404)

   a. generally

   b. cultures

   c. individualistic

   Noun type: _____

PRONOUNS

A pronoun is a word that is used to replace a noun. Once a person, place, thing, or idea is named in a paragraph, you do not need to repeat it every time it is mentioned. Look at the paragraph below. What words would you use to replace the underlined ones?

Kim went to the registrar's office to get a copy of <u>Kim's</u> transcript. <u>Kim</u> asked the registrar about the difference between official and unofficial copies. The registrar told <u>Kim</u> that most students bought one copy of an official transcript and made photocopies of <u>the transcript</u> to send out with <u>the students'</u> résumés. After <u>the students</u> are hired, an employer will ask for official copies of <u>the students'</u> résumés.

Now look at the paragraph below. It is easier and less awkward to read when pronouns replace some of the nouns.

Kim went to the registrar's office to get a copy of <u>her</u> transcript. <u>She</u> asked the registrar about the difference between official and unofficial copies. The registrar told <u>her</u> that most students bought one copy of an official transcript and made photocopies of <u>it</u> to send out with <u>their</u> résumés. After <u>they</u> are hired, an employer will ask for official copies of <u>their</u> résumés.

Thus, after a noun is introduced, a pronoun is used to refer to it. This makes the writing simpler and easier to read. The most common pronouns are:

I, me, my, mine, myself
you, your, yours, yourself, yourselves

she, her, hers, herself
he, him, his, himself
it, its, itself

we, us, our, ours, ourselves
they, them, their, theirs, themselves

who, whom, whose, which, what
this, that, those, these

all, another, any, anybody, anyone, anything, both, each, either, everybody, everyone, everything, few, many, neither, nobody, none, no one, nothing, one, several, some, somebody, someone, something

EXERCISE
A-2

Identifying the Pronoun Reference

Study the pronouns in the sentences below and indicate which nouns have been replaced. The first one has been done for you.

1. Before Sheila McCann donned a baker's apron <u>she</u> didn't know much about baking bread.

   "She" refers to Sheila McCann
   _____

2. "<u>I</u> asked <u>myself</u>, What need in the community could <u>I</u> fill?" recalls McCann.

   _____

3. "Then, <u>I</u> thought, <u>we</u> have no good bread."

   _____

4. After experimenting with some bread recipes, <u>she</u> apprenticed without pay at local bakeries.

   _____

5. McCann observed that "once people switch to the healthful whole grain breads, <u>they</u> are unable to return to the flavorless alternatives."

   _____

6. After nearly a year of research, McCann launched House of Bread (www.Houseofbread.com). <u>She</u> made mistakes, but <u>she</u> did not let them stop <u>her</u>.

   _____

7. One of the greatest challenges, says McCann, was gauging the type, size, and amount of plant assets required to launch and maintain the bakery. <u>She</u> estimates that plant asset costs for a single bakery can exceed $200,000—producing annual sales of about $400,000.

   _____

8. McCann says that maintaining a strong sales-to-assets ratio is crucial to <u>her</u> success.

   _____

9. This includes asset costs ranging from expensive ovens and baking equipment to building and land costs. To be successful, <u>her </u>sales must not only cover these plant asset costs, but also yield a return adequate to pay other expenses and meet the owners' earnings expectations.

_____

10. McCann says that <u>her</u> goal is "To provide customers with the most delicious and healthful bread products." <u>Her</u> annual sales are now projected to exceed $5 million. There aren't many bakeries with dough that rises like that! (Wild)

_____

Getting Ahead in College Box A.2

PERSONAL PRONOUNS

The *pronoun* is a word that refers to and replaces a noun. Like nouns, personal pronouns determine the endings of the verbs that show their action. Below are the pronouns that can act as the subject in sentences. *I, you, he, she,* and *it* represent only one person, place, thing, or idea. *We, you,* and *they* represent two or more.

Singular Pronouns	Plural Pronouns
I	we
you	you (all of you in the audience)
he, she, it	they

Study the groups of singular and plural pronouns and verbs below.

■ How are the endings alike?

■ How are they different?

■ With which pronouns would you use the "s" and with which pronouns would you not use the "s"?

(continued on next page)

(continued from previous page)

■ What rule can you make up that would be true for verbs like these?

_____

_____

Singular	Plural
I wait	we wait
you wait	you wait (collective)
he, she, it waits	they wait

Singular	Plural
I cry	we cry
you cry	you cry (collective)
he, she, it cries	they cry

Singular	Plural
I wish	we wish
you wish	you wish (collective)
he, she, it wishes	they wish

Use the correct form for the word *wish* in each sentence.

1. They _____ (wish, wishes) that the war would end.

2. I _____ (wish, wishes) we had more time to go to the park.

3. He _____ (wish, wishes) that Christmas was every day.

ADJECTIVES

Adjectives are words that describe nouns. They generally come before the noun they describe and answer the questions:

■ Which one?

■ What kind?

■ How many?

Read the sentence below and study the underlined adjectives.

Sixteen endangered whooping cranes arrived home for a winter in Florida.

What do these adjectives tell us about the noun *cranes*?

- *Sixteen* tells us "how many." How many cranes are there? There are sixteen.
- *Endangered* tells us "which ones." Which cranes arrived home in Florida? The endangered ones arrived home.
- *Whooping* tells us "what kind." What kind of cranes are we talking about? We are talking about the whooping cranes.

To figure out which words in a sentence are adjectives, always ask yourself these three questions about the noun: Which one? What kind? How many? If your answer makes sense, then the word is an adjective.

EXERCISE
A-3

Identifying the Adjectives

Identify the adjectives in the following sentences and tell which questions they answer.

Example

Sixteen cranes were raised in captivity over the summer.

Adjective: <u>Sixteen</u>

Question answered: <u>How many cranes?</u>

1. The experimental flock of sixteen cranes was led from Wisconsin to Florida by ultralight planes.

   Adjectives: _____

   Questions answered: _____

2. The flock completed its flight in 49 days. It came from Wisconsin and will winter at the National Wildlife Refuge near Crystal River, Florida.

   Adjectives: _____

   Questions answered: _____

3. This is the second wave of a five-year effort to introduce a migratory flock of whooping cranes.

Adjectives: _____

Questions answered: _____

4. Only a few hundred whooping cranes remain in North America.

Adjectives: _____

Questions answered: _____

5. Establishing a new migratory flock is key to the survival of the species. (Associated Press 8D)

Adjectives: _____

Questions answered: _____

Getting Ahead in College Box A.3

ADJECTIVES

Combine the sentences below by adding the adjectives from the second and third sentences to the first sentence.

Example:

The singer sang a song.

The song was reggae.

The singer sang a reggae song.

1. Can you read a paper?

The paper is on research.

The paper is difficult.

_____

(continued on next page)

2. The coalition helps people.

The coalition is national.

The people are homeless.

_____

3. He scored high on the exam.

The exam was on mathematics.

_____

4. She joined the organization because she wanted to keep the environment from being destroyed.

The organization was Greenpeace.

_____

5. The river empties into the Gulf of Mexico.

The river is the Mississippi.

_____

⊣ VERBS

Verbs have three different functions: showing action, showing being, and helping other verbs.

Verbs show the action in a sentence (run, drive, read).

Action: I _walked_ to school today.

Verbs can also show a state of being. The verbs _is_, _are_, _was_, and _were_ show that something exists or is in a particular condition.

Being: I _am_ here.

Being: We _are_ hungry.

Finally, some verbs are called "helping" verbs because they combine with other verbs that are called main verbs. Sometimes the helping verb stands alone in a sentence; other times it must have a main verb in order to make sense.

Alone: I *have* money.

Needs a main verb: I *have taken* this train before.

Below is a list of helping verbs:

- **Forms of *have*:**
  have, has, had
- **Forms of *do*:**
  do, does, did
- **Forms of *be*:**
  be, am, is, are, was, were, being, been
- **Others:**
  can, could, may, might, must, shall, should, will, would

When we want to say that something happened in the past, we use the **past tense** of a verb. The past tense of a verb usually ends in –ed.

Yesterday I *walked* to school.

They *applied* for a student loan last year.

Last night I *studied* for the psychology exam.

Many past tense verbs do not end in –ed. We call these **irregular verbs**.

I *sold* my old car last week.

Two days ago I *bought* a new one.

This morning my new car *ran* out of gas.

EXERCISE	Identifying the Verb Type
A-4	

Read the story below and tell whether the underlined verb is: (a) an action verb, (b) a being verb, (c) a helping verb, (d) a main verb. The first one has been identified for you.

_____a_____ **1.** Fred's hands perspire as he <u>sits</u> at the keyboard and prepares to type a response to Nina's last correspondence.

_____ **2.** They <u>have</u> known each other for almost three months.

_____ **3.** What started as a very casual acquaintance has <u>blossomed</u> into an important and caring relationship based on common interests, shared humor, mutual understanding, and, most important, love.

_____ **4.** Fred is ready to pop the big question, but he <u>is</u> nervous—in fact, he's downright afraid.

_____ **5.** What if she <u>says</u> no? Or, more frightening, what if she says yes?

_____ **6.** As a confidence builder, Fred <u>rereads</u> the ad that brought the two of them together:

_____ **7.** Attractive, single African American female in early twenties, likes bicycling, body surfing, long walks along the beach on warm moonlit nights seeking young attractive like-minded male for conversation, friendship, and whatever else <u>may</u> develop.

_____ **8.** I <u>am</u> a 5′8 115-pound aerobics instructor who has an open mind and will try almost anything once.

_____ **9.** If you are <u>interested</u>, meet me poolside at the Cybercity Hotel (nonsmokers only, please).

_____ **10.** <u>Ask</u> for Naughty Nina.

_____ **11.** How <u>can</u> Fred pose this important question?

_____ **12.** After all, he <u>has</u> not been totally honest with her.

_____ **13.** He told her that he <u>is</u> vice president of accounting at a major firm but he is only one of 40 assistant accountants who work there.

_____ **14.** They celebrated when he <u>passed</u> the C.P.A. exam a month ago.

_____ **15.** What will she do when she discovers he was actually so <u>frightened</u> that he didn't even take the exam?

_____ **16.** Fred hates to admit it, but much of his relationship with Nina is <u>based</u> on deception.

_____ **17.** Fred takes a deep breath, summons all his courage, and types: Nina, I <u>think</u> it is time we meet in person.

_____ **18.** What <u>do</u> you think? Love, Fred

_____ **19.** Fred's consternation is nothing compared to the humor it produces at the other end when it is <u>received</u> by Nina.

_____ **20.** Nina <u>is</u> neither African American nor an aerobics instructor.

_____ **21.** And although Nina is indeed 5'8" tall, he <u>weighs</u> a little over 175 pounds.

_____ **22.** While Fred <u>may</u> not have taken the C.P.A. exam, "Nina," whose real name is Frank, earned his C.P.A. on his thirty-fifth birthday.

_____ **23.** He and his wife and two daughters <u>celebrated</u> by going out to dinner that night.

_____ **24.** That <u>was</u> 32 years ago. Frank, now retired, gets bored, so while his wife watches television, he plays on the computer.

_____ **25.** For the last three months, he <u>has</u> "surfed the net" dropping in and out of chat rooms under various pseudonyms, including *Wicked Walt*, *The Iceman*, *Lovely Lucy*, and one of his favorites, *Naughty Nina*.

_____ **26.** To date, "Nina" has received over 300 marriage proposals and more than one thousand requests for personal meetings, and has <u>provided</u> dozens of hours of "harmless" entertainment for Frank. (Thompson and Hickey 1–2)

Getting Ahead in College Box A.4

VERB INFINITIVES

A verb **infinitive** is the basic form of the verb. The word "to" always comes before it.

We *like* <u>to dance</u>.

We is a pronoun. *Like* is a verb. *To dance* is a verb in its infinitive form. The infinitive *always comes after another verb* that agrees with the noun or pronoun.

(continued on next page)

Jessica and Tamisha *have* <u>to go</u> to the store.

She *wants* <u>to take</u> the exam tomorrow.

Tell whether or not each sentence below contains an infinitive verb form by writing Y (for yes) or N (for no) on the line provided. If you mark "Y," underline the infinitive verb in that sentence.

_____N_____ **1.** Isabella came from Mexico at age thirteen.

_____ **2.** When my brothers and I were very young, we didn't have much of anything.

_____ **3.** We lived in an adobe hut that my grandparents let my parents borrow.

_____ **4.** My mom used to make us clothes out of old cloth that people would give to her.

_____ **5.** We each had a pair of shoes to wear, but those were just for Sundays when we went to church.

_____ **6.** The rest of the week we would go barefoot, not that we minded.

_____ **7.** We also had very little to eat.

_____ **8.** Sometimes we would go for weeks on tortillas, beans, eggs or soup.

_____ **9.** Everybody helped with the work.

_____ **10.** My father and brothers would get up early to work in the orchards or go looking for work.

_____ **11.** My mother and sisters would clean, sew and when the men came back in the afternoons, prepare fruit and take it to sell in the plaza.

_____ **12.** But one thing was for sure, even though we didn't have much to eat, we would all have breakfast and dinner together, even if it was the same thing for days: eggs and beans.

_____ **13.** Then everyone would go to our parents' room and play games that my mother made up.

(continued on next page)

(continued from previous page)

_____ **14.** Even though we didn't have many things, we were very happy because we had each other.

_____ **15.** Especially, we had the love of our family which made us stronger. (Manis 20)

ADVERBS

Adverbs answer the following questions:

■ When?

■ Where?

■ How?

■ How often?

■ Why?

■ Under what conditions?

■ To what degree?

Most adverbs end in –ly (precisely, accurately, dramatically). Just as adjectives describe nouns, *adverbs* describe verbs. Adverbs also describe adjectives and other adverbs. In the sentence below, "cheerfully" is the adverb and "greeted" is the verb that it modifies.

The speaker <u>cheerfully</u> greeted his audience.

The adverb "cheerfully" describes the verb "greeted." How did the speaker greet his audience? He greeted them cheerfully.

When an adverb describes a verb, it can be placed in several positions in the sentence:

<u>Cheerfully</u> the speaker greeted his audience.

The speaker <u>cheerfully</u> greeted his audience.

The speaker greeted his audience <u>cheerfully</u>.

When adverbs describe adjectives and adverbs, they generally come before the word they describe.

■ **Describing an adjective:**

The post office is <u>terribly</u> busy on Saturdays.

The adverb "terribly" describes the adjective "busy."

■ **Describing an adjective:**

He didn't take that joke <u>very</u> lightly.

The adverb "very" describes the adverb "lightly."

Common adverbs that do not end in –ly include:

very	often	never	always	well
almost	quite	soon	then	there
too	not	just	only	

EXERCISE
A-5

Identifying the Adverb Type

Read each sentence and indicate if the adverb that is underlined describes (a) a verb, (b) an adjective, or (c) another adverb. Then tell which question it answers: When? Where? How? How often? Why? Under what conditions? To what degree?

Example

_____b_____ It is <u>virtually</u> impossible to determine precisely how many people in the United States and around the world have access to personal computers and at some time or another go online to use the Internet.

Question answered: <u>To what degree is it impossible? It is virtually impossible.</u>

_____ 1. The number changes <u>daily</u>—or, more accurately, by the minute.

Question answered: _____

_____ 2. We do know, however, that computers and the World Wide Web have <u>dramatically</u> altered our understanding of the world and how we interact with one another. Think about the fictitious vignette involving Fred and "Nina." Would such deception have been possible before the use of personal computers? Is the hoax perpetuated by "Nina" harmless fun? What are the possible consequences of such a hoax? Would you even categorize the correspondence between Fred and "Nina" as social interaction?

Question answered: _____

_____ 3. Sociologists know that age, race, sex, gender, and social class are but a few of the important variables that <u>significantly</u> affect how people interact in the real world. Do these variables come into play when people interact over the Internet? If so, in what ways? Or, as one television advertisement for the Internet declares, is cyberspace a place where interaction can take place where these social characteristics do not matter?

Question answered: _____

_____ 4. These and other questions <u>immediately</u> spring to mind when the vignette is viewed from a sociological perspective.

Question answered: _____

_____ 5. The vignette also illustrates the first wisdom of sociology . . . . Things are <u>not</u> necessarily what they seem.

Question answered: _____

(Thompson and Hickey 1–2)

Getting Ahead in College Box A.5

ADVERBS

Combine the sentences below by adding the adverbs from the second and third sentences to the first sentence.

(continued on next page)

Example:

The band plays this reggae song well.

They always play well.

<u>The band always plays this reggae song well.</u>

1. Set the computer.

Set it down.

Set it here.

_____

2. Glenn and I go to the football games.

We go often.

_____

3. Michael chose the college based on information he received from the admissions department.

He chose it carefully.

_____

4. Cecilia wears a suit to work.

She wears it usually.

_____

5. We wait for the pool to open.

We wait sometimes.

We wait awhile.

_____

PREPOSITIONS AND PREPOSITIONAL PHRASES

A preposition is a word or phrase that connects a noun or a pronoun to the rest of the sentence. A prepositional phrase starts with the preposition and ends with a noun or pronoun. The prepositional phrase will show direction, place, time, or manner (how something is done).

> The car raced *around the track* (direction) *with tremendous speed* (manner).

> We went *to the mall* (place) *at five o'clock* (time).

> We went *up the mountain* (direction) *on foot* (manner) and skied *down the slope* (direction).

Below is a list of common prepositions:

about	as	beyond	for	of	under
above	at	by	from	off	until
across	before	concerning	in	on	up
after	behind	considering	inside	over	with
against	below	despite	into	since	within
along	beside	down	like	through	without
among	besides	during	near	to	
around	between	except	next	toward	

Sometimes, more than one preposition will head off the phrase and the phrase will end in either a noun or pronoun.

> We could not ride our bikes this week <u>*because of* the rainy weather</u>.

> <u>*According to* a national study</u>, smoking causes about 350,000 deaths every year.

Some common preposition combinations include:

according to	in addition to	on account of
aside from	in back of	prior to
as of	in front of	out of
as well as	in place of	with regard to
because of	in spite of	with respect to
by way of	instead of	

| Getting Ahead in College Box A.6 |

PREPOSITIONAL PHRASES

Combine the sentences below by adding any prepositional phrases to the first sentence.

1. New York is the largest city.

It is in the United States.

<u>New York is the largest city in the United States.</u>

2. It was hot.

It was hot in the city.

It was hot during the day.

_____

3. The skyline is beautiful.

It is beautiful at night.

_____

4. The city lights sparkle.

They sparkle off the water.

The water is of the Hudson River.

They sparkle under the moonlight.

_____

5. One can see the Empire State Building.

One can see it above the skyscrapers.

One can see it from a great distance.

_____

EXERCISE
A-6

Identifying the Prepositional Phrase

Underline the prepositional phrases in the following sentences. The first set has been done for you.

1. <u>Over the past two decades</u>, young women have become more interested <u>in jobs</u> that have been held mostly <u>by men</u>.

2. At the same time, women's progress has been slow in entering and doing well at male-dominated jobs.

3. The percentage of women engineers, lawyers, and doctors increased between 1972 and 1998 in the United States, but it falls far short of equal representation.

4. Women still remain mostly in the less well-paid, traditionally feminine professions of literature, social work, education, and nursing.

5. In all fields, they do not do as well as men; men write more books, make more discoveries, hold more leadership positions, and produce more art work.

6. Ability cannot account for these dramatic differences.

7. Gender-stereotyped messages play a key role instead of ability.

8. Although girls' grades are higher than boys', girls reach secondary school less confident of their ability and more likely to underestimate their achievement.

9. Between tenth and twelfth grade, the percentage of girls in gifted programs decreases.

10. When asked what discouraged them from continuing in gifted classes, the girls named parental and peer pressures and teachers' attitudes as the main causes. (Berk 447)

COPYRIGHT © 2006 BY PEARSON EDUCATION, INC.

| EXERCISE A-7 | Identifying the Function of the Prepositional Phrase |

Identify whether the underlined prepositional phrase shows (a) direction, (b) place, (c) time, or (d) manner (how something is done). The first one has been done for you.

_____c_____ 1. <u>During college</u>, the career ambitions of academically talented young women weaken even more.

_____ 2. <u>In one longitudinal study</u>, high school valedictorians were followed over a 10-year period—through college and <u>into the work world</u>.

_____ 3. <u>By their sophomore year</u>, young women judged themselves to be less intelligent than they thought when they started college, whereas men did not.

_____ 4. Women also shifted their expectations <u>toward less demanding careers</u> because of concerns about combining work with child rearing and questions about their ability.

_____ 5. Even though female valedictorians performed better than their male counterparts <u>in college courses</u>, they achieved at lower levels <u>in their jobs</u>.

_____ 6. The educational ambitions of mathematically talented women went <u>down a great deal</u> during college, as did the number of women majoring in the sciences.

_____ 7. Very few women are <u>in physical-science careers</u>. They make up only 9 percent of employed engineers and physicists.

_____ 8. Young people should be given more career information. <u>In a national study</u> of 1,200 American high school students who were followed for 5 years, it was found that young people of all backgrounds were highly ambitious.

_____ 9. Compared <u>with previous generations</u>, many more expected to graduate from college and enter professional jobs.

_____ 10. But about half did not know <u>about the steps</u> involved in reaching their goal. (Berk 447)

<table>
<tr><td>EXERCISE
A-8</td><td>**Identifying the Prepositional Phrase**</td></tr>
</table>

Underline the prepositional phrases in the following sentences. The first set has been underlined for you.

1. They had only sketchy knowledge <u>of their chosen field,</u> <u>of the educational</u> <u>requirements</u> to enter it, and <u>of the future demand</u> <u>for it.</u>

2. These young people were at risk for becoming "drifting dreamers," failing to make good choices about how to use their efforts wisely.

3. Especially if they entered a community college with plans to transfer to a four- year institution, they frequently found that they did not have the high school background to take the courses they needed.

4. And often they chose courses without checking to make sure that credit would transfer to a four-year college.

5. As a result, some students remained in school for a long period of time, whereas others did not complete their educational plans—for both academic and economic reasons. (Berk 447)

SIMPLE SUBJECTS AND PREDICATES

The *simple subject* of a sentence is a noun or pronoun that names who or what the sentence is about. To find the subject, you would ask:

■ Who is this sentence about?

■ What is this sentence about?

The *simple predicate* of a sentence is the main verb along with its helping verbs. The predicate tells us what action the subject is taking. To find the predicate, you would ask:

■ What is the subject doing?

■ What is happening to the subject?

■ What is said about the subject?

In the sentence below, "economics" is the simple subject. It tells what the sentence is about: economics. The simple predicate is "has grown." It tells us what has happened to the subject: economics has grown.

<u>Economics</u> has, over the last century, grown from a tiny acorn into a mighty oak.

The remaining parts of the sentence add more information about the simple subject and predicate. Let's look at a more complicated sentence.

Under its spreading branches economists find explanations of the gains from international trade, advice on how to reduce unemployment and inflation, formulas for investing your retirement funds, and even proposals for selling the rights to pollute.

This is a long sentence with many nouns and pronouns. How do we know which noun or pronoun is the simple subject? Follow the steps below to learn how:

1. Read the entire sentence.

2. Ask yourself: "Who or what is this sentence about?"

3. Look at the nouns and pronouns. Is it about branches? economists? explanations? trade? advice? unemployment? inflation? formulas? funds? or proposals?

4. Then ask: "What is each of these subjects doing?" and "Does this relate to the whole sentence or just one part of the sentence?" The simple subject should relate to the whole sentence.

5. Try to match the possibilities with the subject.

■ **What are the branches doing?**

The branches are spreading.

■ **Is this sentence about branches spreading?**

Are the branches giving advice on how to reduce unemployment?

Are the branches making formulas for investing retirement funds?

Are the branches giving proposals for selling the rights to pollute?

We can say "no" to all of these questions about "branches." Thus, we know that "branches" is not the simple subject. However, if we ask these questions with the noun "economists" in mind, the information suddenly makes sense.

■ **Is this sentence about** *economists*?

■ **What are the economists doing?**

The economists find—

■ **What are the economists finding?**

They are finding:

- explanations of the gains from international trade.
- advice on how to reduce unemployment and inflation.
- formulas for investing your retirement funds.
- proposals for selling the rights to pollute.

It makes sense that the economists are finding all of these things. Thus, the simple subject is "economists" and the simple predicate is "find."

EXERCISE
A-9

Identifying the Simple Subject and Predicate

Find the simple subject and simple predicate. Underline the simple subject once and the simple predicate twice. The first set has been underlined for you.

1. Throughout the world, <u>economists</u> <u>are laboring</u> to collect data and to improve our understanding of economic trends.

2. What is the economists' purpose?

3. The ultimate goal of economic science is to improve the living conditions of people in their everyday lives.

4. Higher incomes mean good food, warm houses, and hot water.

5. They mean safe drinking water and inoculations against the diseases.

Getting Ahead in College Box A.7

COMPOUND SUBJECTS

Some sentences have two or more simple subjects. We call these compound subjects. They are joined by words like "but," "and," and "or." You can tell if a sentence has a compound subject if each simple subject can stand alone and make sense with the rest of the sentence.

Example

Webmaster and *digital librarian* are jobs that did not exist 10 years ago.

Webmaster is a job that did not exist 10 years ago.

Digital librarian is a job that did not exist 10 years ago.

Read the following sentence and identify three simple subjects and write them in the spaces below.

Hispanics, African Americans, and Asian Americans are projected to make up approximately 27 percent of the workforce by the year 2005.

_____   _____   _____

COMPLETE SUBJECTS AND PREDICATES

The simple subject and simple predicate are the heart of a sentence. Look at the sentence below:

The Metropolitan Museum of Art is closed this week.

In this example, "museum" is the simple subject and "is closed" is the simple predicate. We could ask and answer:

■ What is closed?

■ The museum is closed.

The **complete subject** of a sentence is made up of the simple subject (noun or pronoun) and the words that describe it. To find the complete subject, you would locate the verb and ask who or what is doing this action.

The Metropolitan Museum of Art is closed this week.

Ask: Who or what is closed this week?

Answer: The Metropolitan Museum of Art is closed this week.

Thus, the complete subject is "the Metropolitan Museum of Art."
The **complete predicate** is made up of the simple predicate (the main verb + helping verbs) and the words that describe them. After you find the subject, the predicate is the remaining part of the sentence.

(The Metropolitan *Museum* of Art)   (*is closed* this week.)
        complete subject   complete predicate

EXERCISE
A-10

Locating the Complete Subject and Predicate

Highlight the simple subject and the simple predicate. Then, underline the complete subject once and complete predicate twice. The first term has been identified for you.

1. Higher incomes mean even more.

2. They allow governments to build schools so that young people can learn to read.

3. As incomes rise further, nations can afford deep scientific inquiries into biology to discover vaccines against diseases.

4. With the resources from economic growth, talented artists have the opportunity to write poetry and compose music.

5. Freedom from hunger, disease, and the elements is a universal human goal.

SENTENCE PATTERNS

Read the sentence below. Does it make sense?

Students by with inspired goals connected become if college in successful they long-term that college are study.

It's not easy to understand the above sentence because the words are scrambled; the sentence has no order. We know, from studying English, that sentences have certain structures, and we are used to seeing words arranged within these structures (e.g., nouns are usually followed by verbs; prepositions begin phrases; adjectives come before nouns).

Look again at this sentence when it is organized in a way that we would expect.

> Students become successful in college if they are inspired by long-term goals that are connected with college study.

Most of us would agree that the unscrambled sentence is faster and easier to read.

The organization of ideas in a sentence is called the **sentence pattern**. If you do *not* look for the organizational pattern of the sentence while you read, you may find yourself reading words without thinking about their meaning. We will discuss the four most basic sentence patterns:

- subject–verb
- subject–verb–direct object
- subject–verb–direct object–indirect object
- subject–verb–complement

Subject–Verb Pattern

The *subject–verb* sentence pattern includes a subject (the noun or phrase the sentence is about) and a verb (what the subject is doing). Look at the example below:

> We sang.

What noun or phrase is the sentence about? *We*. What did *we* do? *Sang*. "We" is the subject and "sang" is the verb.

Subject–Verb–Direct Object Pattern

The *subject–verb–direct object* sentence pattern is similar to the subject–verb pattern but includes a direct object. A **direct object** is a word or word group that receives the action.

> We sang songs.

"Songs" is the direct object. It answers the question "What did we sing?" "We" is the subject, "sang" is the verb, and "songs" is the direct object.

Subject–Verb–Direct Object–Indirect Object Pattern

The *subject–verb–direct object–indirect object* sentence pattern adds an indirect object. An **indirect object** is a word or word group that tells *to whom* or *for whom* the action was done.

We sang songs to the audience.

To whom did we sing these songs? "We" is the subject, "sang" is the verb, "songs" is the direct object, and "audience" is the indirect object.

Subject–Verb–Complement Pattern

In the *subject–verb–complement* sentence pattern, a word or word group renames or describes the subject.

This song is *beautiful*.

"Beautiful" describes the subject "song." "Song" is the subject, "is" is the verb, and "beautiful" is the subject complement.

This song is a *poem*.

"Poem" renames the subject "song." "Song" is the subject, "is" is the verb, and "poem" is the subject complement.

EXERCISE
A-11

Identifying the Sentence Pattern

Unscramble each of the sentences below and identify the sentence pattern. The first one has been done for you.

1. is difficult biology a subject
   Biology is a difficult subject.
   Subject–verb–complement

2. exam students biology the for studied the

   _____

   _____

3. studied students the

_____

_____

4. gave the to professor the biology us exam

_____

_____

5. like we biology

_____

_____

EXERCISE
A-12

Identifying the Sentence Pattern

Identify the sentence patterns. The first one has been identified for you.

_____d_____ **1.** Listening is an active process.
   a. subject–verb
   b. subject–verb–direct object
   c. subject–verb–direct object–indirect object
   d. subject–verb–complement

_____ **2.** You should ask questions to clarify what the speaker means.
   a. subject–verb
   b. subject–verb–direct object
   c. subject–verb–direct object–indirect object
   d. subject–verb–complement

_____ **3.** The speaker should ask questions of the audience.
   a. subject–verb
   b. subject–verb–direct object

    c. subject–verb–direct object–indirect object

    d. subject–verb–complement

_____ **4.** Questions are the key to understanding and remembering what you hear.
    a. subject–verb

    b. subject–verb–direct object

    c. subject–verb–direct object–indirect object

    d. subject–verb–complement

_____ **5.** We always listen.
    a. subject–verb

    b. subject–verb–direct object

    c. subject–verb–direct object–indirect object

    d. subject–verb–complement

A Reading in Geography

Did you know that Brazil is the fifth largest country in the world—almost as large as the United States? Read the following selection to find out more about Brazil. As you read, underline the simple subject once and the simple predicate twice in each sentence. After reading, complete the comprehension questions at the end.

Vocabulary in Context

Complete the vocabulary exercises first to become familiar with the new terms The first term has been identified for you.

    a. extensive—far reaching

    b. administratively—as managed by the government

    c. equatorial—having to do with the equator

    d. verdant—green and leafy

    e. confluence—a joining together

_____a_____ **1.** Brazil has an _____ coastline; it borders the Atlantic Ocean and is 4,578 miles long.

_____ **2.** With respect to government and political boundaries, or
_____, Brazil is broken up into 26 states and one fed-
eral district.

_____ **3.** The Amazon Basin has an abundance of leafy green trees. It is
the most _____ area in the country.

_____ **4.** Brazil's land mass is so large that it covers many different climates. Its climates include tropical, _____, semi-arid,
highland tropical, and subtropical.

_____ **5.** The Amazon joins together with the Atlantic Ocean. The
point at which they meet is called their _____.

Brazil

[1] <u>Brazil</u>, officially the Federative Republic of Brazil, or in Portuguese the
Republica Federativa do Brasil, <u>is located</u> in South America. It borders
the Atlantic Ocean, which gives the country an **extensive** coastline of
4,578 miles. Brazil is the largest country in Latin America with
3,286,470 square miles of land, occupying nearly half of the continent
of South America. Its landmass is slightly smaller than the United
States, making it the fifth largest country in the world. Besides the
Atlantic Ocean, Brazil's border touches ten different countries. These
include the French Guiana, Suriname, Guyana, Venezuela, and
Colombia, which all are located to the North of Brazil, Uruguay and
Argentina to the South, and Paraguay, Bolivia, and Peru to the West.
Brazil has a population of approximately 170 million. Currently, the
president of Brazil is Fernando Henrique Cardoso. As president, he
functions as both the chief of state and head of government.
Administratively, Brazil is broken up into 26 states and one federal
district. Brazil's capital is Brasilia, located in the southern portion of
Brazil's central region.

[2]   Brazil has a varied climate, including areas classified as
equatorial, tropical, semi-arid, highland tropical, and subtropical.
The areas that receive large amounts of rain, such as the Amazon
Basin have **verdant** and lush evergreen trees, while in semi-arid
places such as the northeast, a dry bush predominates. The Pantanal
Mato-Grossense, which is also one of the worlds' largest biological
reserves, is a plain located in the western portion of the center of the
country made up of tall grasses, weeds, and widely dispersed trees.

[3]   In addition to its long coast on the Atlantic Ocean, Brazil contains two river systems that shape its distinctive geography, the Amazon and San Francisco Rivers. Although not as famous as the Amazon, the San Francisco River is the largest river completely within Brazil, flowing over 1,000 miles from the Brazilian Highlands to its **confluence** with the Atlantic Ocean. (Farr and Hammers 29–30)

Comprehension Questions

_____c_____ 1. Brazil is the

a. largest country in the world.

b. second largest country in the world.

c. fifth largest country in the world.

d. tenth largest country in the world.

_____ 2. How many states does Brazil have?

a. 26

b. 52

c. 170

d. 0; Brazil has federal districts instead of states.

_____ 3. The largest river in Brazil is named:

a. the Brazilia River.

b. the Amazon River.

c. the San Francisco River.

d. the Pantanal Mato-Grossense River.

_____ 4. Brazil is:

a. much smaller than the United States.

b. about the same size as the United States.

c. slightly larger than the United States.

d. much larger than the United States.

_____ **5.** "Republica Federativa do Brasil" means the:

     a. Brazilian Republic.

     b. Brazilian Federation.

     c. Republic of Brazil.

     d. Federative Republic of Brazil.

Visual Literacy Box A.1 ● ● ● ● ● ● ● ● ● ● ● ● ● ● ●

Mapping Geographic Information

Mapping can help you organize and visualize information so that you can better understand and remember it. Read the sentences below and then finish the map.

Brazil's border touches ten different countries. These include the French Guiana, Suriname, Guyana, Venezuela, and Colombia, which all are located to the North of Brazil, Uruguay and Argentina to the South, and Paraguay, Bolivia, and Peru to the West.

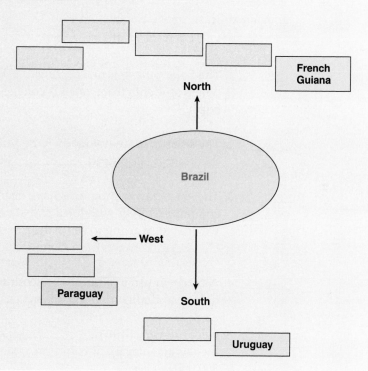

A Reading in Chemistry

Did you know that houses, cars, and even boats could be powered by energy from the sun? Read the following selection to find out more about this type of energy. As you read, underline the simple subject once and simple predicate twice in each sentence. After reading, complete the comprehension questions at the end.

Vocabulary in Context

Complete the vocabulary exercise first to become familiar with the new terms. The first term has been identified for you.

a. intercollegiate—between or among colleges

b. vanguard—forefront, leading edge, frontrunner

c. adequate—enough

d. photovoltaic—having to do with solar power

e. minimal—least, smallest, minimum

_____a_____ 1. The Solar Splash is an _____ boat competition in which students from various colleges design and race solar boats.

_____ 2. The solar cars are not ready to be put on the roads in spite of their cutting edge and _____ designs.

_____ 3. The solar power programs have been supported by private companies along with local and state governments. However, we are still waiting to see if the program will receive _____ funds from Congress to keep it going.

_____ 4. Already in use in a number of countries, _____ technology is challenging the oil and gas industries.

_____ 5. Needing very little or _____ maintenance, a 200-megawatt solar plant could provide household power for 300,000 people.

Photovoltaics: Plugging in the Sun

[1] The largest solar <u>installation</u> in the United States, located in Carrisa Plains, CA, <u>was built</u> by ARCO Solar, Inc. and Pacific Gas and Electric Company. It generates about seven megawatts at peak power. Although this generating capacity is small compared to that of fossil fuel, nuclear, and hydroelectric plants, much larger solar installations are expected in the future. A 200-megawatt plant, which could provide household power for 300,000 people, could be erected on a square mile of land at relatively modest capital expense and **minimal** maintenance. At currently attainable levels of operating efficiency, all the electricity needs of the United States could be supplied by a photovoltaic generating station covering an area of 85 miles by 85 miles, roughly the area of New Jersey.

[2] **Photovoltaic** technology is already in use in a number of countries. From small, remote villages in developing countries to upscale suburbs in Japan and the United States, 500,000 homeowners worldwide use solar cells to generate their own electricity. In sunny Sacramento, CA, the Municipal Utility District has constructed an array of 1600 photovoltaic cells that produces two megawatts (2×10^6 watts) of electricity, sufficient to serve 600 homes. An additional 420 homes have rooftop photovoltaic systems. The homeowners sell back excess electricity to the utility company. The district has voted to close down its nuclear reactors in favor of using photovoltaics and other "cleaner" energy technologies. Aided by generous tax credits, over 23,000 homes in Japan have rooftop solar units, installed to overcome the high cost of electricity.

[3] The European Union and the United States are partners in the "Million Roofs" program, an initiative to install a million rooftop photovoltaic systems by 2110. The U.S. program proposes a 15% tax credit and funds to subsidize partnerships among builders, utilities, and local governments. Already supported by private companies, as well as local and state governments, it remains to be seen whether the program will receive **adequate** funds from Congress to achieve the goal. A study in western Germany pointed out that half the electricity needs of that region could be met using rooftop solar cells.

[4] Solar cells even power cars. Sunrayce USA, a nine-day, 1250-mile race sponsored by the U.S. Department of Energy and private corporations, has become a popular activity for engineering students. Student teams design, build, test, and drive cars that are powered only by photovoltaic cells. In spite of their **vanguard** designs, the cars are

not ready to be put on the roads for everyday use. The World Solar Challenge, a 1865-mile race across Australia, from Darwin in the north to Adelaide in the south, attracts commercial entrants. In the 1996 race, a car built by Honda using photovoltaic cells manufactured in Australia covered the course in 35.5 hours, for a record average speed of 53.1 miles per hour. There is also an **intercollegiate** solar boat competition called Solar Splash. In addition, an airplane powered only by battery-charging amorphous (non-crystalline) silicon solar cells has flown more than 2400 miles in less than 120 hours, and a solar-powered boat has made its appearance. (Stanitski et al. 325–26)

Comprehension Questions

Unscramble each sentence below and identify its sentence pattern. The first one has been done for you.

_____c_____ **1.** company homeowners utility the electricity excess back sell the to

The homeowners sell back excess electricity to the utility company.

    a. subject–verb

    b. subject–verb–direct object

    c. subject–verb–direct object–indirect object

    d. subject–verb–complement

_____ **2.** peak it power generates at seven about megawatts

_____

    a. subject–verb

    b. subject–verb–direct object

    c. subject–verb–direct object–indirect object

    d. subject–verb–complement

_____ **3.** photovoltaic is technology already use in a in number countries of

_____

a. subject–verb

b. subject–verb–direct object

c. subject–verb–direct object–indirect object

d. subject–verb–complement

_____ **4.** cells power cars solar even

_____

a. subject–verb

b. subject–verb–direct object

c. subject–verb–direct object–indirect object

d. subject–verb–complement

_____ **5.** engineering Sunrayce become students has for popular a USA activity

_____

a. subject–verb

b. subject–verb–direct object

c. subject–verb–direct object–indirect object

d. subject–verb–complement

Getting Ahead in College Box A.8

THE PRONUNCIATION OF VOCABULARY

When two or three consonants are grouped together, the combination of the letters makes one sound, although each letter can still be heard within that sound. For example, the *p* and the *l* sounds in please, plan, and play are blended together to make one sound. Thus, they are called consonant blends. Using the following examples as a pronunciation guide, list the words in each sentence that have blends and underline the blend.

cr	as in	crop
dr	as in	drive
str	as in	string

(continued on next page)

(continued from previous page)

sm	as in	**sm**ell
tr	as in	**tr**ain
fr	as in	**fr**eeze

1. In sunny Sacramento, CA, the Municipal Utility District has constructed an array of 1600 photovoltaic cells that produces two megawatts ($2\text{X}10^6$ watts) of electricity.
   Sa<u>c</u>ramento
   di<u>str</u>ict
   con<u>str</u>ucted
   elec<u>tr</u>icity

2. Although this generating capacity is small compared to that of fossil fuel, nuclear, and hydroelectric plants, much larger solar installations are expected in the future.

   _____

   _____

   _____

   _____

3. The World Solar Challenge, a 1865-mile race across Australia, from Darwin in the north to Adelaide in the south, attracts commercial entrants.

   _____

   _____

   _____

   _____

A Reading in Psychology

What makes love last? After 20 years of research, one psychologist believes he has the answer. Read the passage below to find out why marriages succeed or fail. As you read, underline the simple subject once and the simple predicate twice in each sentence. After reading, complete the comprehension exercise at the end.

Vocabulary in Context

Complete the vocabulary exercise first to become familiar with the new terms. The first one has been done for you.

a. **empirical**—backed by proof; based on experience or observation

b. **colleagues**—people you work with

c. **contemptuous**—scornful; with disdain or disrespect

d. **conventional**—usual, standard, regular, traditional

e. **longevity**—long life; prolonged existence

_____d_____ 1. Psychologists are discovering that much of the standard and traditional information they believed to be true is simply wrong; _____ wisdom failed them in their counseling practices.

_____ 2. Gottman and his co-workers or _____ have been intensely observing what happens when couples interact.

_____ 3. How long your relationship lasts, or its _____, depends primarily on your being five times as nice as you are nasty to each other.

_____ 4. A critical, negative, and _____ husband actually makes women physically ill.

_____ 5. John Gottman began to do scientific research on the subject of marriage counseling because he believed that almost none of the theory and practice was based on _____ scientific research.

What Makes Love Last?

[1] Long-lasting <u>marriages</u> <u>are increasingly rare</u>. Not only do more than 50 percent of all first marriages in the United States end in divorce (make that 60 percent for repeat attempts), but fewer people are even

bothering to tie the slippery knot in the first place. One fourth of Americans eighteen or older—about 41 million people—have never married at all. In 1970, that figure was only one sixth.

[2] But even while millions of couples march down the aisle only to pass through the therapist's office and into divorce court, a quiet revolution is taking place when it comes to understanding how long-term love really works. Inside the laboratories of the Family Formation Project at the University of Washington in Seattle, affectionately dubbed the Love Lab, research psychologists are putting our most cherished relationship theories under the scientific microscope. What they are discovering is that much of what we regard as **conventional** wisdom is simply wrong.

[3] "Almost none of our theory and practice in marital therapy is founded on **empirical** scientific research," contends the Love Lab's head, John Gottman, an award-winning research psychologist trained both as a therapist and a mathematician. Indeed, it is this lack of solid research, Gottman believes, that contributes to a discouraging statistic. For 50 percent of married couples who enter therapy, divorce is still the end result.

[4] Gottman believes that, although relationship counseling has helped many people, much of it just doesn't work. Not satisfied with warm and fuzzy ideas about how to "get the love you want," Gottman is scouting for numbers, data, proof. And he is finding it.

[5] For the past twenty years, in a laboratory equipped with video cameras, EKGs, and an array of custom-designed instruments, Gottman and his colleagues have been intensely observing what happens when couples interact. He watches them talk. He watches them fight. He watches them hash out problems and reaffirm their love. He records facial expressions and self-reported emotions, heart rhythms and blood chemistry. He tests urine, memories, and couples' ability to interpret each other's emotional cues. Then he pours his data, like so many puzzle pieces, into a computer. The resulting picture, he says, is so clear and detailed it's like "a CAT scan of a living relationship."

[6] What Gottman and his colleagues have discovered and summarized for popular audiences in a new book, *Why Marriages Succeed or Fail*, is mind-boggling in its very simplicity. His conclusion: Couples who stay together are . . . well . . . nice to each other more often than not. "Satisfied couples," claims Gottman, "maintained a five-to-one ration of positive to negative moments" in their relationship. Couples heading for divorce, on the other hand, allow that ratio to slip below one-to-one.

[7]   Gottman contends that many aspects of wedded life often considered critical to long-term success—how intensely people fight; whether they face conflict or avoid it; how well they solve problems; how compatible they are socially, financially, even sexually—are less important than people (including therapists) tend to think. In fact, Gottman believes, none of these things matter to a marriage's **longevity** as much as maintaining the crucial ratio of five to one.

[8]   If it's hard to believe that the longevity of your relationship depends primarily on your being five times as nice as you are nasty to each other, some of Gottman's other conclusions may be even more surprising. For example:

- Wildly explosive relationships that vacillate between heated arguments and passionate reconciliations can be as happy—and long-lasting—as those that seem more emotionally stable. They may even be more exciting and intimate.

- Emotionally inexpressive marriages, which may seem like repressed volcanoes destined to explode, are actually very successful—so long as the couple maintains that five-to-one ratio in what they do express to each other. In fact, too much emotional catharsis among such couples can "scare the hell out of them," says Gottman.

- Couples who start out complaining about each other have some of the most stable marriages over time, while those who don't fight early on are more likely to hit the rocky shoals of divorce.

- Fighting, whether rare or frequent, is sometimes the healthiest thing a couple can do for their relationship. In fact, blunt anger, appropriately expressed, "seems to immunize marriages against deterioration."

- In happy marriages, there are no discernible gender differences in terms of the quantity and quality of emotional expression. In fact, men in happy marriages are more likely to reveal intimate personal information about themselves than women. (When conflicts erupt, however, profound gender differences emerge.)

- Men who do housework are likely to have happier marriages, greater physical health, even better sex lives than men who don't. (This piece of news alone could cause a run on aprons.)

- Women are made physically sick by a relentlessly unresponsive or emotionally **contemptuous** husband. Gottman's researchers can

even tell just how sick: They can predict the number of infectious diseases women in such marriages will suffer over a four-year period.

■ How warmly you remember the story of your relationship foretells
your chances for staying together. In one study that involved taking
oral histories from couples about the unfolding of their relationship,
psychologists were able to predict—with an astonishing 94 percent
accuracy—which couples would be divorced within three years
(Atkisson).

SENTENCE PATTERNS

Unscramble each sentence below and identify its sentence pattern.

_____d_____ **1.** rare long-lasting are marriages increasingly

Long-lasting marriages are increasingly rare.

    a. subject—verb

    b. subject—verb—direct object

    c. subject—verb—direct object—indirect object

    d. subject—verb—complement

_____ **2.** watches talk he them

_____

    a. subject—verb

    b. subject—verb—direct object

    c. subject—verb—direct object—indirect object

    d. subject—verb—complement

_____ **3.** problems he out them hash watches

_____

    a. subject—verb

    b. subject—verb—direct object

    c. subject—verb—direct object—indirect object

    d. subject—verb—complement

_____ **4.** into he a his data then computer pours

_____

a. subject—verb

b. subject—verb—direct object

c. subject—verb—direct object—indirect object

d. subject—verb—complement

_____ **5.** who together nice each more often not than couples stay are to other

_____

a. subject—verb

b. subject—verb—direct object

c. subject—verb—direct object—indirect object

d. subject—verb—complement

Comprehension Questions

_____ **1.** What percentage of Americans 18 or older have never married?

a. 1 %

b. 10%

c. 25%

d. 50%

_____ **2.** After much research, Gottman found that:

a. couples who fight most often get divorced.

b. couples who stay together are nice to each other more often than not.

c. couples who never fight get divorces most often.

d. couples who start out complaining about each other usually get divorced.

_____ **3.** How long your relationship lasts depends on your being _____ as nice as you are nasty to each other.

a. just

b. twice

c. three times

d. five times

_____ **4.** When married to an unresponsive or critical husband, women become:

    a. unresponsive.

    b. just as critical.

    c. physically sick.

    d. depressed.

_____ **5.** Psychologists were able to predict (with 94 percent accuracy) which couples would be divorced within three years by:

    a. how often they fight.

    b. how bluntly they express their anger.

    c. how often men do housework.

    d. how warmly they tell about how they met each other.

Visual Literacy Box A.2 ●●●●●●●●●●●●●●●

Mapping Scientific Information

Finish the map based on the information in the sentences below.

Solar cells even power cars. Sunrayce USA, a nine-day, 1250-mile race sponsored by the U.S. Department of Energy and private corporations, has become a popular activity for engineering students. Student teams design, build, test, and drive cars that are powered only by photovoltaic cells. In spite of their vanguard designs, the cars are not ready to be put on the roads for everyday use. The World Solar Challenge, an 1865-mile race across Australia, from Darwin in the north to Adelaide in the south, attracts commercial entrants. In the 1996 race, a car built by Honda using photovoltaic cells manufactured in Australia covered the course in 35.5 hours, for a record average speed of 53.1 miles per hour. There is also an intercollegiate solar boat competition called Solar Splash. In addition, an airplane powered only by battery-charging amorphous (non-crystalline) silicon solar cells has flown more than 2400 miles in less than 120 hours, and a solar-powered boat has made its appearance.

(continued on next page)

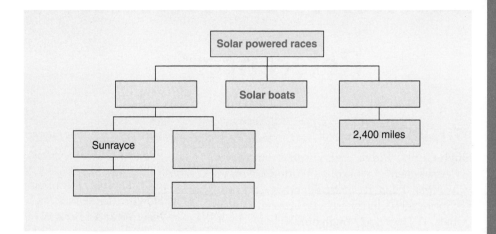

References

INTRODUCTION

Singh-Gupta, Vidya and Eileen Troutt-Ervin. "Assessment of Workplace Writing," *Journal of Vocational and Technical Education*, 13, no. 2 (Spring 1997), http://scholar.lib.vt.edu/ejournals/JVTE/v13n2/Singh.html.

Stanley, Thomas J., and William D. Danko. *The Millionaire Next Door*. Atlanta: Longstreet. 1996.

CHAPTER 2

Barker, Larry L., and Deborah Roach Gaut. *Communication*. 8th ed. Boston: Allyn and Bacon, 2002.

Manis, Robert. *The Marriage and Family Workbook*. Boston: Allyn and Bacon, 2001.

Stanitski, Conrad L., Lucy Pryde Eubanks, Catherine H. Middlecamp, and Wilmer J. Stratton. *Chemistry in Context: Applying Chemistry to Society*, 3rd ed. Boston: McGraw-Hill, 2000.

CHAPTER 3

Barker, Larry L., and Deborah Roach Gaut. *Communication*. 8th ed. Boston: Allyn and Bacon, 2002.

Bennett, Jeffrey, Megan Donahue, Nicholas Schneider, and Mark Voit. *The Cosmic Perspective*. Menlo Park: Addison Wesley Longman, 1999.

Berk, Laura E. *Development through the Lifespan*. 2nd ed. Boston: Allyn and Bacon, 2001.

Davidson, J. Kenneth, Sr., and Nelwyn B. Moore. *Marriage and Family: Change and Continuity*. Boston: Allyn and Bacon, 1996.

DeVito, Joseph A. *The Interpersonal Communication Book*. 8th ed. New York: Addison Wesley Longman, 1998.

Hewitt, Paul G., John Suchocki, and Leslie A. Hewitt. *Conceptual Physical Science*. 2nd ed. New York: Addison Wesley Longman, 1999.

Kerman, Joseph, Gary Tomlinson, and Vivian Kerman. *Listen*, 4th ed. Boston: Bedford/St. Martin's, 2000.

Parkay, Forrest W., and Beverly Hardcastle Stanford. *Becoming a Teacher*. 5th ed. Boston: Allyn and Bacon, 2001.

Samuelson, Paul A., and William D. Nordhaus. *Macroeconomics*. 17th ed. New York: McGraw-Hill, 2001.

CHAPTER 4

Barker, Larry L., and Deborah Roach Gaut. *Communication*. 8th ed. Boston: Allyn and Bacon, 2002.

Berman, Claire, "When Children of Divorce Become Parents," *Parents*. Bruner and Jahr USA Publishing, July 1992.

Campbell, Neil A., Lawrence G. Mitchell, and Jane B. Reece. *Biology: Concepts and Connections*. 3rd ed. San Francisco: Benjamin/Cummings, 2000.

DeVito, Joseph A. *The Interpersonal Communication Book*. 8th ed. New York: Addison Wesley Longman, 1998.

Farr, Grant, and Corie Hammers. *Global Societies to Accompany Sociology: Changing Societies in a Diverse World*. 4th ed. Boston: Allyn and Bacon, 2001.

Hewitt, Paul G., John Suchocki, and Leslie A. Hewitt. *Conceptual Physical Science*. 2nd ed. New York: Addison Wesley Longman, 1999.

Kottak, Conrad Phillip. *Mirror for Humanity*, 3rd ed. New York: McGraw-Hill, 2003.

Nash, Gary B., Julie Roy Jeffrey, John R. Howe, Peter J. Frederick, Allen F. Davis, and Allan M. Winkler. *The American People: Creating a Nation and a Society*. New York: Addison Wesley, 2000.

Pulver, John C., "Birth Order and Family Differences," from *The Marriage and Family Workbook: An Interactive Reader, Text, and Workbook* by Robert Manis. Boston: Allyn and Bacon, 2001.

Stanitski, Conrad L., Lucy Pryde Eubanks, Catherine H. Middlecamp, and Wilmer J. Stratton. *Chemistry in Context: Applying Chemistry to Society*, 3rd ed. Boston: McGraw-Hill, 2000.

CHAPTER 5

Barker, Larry L., and Deborah Roach Gaut. *Communication*. 8th ed. Boston: Allyn and Bacon, 2002.

Campbell, Neil A., Lawrence G. Mitchell, and Jane B. Reece. *Biology: Concepts and Connections*. 3rd ed. San Francisco: Benjamin/Cummings, 2000.

DeVito, Joseph A. *The Interpersonal Communication Book*. 8th ed. New York: Addison Wesley Longman, 1998.

Franzoi, Stephen L., *Social Psychology*. 3rd ed. Boston: McGraw-Hill, 2003.

Pulsipher, Lidia Mihelic, and Alex Pulsipher, *World Regional Geography*, 2nd ed. New York: W. H. Freeman and Company, 2002.

Thompson, William E., and Joseph V. Hickey. *Society in Focus: An Introduction to Sociology*, 4th ed. Boston: Allyn and Bacon, 2001.

Troyka, Lynn Quitman, *Quick Access: Reference for Writers*. Upper Saddle River, N.J.: Prentice-Hall, 2001.

Weiten, Wayne. *Psychology: Themes and Variations*, 5th ed. Belmont, Calif.: Wadsworth-Thomson Learning, 2002.

X, Malcolm. "A Homemade Education," from *The Autobiography of Malcolm X*, by Malcolm X and Alex Haley, New York: Random House, 1964 by Alex Haley and Malcolm X. © 1965 by Alex Haley and Betty Shabazz.

CHAPTER 6

Adler, Ronald B., and George Rodman. *Understanding Human Communication*, 8th ed. New York: Oxford University Press, 2003.

Atkisson, Alan, "What Makes Love Last?" *New Age Journal* (now *Body & Soul*), September/October 1994.

Berk, Laura E. *Development through the Lifespan*. 2nd ed. Boston: Allyn and Bacon, 2001.

Bryjak, George J., and Michael P. Soroka. *Sociology: Changing Societies in a Diverse World*. 4th ed. Boston: Allyn and Bacon, 2001.

Campbell, Neil A., Lawrence G. Mitchell, and Jane B. Reece. *Biology: Concepts and Connections*. 3rd ed. San Francisco: Benjamin/Cummings, 2000.

Davidson, J. Kenneth, Sr., and Nelwyn B. Moore. *Marriage and Family: Change and Continuity*. Boston: Allyn and Bacon, 1996.

DeVito, Joseph A. *Essentials of Human Communication*. 3rd ed. New York: Addison Wesley Longman, 1999.

Farr, Grant, and Corie Hammers. *Global Societies to Accompany Sociology: Changing Societies in a Diverse World*. 4th ed. Boston: Allyn and Bacon, 2001.

Franzoi, Stephen L., *Social Psychology*. 3rd ed. Boston: McGraw-Hill, 2003.

Gaines, Larry K., Michael Kaune, and Roger LeRoy Miller. *Criminal Justice in Action: The Core*. Belmont: Wadsworth/Thomson Learning, 2001.

Kornblum, William and Carolyn D. Smith. *Sociology: The Central Questions*, 2nd ed. Orlando, Fla.: Harcourt, 2002.

Hewitt, Paul G., John Suchocki, and Leslie A. Hewitt. *Conceptual Physical Science*. 2nd ed. New York: Addison Wesley Longman, 1999.

Nash, Gary B., Julie Roy Jeffrey, John R. Howe, Peter J. Frederick, Allen F. Davis, and Allan M. Winkler. *The American People: Creating a Nation and a Society*. New York: Addison Wesley, 2000.

Purves, William K., David Sadava, Gordon H. Orians, and H. Craig Heller. *Life: The Science of Biology*, 6th ed. Sunderland, Mass.: Sinauer Associates, 2001.

Smith, Robert Leo, and Thomas M. Smith. *Elements of Ecology*. 4th ed. New York: Addison Wesley Longman, 2000.

Stanley, Thomas J., and William D. Danko. *The Millionaire Next Door*. Atlanta: Longstreet. 1996.

Stanitski, Conrad L., Lucy Pryde Eubanks, Catherine H. Middlecamp, and Wilmer J. Stratton. *Chemistry in Context: Applying Chemistry to Society*, 3rd ed. Boston: McGraw-Hill, 2000.

Whitney, Eleanor Noss and Sharon Rady Rolfes. *Understanding Nutrition*, 9th ed. Belmont, Calif.: Wadsworth/Thomson Learning, 2002.

CHAPTER 7

DeVito, Joseph A. *The Interpersonal Communication Book*. 8th ed. New York: Addison Wesley Longman, 1998.

Garraty, John A., and Mark C. Carnes. *The American Nation: A History of the United States*. 10th ed. New York: Addison Wesley Longman, 2000.

Nash, Gary B., Julie Roy Jeffrey, John R. Howe, Peter J. Frederick, Allen F. Davis, and Allan M. Winkler. *The American People: Creating a Nation and a Society*. New York: Addison Wesley, 2000.

Stanitski, Conrad L., Lucy Pryde Eubanks, Catherine H. Middlecamp, and Wilmer J. Strat-

ton. *Chemistry in Context: Applying Chemistry to Society*, 3rd ed. Boston: McGraw-Hill, 2000.

CHAPTER 8

Hales, Dianne. *An Invitation to Health*. Belmont, Calif.: Wadsworth, 2002.

Henslin, James M. *Essentials of Sociology: A Down-to-Earth Approach*. 4th ed. Boston: Allyn and Bacon, 2002.

Hewitt, Paul G., John Suchocki, and Leslie A. Hewitt. *Conceptual Physical Science*. 2nd ed. New York: Addison Wesley Longman, 1999.

Mac, Bernie. *Maybe You Never Cry Again*. New York: Penguin, 2003.

Males, Mike. "Stop Blaming and TV." *The Progressive*. Madison, WI. www.progressive.com.

Ury, William L. *The Third Side: Why We Fight and How We Can Stop*, previously published as *Getting to Peace*. New York: Penguin, 2000.

CHAPTER 9

Barker, Larry L., and Deborah Roach Gaut. *Communication*. 8th ed. Boston: Allyn and Bacon, 2002.

Bryjak, George J., and Michael P. Soroka. *Sociology: Changing Societies in a Diverse World*. 4th ed. Boston: Allyn and Bacon, 2001.

DeVito, Joseph A. *Essentials of Human Communication*. 3rd ed. New York: Addison Wesley Longman, 1999.

Gordon, Lori. "On Communication Styles in Marriage and Family." *Psychology Today Magazine*. New York: Sussex Publishers, 1993.

Haddon, Dayle. *The 5 Principles of Ageless Living*. New York: Atria, 2003.

Hewitt, Paul G., John Suchocki, and Leslie A. Hewitt. *Conceptual Physical Science*. 2nd ed. New York: Addison Wesley Longman, 1999.

Manis, Robert. *The Marriage and Family Workbook*. Boston: Allyn and Bacon, 2001.

Melendez, Miguel. *We Took the Streets: Fighting for Latino Rights with the Young Lords*. New York: St. Martin's Press, 2003.

Whitney, Eleanor Noss and Sharon Rady Rolfes. *Understanding Nutrition*, 9th ed. Belmont, Calif.: Wadsworth/Thomson Learning, 2002.

CHAPTER 10

Berk, Laura E. *Development through the Lifespan*. 2nd ed. Boston: Allyn and Bacon, 2001.

Campbell, Neil A., Lawrence G. Mitchell, and Jane B. Reece. *Biology: Concepts and Connections*. 3rd ed. San Francisco: Benjamin/Cummings, 2000.

DeVito, Joseph A. *The Interpersonal Communication Book*. 8th ed. New York: Addison Wesley Longman, 1998.

Edwards, George C. III, Martin P. Wattenberg, and Robert L. Lineberry. *Government in America: People, Politics, and Policy*. 9th ed. New York, Addison Wesley Longman, 2000.

Henslin, James M. *Essentials of Sociology: A Down-to-Earth Approach*. 4th ed. Boston: Allyn and Bacon, 2002.

Hewitt, Paul G., John Suchocki, and Leslie A. Hewitt. *Conceptual Physical Science*. 2nd ed. New York: Addison Wesley Longman, 1999.

CHAPTER 11

Campbell, Neil A., Lawrence G. Mitchell, and Jane B. Reece. *Biology: Concepts and Connections*. 3rd ed. San Francisco: Benjamin/Cummings, 2000.

DeVito, Joseph A. *The Interpersonal Communication Book*. 8th ed. New York: Addison Wesley Longman, 1998.

Edwards, George C. III, Martin P. Wattenberg, and Robert L. Lineberry. *Government in America: People, Politics, and Policy*. 9th ed. New York, Addison Wesley Longman, 2000.

Nolting, Paul. *Math Study Skills Workbook*. Boston: Houghton Mifflin, 2001.

CHAPTER 12

Associated Press. "Endangered Cranes Reach Florida Coast." *USA Today* 2 Dec. 2002: 8D.

Atkisson, Alan. What Makes Love Last?" *New Age Journal* (now Body & Soul), September/October, 1994.

Berk, Laura E. *Development through the Lifespan*. 2nd ed. Boston: Allyn and Bacon, 2001.

Campbell, Neil A., Lawrence G. Mitchell, and Jane B. Reece. *Biology: Concepts and Connections*. 3rd ed. San Francisco: Benjamin/Cummings, 2000.

Edwards, George C. III, Martin P. Wattenberg, and Robert L. Lineberry. *Government in America: People, Politics, and Policy*. 9th ed. New York, Addison Wesley Longman, 2000.

Haddon, Dayle. *The 5 Principles of Ageless Living*. New York: Atria, 2003.

Lefrancois, Guy R. *The Lifespan*. 3rd ed. Belmont: Wadsworth, 1990.

Ridder, Knight. "UFO True Believer: Sure the Truth Is out There," from *The Express Times*. August 11, 2003, C-1.

APPENDIX

Associated Press. "Endangered Cranes Reach Florida Coast." *USA Today* 2 Dec. 2002: 8D.

Atkisson, Alan. "What Makes Love Last?" *New Age Journal* (now Body & Soul), September/October, 1994.

Farr, Grant, and Corie Hammers. *Global Societies to Accompany Sociology: Changing Societies in a Diverse World*. 4th ed. Boston: Allyn and Bacon, 2001.

Manis, Robert. *The Marriage and Family Workbook*. Boston: Allyn and Bacon, 2001.

Samuelson, Paul A., and William D. Nordhaus. *Macroeconomics*. 17th ed. New York: McGraw-Hill, 2001.

Stanitski, Conrad L., Lucy Pryde Eubanks, Catherine H. Middlecamp, and Wilmer J. Stratton. *Chemistry in Context: Applying Chemistry to Society*, 3rd ed. Boston: McGraw-Hill, 2000.

Thompson, William E. and Joseph V. Hickey. *Society in Focus: An Introduction to Sociology*, 4th ed. Boston: Allyn and Bacon, 2002.

Wild, John J. *Financial Accounting*, 2nd ed. Vol. 2. Boston: McGraw-Hill, 2003.

Index